A-Level English Language & Literature

CloudLearn Ltd

Specification Code: 9EL0
First Teaching: 2015
First Assessment: 2017

A Level English Language & Literature

Published and Distributed by:
OSC Ltd.

Publication Date   August 2015
Edition Number   2015/01

Contents

Introduction to English Language & Literature

Welcome to your CloudLearn A-Level English Language & Literature course!

English Language & Literature takes an integrated approach to the study of these two subjects. In this course, we will be learning how authors construct both fiction and non-fiction texts. Through learning more about the English language and how it can be used, we can begin to think about the choices that writers make and how they decide which words to use. We can start to think about the power of language and the impressions that words convey, sometimes without us really noticing. This can help us learn how to read critically.

The study of literature can also be approached through our ideas about language. Through literary study, we can enhance our appreciation of authors and how they work. We can explore the many levels of meaning within a literary text and analyse how the author creates meaning through the use of language. This can enhance our understanding of an author's work and how it creates an impression on a reader.

In this way, the study of English Language and Literature can be much more than another A-Level subject and it can have wider applications outside of academic assessment. Indeed, we hope that studying this course will help you to think more about the words that we use every day, and to think critically about the many ways in which ideas can be conveyed.

Studying with CloudLearn

CloudLearn are specialists in distance learning. Our courses are designed to help you study independently, at a time to suit you. We understand that you require guidance, support and advice in order that you can approach the examinations with confidence.

This course has been designed with the needs of the A-Level specification in mind, and so is tailored to the requirements of the examination. You will find that all the study tasks, all the Tutor Marked Assignments (TMAs) and all the study advice given is structured around the expectations of the examination format.

Following the A-Level reforms of 2015, all A-Level exams and coursework are now taken in the same year. Normally, students study for A-Level over a two year period. There are no longer any exams at the end of the first year. Instead, all of the exams are now taken in May/June of the second year, at the end of the course.

This is more challenging for distance learning students, as you will need to remember the content of the course for a longer period of time. To help you, this course has been devised so that there is repetition of key ideas and material, so that you are well prepared for the exams.

In this introductory section, we will look at: how to study this course; how to enter for the exams; the structure of the Edexcel English Language & Literature A-Level; how to plan your time; and how to develop your study skills.

How to Study this Course

Now that you have received your course materials, you can start whenever you like!

Begin by reading through this introductory material. This will help you to gain an overview of A-Level English Language & Literature.

Read carefully through the information in this section. You may want to keep referring back to this material, so that you know what stage you are working on and how the units fit together.

Once you have read through the introduction and gained an overview of the A-Level, then you will reach the first topic.

Topics

This course is divided into topics, and each topic is focussed on particular Aims and Objectives. You can think of each topic as a lesson. You need to study the topics in order, as they build on each other to guide you towards the exams.

Work through each topic, one at a time, reading the study material and completing the Tasks as you work through.

Self-Assessment Tasks

Each topic contains Tasks. Some of these Tasks will ask you to read a particular section or chapter. Some will include questions to answer.

Each Task has a commentary, which is a form of model answer. These commentaries are designed to help you gauge your progress. However, do not worry if your answer doesn't match the commentary exactly. So long as you are making close references to the text, then there is plenty of scope for different interpretations in literature.

These Tasks are part of the self-directed learning process. You are free to complete them at your own pace. They do not need to be marked by your tutor.

Tutor Marked Assignments (TMAs)

At certain points in the course, you will find Tutor Marked Assignment (TMAs). These are pieces of work that your tutor will mark for you and give you feedback on.

You will need to type these TMAs and upload them to your tutor for marking as Word documents or Rich Text Files. Your tutor will mark and return your work to you, usually within 7-10 days.

There are no deadlines for these TMAs and they do not count towards the formal A-Level assessment. However, they are designed to help you gain valuable experience in answering examination-style questions and to get feedback on your work.

These TMAs can only be marked once by your tutor (no re-drafts) so try your best first time.

Contacting your Tutor

When you register your tutor support, you will receive a Welcome Letter containing the contact details of your tutor.

You can contact your tutor by email. She will mark and return your Tutor Marked Assignments to you and answer any questions that you may have about the course. Please allow 24-72 hours for a response to enquiries and 7-10 days for the return of written work. Response times can occasionally be longer than this at busy times or in holiday periods.

When you email your tutor, please include your full name, and what subject you are studying (English Literature or Language & Literature).

(Please note that your tutor will not be able to contact you by telephone or any other means.)

Entering for the Exams as a Private Candidate

Private candidates are students who enter for the exam independently. They arrange to sit their exams at a local school or college (called an exam centre).

As a private candidate, it is your responsibility to make the arrangements to enter for the exams. This can sound daunting, but it is easier than it first appears.

You should enter for the exams as soon as you can. This is because it can take time to find an exam centre, and because you will need some materials that are provided to candidates by the exam board (Edexcel) via your exam centre.

You will need to make the arrangements with your exam centre yourself. As this involves arranging a meeting in person with an exams officer, your tutor cannot help you with this.

The first stage is to find an exam centre.

Finding an Exam Centre

A-Level English Language & Literature has a coursework component. We therefore recommend that you choose one of CloudLearn's recommended exam centres.

Telephone the centre nearest to you and ask to register for:

Pearson Edexcel A-Level English Language & Literature (9EL0)

You will need to arrange an appointment so that you can meet with the exams officer, sign the entry forms, and pay the entry fee. You will need to take ID with you when you go to register. If you are carrying over any marks (e.g. if you have already taken part of this exam or are re-sitting) then you will also need to discuss this with your centre. You should also discuss any access requirements you may have with the centre when you telephone.

When you register, you should also tell your exams officer that you will need to order you a copy of the Edexcel publication:

Voices in Speech and Writing: An Anthology

This anthology should be provided free of charge to all candidates who enter for the exam.

(Please note that your tutor cannot help you make these arrangements with your exam centre and that your tutor cannot contact your exam centre for you.)

Authentication of Coursework

When you register, your exam centre may ask you about coursework authentication.

Coursework authentication is a process by which a qualified person signs a declaration to say that your coursework is your own unaided work.

For those students registering at one of our recommended exam centres, your tutor will be happy to write a letter for you in order to authenticate your coursework (so long as she has seen enough of your work beforehand to know that it is your own work). If your centre asks you for the details of your authenticator, you can provide your tutor's details.

We will look at coursework further in the next section, as we overview the components of A-Level English Language & Literature.

Edexcel A Level English Language & Literature (9EL0)

All A-Level courses are now linear. This means that all exams must be taken and coursework must be submitted in the same year. The exams are only held in May/June (once per year). The first exams for this A-Level will be held in May/June 2017.

The Edexcel A-Level in English Language & Literature has two components plus coursework. These are as follows:

- Component 1 - Voices in Speech and Writing
- Component 2 - Varieties in Language and Literature
- Coursework - Creating and Investigating Texts

We will now look at each of these in more detail.

Component 1 - Voices in Speech and Writing

For this component, will look at how voices are conveyed in texts. We will look at the Edexcel publication *Voices in Speech and Writing: An Anthology* and explore the way that the selected authors convey a sense of voice. We will then study a drama text. This will be Arthur Miller's *All My Sons*.

This component is assessed by a written exam, lasting 2 hours and 30 minutes. There will be two sections.

In Section A, you will answer a comparative essay question. This question will ask you to compare one of the texts that you have studied as part of the anthology with an unseen extract selected from 20th or 21st century sources.

In Section B, you will answer one extract-based question on our chosen drama text: *All My Sons*. You will be allowed to take a clean (unmarked) copy of the text into the exam with you.

The total number of available marks for the paper is 50. These are divided evenly between the sections so that Section A is worth a maximum of 25 marks and Section B is also worth a maximum of 25 marks.

Component 1 is worth 40% of the total A-Level

Component 2 - Varieties in Language and Literature

For Component 2, we will be studying a range of texts based around the theme of Encounters. We will practice reading non-fiction prose texts on this theme. We will then study two literary texts. These texts will be:

Emily Bronte - *Wuthering Heights*
Angela Carter - *The Bloody Chamber*

This component is assessed by a 2 hour 30 minute written exam.

In Section A, you will answer a essay question cn an unseen extract on the theme of encounters. This section will be worth 20 marks.

In Section B, you will answer a comparative essay question on our studied texts. You will be allowed to take clean (unmarked) copies of the texts into the exam with you. This section will be worth 30 marks.

This component is worth 40% of the total A-Level.

Coursework - Investigating and Creating Texts

For the coursework component of A-Level Language & Literature, you will study one non-fiction text and one fiction text. These texts will be thematically linked.

You will then complete two pieces of original writing. One will be a piece of fiction writing and one will be a piece of creative non-fiction.

You will also complete a separate analytical commentary that reflects on the texts that you have studied and the pieces of original writing that you have produced.

The coursework component is worth 20% of the total A-Level.

Summary

The table below shows an overall summary of the A-Level English Language & Literature course:

Component	Exam Duration	Percentage of Total A-Level
Component 1 - Voices in Speech and Writing	2hours30min	40%
Component 2 - Varieties in Language and Literature	2hours30min	40%
Coursework	-	20%

You will also notice that you are allowed to take copies of the texts into the exams with you.

Therefore, I would strongly suggest that you buy copies of these texts. All of these texts are available inexpensively.

However, you should also note that you can only take **clean** copies of the texts into the exam. Clean means not marked or annotated in any way. Be aware of this if buying a second-hand copy, as you will need to check that the book has not been annotated by a previous owner. You must remember not to write on or mark your exam copies. If you really feel you need to, then you could always buy two copies, one to write on and one to keep clean for the exam.

There is a summary of the texts you will need at the end of this introduction.

Coursework

English Language & Literature A-Level contains a coursework component. CloudLearn has made arrangements with our recommended exam centres for you to complete your coursework as a private candidate.

If you choose one of our recommended centres, then you should follow the coursework directions given in this course.

In this course will be studying two coursework texts: *Grayson Perry: Portrait of the Artist as a Young Girl* and *The Importance of Being Earnest*. You will select your coursework tasks from the list provided in these course materials. You tutor will be able to look at the first draft of your coursework and give you feedback on it.

Your tutor will also authenticate your coursework for you (provided that she is satisfied that it is your own unaided work). She will do this by writing a letter to your exam centre to accompany your coursework. Your coursework will then be submitted to your exam centre and the teachers at your exam centre will mark your work.

For most exam centres, the coursework deadline will be in May, but it can vary between centres. You should check your exam centre's coursework deadline when you register.

If you follow the suggested course structure outlined in the next section, ther you should have your coursework completed well before the deadline and have plerty of time available for authentication. However, it is your own responsibility to make sure that you meet your coursework deadline.

Other Exam Centres

Please note that if you choose a different exam centre to those recommended by CloudLearn then you will need to make your own coursework arrangements with that centre directly.

Other centres may have their own coursework requirements and you should discuss these arrangements as soon as you register. Your tutor will not be able to help you to make these coursework arrangements.

For this reason, we strongly suggest that you select one of CloudLearn's recommended exam centres.

Plagiarism

Your work must be your own work. This means it must be written in your own words.

Copying from these course materials, from the internet, or downloading free essays are all forms of plagiarism. Do not copy any materials! You should also make sure that any quotations or ideas from critics are properly referenced.

Your tutor has been trained in how to detect plagiarism. She will also use anti-plagiarism software to check your coursework.

If plagiarism is detected then your tutor will not be able to authenticate your work. Candidates who commit plagiarism may also be disqualified from their exams.

Therefore, please make sure that you are always writing your essays using your own words and your own ideas. So long as you do this, you have nothing to worry about.

The Edexcel Website

The Edexcel website contains lots of helpful information and advice. As well as information on entering for your exam, you will also find past-papers, mark-schemes and examination reports. Make as much use of the website as possible.

Task

You can download the Edexcel English Language & Literature specification from this website:

http://qualifications.pearson.com/en/qualifications/edexcel-a-levels/english-language-and-literature-2015.html

It is a good idea to read through this material and become familiar with it. You will need to keep referring to it as we go through the course.

There is no commentary on this activity.

The Assessment Objectives: What are the Examiners Looking For?

The Edexcel examiners will apply five Assessment Objectives when reading your work. These Assessment Objectives are known as AO1, AO2, AO3, AO4 and AO5.

Students must:

AO1	Apply concepts and methods from integrated linguistic and literary study as appropriate, using associated terminology and coherent written expression
AO2	Analyse ways in which meanings are shaped in literary texts
AO3	Demonstrate understanding of the significance and influence of the contexts in which literary texts are produced and received
AO4	Explore connections across texts, informed by linguistic and literary concepts and methods
AO5	Demonstrate expertise and creativity in the use of English to communicate in different ways

What Does This Mean?

The AOs specify the skills and approaches that you are required to develop in A-level English Language & Literature. It is therefore useful for you to have an idea of what they mean in practice.

AO1

AO1 comprises two elements: the quality of your written work and your knowledge of relevant terminology. We will be learning the terminology of English Language and Literature as we work through the course. Where possible, new terminology will be placed in text boxes for ease of explanation.

The quality of your written communication is also important to exam success.

At the most basic level, you must write legibly in the exam. This might take more practice that you think, especially if you have become used to using a computer rather than writing by hand.

You must use accurate spelling, grammar and punctuation. You should already be familiar with the use of the comma, full-stop and apostrophe. You should also be able to write in sentences and paragraphs. You will also need an understanding of grammar, including parts of speech such as nouns, verbs, pronouns and adjectives. Above all, you must be able to express what you mean.

If you feel that you may have difficulties with your written communication or you are unfamiliar with any of the concepts above, please undertake some further reading on the subject. You will find many good books on grammar, punctuation and style in any local library.

AO2

This AO assesses your understanding of how a text is constructed by the author. This is, arguably, the most important aspect of the study of any text and you will quickly become adept at appreciating literary and linguistic techniques.

AO3

AO3 explores how the understanding of texts can be dependent on context. You will need to be able to apply relevant contextual factors in your interpretation of a text. Relevant contextual factors might include the political or social context of a text, or the role of genre and audience.

> **Terminology**
>
> **Context** – The context of a text is those circumstances surrounding a text and which affect its interpretation. It is sometimes divided into Context of Production and Context of Reception.
>
> **Context of Production** – This includes all the circumstances influencing how the text was written. For example they might include the socio-political situation at the time of writing, or events in the personal life of the author.
>
> **Context of Reception** – This is concerned with the circumstances surrounding how the text has been received by an audience either at the time of publication or by later readers. A text often resists its specific context of production and goes on to speak to new generations of readers in new ways. A literary text can even take on interpretations beyond that intended by the author. For this reason, some literary critics believe that context of reception more important that context of production. This is a good example of how interpretation is central to the study of English Literature.

AO4

This assessment objective assesses your ability to make connections between different texts. There are many ways to connect different texts, for example, through the use of a specific literary concept, or through shared linguistic features.

AO5

AO5 requires you to show your ability to communicate effectively and creatively. This AO will be assessed in the coursework component.

How is English Marked?

Unlike other subjects that you may have studied, English Language & Literature is not marked using a checklist of points. Instead, your answer will be marked according to its overall quality.

When marking an answer, an examiner uses a marking grid. The marking grid is divided into levels, and gives a description of the features of an answer of that level.

The student's answer is then compared to the features of each level and placed into the level that fits it best.

Within the level, marks can be awarded or deducted based on the quality of the answer and how well the features of that level are met.

Level 1 is the lowest level and Level 5 is the highest level.

The table below is a broad guide to the features of the levels. There is a full description of the levels in the Sample Assessment Materials on the Edexcel website.

Level 1	Descriptive	Answers of this level use a narrative or descriptive approach and show little understanding of how authors craft texts. They will show a limited range of terminology and there will be frequent errors. They may describe some contextual factors, but not the significance of these factors. They may treat the texts separately.
Level 2	General Understanding	Answers of this level make some general points. They apply some general understanding of an author's use of techniques. They will describe general contextual factors. They will have lapses in the use of terminology. They will state obvious similarities and differences between texts and make some general links between them.
Level 3	Clear Relevant Application	Answers of this level offer a relevant and logically structured response. They use terminology accurately. They have a clear understanding of how meaning is shaped by literary and linguistic features and can support this with clear examples. They explain the significance and influence of contextual factors. They identify relevant connections between texts.
Level 4	Discriminating Controlled Application	Answers of this level show a controlled application of concepts and methods, supported with well-chosen examples. Answers will be well-structured. They will analyse the effects of linguistic and literary features and show an awareness of subtlety and nuance. They will make discriminating comments on how texts are affected by context. They will analyse connections across texts.
Level 5	Critical Evaluative Application	Answers at this level present a critical application of concepts and methods with sustained textual examples. They will use a sophisticated structure and expression and appropriate technology. They will show a critical evaluation of literary and linguistic choices and evaluate how these shape meaning. They will examine the multi-layered nature of texts and the nuances of context. They will evaluate connections across texts.

To achieve a high level, a student must demonstrate a sophisticated approach with a very good understanding and use of appropriate terminology.

In the next section, we will look at how to write good essays and other study skills for English Language & Literature.

Task

There is a more detailed version of the marking grid above on page 21 of the Edexcel English Language & Literature specification on the Edexcel website. This is the grid that the examiner will use to mark your coursework.

Take a few minutes to look at the grid and familiarise yourself with the different levels. This will give you an idea of the quality of answer that you should aim for.

Study Skills for English Language & Literature

You may be returning to education after a break or fitting in study around other commitments. In either case, adopting good study habits at the outset will help you in the long run. Here are some tips.

1) Find a quiet place to study where you can concentrate. You might find that even half an hour of concentrated learning is more productive than several hours in an environment with many distractions.

2) You may find it easier to study if you have a suitable place to work. A desk with a computer and nearby space to store books and course materials is ideal, but not always possible. If you do not have space for a home office, try to find another method of creating a study space. You may be able to use the kitchen table, living room or bedroom at particular times during the day. You may therefore find it helpful to make a portable study space by keeping all of your study materials together in a large plastic box (or something similar). This means you can work in different places when they are available and move around without losing important items or using up study time in searching for books, paper, etc.

3) Try to find a place where you will not be disturbed. If necessary, tell the other people that you live with that you are not to be interrupted when you are studying unless it is very important. You may also want to deactivate instant messaging and other distractions during your study time.

4) Many students also find it helpful to develop a study routine. Finding the best time to study will depend on when you feel you are most able to concentrate. This decision will involve a number of personal and lifestyle factors and is best found through trial and error. Some people like to wake up early and study for an hour before going to work. Other people are night owls, who may like to work late at night. Alternatively, you may find that you are thinking of ideas on your commute home, and decide to begin studying as soon as you get in. You should experiment with studying at different times of the day, to see when you feel most effective.

4) Relax! Remember to take regular breaks from study, particularly when revising. Concentration can wane if you work for too long, or try to work when you are over-tired. You should aim for at least a five minute break for every forty-five minutes of study. It is important to take breaks and to leave time for other activities, so as not to become anxious or stressed. The study of English should be fun. Enjoy it!

Taking Notes

Fortunately, English Language & Literature is not an information-heavy subject, and there is very little that you will need to memorise. However, as the exams are held at the end of the course, you will need to have a good understanding of the material you learn and you will need to keep looking over your notes, so that you can keep your knowledge active in your mind over the two years of the course.

The best study practices are active (such as taking-notes) rather than passive (just reading). Taking notes can help you to process the information you read, so that you are absorbing what you learn. Notes will also come in useful when you come to revise for the exam.

You can write on this course itself, but remember that you must not write on the texts. Therefore you may like to take separate notes. This will help you when you revise for the exams.

For example, you could try writing index cards. This will require you to think about and summarise the information as you write it down. You could even try to remember some of the information, write it down, and then check your recollection. Another method is to write notes to yourself in the margins or around the headings of your own notes, or on the course itself. These could be short, one sentence or keyword summaries of the ideas in that paragraph or chapter. Making these notes will make you think about the information and summarise it. It will also jog your memory as you revise the full text.

Another popular note-taking method is called mind mapping. Mind mapping uses colours, drawings and symbols. It is a creative process, helping you to remember and link ideas together. You begin by writing down the central topic in the centre of a blank page and then write down all the connected ideas around it (like a spider diagram). The advantage of this is that you are constantly thinking about the ideas and concepts, and you are learning to make links between them.

The note-taking method you use is a personal choice, and you should try several different methods to find the one that works best for you. The most important thing is that your note-taking should be as active and as creative as possible to help you remember the information.

Keep your notes where you can refer to them easily. For example, you might like to use record cards or a ring binder. You can use any system that works for you but make sure that you can access your notes on particular topics easily. This will also help you when you come to revise.

Answering Questions in English Language & Literature

Writing well is an important skill in English Language & Literature. However good your ideas are, you will need to be able to express them well in order to gain marks. It is very important that you focus on answering the question that is asked; do not simply explain what happens in the novel. To do this, you will need to write analytically.

Writing Analytically

Writing analytically involves thinking about how a writer has created a text. It is about understanding the process of the writer's craft.

A good way to make sure that you are writing analytically is to keep thinking about the author and what she or he is trying to achieve. You need to look in detail at literary and linguistic techniques and think about why the author has chosen to use that particular technique. Why is this technique useful? What effect does it create for the reader?

Keep using analytical phrases such as 'this shows that' in order to draw attention to the writer's writing process and the construction of the text.

For example:

In this chapter, [the author] uses [named literary technique] in an interesting way. He begins with ... then uses ... to look at ... . This creates the impression that ... .

The author's use of [linguistic feature] is also interesting.. .. An example of this is ... . This shows that ... and creates the sense that ... .

Make Each Paragraph Count

A good method to make sure that you are writing analytically as you answer questions is to construct each paragraph using the format: Point; Evidence; Elaboration; Link.

For each paragraph:

Point	Make one clear point per paragraph
Evidence	Use a quotation from the text, or a reference to a technique, the structure of the novel, or a character or event, to illustrate the point you have made
Elaboration	Explore the point in more detail, thinking about why and how the author has used this technique and how this fits into the wider context. Remember to use lots of analytical language, such as "this shows that" and "this creates the effect that". This will help ensure that you are always analysing the text
Link	Link your point back to the overall question title, or into your next point.

This is called the PEEL structure. Once you become familiar with it, then you can vary it. But it is a useful format that you can use to make sure that you are always writing analytically.

Once you have mastered analytical writing, you need to make sure that your individual paragraphs work together to form a well-structured essay. English literature is assessed through essay writing. The best essays are well-structured, relevant, and have a clear overall line of argument.

Planning and Structuring an Essay

Thinking about the question and planning the essay before you begin writing is essential to develop a clear structure. You should always plan an essay before you begin writing. In an exam, you should spend about five minutes of the exam planning your essay.

1) First, pick out the key words in the question. You may find it helpful to underline these words. Work out exactly what the question is asking. Remember that you must answer the question that is asked and that you must answer it as fully and relevantly as you can.

2) Next, begin planning your answer. You might like to use a spider diagram to plan your essay or to simply write some brief notes. Consider your argument and the points that you want to make, and then begin to order them. Make sure that every point is relevant to the question. Find examples from the texts to back up each of your points. Planning this out before you begin to write will give your essay structure.

3) Begin with an Introduction. The introduction should set out your argument clearly and concisely. Explain what you will be saying in the essay.

4) Each following paragraph should consider one point of your argument. Give an example for each point. Develop each point fully before moving on.

5) Structure your essay so that the points follow on from each other. This helps the argument to flow and makes the essay more persuasive. You might group similar topics together or use similarities of structure or language to draw comparisons. Use linking phrases such as 'moreover,' or 'on the other hand,' to link paragraphs together.

6) Finish your essay with a conclusion. Briefly summarise your argument and give your final answer to the question. Give a balanced answer to the question.

Essay writing is a learned skill and, as with all things, practise makes perfect. Over this course, you will get plenty of practice at answering essay questions in English Literature.

Using Quotations

All the points that you make in your essays must be backed up by examples. The examples that you use may be direct quotations from the text, or quotations from the opinions of critics.

Quoting directly from the text is essential in English Language & Literature. You may take **clean** copies of your texts into the exam with you, so you will not need to memorise any quotations, although you should be familiar enough with the text that you can find any material you want to refer to quickly.

When you use quotations from the text, you must remember to analyse and explain the quote and how it supports your argument. It is usually (though not always) better to use short quotations. Ideally they should form part of your own sentence.

Examples:

> Details such as the 'heavy velvet curtains', 'red figured wallpaper' and 'black satin, embroidered with tears of pearl' all work to create a lush gothic setting.

As Cathy says, she cannot explain her feelings 'distinctly' but says that 'I'll give you a feeling of how I feel'. In many ways, this is more powerful than a simple relation of her thoughts, because it relies on the reader forming their own understanding of the dream's meaning.

It is also acceptable to reference events, characters, places etc. without direct quotation from the text. This can be especially useful when discussing narrative forms.

Example:

Bronte's use of two narrators creates an unusual structure. She typically draws attention to the presence of the narrators at the beginning or end of a chapter. This does not impeded the flow of the story, but it does remind us, periodically, of the presence of the narrators and of their competing views of events. This means that the reader is always thinking critically about the story. It encourages us to think for ourselves about the meaning of the events related.

You may also use quotations from critics to support your points. However, if you do, you must also go on to support and explain the quote, so it is important to make sure that you fully understand what the critic is saying. Try to follow the quotation with an example from the text.

Example:

Gilbert and Gubar see this as a difficulty in forming a stable identity that all women experience. They argue that 'Just as triumphant self discovery is the ultimate goal of the male *Bildungsroman*, anxious self-denial, Bronte suggests, is the ultimate product of female education.'[1] Cathy's carved rehearsal of the names 'Catherine Heathcliff' and 'Catherine Linton' on her windowsill shows her inability to choose between these identities. Whichever she chooses, it will mean the exclusion of the other and lead to a fragmentation of her self.

---

[1] Sandra M. Gilbert and Susan Gubar 'Looking Oppositely: Emily Bronte's Bible of Hell' in *The Madwoman in the Attic: The Woman Writer and the Nineteenth-Century Literary Imagination* (Yale Nota Bene, Second Edition, 2000) p. 276

You can also use an example to contradict a critical argument. When you use quotations from critics, remember that you do not have to agree with them. The examiner is interested in your opinion, so don't be afraid to say what you think.

Example:

Patricia Dunker, writing in 1984, believed that the original sexism of the fairy tale was too powerful to overcome and that as 'the carrier of ideology, proves too complex and pervasive to avoid'.[2] However, this seems to ignore the critical re-evaluation that Carter makes of the original tales, for example in the rescue by the mother in 'The Bloody Chamber'.

If, in the exam, you want to discuss the opinion of a critic but you cannot remember the full quotation, you can refer to the argument in general terms.

Example:

The critic Patricia Dunker believes that sexism is so inherent in the ideology of the fairy tale that it is impossible to avoid, even by re-working the tale.

Finally, it is important not to use a critical quotation if you are not sure what it means, or if it doesn't fit your argument. Never try to 'shoehorn' an irrelevant quotation into an exam essay.

---

[2] Patricia Dunker 'Re-Imagining the Fairy Tales: Angela Carter's Bloody Chamber' cited in Steve Roberts *The Bloody Chamber York Notes Advanced* (York Press, 2008) p. 106

How to Plan your Studies

Students often ask how they should plan their studies. As distance learning is flexible, and you can study at your own pace, there is no set way to study these course materials, and there are no deadlines. You can plan your study around your own schedule and work at times to suit you.

However, as we have mentioned, all A-Level courses are now linear. This means that all exams must be taken and coursework must be submitted in the same academic year.

This means that the examination window is now quite narrow, so you will need to time your studies so that you can complete all the exams in your chosen year. Most students study for their A-Levels over two years, and take the exams at the end of those two years. (Note that academic years usually begin in September and end in June.)

Therefore, to help you plan your time, we have prepared this guideline to help you know when you should have reached each stage.

The majority of students enrol in September, so we have prepared the table below based on that assumption. However, if you have enrolled at another time of year, you can still begin your course straight away. We will offer you advice on how to plan this in the next section, but you should still read the information below.

Suggested time plan for a student who enrols in September:

Autumn Term of Year 1 (Sept-January)	Understanding English Language Component 1 - Voices in Speech and Writing: The Anthology
Spring Term of Year 1 (January-April)	Component 1 - Voices in Speech and Writing: All My Sons
Summer Term of Year 1 (April-June)	Coursework
Autumn Term of Year 2 (Sept-January)	Component 2 - Varieties in Language and Literature: Unseen Texts Component 2 - Varieties in Language and Literature: Wuthering Heights
Spring Term of Year 2 (January-March)	Component 2 - Varieties in Language and Literature: The Bloody Chamber
Summer Term of Year 2 (March-May/June)	Revision

If you follow this time plan, then you can be sure that you will have covered all the material within the two years.

You can therefore look at these dates as goals for where you should be at the end of each term, and use these goals to plan your studies.

Some students like to make a detailed study plan. They look at the number of topics in each component, divide them by the number of weeks in each term, and then aim to complete that set number of topics per week.

Other students prefer to work more flexibly. They may study more or less per week depending on what suits them and their other commitments. Their overall aim is the same, but they work more flexibly to achieve it.

Either of these methods can work very well, and which you choose is a matter of personal preference. However, we do recommend that you check from time to time to make sure that you are on track for the suggested goals in the table above.

For students starting at other times of the year

If you start at a different time of year, then you will have to adjust this plan so that you can complete your work in the time available.

The first stage is to decide which year to take your exams. If you begin in January 2016, for example, then you might want to sit the exams in May/June 2018, giving you a slightly shorter study time of 16 (instead of 24 months). You will therefore need to work a little faster than other students.

Alternatively, you might decide to wait until May/June 2019 (giving 28 months of study time). This will give you more time to complete your course and you can work at a slower pace.

Tutor support lasts for 24 months and more tutor support can be purchased if necessary.

To calculate how quickly you will need to work to complete your studies in the time allowed, you will need to create a personal timescale. For example, if you begin the course in November, then you might want to catch up by working very hard to complete Component 1 in only 2 months (instead of 4 months) and then follow the standard plan above. Alternatively, you might want to create your own timescale, by working on each component over 3 months (instead of 4).

You can always calculate how fast you need to work by looking at the number of components to complete and the time available.

For example:

12 months / 3 components = 4 months per component

You can then break this down further to look at the number of topics left to complete in the time available. This is also a useful calculation if you fall behind.

For example:

total no. topics in component / number weeks = no. topics to complete per week

You can then use this to calculate how many topics you will need to complete per week.

We hope that you don't find this too confusing. You are entirely free to work at your own pace, but we find that many students ask us to provide guidance on how fast they should be working. We hope that this section helps you to understand how to gauge your progress.

Unlike school, your tutor won't be able to remind you of deadlines, or keep tabs on your progress, so you will need to be well-organised and take control of your own learning.

FAQ

Can my tutor help me find an exam centre?

Unfortunately not. As this involves phoning centres and making an appointment, your tutor cannot make these arrangements for you. We recommend choosing one of the centres recommended on the CloudLearn website.

When is the coursework deadline?

The coursework deadline varies between exam centres. You should check with you exam centre when you need to submit coursework by. For most exam centres, the deadline is late April or early May.

How much work do you need to see before you can authenticate my coursework?

You tutor would like to see 2 TMAs and your coursework draft prior to authentication.

When are the TMAs due?

There are no deadlines for TMAs and you are free to work at your own pace.

Can I redraft and resubmit my TMA?

Like the exam, each TMA can only be marked once by your tutor (no re-drafts) so try your best first time.

Can my tutor mark additional work / past papers?

Unfortunately not. Only the TMAs will be marked as part of the course.

Can my tutor predict my grade for my UCAS form?

Yes, provided she has seen enough of your work to do so. You tutor will only be able to predict your grade after she has seen at least 2 TMAs. However, you should note that predicted grades are only *predictions*, based on the work you have competed so far. They are not a guarantee of the grade that you will actually get.

You should also note that your tutor will predict your grade based on what she thinks you are likely to get. She cannot predict you a specific grade.

If you will need a predicted grade for your UCAS application, then you should discuss this with your tutor.

Can my tutor write me a UCAS reference?

The UCAS reference is a very important part of your application and institutions may make their decision based on what your tutor says about you. They are also long references, of around 700 words.

The difficulty is therefore that your tutor will have only known you for a brief time through email contact, and therefore she will struggle to find enough to say about you to fill the reference. Unfortunately, it can be actively damaging to say very little on a reference and this could limit your chances for your chosen place.

The best person to write a reference for you is someone who knows you well through a context in which you have been actively and enthusiastically involved. Good choices of referee include a class tutor or year head (who has taught and known you for several years), and employer, a sports coach, a religious leader, a leader of a voluntary organisation (such as a Scout or Guide leader, etc.).

If you have no-one else who can write a reference for you, then your tutor may be able to write one for you. You should discuss this with her.

List of Texts

You can buy any edition of these texts. However I would recommend that you buy new copies. This way you know that they will be clean and unmarked.

Remember not to write anything at all on your copies of the texts. You must not highlight, underline or mark the texts in any way, or you will not be allowed to take them into the exam with you.

You will need:

Component 1

- Voices in Speech and Writing: An Anthology

  (This is available from Edexcel and you will need to order a copy from your exam

  centre.)

- Arthur Miller *All My Sons*

Component 2

- Emily Bronte *Wuthering Heights*

- Angela Carter *The Bloody Chamber*

  (This is sometimes called *The Bloody Chamber and Other Stories*)

Coursework

For your coursework, you will study one fiction text and one non-fiction text. On our course, we will study:

- Oscar Wilde *The Importance of Being Earnest*

- Wendy Jones *Grayson Perry: A Portrait of the Artist as a Young Girl* (Vintage Books,

  London, 2007)

Hopefully, this introduction has whetted your appetite and you are now feeling confident and ready to begin your studies. In the next section, we will start by introducing the skills of English Language and Literature.

Enjoy Your Reading!

Introduction to English Language and Literature

Topic 1 – Revising GCSE Grammar

Introduction

In this topic, we will revise the basic of English grammar.

Aims and Objectives

- To revise the basics of English grammar

The Basics of Grammar

In order to study A-Level English Language & Literature effectively, candidates should ideally have a pass in GCSE English, or equivalent. Although it is not *necessary* for candidates to have achieved this qualification, it is certainly the case that A-Level English Language & Literature builds on the skills and materials covered at GCSE. If you already have GCSE (or equivalent) in English, but you feel that your skills might need brushing up, or if you don't have GCSE (or equivalent), then I recommend the following:

- Ensure you are familiar with the following terms for the parts of speech: **verb**, **noun**, **pronoun**, **adjective** and **adverb**. (Then read the information provided below).
- Check you are familiar with the common rules and conventions of punctuation. It is advised that you check over your understanding of the use of: **full stops**, **commas**, **quotation marks**, **semi colons**, **colons**, **exclamation marks** and **question marks**.
- Remember, you are marked on the quality of your written English in the examination, as well as the content of your answer. You therefore need to become comfortable with standard punctuation, and be a confident speller. Practice is the best way to ensure this.

Grammatical Overview

You will be pleased to hear that you are not required to become a linguistic expert in order to be successful in A-Level English. However, you are expected to be able to handle some technical grammatical terms with the primary purpose of aiding your textual analysis. So, being able to identify nouns, verbs, pronouns, adverbs and adjectives in a sentence will help you to better appreciate how an author has created particular effects in his or her writing.

Nouns

These are words that name 'things' whether 'abstract' (like love, justice, beauty or truth – things which are not objects or items) or 'concrete' (like table, chair, laptop – things which are). You can usually recognise a noun by the definite (the) or indefinite article (a/an) which is placed before it, though in the rules of English grammar you do not always need an article in front of a noun.

Nouns are often used as either the subject or object of a sentence, in English. To explain this further, look at the following examples:

1. The dog ate the cat
2. The cat ate the dog

Subject

The subject of a sentence is the person or thing (in sentence 1, the dog; in sentence 2, the cat) who is doing the action of the main verb. The verb in sentences 1 and 2 is 'ate' from the verb 'to eat'. In sentence 1, it is the dog which is eating. In sentence 2 it is the cat.

Object

The object of a sentence is the person or thing (in sentence 1, the cat; in sentence 2, the dog) which is being acted upon. The verb is from 'to eat', and in sentence 1, it is the cat which is being eaten. In sentence 2, it is the dog.

How do we know, from these sentences, whether the dog or the cat is the subject or the object?

In English, we know this by **syntax**. Syntax is word order or word position within the sentence.

In English, the subject of the main verb will almost always come **before** the main verb. Also, the object of the main verb will almost always come **after** the main verb.

Therefore, Standard English syntax in statements is as follows:

Subject – Verb – Object

It is important to understand that this formation is not the same in all languages and not all languages use syntax (remember, this means word position or word order) to show the subject or object relationship.

Pronouns

These are words which replace a noun in a sentence. This means that they are grammatically like nouns. What that means is that they can function as subjects or objects of verbs, like nouns can.

Personal pronouns are: I, you, he, she, it, we, you and they as subjects, whereas me, you, him, her, it, us, you or them are the same pronouns, but as the object. For example:

1.   I [subject] like him [object]

2.   He [subject] likes me [object]

I/me both refer to the first person singular.

Him/he both refer to the third person singular in the masculine.

It is also possible to show possession (ownership) with pronouns: my, your, his, her, its, our, your or the, or mine, yours, his, hers, its, ours, yours or theirs.

We can also categorize pronouns into singular or plural:

Singular	Plural
I	We
You	You
She, he, it	They

And into first, second or third person:

First Person	Second Person	Third Person
I	You	She, he, it
We	You	They

Thus, we can define any pronoun as singular or plural and first, second or third Person.

In literature, if the narrative is described as being 'in the first person' it means that it uses the form 'I' - the **first person singular pronoun**. In other words, the first person narrator is also a character in the story.

If a narrative is described as being 'in the third person' (probably the most common narrative form) it means that it describes the characters as 'he' and 'she' - the **third person singular pronouns**.

Verbs

These are 'doing' words and typically describe actions or states. They are fairly easy to recognise in English since it is a largely uninflected language and has few grammatical endings.

For example, verbs may end in –s as in 'he works' or –ing as in 'working' or –ed as in 'worked'. Works, working and worked are all inflections of the verb 'to work', which is a regular verb because it follows this familiar pattern. The most important irregular verb in English is the verb 'to be' which can come in the form: is, be, am, are, being or has been, was or were. As in many languages, it does not follow the regular verb pattern though it is probably the most common of all the verbs.

Verb Tenses

It is important that you can identify different tenses, and that you understand how they are used in English.

Present Simple (many uses, including for general statements)

PERSON	VERB
I	Play
You (singular)	Play
He, she, it	Plays
We	Play
You (plural)	Play
They	Play

Example: I play with the ball in the street (This describes a general or global state of affairs).

Present Continuous (for on-going present action)

PERSON	VERB
I	Am playing
You (singular)	Are playing
She, he, it	Is playing
We	Are playing
You (plural)	Are playing
They	Are playing

Example: I am playing with a ball in the street (This describes something that is happening right now).

Past Continuous (for on-going or continuing past action)

PERSON	VERB
I	Was playing
You (singular)	Were playing
He, she, it	Was playing
We	Were playing
You (plural)	Were playing
They	Were playing

Example: They were playing with the ball in the street (This action was on-going in the past).

Past Simple (for finished and completed past action)

PERSON	VERB
I	Played
You (singular)	Played
She, he it	Played
We	Played
You (plural)	Played
They	Played

They played with a ball in the street (This is a completed or finished action in the past).

Present Perfect (for past actions which still have a reference in the present)

PERSON	VERB
I	Have played
You (singular)	Have played
He, she, it	Has played
We	Have played
You (plural)	Have played
They	Have played

Example: I have played with a ball in the street, but I don't like doing it now (This describes a past action which still has a relevance or reference to a present state)

Past Perfect (for past actions that took place before other past actions, which are referred to in the simple past)

PERSON	VERB
I	Had played
You (singular)	Had played
He, she, it	Had played
We	Had played
You (plural)	Had played
They	Had played

Example: I ate my dinner after I had played with a ball in the street.

As you will have noted from the examples above, in English (in common with many other European languages), there are six 'parts' of the verb. This means that there are six different ways of expressing a verb, depending on who the 'person' is performing the action. These parts are:

I; you (singular); He, she or it; We; you (plural) or they.

In many other languages, you would find a great difference between, for example, 'I play' and 'We play', where the 'person' varies but the tense stays the same.

However, in English, notice instead the similarities: the only different example is the third person singular:

He, she or it plays, which ends '–s'.

This lack of complexity is a key characteristic of English as a language.

Active and Passive

Verbs can also be in the active or in the passive. All the verbs in the tables above are in the active. In the passive, the 'direction' of the action is reversed. For example:

I hit (active)
I am hit (passive)

They eat (active)
They are eaten (passive)

She sends (active)
She is sent (passive)

We see (active)
We are seen (passive)

Adjectives

These are words that describe, or 'qualify', a noun. They are typically placed before a noun in Standard English word order: a **pretty** dress, a **blue** table and so on. It is possible to use more than one to describe a noun, for example: a **pretty blue** table. Notice how the word order, or **syntax**, matters, here. For example, in English, we would **not** say 'a blue pretty table'.

There is a rule that governs the order in which adjectives are placed before the noun in English. That rule is as follows:

1) Number always comes first – that is, how many of the thing in question there are
2) Opinion about the noun is second – for example, an adjective such as 'beautiful' which is a judgement label applied by the speaker
3) Size is third – that is, a reference to whether the thing is large or small
4) Age is fourth – that is, a reference to whether the thing is young or old

5) Shape is fifth – that is, round, rectangular, triangular or any other shape designation

6) Colour is sixth – any colour word is also an adjective

7) Proper adjective – that is, nationality or place of origin, such as French or British. These are adjectives derived from the proper nouns France and Britain respectively

8) Purpose or qualifier – that is, a word that defines more closely the function of the thing. An example would be 'racing' in 'racing' car. The qualifier 'racing' categorises 'car' in this case.

An example of this in practice would be as follows:

Two beautiful small old rectangular blue French writing tables

Not Writing small beautiful rectangular French blue old two tables

The 'wrongness' of the second example, where only the word order has been shifted, shows us the huge importance **syntax** plays in English. In contrast, in many other languages, the ordering of multiple adjectives placed before the noun is much less strict, and as such the second example would 'feel' less wrong in another language compared to English.

Adjectives come in comparative and superlative forms, as well. Big is a regular adjective, **bigger** is the comparative and **biggest** is the superlative. Some adjectives are irregular, such as bad. The comparative is **worse** and the superlative is **worst**. It is irregular because it does not follow the –er and –est pattern of a regular adjective. Comparatives are used to compare two people or things, e.g. He is taller than me. Superlatives are used to compare more than two people or things, e.g. He is the tallest in the class.

Task

Look at the following, and complete the table:

Adjective	Comparative	Superlative
Pretty Good		

Now try and think of 10 more adjectives, and include them in this table along with their comparative and superlative forms.

Commentary

For this task, 'Pretty' is regular, but 'Good' is irregular. The comparative and superlative forms are as follows, and I have also added a few more adjectives to the table:

Adjective	Comparative	Superlative
Pretty	Prettier	Prettiest
Good	Better	Best
Tall	Taller	Tallest
Short	Shorter	Shortest
Big	Bigger	Biggest
Small	Smaller	Smallest
Cold	Colder	Coldest
Hot	Hotter	Hottest
Happy	Happier	Happiest
Strange	Stranger	Strangest
Unusual	More unusual	Most unusual
Excellent	More excellent	Most excellent

Adverbs

These are words which describe, or qualify, a verb. They can be placed more flexibly in the sentence; the following are both possibilities:

Quietly, he went
He went **quietly**.

Adverbs typically end in –ly, though not always, as in:

He could run **fast**

Adverbs can also be comparative (**more quietly** or **faster**) and superlative (**the quietest** or **the fastest**).

Task

Here is a short section of dialogue from *The Importance of Being Earnest* by Oscar Wilde. Read it carefully, and write down all the examples of nouns, verbs, adjectives, adverbs and pronouns that you can, and then read the commentary below.

Algernon: That is quite a different matter. She is my aunt. (*Takes plates from below.*) Have some bread and butter. The bread and butter is for Gwendolen. Gwendolen is devoted to bread and butter.

Jack: (*advancing to table and helping himself*). And very good bread and butter it is too.

Commentary

You should have found some examples of nouns, such as: Algernon, Gwendolyn, Jack, aunt, bread, butter, matter or plates. There are also verbs, such as: is, have, takes, advancing and helping. The adjectives include: good, different. The pronouns are: she, it, my. There was one adverb: quite.

Hopefully you didn't find it too difficult to categorize the word types in this exercise, but if you found this troublesome then I suggest you spend a little more time familiarizing yourself with nouns, verbs, adjectives, adverbs and pronouns by rereading this information and practicing language analysis a little more.

Sentence Type

As already discussed, syntax is the study of sentence structure, or how words fit together. Clearly, language is more than just disassociated words: it is word relationships which form into sentences, then paragraphs, and finally complete texts.

As you know, English is not particularly grammatically complex, since it is a relatively uninflected language, it is more so with regard to its syntax. In order to analyze the set texts, you need to be aware of some of the main features of English syntax, as follows.

Sentences are the organization of individual words. They can be as varied as you like in terms of content and meaning, but broadly fall into one of four functions, which are:

- Statements (declaring information)
- Interrogations (asking a question)
- Imperatives (giving an order or command)
- Exclamations (conveys intense emotions such as anger, surprise, joy or shock).

Task

Read the sentences that follow carefully, and categorise them as a statement, interrogation, imperative or exclamation.

1. Where are you going?
2. I'm going to the library.
3. Go to the library!
4. What?!

Task

Taking the statement: 'She's happy' modify it by changing the word order, punctuation or syntax in order to transform it into an example of an interrogation, imperative and exclamation.

Commentary

'She's happy' is a statement. The interrogation: 'Is she happy?' is an acceptable transformation. For the imperative, you might have: 'Be happy!' and the exclamation could be: 'She's very happy!' to express joy or surprise as indicated by the exclamation mark.

Besides typically having one of these four functions, sentences can also be analysed in terms of their syntactical complexity. (Though this is not the same as whether they are difficult to understand). As such, we have sentences which are simple, compound and complex based on the number of clauses in the sentence and the relationship between them. Read the information that follows and then attempt the next task.

Simple Sentences

Simple Sentences have only one main clause. This means that there is one subject (the person or thing doing the verb) and one main verb. An example of this is: 'The man wrote.' Here, we have the main verb in the past tense, wrote, and the man doing the writing, who is the subject. Often, simple sentences are also short sentences, but this is not necessarily the case. Simple sentences are direct and blunt, and can create a striking impact if mixed in with more complex ones.

Compound Sentences

Compound sentences have two or more clauses, linked by a co-ordinating conjunction such as 'and' or 'but'. For example: 'He went out the door and tripped over the pavement'. Here we have two main verbs, went out and tripped over, in each of the two clauses linked by 'and', though the subject 'he' remains the same in each.

Complex Sentences

Complex sentences also have two or more clauses, like compounds, but are linked by the subordinating conjunctions like 'although', 'when', 'if' or 'because'. These subordinating conjunctions have the effect of placing the clauses in a dependent hierarchy, so one is primary and the others secondary. For example: 'Although it was cold, they still went outside'. Here, the important information as contained in the main clause is 'they still went outside' whereas the secondary clause is 'although it was cold' which contains information subordinate to that of the main clause.

Task

Write three examples of your own of a simple sentence, a complex sentence and a compound sentence. When you have done that, try and get into the habit of noticing further examples of these from your day to day reading and speaking. By doing this, you will be starting to practice the skills of language analysis!

Commentary

Here are some examples of simple sentences:

She was cold.
It was dark.
He ran.

Here are some examples of compound sentences:

She felt cold and she put on a jumper.
It was dark and he put the light on.
He ran but tripped over a log.

Here are some complex sentences:

Despite the cold, she felt happy.
Although it was nearly dark, the dog needed walking.
If I see a monster, I will run away.

Topic 2 – Introduction to English Language for A-Level

Introduction

In this section, we will start thinking about English as a language. We will think about how sentences are constructed and how authors use linguistic techniques.

Aims and Objectives

- To start thinking about English as a language

Reading English

At first glance, studying English Language seems relatively straightforward. After all, we use the English language every day. We speak, read and write English, often without really thinking about it. We have learned to understand English by a strange form of osmosis, absorbing its nuances on an intuitive level. Indeed, many aspects of our language are taken for granted and we hardly notice how complex and sophisticated the English language really is, or can be.

However, in order to write about how English is used and in order to analyse and unpick the ways in which sentences are constructed, then we need to learn a whole new terminology.

Linguistics is the study of language. It is itself another kind of language with its own set of words.

In this section, we will be learning some of this vocabulary.

Linguistic Terminology for A-Level

The Edexcel A-Level English Language and Literature specification requires you to have some basic familiarity with the following linguistic terms:

- phonetics, phonology and prosodics
- grammar and morphology
- lexis and semantics
- pragmatics
- discourse

In this section, we will introduce these ideas.

Phonetics, Phonology and Prosodics

Phonetics is the study of spoken sounds and phonology is the study of sounds in a particular language.

In phonetics, a linguist might study spoken sounds in different languages using the International Phonetic Alphabet. A phonologist studying English might look at how these sounds are combined to form English words. There are around 44 sounds in English and these can be combined to form well over 250,000 words![3]

If you go on to study English Language or Linguistics at university, you will learn about how sounds are formed and represented. However, a detailed study of this is not required for A-Level. Instead, we will mainly be looking at aspects of spoken language such as accent and dialect.

---

[3] The exact number of words in the English language is unknown, mainly due to difficulties in classifying what 'word' might include. This conservative estimate of over a quarter of a million words comes from the OED in an article at http://www.oxforddictionaries.com/words/how-many-words-are-there-in-the-english-language

Phonetics and phonology can also help us to distinguish between 'real life' speech and the scripted speech used in drama. These aspects of phonetics and phonology will become important when we consider the idea of voice and look at how it is created.

Another important feature of spoken language and how a sense of voice is created is the concept of prosodics. Prosodics can be thought of as the way that spoken sounds are organised to create additional meanings. For example, we might find that we speak very quickly when we are excited and more slowly if we are tired. Someone listening to us would then be able to tell how we felt from listening to the speed of our speech.

Intonation is another aspect of prosodics. Think of the phrase:

"Yeah, right."

This could have totally different meanings depending on how it is intoned. It could be an enthusiastic response to a question or suggestion. However, if a mocking tone was used, then it could be sarcastic. (When we represent speech in writing, we can use grammar and punctuation to make meanings like this clearer. For example, the enthusiastic response could be more strongly suggested by using an exclamation mark.)

Prosodics also includes the way that particular words in a sentence might be emphasised (**stressed**) and how this affects meaning.
Consider the statement:

"I want to go swimming next week."

Here, the meaning can be altered depending on where the stress falls. If *I* is stressed, then this emphasises the fact that this is what the speaker wants to do. If *next week* is stressed then the timing of the activity is shown to be more important. If the stress falls on *want* then this creates the impression that the speaker is a bit bratty or spoilt.

An author might represent these features of intonation by italicising emphasised words. Therefore, you can see that emphasis can create some sense of the speaker's voice and meaning, even though we cannot hear them and we can only read the words as written.

In this way, although we will be looking at written examples of English language, understanding how different features of spoken English are used and represented can help us to gain a good idea of voice and how it can be conveyed.

Task

Write a short definition of the following linguistic terms:

- Phonetics
- Phonology
- Prosody

If you find this difficult, use a dictionary to help you.

Commentary

Phonetics is the study of spoken sounds.

Phonology is the study of spoken sounds in a particular language.

Prosody is the patterns of stress and intonation in a language.

from the previous topic. However, the word 'morphology' may be new to you.

Morphemes are the smallest units of language and **morphology** is the study of these units. A morpheme can be a whole word or part of a word. Think of the following words:

- Cat
- Kind
- Dogs
- Unkind

Some of these words can be broken down into smaller units of meaning. For example:

Dog + -s = Dogs

In this example, the plural form of dog is made by adding an -s to the end of the word. Here dog is a morpheme and -s is a morpheme. Dog, however, is also a word on its own. -S is not a whole word on its own. Therefore we say that Dog is a **free morpheme** and that -s is a **bound morpheme**. In English, many words use the bound morpheme -s to form their plural.

Here is another example:

Cat + -s = Cats

This use of morphemes changes the form of the word 'cat' from singular (cat) to plural (cats). 'Cat' refers to a single cat; 'cats' refers to more than one cat. However, the concept of *cat* is unchanged. This is called **inflectional morphology**.

In **derivational morphology**, morphemes are used to create new words. Here are some examples of this use of morphemes:

Un- + Kind = Unkind
Kind + -ness = Kindness

Here the bound morphemes un- and -ness can be added to kind to change its meaning. This type of bound morpheme is called an **affix**. The morpheme un- goes before the free morpheme and is called a **prefix**. The morpheme -ness goes after a word and is known as a **suffix**.

Some authors have used morphemes to form their own original words, sometimes called neologisms. For example, the author Thomas Hardy used the word 'uncoffined' in his poem Drummer Hodge and the word 'unkissed' in his poem Her Father.

Although these words are not in a dictionary, the morphological structure of English means that we can quite easily understand what they mean.

Task
Identify the morphemes in the words below:

Box
Boxes
Child
Childish
Unkind
Kindly
Kindness

Commentary

Free morphemes:
Box
Kind
Child

Bound morphemes:
-es
-ish
un-
-ly
-ness

Lexis and Semantics

Semantics is described as the study of meaning. In this context, we are referring to the way that words act as signifiers that represent a particular concept. Words are not the only way that ideas can be represented. Other signs that act as signifiers might include mathematical symbols or road signs.

In English Language and Literature, however, we are mostly concerned with the way that a writer chooses words. We are therefore concerned with the way that some words have particular connotations and that the words that an author chooses create a particular effect on the reader.

Think of the following:
- Green
- Red

These words are used to describe colours. They could be used quite straightforwardly as adjectives (modifiers) to describe how something looks, for example, 'a red car' or 'a green dress'.

However, these words might have other connotations as well. Green is associated with nature, with the countryside, and with the environmentalist movement (such as The Green Party). Red might be associated with danger or with passionate love.

In this way, words can mean more than it immediately appears and writers can use this to create particular effects. In The Great Gatsby, F. Scott Fitzgerald uses colours to create additional layers of meaning in the novel.

For example, Gatsby associates his lost love Daisy with a green light at the end of her dock. The colour green here has a symbolic meaning that goes beyond a literal description of the colour and we might read this green light as representing a lost Eden or a kind of paradise. Fitzgerald did not choose to make the light red or yellow and it would not have had this same meaning if he had done so.

You should also note that sometimes words are combined into phrases where they no longer act as individual words. Take as an example the phrase 'a red flag'. This can be read in two ways. It has a literal meaning, to describe a flag that is red, as in this example:

I put a red flag on the top of my sandcastle.

However, it also means 'a warning', possibly due to the use of red flags in C16th naval warfare. Consider this example:

"He kept saying he had to work late. That should've been a red flag right there."

Here the speaker is using the term 'a red flag' in this second sense, to mean a warning. Here, the three words 'a red flag' cannot be separated because they work together to create the accepted meaning.

For this reason, some linguists prefer to use the term **lexemes** to refer to a unit of meaning, whether this is an individual word or a phrase that cannot be divided.

Pragmatics

As we have seen in the examples above, words can have multiple meanings and connotations. Semantics tends to view these meanings as encoded in our language and accessible to us as part of our shared culture as speakers of English. For example, the way that the colour green is associated with nature is an idea that we pick up on through its frequent repetition in language and culture.

Pragmatics is a sub-species of semantics that emphasises the importance of context in interpreting meaning. These contextual factors are non-linguistic. They might include all the circumstances in which a phrase is spoken, the social relationship of the speakers, their presumed intent, etc. Pragmatics explores how the context helps to avoid potential ambiguities in spoken language.

An example of this might be the sentence:

You are green!

This is an ambiguous statement and we would need to use contextual factors to interpret it. For example, a child could say this to their mum after drawing a picture of her in green crayon. Alternatively, if it was said in a nightclub where the speakers were standing under a green light, then it could refer to the way that the green light made their skin tone appear differently. If a friend was helping you to dye your hair green, then they might say this to tell you that the colour had taken successfully.

There are also other potential meanings that use the non-literal attributes of the word green. Green can also mean inexperienced and this could therefore be a statement criticising someone's naivety. It could make reference to the idea of a green light to mean something like 'you're good to go'. Another example would be to use the statement as a compliment to someone's environmental awareness.

"I try to cycle or walk as much as possible."
"You are green!"

In this way, contextual factors can completely alter the meaning of a phrase. Indeed, some linguists would argue that context is always central to interpretation and perhaps more so than has always been realised. They might even go as far as to argue that pronouns, particularly 'I' and 'you', have no meaning without context.

Context can also become important when considering how different groups of people speak to each other. For example, the way you speak to your friends is likely to be very different to the way you would speak to a teacher at school. These types of considerations also become important when we consider the use and conventions of different genres of writing. We will be looking at genre and voice in Component 1.

Discourse

The conventions of genre are also described using the linguistic term **discourse**. In this sense, discourse refers to the way that different types of texts use particular features. This can include using a particular design or layout.

For example, a newspaper article will usually have a heading in larger print at the beginning of the article. A website might have a banner at the top of every page.

We will look at the conventions of different genres in detail in Component 1.

Task

Thinking about English as a language is a difficult skill and can seem quite alien at first. If you find the ideas in this section difficult, it may help you to read a textbook on English Language.

We would recommend:

Sarah Thorne *Mastering Advanced English Language* (Palgrave Macmillan, Second Edition, 2008). ISBN: 978-1403994837

Adrian Beard (ed.) *Working with Texts: A Core Introduction to Language Analysis* (Routledge, Third Edition, 2008) ISBN: 978-0415414241

Topic 3 – Introduction to Literary Terms

Introduction

In this topic, we will learn some of the literary terms used in the study of English Literature.

Aims and Objectives

- To review some literary terms that will be useful to you in the study of English Literature

Introduction to Literary Terms

In this topic, we will learn some of the literary terms used in the study of English Literature. Some of these terms may be familiar to you from GCSE and some from your wider reading. Some may be new to you.

More of the terms from this section will be applicable to literary works (novels, short stories, drama and poetry). However, non-fiction writers can also use these techniques. For example, figurative language can be used to add colour and interest to a non-fiction article as well as a fiction short story.

We will start by considering some of the main features of fictional works. You will probably be familiar with these terms.

Narrator

The narrator is the person who tells the story. Sometimes this is a character in the story, who tells the story from their own perspective, using the first person pronoun 'I'. Sometimes the story is told from the perspective of an omniscient narrator. This is a narrator who relates the events of the novel, but is not themselves a character. This third person narrator may know all the events of the novel and have access to the inner thoughts of all the characters.

Vocabulary

First Person – A story told from the perspective of a single character, using the form 'I' throughout. These are described as First Person narratives. It is important to remember that the narrator is a character in the novel and not the author.

Third Person – A story told using the Third Person form. These types of stories use the characters names and the appropriate pronouns for example: 'Sarah said' or 'He walked.' The story can be told from the perspective of an omniscient narrator. This can be focalised through the point of view of a particular character. It may even switch points of view between different characters.

Point of View

Sometimes, a third person narrator is not omniscient and the story is told from the point of view of one particular character. For example, the narrative may use the form 'Sarah said' but all the information and thoughts are told from the point of view of Sarah. The reader would not be told any information that Sarah herself did not know.

If the story is told from Sarah's point of view in this way, then the readers are likely to sympathise with Sarah. Although the narrative may be written in the third person, it is subjectively from Sarah's point of view. Sarah is the focus of the novel. Another term used in English Literature to define point of view is focalisation.

The point of view of a novel is not always consistent and sometimes different points of view might be used. For example, different chapters might be told from the point of view of different characters. This gives us interesting, alternative viewpoints and at its most sophisticated, it can be used to create unreliable, shifting perspectives that question the events of the novel.

In this way, the point of view that a story is told from can have an important effect on the way that we read the events. How much we know affects how we interpret the story and which characters we sympathise with. Since we usually sympathise with the character whose eyes we look through, an author can change our perceptions by changing the perspective of the story.

Characterisation

Characters in texts are not 'real' people, but are insteac constructed by an author. However, to give them a sense of reality, each character will have their own distinct personality traits. The way that an author does this is called characterisation.

Characterisation often begins with a name. Again, in real-life names can seem fairly arbitrary but in a novel or poem the character names, like everything else in the text, are deliberately chosen. A character's name can be used to give a sense of social class or ethnicity. Names can also have a double meaning, or convey a certain characteristic

Authors also spend time describing the physical characteristics of characters. An author may intend a characters appearance to tell us something about them. The way they look can often be read as a sign of their inner person.

A first person narrator is also a character in a novel. It is important to remember that the narrator will have their own personality that influences what they say. They may be unreliable.

Character and Speech

Character can also be conveyed through the way the characters speak to each other, what they say and, sometimes, what they don't say.

At the most basic level, speech can be used to denote social class and position. A working class character, for example, might use a form of dialect rather than standard English. Dialect can also be used to indicate a geographical region for the character's origin.

An author can also use dialogue to tell us more sophisticated things about the characters, through the way that they speak to each other. What characters do not say can also be significant. Characters can also say things indirectly, through implication.

Characters can also describe their own feelings and thoughts in their conversations with the other characters. There may be a contradiction between what a character says about themselves and how their actions are interpreted by other characters, particularly an unreliable narrator.

Setting

In some novels, the setting has a presence that is almost as strong as that of the characters. These settings create a memorable effect on the reader and can form a large part of our enjoyment of a work.

The location can be a real place, a real place in the past or a completely fictional environment, such as a distant planet. Scenes and places in stories usually have a greater significance, however, than merely being a setting for the action. Indeed, these locations form part of the way that the story is told.

It is important to note that even a real place in a story can never be a wholly neutral description of that place. Instead, as we discussed earlier, fiction can only represent the world. The author will always emphasise and minimise certain aspects of any environment and this can be either a conscious or an unconscious part of the writing process.

Settings of stories can also have a wider significance. Indeed, place can often be used by a writer to draw attention to a particular reading of the text. A short story about a lonely man, for example, might use a location such as a lighthouse to emphasise his isolation. In this way, settings can often be symbolic. We will look at symbolism in the next section.

Imagery

There is another aspect of language use we need to consider in order to start learning about literary analysis. This is the use of imagery, or the way in which an author 'draws' pictures and images by using words.

Imagery can be literal or figurative. If it is literal, it means that the words are direct, straightforward descriptions of people or events. The writing is realistic, and it is typically this type of language which enables writers to explain plot development. Figurative language is not meant to be read literally but rather invites a comparison between one thing that is described and something else in order to give us greater insight into what the writer is really trying to communicate.

Figurative language is expressed by some particular techniques, such as: similes, metaphors, personifications and symbolism.

Simile

This is saying one thing is **like** or **as** another. Some similes are so familiar that they have become clichés: 'The clouds were **like** fluffy balls of cotton wool' is an example of a common comparative description. Also, 'she was **as** beautiful **as** a rose' is another common literary simile that has become a cliché.

In future, you may wish to listen out to how language is used day-to-day in ordinary contexts, to see if you can notice any common similes in conversation.

Metaphor

This is a direct comparison drawn between two different things, as if the first thing really is the second. There is no use of 'like' or 'as' as in similes. For example: 'She was a shadow of her former self.'

In this sentence, we are not expected to read the metaphor literally. The woman is not really a shadow: rather we are invited to imagine that the character has gone through a trauma of magnitude enough to make her seem insubstantial, like a ghost.

Remember, in spoken English both similes and metaphors are used all the time, often in the form of **idiom**.

An idiom is a phrase which has a particular and specific meaning which is not directly related to the immediate words used. They are used in many contexts and for many different purposes.

An example: 'You're pulling my leg!'

Most native speakers of English would understand that this means that the speaker doesn't believe what is being said, or that they think they are being teased. This phrase has a fixed meaning, although that meaning has no obvious connection to the words used. It's not immediately clear why this phrase has become commonplace or what teasing has to do with legs.

English has many idioms. You may like to search online or in other reference books for more examples if you are interested in this aspect of language use.

Personification

In personification, the author attributes human characteristics to something non-human. For example:

'The building stared back defiantly'

'Staring defiantly' is something that people do, but not buildings. This is personifying the building to convey the feeling or mood of the situation. In this case, the mood being conveyed is that of anger or rebellion. This image might therefore be used to describe a teenage character who doesn't want to return home after an argument but knows that they have to. This can be an effective and sophisticated writing technique if used well.

Symbolism

This is a important literary device. It is the use of an object, action or situation to represent something beyond its ordinary and basic level meaning. For example, the colour white has symbolic connotations of purity and innocence, and the colour black has those of despair, evil, death and gloom. If an author is using these colours in a symbolic way, then perhaps a character would change their clothing from black to white, or white to black, in order communicate something new about the changing emotions of that person, or the changing nature of the situation they are in.

Students often ask about the difference between metaphor and symbolism. The answer is that a symbol is actually present in the text. We saw in the section on setting that a lighthouse can be used to symbolise isolation and loneliness. If a character actually lives in a lighthouse, this is a symbol. If a character lives in a tower block that is described as 'a tall lighthouse above the sea of roofs', this is a metaphor. Both may represent the character's isolation.

Some symbols are easily discernible and some are more complex. Readers may debate the meaning of a particular symbols and different readers may interpret them in different ways. Some readers may find symbols in a text that the author tells us s/he did not intend. The extent to which we can know the mind of an author is an interesting debate within the academic discipline of English Literature.

Vocabulary Summary

Imagery – the use of visually descriptive or figurative language. Imagery is used to set the scene and to create images of a time, place or person in the reader's mind. It can be the use of simple, sensory description or it can be more complex and involve multiple layers of additional meanings.
Simile – a straightforward comparison that always included the words 'like' or 'as'. For example, "her hair was as black as a raven's feathers".
Metaphor – the use of one thing to 'stand in' for something else. An example is the phrase "raven haired", where a raven represents the colour black.
Symbolism – A symbol is both a thing in itself and the meaning which has attached to that thing through persistent representation. Symbolism is culturally specific. A raven, for example, is a symbol of death and ill-omen in Anglo-American culture. However, in Norse mythology and art, a raven is a symbol for Odin.

Literary Techniques

There are a few further literary techniques that we will look at briefly before we move onto the first unit. These are onomatopoeia, alliteration, consonance and assonance.

In **onomatopoeia**, the word used also suggests the sound that it describes. It is often used for animal noises such as 'meow' for a cat or 'neigh' for a horse. Many other words also sound like what they describe. A common example is the word splash. Mechanical sounds are also often imitated in this way. An example is the word 'buzz'. which describes the sound that it makes.

Alliteration is another technique that we will encounter in many texts. In **alliteration**, a particular sound is repeated at the start of a series of words. The rhyme 'Peter Piper picked a peck of pickled peppers' is an example of alliteration. Alliteration is closely related to the technique of **consonance** where a consonant sound is repeated, though not at the start of the word, for example in the phrase 'pitter patter'. It is also related to **assonance**, where a vowel sound is repeated, for example between the words you and blue.

Personification - The attribution of human characteristics to something non-human.

Onomatopoeia – A word that suggests the sound that it describes. For example 'meow' suggests the sound made by a cat. 'Buzz' is another

Alliteration - The use of the same letter or sound at the beginnings of adjacent or closely connected words.

Application

Although thinking about linguistic and literary features is important, try not to get too bogged down in them. English language and literature is not a memory test and you shouldn't spend lots of time memorising technical terms. Instead, you should think of these as tools to help you to read closely.

You need to go beyond just identifying and listing the techniques used and there are no marks for what the examiners call 'feature spotting'. Instead, the idea is to look at how the author uses these techniques to create a particular effect. Every time you mention a linguistic or literary feature, make sure that you go on to say why the writer has used this feature and what effect s/he hopes to create. Keep using lots of analytical phrases, such as 'this shows that' and 'this suggests' to make sure that you are really looking in detail at the techniques that an author uses.

An example of how to write about features in this way is:

> *Within this dialogue, Bronte's use of linguistic features helps to characterise Heathcliff.*
>
> *This creates the effect that ...*

This is called analytical writing and we will be practising writing in this way throughout the course. The aim is to think about how authors and why an author has chosen a particular technique and the effect that this creates on the reader.

In this way, try to think of the terminology shown in this section as a way to help you think about a text and to inform your personal responses.

The goal of English Language and Literature is to open up meanings and comparisons, rather than to answer with a simplistic answer. There are no straightforward or definitive answers in English. Your role is to explore the different ways that authors create meanings. There are no strictly right or wrong answers, so long as you are making references to the text and using linguistic terminology accurately.

Task

Add the new terms from this section into your glossary of terms.

When you feel confident with this section, you are ready to move onto the first unit.

Component 1:
Voices in Speech and Writing

Topic 1 – Component 1: Voices in Speech and Writing

Introduction

In this topic, we will gain an overview of the first component of A-Level Language and Literature: Voices in Speech and Writing.

Aims and Objectives

- To think about the requirements of this component
- To learn what you will be asked to do in the Component 1 exam

Component 1: Voices in Speech and Writing

Voices in Speech and Writing is the first component of A-Level English Language and Literature. We will be thinking about the idea of voice and we will be looking at the use of voices in both literary and non-literary texts.

In this component, we will study two texts. These are the Edexcel anthology *Voices in Speech and Writing: An Anthology* and the drama text *All My Sons* by the playwright Arthur Miller.

You will need copies of these texts. The Edexcel Anthology will be available from your exam centre and you should ask your exams officer to order one for you when you register to take your exams. You can buy any edition of *All My Sons*. You will be allowed to take *All My Sons* into the exam with you, so long as your copy is completely clean and have not been marked or annotated in any way. In other words, you must not write anything on your copy of the text, or you will not be allowed to take it into the exam with you.

The Component 1 exam has two sections. Section A will be based around one of the non-fiction texts that we will study as part of the Anthology. In Section B, you will focus on the chosen drama text: *All My Sons*.

Section A - Voices in 20th and 21st Century Texts

In Section A, you will be asked to compare one of the extracts from the Anthology to an unseen text. You will answer an essay question comparing how the authors create a sense of voice. Text A will be an unseen text that you have not read before. Text B will be a text that you have already studied. Text A and Text B will be printed in the Source Booklet which you will find on your desk at the start of the exam.

Section B - Drama Texts

Section B will ask you to answer a question on a drama text. We will be studying *All My Sons* and you will answer the question on this play. An extract from the play will be printed in the Source Booklet. You will be asked to write an essay comparing the use of language in this extract with other parts of the play. You will be able to take your copy of *All My Sons* into the exam with you.

Overview

In the exam you will be given two booklets. One will be a source booklet containing the extracts for you to read. The other will be a question booklet containing the exam questions.

The exam will last 2 hours and 30 minutes. It is worth 40% of the total A-Level.

Topic 2 – Section A - Voices in Speech and Writing: An Anthology

Introduction

In this topic, we will learn what you will need to do in Section A of the Component 1 exam.

Aims and Objectives

- To learn what you will need to do in Section A of the Component 1 exam

Voices in Speech and Writing: An Anthology

Our work for Section A of Component 1 will be based on the Edexcel publication *Voices in Speech and Writing: An Anthology*. This can be ordered in by your exam centre and you should ask your exams officer to order a copy of the anthology for you when you register to take your exams.

The anthology contains a variety of texts from a variety of genres. These include literary, non-literary and digital texts. We will be studying these texts to explore how the authors create a sense of voice. Through examining the texts in detail, you will develop your skills of close reading, and learn how to approach texts critically.

You will also be encouraged to explore the texts by making connections between them. This will help you to think about how texts relate to each other, and how authors are influenced by the genre they are working in and by their wider context. The texts in the anthology have been chosen by Edexcel to show a variety of voices drawn from a wide range of backgrounds and perspectives.

The overall aim of our reading is to use our knowledge of linguistic and literary techniques to analyse how an author creates a sense of identity and persona within a text. By thinking about how authors construct texts, we can make a critical and evaluative assessment of the texts we read. This is a useful skill for everyday life, as well as the A-Level exam.

Section A of Component 1

As we saw in the last topic, in Section A you will be asked to compare one of the extracts from the Anthology to an unseen text. You will answer an essay question comparing how the authors create a sense of voice. Text A will be an unseen text that you have not read before. Text B will be a text from the anthology that you have already studied. Text A and Text B will be printed in the Source Booklet which you will find on your desk at the start of the exam.

This means that you will not need to take your anthology into the exam with you, so you can write on it if you want to.

The question on the exam paper will be phrased in the format:

SECTION A: Voices in 20th and 21st Century Texts

Read Text A on pages [X-X] and Text B on pages [X-X] before answering Question 1 in the space provided.

Question 1:

Compare the ways in which the speaker and writer create a sense of voice as they describe their experiences. In your answer you must consider linguistic and literary features, drawing upon your knowledge of genre conventions and context.

N.B. [X-X] indicates a range of page numbers. These will be specified on the exam paper i.e. Pages 2-3 etc.

What Does This Mean?

There are five main parts of this question that you need to address. These are highlighted in bold below:

Compare the ways in which the speaker and writer **create a sense of voice** as they describe their experiences. In your answer you must **consider linguistic and literary features**, drawing upon your knowledge of **genre conventions** and **context**.

Compare

The word 'compare' means that you will need to make comparisons and connections between texts. By making comparisons, we can learn more about how each author creates an individual sense of voice. We can also think about how the voices of diverse authors are similar and different.

You will need to use comparative phrases such as 'similarly', 'differently', 'on the other hand', 'by contrast' and 'in comparison'.

A Sense of Voice

The focus of Section A is voices. We are mainly interested in how an author creates a sense of their own identity and personality. We will explore this further in the next topic.

Linguistic and Literary Features

Linguistic and literary features are techniques that create a particular impression on the reader. Different techniques can create different impressions on the reader and the author will therefore make choices as to how to phrase a piece in order to encourage the reader to respond a certain way.

Identifying these literary and linguistic features and using the correct terminology to describe them is one of the core skill of integrated English Language and Literature.

Genre Conventions

Each of the genres in the anthology has its own features. For example, a newspaper article will have typographical features such as the use of a heading and maybe a sub-heading. Broadsheet newspaper article will also usually have common language features, for example the use of a higher register and more sophisticated vocabulary than a tabloid newspaper.

You should notice therefore that these features are always comparative and that one genre is often defined in comparison to another. In other words, each genre has features that make it similar and different to another. We will be comparing features of the same genre and different genres as part of our analysis of voice.

Context

The context of a text is all the circumstance that surround that text. This means that you will need to consider how an author is influenced by the world around them and how different authors may have had different influences. These influences could include (amongst many others) the time period of writing, their culture or ethnicity or their social background. These influences can affect their voice and persona.

We will look at this further in the next topic.

Task

If you have not already done so, now is a good time to register for your exams. You will need a copy of the anthology for the rest of this section.

Topic 3 – Voices

Introduction

In this topic, we will look at the concept of voice. We will think about what we mean by 'voice' and how voices are constructed.

Aims and Objectives

- To start exploring the concept of voice

What Do We Mean By 'Voice'?

When we think about voice, what do we mean? We might think at first of our own voice: our pitch; our accent; and the way we phrase what we say. But is our own voice always the same? Do we speak the same way when we talk to our friends as when we talk to our parents? Do we speak differently when we are talking to a teacher, attending a job interview or visiting an elderly relative?

The more we think about it, the more we might start to think that we actually have different voices, and that each of these voices reflects a slightly different identity. In this way, we might say that our voices are constructed, and that they are designed to display a particular identity or persona.

Writers also create a sense of voice. This creates a sense of the writer as a person and it informs the way that we read their work. We may sometimes feel that we like the writer and that we enjoy reading their work. This may mean that we are more likely to agree with what they say. Alternatively, we may sometimes dislike the writer and find what they say provocative, and this may be partly due to their persona. In all cases, the writer is expressing a sense of voice and identity.

In this component, we will be studying how writers create a sense of voice in their work. All voices are constructed, so it is possible for us to look at how a particular writer has created this sense of identity through their choice of language and through their use of literary or linguistic techniques.

Voice, Text and Genre

In a well-crafted text, we may get a strong sense of the writer's voice. This may be expressed in different ways, depending on the genre or mode of writing.

In this component, we will be looking at literary, non-literary and digital texts drawn from several different genres. Different genres have their own conventions.

The Voices Anthology contains examples of texts from several different genres. These genres are:

- Article
- Autobiography/Biography
- Diary/Memoir
- Digital Texts (Blog and Podcast)
- Interview
- Radio drama/Screenplay
- Reportage
- Review
- Speech
- Travelogue

You will notice that these types of writing are sometimes very different from each other. For example, the author of an article will be writing for a large audience and they will be likely to alter their voice accordingly. On the other hand, a diary might be a personal document intended to describe the writer's day-to-day experiences and it might not be intended to be read by anyone else at all. We might at first assume, therefore, that the voice of a diarist is more 'honest', while the article author will adopt a public persona.

In this way, you will see that the way that voice is constructed is connected to the genre of the text. Some writers create a very strong sense of identity and we may even be able to 'hear' the author, as if they were speaking to us directly. In other types of prose, we might hear the voices of characters indirectly, for example, the way that speech is reported in a novel. We will look in more detail at the characteristics of each genre as we work through the texts.

Some of the genres that we will be looking at are designed to be listened to, rather than read, and this will also affect how we hear the voices within the text. For example, although we will be reading speeches, they are actually designed to be spoken aloud to an audience. The speaker's skills of presentation (known as oration) will therefore be important, even though it is difficult to grasp this from the text alone.

Dramatic texts (such as radio plays) are also designed to be listened to, rather than read, and the actors will speak the lines and add emphasis to the words in order to bring out their meaning. In a play, the speech is usually meant to sound immediate and spontaneous, as if the characters are speaking to each other and we are watching, even though the words are actually carefully scripted.

For Edexcel A-Level English Language and Literature, we will not be looking at the features of speech and the representation of spontaneous speech in a lot of detail. However, it is recommended that you learn some of the terms used to analyse speech, in order to help you to write about the way that naturalistic speech is presented.

The table overleaf shows a glossary of terms that you should become familiar with. Gaining an overview of the features of speech at this stage will help you to think in terms of 'voice' as we work through this component.

This table of terms is based on that provided by Edexcel[4].

Feature / Term	Definition / Example	Function / Effect
Accent	A distinctive way of pronouncing a language	Can indicate the regional origin or social class of a speaker
Address	How people refer to or 'address' each other. (Examples include 'mum'/'madam'/'mother')	Indicates status/relationship/ class/role/gender/inclusion/ exclusion, etc.
Adjacency pairs	Exchanges between different speakers that are connected and that have expected responses (For example, the question "Where are you? expects a reply that answers this question, like: "I'm in the supermarket")	Keeps conversation flowing. Establishes and sustains/disrupts the pattern of conversation (turn-taking). Indicates power/dominance/ compliance/co-operation. To disrupt the usual pattern can indicate deliberate rudeness or disinterest.
Agenda	The topic or subject of the conversation	Indicates levels of co-operation/ agreement/disagreement/ dominance/compliance, etc.
Back Channel features/Co-operative signals	Words, phrases and non-verbal utterances used by a listener (e.g. 'I see', 'oh', 'uh huh', 'really') which indicate they agree or want to heat more. Used by the listener to give feedback to a speaker that the message is being followed and understood	Indicates co-operation, and permission to continue with the agenda
Backtracking	Interruption of the sequence of an utterance to include information that should have been included earlier	Indicates how speakers monitor what they say, and levels of correction and/or clarification
Contraction	A reduced form often marked by an apostrophe (in writing) e.g. can't, he'll, might've	Lowers formality and speeds up the interaction
Deixis/deictics	Devices which make sure that a listener knows what, where and to whom an	Indicates co-operation, monitoring, awareness of

[4] Edexcel Getting Started Guide at http://qualifications.pearson.com/en/qualifications/edexcel-a-levels/english-language-and-literature-2015.coursematerials.html#filterQuery=Pearson-UK:Category%2FTeaching-and-learning-materials

	utterance refers. Examples include: 'this', 'that', 'there'	context and awareness of audience
Dialect	Elements of speech other than sound (grammar and vocabulary) that are distinctive to a regional or social use of language	Indicates social or regional background of a speaker
Discourse markers	Words and phrases that signal the relationship and connections between utterances. Examples include: 'first', 'now', 'on the other hand'	Indicate connections/relationship between utterances, and signposts to the listener
Elision	The omission or slurring [eliding] of one or more sounds or syllables – e.g. 'gonna'	Lowers formality and speeds up the interaction
Ellipsis	The omission of part of a grammatical structure – e.g. 'You okay?'	Conveys a more casual and informal tone
False start	When a speaker begins an utterance, then either repeats or reformulates it	Indicates self-correction and monitoring
Filler	Used to gain thinking time (sometimes called 'voiced pause'). Examples include: 'er', 'um', 'well'	Enables a speaker to pause and gain time to think
Hedges	Vague words or phrases that are used to soften the force of how something is said. Examples include: 'perhaps', 'maybe', 'sort of'	Indicate politeness, uncertainty and co-operation
Idiolect	Features that make up a personal language profile/individual style of speaking.	N/A
Monitoring talk	Words or phrases used to check or comment on what is being said. Examples include: 'do you see what I mean?' 'I think we've been here before.'	Checks that the speaker has been understood; comments on another's speech; reviews a conversation at any given point
Paralinguistic features	Features that enhance the meaning of spoken language, but are not part of the language itself. For	Add additional layers of meaning and may help ensure the listener's understanding

	example, hand gestures and facial expressions	
Phatic talk	Formulaic utterances with stock responses used to establish or maintain personal relationships. Examples include: 'How are you?' 'Fine, thank you.'	Indicates politeness and co-operation, and keeps conversation flowing
Repair	The process by which a speaker recognizes a speech error and repeats what has been said with some sort of correction	Clarifies or corrects the point being made. Can indicate lack of confidence/security
Simultaneous speech	Occurs when two people say the same thing at the same time, usually in the form of overlap	Can indicate engagement, or more negatively, impatience
Tag questions	Familiar questions, sometimes rhetorical, that are added to a declarative sentence to turn it into a question. Examples include: 'Don't you …?' 'Isn't it …?'	Indicate co-operation and invitation to respond
Vague language	Statements that sound imprecise and unassertive e.g. 'and so on', 'whatever', 'and stuff'	Indicates uncertainty. Lowers formality
Vocative	Names, titles, terms of address – used in the initial position such as 'Mum, can I …?'	Helps to create a personal relationship between speakers and encourage interaction

This list provides a useful summary of some of the features of spoken language. You will find it useful to add your own features to this list as you work through this section.

Task

Using a blank sheet of A4 paper, make a table (similar to that above) using the following headings:

Feature	Definition / Example	Function / Effect

Use this to keep a record of new literary or linguistic terms that you come across. This glossary table will help you to remember new terms and will also be useful when you come to revise for the exam.

(There is no commentary on this activity.)

Topic 4 – Thinking about Texts and Contexts

Introduction

In this topic, we will think further about the way that all the circumstances surrounding a text can affect the voice that a writer chooses to use.

Aims and Objectives

- To think about the influence of genre
- To understand texts in terms of their purpose and audience
- To think about the role of context, attitudes and values

Genre

In the previous topic, we looked at how the genre of a text can influence the way that the writer constructs a sense of voice. We looked at how an article might be written for a large audience, and therefore the writer might adopt a public persona, whereas a diary might be written for no audience and have a more personal tone.

Following on from this idea, we will now think further about the way that different considerations can affect the writer's choice of voice. Some of these considerations are:

- Genre
- Audience
- Purpose
- Context
- Attitudes and Values

In this topic, we will look at how these different factors can influence a text. Although we will initially look at each in turn, it is important not to separate them out too artificially, as there is a lot of overlap between them. A text will be a product of all of these considerations, and should be seen as a sum of its many parts.

Audience

The expected audience will affect the writer's choices. When writing an article, for example, an author will need to think about the audience that s/he is writing for. For example, s/he might be writing for a broadsheet newspaper whose readership are assumed to be well-educated. The author will therefore use quite a sophisticated vocabulary, and may include detailed or complex information as part of the argument. The author might choose a voice that s/he believes will match that of their audience. For example, the author might also present themselves as well-educated and professional, in order to build rapport with their imagined readers.

If the same writer was writing an article for teenagers, s/he might adopt a very different style and tone. The author might assume that the teenage audience would not have as sophisticated a vocabulary as adults and might use simpler words. S/he might explain the concepts discussed, instead of assuming that the audience would already know what they mean. The author might also attempt to use a friendlier or more chatty tone, in order to appeal to the audience by creating a more accessible voice.

These are two examples of very different audiences. There can also be very subtle differences between audiences, and a perceptive writer will incorporate an awareness of these differences into the voice they use for their text.

Purpose

Closely related to both audience and genre, is the idea of purpose. Writers will always have particular intentions when they begin writing. Sometimes these purposes are classified as: to persuade; to inform; to instruct; or to entertain. (You may have come across these distinctions at GCSE.) However, there is considerable overlap between these purposes, and texts are often written for more than one reason.

For example, a newspaper article might be written to inform the newspaper's readers of a particular newsworthy event, for example a recent government announcement of a change of policy. This article could therefore be written to inform. However, it might also be written to persuade the audience to a particular view, depending on whether the journalist (and their editor) agree with this change of policy or not.

A review of a new film will also be written for several purposes. It might be written to entertain, but will also attempt to persuade the audience to the writer's view of the film.

The purpose of a text can therefore affect the author's choice of voice. Many writers may decide that if the readers like them, then they are more likely to agree with their views and they may therefore try to create a very likeable, personable voice. Another approach might be to present themselves as an expert in a particular field, perhaps adopting a scholarly tone, in order to make their view sound more convincing.

Context

Context is everything that happens around a text. This will include a wide range of factors and can be everything from the historical period in which a text is written to the author's own personal circumstances.

Another way of thinking about context is as all the factors that affect how the audience will consume a text. For example, a text that gives a very conventional or commonplace view will usually be relatively uncontroversial. A text that gives a unusual viewpoint may be challenged by readers.

Again, this will depend on the audience. The Telegraph is a newspaper that promotes conservative views, so a left-wing viewpoint is likely to prove controversial amongst its readership. In the opposite way, a Marxist literary journal would expect its authors and readers to share that viewpoint and would find the conservative ideas expressed in The Telegraph distasteful.

Often there is a difference between the context of production and the context of reception, especially for historical texts. The way that a text would have been read when it was first written and the way it is read today can often be very different, because of a change in cultural ideas, attitudes and values.

Attitudes and Values

We all have particular attitudes and values, whether we always realise it or not. These attitudes are usually the result of the environment around us, such as our social class, culture and upbringing.

Sometimes a writer will expressly argue towards a particular cultural, social or religious viewpoint. This will usually be when the writer is trying to persuade the audience to their view. At other times, these attitudes will be more subtle and may not be immediately obvious. As readers, however, it will be our job to look carefully at what the writer says and at what this says about them.

A writer may not always be aware of these attitudes and values within their own work. We sometimes call these unconscious biases.

Putting It All Together

In this way, the genre, audience, purpose and context will all affect the choices that a writer makes when constructing his or her voice.

In other words, these aspects of a text should not be looked at in isolation. Instead, we need to use our knowledge of different genres, audiences, purposes and contexts to look at how and why the writer has chosen to present themselves in a particular way.

For example, we know that a blog post will usually be written in a less formal style than a broadsheet news article. We know that the blog writer will choose to write in this style because it suits their likely audience (online surfers, who may not spend a long time reading the blog) and purpose (probably primarily to entertain). The tone is therefore likely to be chatty and personal and use an informal register.

As we work through the texts in the anthology, we will learn how to recognise the different features of texts and to look at how the author creates a sense of voice.

In the next topic, we will start exploring the genre of diary/memoir.

Task

This component requires the ability to get a sense of an author's voice and how it is constructed.

The best way to do this is to get lots of practice through reading widely.

You should try to read as much as possible. Try to read at least one newspaper a week and take every opportunity to read examples of texts from the genres of the anthology.

The more you read different examples of different authors in each genre, the better you will be able to get a sense of their different voices and how these are constructed.

Topic 5 – Diary and Memoir

Introduction

In this topic, we will begin looking at the anthology texts. We will begin with the genre of diary and memoir.

Aims and Objectives

- To learn about diary and memoir as a genre
- To examine the audience and purpose of our studied texts

Diary and Memoir

Although it is not the first genre in the anthology, in our course we will start by studying the genre of diary and memoir.

Diaries and memoirs are both forms of writing in which people record the experiences and events of their lives. A diary is normally written every day and records the events of that day. This might include the writer's thoughts and feelings as well as anything that has happened to them that day, whether happy or sad. In most cases, a diary is not intended to be published and it is usually a personal document. It may therefore have a confessional tone and the writer may describe feelings or events that they would not talk or write about in public.

However, many diarists will be aware that there is the possibility that their diary will be found and read, and they may therefore hide some of their more intense emotions or present a particular impression of events. For example, many young people keep a diary, but they might use a code to stop it from being read by brothers, sisters or parents.

Sometimes a dairy might be written by a politician, celebrity or other public figure. This type of diary might always be intended for publication and might therefore present the writer's own side of events, for example a politician's thoughts about a difficult political decision or a celebrity's view of their high-profile break-up. In this case, the author is likely to try to present themselves in a positive light. Even if not originally intended for publication, true honesty is difficult to achieve and there may always be an element of self-delusion in how we write about ourselves. In this way, although we might assume that the writer is being honest about their thoughts and feelings, they may still put considerable thought into the voice they create.

Memoirs are similar to diaries in that they are written from an individual's own point of view. A memoir will usually look back at a particular part of an individual's life, such as a summer from their childhood or a time when they lived abroad, and it will often recount their memories and experiences of that time. They are usually written after the events and may use material from the individual's diaries of the time. Because memoirs are written about the past, however, there will always be a level of distance and a memoir is often less immediate than a diary.

Diaries and memoirs can often be useful historical resources, as they can help us to understand the events of the past from a particular person's perspective.

The Anthology Texts

Your anthology contains two diary/memoir texts. These are:

- What I Did in 2003 by Alan Bennett; and
- An Eye-Witness Account Written by a Young Radio Reporter in the First World War

These texts are in Section 3 on pp.14-16 of the anthology.

Task

Read the text by Alan Bennett and answer the following questions:

1) Think about the title 'What I did in 2003'. What does this choice of title suggest to you?

2) Write 3-5 sentences on your initial impressions of Bennett based on this text. Use examples from the text to support your points.

3) Is this a genuine diary?

Commentary

1) The title 'What I Did in 2003' is reminiscent of the type of school essay many children complete in primary school, often with the title 'What I Did in the School Holidays'. This type of activity would have been very familiar to schoolchildren of Bennett's generation. Here, Bennett is using this reference humorously. The title both illustrates the pointless or banal nature of the original classroom activity, and seems slightly self-deprecating. After all, if a whole year can be written about this way, did very much of interest happen?

2) We get quite a strong sense of Bennett's voice and personality from this text. His tone is light-hearted and warm, and he is often mildly amused and amusing, such as in the line 'at 78 and with an artificial hip, it's not something I feel I should be doing'. He displays some mild cynicism and annoyance at times, such as reference to the 'unctuous telephone calls' and the way the closure of the abbey 'infuriates us both'. We are given insights into his current life and his childhood, particularly in the specific place names, and this gives a sense of him as being a real person. We get an impression of his mildly rebellious nature in how he was 'happy to outwit authority'.

3) This is a difficult question to answer definitively, and there are arguments for either view. It is certainly laid out as a diary, with specific dates given for the entries, and it is unlikely that Bennett could've remembered this level of detail if he was writing a long time after these events occurred. However, there is a strong sense of the presence of an audience here, and it is clear that this was never written as a personal diary. For example, Bennett obviously knows who 'his old Oxford supervisor' was, without needing to give his name, and this is therefore obviously intended for a wider audience. We might also suspect that a genuine diary entry might include a more emotional response to the death of a friend and colleague, instead of a rather glib, if amusing, anecdote.

About Alan Bennett

Alan Bennett is a well-known playwright. He is known for his often comic portrayals of working class characters in the popular drama series Talking Heads. He is himself of working class origins, but was accepted to Oxford University after studying at Grammar School. He often uses his social background in his writing. His play *The History Boys* is quite a popular text for A-Level study.

Given that Alan Bennett was already a famous person, we might imagine that this diary was always intended for publication, and the context and sense of voice that Bennett creates tends to support this view. We might also suppose that he would have a ready audience for his published diary. Our next text is quite different.

Task

Read Text 3.2: An Eye-Witness Account Written by a Young Radio Reporter in the First World War.

Thinking about the ideas we looked at in the previous topic, try to complete the following comparison table:

	Audience	Purpose
What I Did in 2003?		
Neyland's Eye Witness Account		

Commentary

The aim of this task is to help you start to think about comparing texts. This will help you prepare for reading an unseen text in the exam.

Text	Audience	Purpose
What I Did in 2003?	General readers; People interested in Alan Bennett and his work	To entertain readers; Possibly to record and share views and everyday experiences of life

We get a sense of this from Bennett's use of amusing anecdotes (climbing over a fence, etc.) and from his attention to detail (place names, etc.) |
| Neyland's Eye-Witness Account | People interested in the First World War; People interested in soldiers' personal experiences of war | To record the realities of war and to share personal experiences

We get a sense of this from the writer's accuracy, attention to detail and use of technical language, e.g. 'sapper', 'Verey lights'. Neyland's experience of war is also described in quite a straightforward and unemotional way, which contrasts with many other firsthand accounts. He also communicates his strong sense of duty and h s desire to 'play a real part in the Great War' and this suggests his |

		purpose is also to persuade others to his more heroic/stoic view of the First World War.

We will return to Neyland's account again in the next topic, where we will look at the genre of autobiography/biography.

Topic 6 – Autobiography / Biography

Introduction

In this topic, we will start looking at the genre of autobiography and biography.

Aims and Objectives

- To learn about the genres of autobiography and biography
- To start looking at our texts for this section

Autobiography / Biography

Autobiography and biography have several similarities to diaries and memoirs. They are also concerned with the lives of individuals. An autobiography is an account of a person's life, written by that person. It is similar to a memoir in that it may include personal views and reminiscences, but it deals with a person's life as a whole, rather than a selected part of it.

Biographies are written by professional writers who choose subjects to write about. They may interview the person (if they are still alive) or they may collect historical documents, such as the person's diaries or letters. A biography is not necessarily written from the perspective of its subject, but it will focus on them and therefore is likely to include a lot of material from their point of view. Not all biographers actually like their subjects, however, and some can be critical.

There is some area of overlap between biography and autobiography when a 'ghost writer' is involved. A ghost writer is a professional author who is hired (usually by a publishing company) to prepare an 'autobiography' of a famous celebrity. The ghost writer will usually interview the celebrity to get an idea of the events of their life from their perspective and an idea of their voice. The writer will then write the autobiography from the perspective of the celebrity using the first person pronoun 'I'.

Autobiographies and biographies are intended for publication and this makes them different to some diaries.

De Profundis

The anthology text by Wilde is an excerpt from De Profundis. This text is a long, autobiographical letter written to Lord Alfred Douglas. It describes Wilde's spiritual growth through the experience of his trials and imprisonment. De Profundis is Latin for 'from the depths'.

In this text, Wilde describes how he has come to accept the events that have happened to him. He views suffering as a spiritual experience and values humility. In the full length letter, he comes to identify Christ with the figure of the artist and goes on to say that experience and art are one and that whatever happens to one person, happens to oneself. He argues in favour of accepting negative experiences and transforming them into something good.

Me & Mom & Me

Me & Mom & Me is Maya Angelou's seventh and final autobiography. In it, Angelou describes her relationship with her mother, Vivian Baxter. The first section Me & Mom details her early life and her difficult early relationship with her mother, while the second section, Mom & Me, explores the loving and supportive relationship that developed between the women as adults.

The autobiography was published close to Mother's Day just before Angelou's 85th birthday. Reviewers have praised the work, calling it 'a tender read and a lovely tribute'[5] and a 'tightly strung, finely tuned memoir'[6].

Task

Read the texts on pp. 11-13 of the anthology. Make notes on any significant features that you notice.

Following on from the activity that we completed in the last unit, complete the table below, adding information for the texts in this section. You will also need to use the notes you made on context in the previous task.

Text	Audience	Purpose	Context
What I Did in 2003?			
Neyland's Eyewitness Account			
De Profundis			

---

[5] Marjorie Kehe of The Christian Science Monitor, 2014 cited Wikipedia
<https://en.wikipedia.org/wiki/Mom_%26_Me_%26_Mom> accessed 21/06/2015
[6] Kirkus Review of Books, 2013 cited Wikipeadia < https://en.wikipedia.org/wiki/Mom_%26_Me_%26_Mom>
accessed 21/06/2015

Me & Mom & Me			

Commentary

Text	Audience	Purpose	Context
What I Did in 2003?	General readers; People interested in Alan Bennett and his work.	To entertain readers; Possibly to record and share views and everyday experiences of life. We get a sense of this from Bennett's use of amusing anecdotes (climbing over a fence, etc.) and from his attention to detail (place names, etc.)	Bennett's role as a well-known figure. Personal friendships with well-known actors, celebrities.

Yorkshire context as part of author's identity. Multiple references to places in Yorkshire. |
| Neyland's Eyewitness Account | People interested in the First World War; People interested in soldiers' personal experiences of war. | To record the realities of war and to share personal experiences. We get a sense of this from the writer's accuracy, attention to detail and use of technical language, e.g. 'sapper', 'Verey | The First World War as a major world event. The harrowing experiences of young soldiers and individual reactions to events. |

		lights'. Neyland's experience of war is also described in quite a straightforward and unemotional way, which contrasts with many other firsthand accounts. He also communicates his strong sense of duty and his desire to 'play a real part in the Great War' and this suggests his purpose is also to persuade others to his more heroic/stoic view of the First World War.	Context of writing/publication (1930). Changing context today. Do we still have the same attitudes to duty?
De Profundis	People interested in Wilde and his writing; people interested in philosophy; people interested in the effects of prison on inmates.	To explain insights gained whilst in prison; to reconnect with Alfred Lord Douglas.	The background of Wilde's trials and homosexuality. His status as a famous figure in Victorian high society. Different attitudes to Wilde today.
Me & Mom & Me	General readers of autobiography; people interested in Angelou and her work; people interested in family relationships and motherhood.	To explore her relationship with her mother; perhaps to help other families who have experienced difficult relationships.	Angelou's role in the Civil Rights Movement and as a supporter of women's rights. Her important status as a well-known, public figure and as a black female author. American context (spelling of 'mom' and 'favorite') . Reference to

			American foods, such as 'hotdog'.

Topic 7 – Reportage

Introduction

In this topic, we will look at the genre of reportage.

Aims and Objectives

- To learn about reportage
- To study the two reportage texts in the anthology

Reportage

Reportage is a first-hand account of an event. It has certain similarities to a diary entry, memoir or autobiography, as it is often a personal commentary on events as they unfold. However, reportage is usually associated with the media and journalism. An example could be a live news report by a journalist at the scene of a natural disaster or a printed account by an aid worker describing the situation in a refugee camp.

There are two Reportage texts in your anthology. These are:

- 7.1 Chris Rainier: Tsunami Eyewitness Account by Nat Geo Photographer
- 7.2 Jessica Read: Experience: I Survived An Earthquake While Scuba Diving

---

Task

Read Text 7.1 Chris Rainier: Tsunami Eyewitness Account by Nat Geo Photographer

---

Tsunami Eyewitness Account by Nat Geo Photographer

This text describes the photographer Chris Rainier's experience of the days following the tsunami in Indonesia in 2005. Chris Rainier would have first communicated this as a spoken text and it has been recorded in writing for The National Geographic News. We can see from the way that the text is presented here that it would have been available on their website. National Geographic is an American publication that is mainly interested in nature, science and world travel.

The author mostly uses the first person to describe his experiences, such as in the vivid phrase 'everywhere I go I have to be careful I don't step on a corpse'. This creates a strong sense of immediacy. He also includes the reader at strategic points. He uses the first person plural in the phrase 'because we grew up with the images' in order to make a comparison that he feels the audience will understand and to include them in his experience. Significantly, this is used in the first line, to build an immediate rapport with the reader.

The text uses a mixture of factual, statistical information, such as 'the government has confirmed 95000 dead' and more impressionistic accounts, that convey the author's own experience, such as his comparison to the work of the painter Hieronymus Bosch. There is some overlap between these areas where figures are stated, but somewhat vaguely, such as 'some 200 charities' and 'some 10 square miles' and 'something like 30,000 bodies'. This might reflect the fact that it is more difficult to get information on the ground or that the scale of the situation makes it difficult to be precise.

The semantic field is drawn from disaster with many references to 'exposed bodies', 'deep wounds', 'decaying' and 'dying' and the article is very emotive. Powerful phrases are used to show the scale of the disaster, such as 'the horror of this place' and 'we see people with deep lacerations that have been covered with a dirty rag'.

The article is divided by the sub-heading question 'Are the emergency supplies of food and medicine getting through to the people?' This foregrounds the existence of the 'massive amount of money raised in the US and other countries' and the author identifies that the main difficulty is the logistics of getting needed help to injured and displaced people.

The overall tone of the article, however, shows the task as difficult but hopeful. The author tries to balance the horror with a sense of hope. The phrase 'So many people are here and so much assistance is coming in' uses repetition of 'so many / so much' to emphasise abundance. He emphasises the presence of the US military, the UN, and charity organisations several times and he tells the audience that people come up to hug and thank him for his help.

Although the situation is clearly very serious, we might argue that this article tends towards some cautious optimism. This is shown in the final line 'the challenge is to stabilise their communities and set up new places for them to live' . This again seems to suggest that the task is perceived as difficult, but not impossible, and seems to look forward to the future and to the expected eventual success of the relief program.

Task

Are there any attitudes and values on display in this text? Can you account for this through a consideration of context?

Commentary

National Geographic is an American publication and there is a lot of emphasis on the American participation in the relief effort here. The author mentions the role of the US military several times and states 'how everyone is very impressed' with their help. He explains how they work 'from dawn to dusk', using a cliché to reinforce and emphasise his point.

Indeed, the author shows a very pro-America stance here. The reference to monies 'raised in the U.S. and other countries' might be thought to minimise the efforts of non-American countries and we might suggest that a phrase such as 'worldwide relief fund' would have been more neutral and inclusive. The phrase 'They appreciate America's help' could be thought of as quite patronising.

Some of this could be explained through reference to the American publication of the article and also to America's participation in/instigation of recent wars (in 2005). This is shown in the phrase 'The U.S. military is being well-received', which draws attention to the fact that American foreign policy hadn't generally been very popular in many countries at this time.

Experience: I Survived An Earthquake While Scuba Diving

This text describes how the author experienced an earthquake while scuba diving in the Philippines. It first appeared in the Guardian Weekend Magazine, both in print and on their website. We can see that this text is taken from the online version of the magazine, contained in the Life and Style section. The purpose of this piece of reportage is to inform and entertain.

As a first-hand account, the author uses the first person throughout, and this makes it clear that she is drawing from her own experience. The article is structured so that it forms a clear narrative. It has an introduction, a beginning, a middle, an end and a conclusion. Each section of the piece is separated by a discourse marker, such as 'Last October', 'After nearly 45 minutes' and 'back in the boat'. These further create a sense of narrative progression and help to orientate the reader.

In the introduction where the author explains her background in scuba diving and how she usually enjoys diving as a relaxing activity. She emphasises that it is normally a peaceful activity through the use of the words 'calmness of being submerged'. The adjective pre-modifiers 'hypnotic' and 'quiet' in 'hypnotic sound' and 'quiet clicks' further emphasise that diving is usually tranquil. This sets up the rest of the piece, which as we know from the title, will not be about a relaxing dive.

She then begins with an explanation of the diving holiday she was on, and a short description of how the day began. She explains how 'after breakfast we boarded the boat with seven other advanced divers' and this has a simple, matter-of-fact tone.

Next, the author explains what happened on the dive itself. This draws on her sensory experience, and shows the author what she heard, saw and felt. Details such as 'a low rumble like an engine' help the reader to imagine what the sound was like, and the choice of simile used here compares the sound to one that all readers will be able to imagine easily. She also explains the confusion they felt before they know what was happening and says that 'The situation felt sinister and dangerous'. This phrase creates some tension, even though as readers we already know the cause of the sound and that the author survives the incident.

The end of the story comes as the author describes how they discovered they had witnessed an earthquake. This section is more factual, as the author now has access to reports of the incident. It includes more detailed information and technical terms, such as 'huge earthquake, measuring 7.2 on the Richter scale' and 'epicentre'. The author also realises that this incident was much more serious for many others than it was for the divers and she described how they were 'horrified' to hear that 'more than 200 people had died, with 1,000 injured'. Some of the language choices here are associated with the semantic felid of war, such as 'underwater bomb', 'enveloped', 'mushrooming' '30 Hiroshima bombs' and these words are used to show the power of nature 'at its most stunning, and most ferocious'.

There is a final conclusion where the author reveals how she had almost attended hospital that day for an earache. If she had done so, she would likely have been killed or injured in the earthquake. This gives a final sense of a tragedy avoided and of the author's good fortune in surviving these events.

Task

Think back to Text 3.2 Neyland's Eye-witness account written by a young radio operator in the First World War.

How are these two genres similar and different?

Commentary

Both of these texts are first-person accounts and both are told from a first-person perspective. They both describe the author's real-life experiences, and give a sense of what it was like to live the reported events. Furthermore, there are some similarities of content in that they both describe terrifying situations where the authors experienced physical danger.

Memoirs generally deal with a particular time in an author's life, generally looking back on the events from a time in the future, at a later stage of the author's life. Reportage is usually part of the news media and is more concerned with recent events. This is shown in these two texts where Neyland begins his account with 'At the age of eighteen', while Read describes events of 'Last October'.

Due to this time difference, the authors also have a different perspective on the events. Neyland's account was published 10 years after the end of the war and he has had more time for reflection than Read. Neyland draws significance from the fact that he was a participant in world events and he feels that he made a contribution to his country by doing his duty in war.

For Jessica Read, this was a terrifying incident where she might have been killed. For her, this was in many ways a random event and she feels she was lucky to survive. For her, it shows the power of nature. Her views of the event may change over time, and it may seem either less or more important to her at a later time in her life.

Topic 8 – Interviews

Introduction

In this topic, we will look at the two texts of interviews.

Aims and Objectives

- To learn about how voice is created in interviews
- To consider how far interviews are scripted in advance

Interviews

Interviews could be thought of as similar in some ways to memoirs or autobiographies, since they also deal with the experiences of real individuals speaking in their own voice. However, like the other genres we have looked at, the participants will still try to create a sense of voice and identity.

Interviews are usually conducted by an interviewer who asks the interviewee questions. There are many types of interviews. For example, a celebrity might be interviewed by a chat show host, an eyewitness might be interviewed by a TV reporter, the police may interview a suspect, or a candidate could attend a job interview.

It is important to remember that interview questions and answers are originally spoken and listened to (rather than written and read) and some information might be conveyed by gesture or facial expression. The interview may be recorded and/or broadcast and then a transcription made of the recording.

In this section, we will look at two interview texts. These are:

- 5.1 BBC Panorama interview between Martin Bashir and Princess Diana
- 5.2 Jay Leno's interview with President Obama

We will again look at how a sense of voice is created and at how the interviewer extracts information by using different types of questions.

The BBC Panorama Interview

Text 5.1 (on page 19 of your anthology) is a transcript of part of the Panorama interview between journalist Martin Bashir and Princess Diana. This was a significant television event, which received very high ratings when it was broadcast in 1995. Diana was a very high profile public personality, and the interview followed in the wake of a bestselling book called Diana: Her True Story, which described the Princess's unhappiness. At that time, Diana and Prince Charles were undergoing difficulties in their marriage and they divorced the year after (1996).

Task

Read Text 5.1 on page 19 of your anthology.

Make notes (on a separate piece of paper) of anything interesting that you notice.

Commentary

You will notice several interesting features about this interview.

These are some of the features that you might have noticed.

Register

Diana uses a mixture of informal and formal language here. Diana's voice uses mainly standard English, with a relatively sophisticated vocabulary. Phrases such as 'alleviate this doubt' use a relatively high register and sophisticated vocabulary. Other phrases, such as 'you know' and 'whatever', are much less formal, as perhaps suits her role as the 'people's princess'. This mixture of styles therefore shows an awareness of different audiences.

Repetition

Diana uses a lot of repetition in this interview. Some examples are: 'I know I can, I know I can, yes' and 'They don't care. People don't care.' Repetition can be used in this way to add emphasis. By repeating a word of phrase a speaker or writer can draw attention to it, or reinforce their point.

Extended Repetition

Repetition can also be used to form patterns in the text. There are several examples of this effect within this interview. The word 'whatever' is used three times. This adds emphasis. The repetition of 3 words or phrases together is known as a 'list of 3', 'rule of 3' or sometimes as 'triadic structure'.

There are also two examples of a 'list of 4' or 'quadratic structure' in this interview. Quadratic structure means repetition in groups of four. These are:

"to give affection, to make them feel important, to support them, to give them light in their dark tunnels"

and

"people's emotions, people's insecurities, people's distress, people's hopes and dreams."

Again, this type of repetition adds emphasis to words. The choice of words that Diana repeats here emphasises her commitment to human beings and their emotional lives. Note that there is repetition of 'people's' which shows the importance that Diana places on her idea of ordinary people' and that there is repetition of verbs associated with generosity e.g. 'to give... to make... to support... to give...' The pattern is also pleasing to the ear, and adds a sense of symmetry and balance to the sentence. This is a rhetorical effect often associated with political speeches.

Vocabulary

Rhetorical Device - A rhetorical device is a technique used to create a particular effect on an audience. Repetition is a common rhetorical device.

Repetition - Repetition is the repeating of a word in order to add emphasis.

Listing - Listing is a general term used for the technique of making lists. Lists can emphasise and reinforce an idea through repetition. For example, a politician might list election promises in the form: 'We will..., we will..., we will...'. When a particular number of items is listed, this can be called a 'list of X' (where X is the number of items.)

List of 3 - This is a type of repetition where the same word or words are repeated 3 times. It is also sometimes known as the 'rule of 3' or 'triadic structure'.

List of 4 - This is a type of repetition where the same word or words are repeated 4 times. It is also sometimes known as 'quadratic structure'.

Use of Metaphor and Cliché

Diana uses metaphors several times in this interview. When she speaks about helping 'to give them light in their dark tunnels' she is not speaking literally and the light and the dark tunnels are metaphors. She will bring a metaphorical light to illuminate the metaphorical darkness of sadness or distress.

This is a well-worn phrase that most people will have heard before. When a metaphor is used many times in this way, it becomes a cliché. A cliché is a phrase that has become overused to the point where it is considered trite.

In fiction or poetry, clichés are generally avoided and authors look for fresh and imaginative ways to express ideas. Indeed, using clichés can make an author look, uninspired, inexperienced or lazy.

There are two more phrases in this interview that might be thought of as clichés. These are:

"the seed is there, and I hope it will grow"

"knowledge is power"

Although phrases such as this are generally thought of as tired and unoriginal, they do have an effect on the reader. Indeed, sometimes a listener might identify with a speaker after hearing them express ideas that the listener has heard before, and this could create a sense of familiarity. It could also create a sense that the speaker is ordinary or 'normal' and help the listener to identify with them. By using the same phrases that everyone uses in speech, Diana seems more 'down-to-earth' than she would do if she used highly creative or unusual metaphors to describe her feelings. In this way, the use of clichés can be thought to contribute to a sense of voice here.

Simile - A straightforward comparison that always includes the words like or as. For example, 'her hair was as black as a raven's feathers'.

Metaphor - A metaphor is an comparison where one thing to 'stands in' for something else. An example would be 'raven haired', where a raven represents the colour black.

Idiom - An idiom is a phrase or expression with a fixed meaning. This meaning is often different to the natural meaning of the words used. For example, 'raining cats and dogs' means raining heavily, even though this has no obvious connection to cats or dogs. There are lots of idioms in the English Language, and they prove very challenging for non-native speakers.

Cliché - A cliché is a phrase that began as an original or unusual expression, but which has since become overused. An example is the phrase 'she was as beautiful as a rose'.

Types of Questions

We can also get a sense of Martin Bashir's voice in this interview. Bashir is asking the questions, so his speech is generally quite brief. However, we can get some sense of his voice and of his interview technique.

This is quite a polite and formal interview. Most of the questioning is relatively gentle and unaggressive. Most of the questions are quite short and designed to elicit more information, for example 'Why do you think that?' or to clarify Diana's meaning, such as 'When you say indifferent, what do you mean?'

In asking this question, Bashir is also giving Diana the opportunity to say something more positive about the general public. It might be thought of as criticism to say that people are 'indifferent' to an issue, but here Bashir gives Diana the chance to explain that she doesn't think that it is their fault that they are bored with the monarchy, but rather the result of being 'force-fed'.

Bashir asks some questions that are longer and that might be considered slightly more critical. The question opener 'up until you came into this family' suggests a causal relationship between Diana's entry into the royal family and their unpopularity. However, you might also consider whether this question is softened by 'do you feel', which emphasises Diana's personal feelings and 'at all to blame' which is arguably softer than 'to blame'. There are certainly more aggressive ways to ask this question, if Bashir had wanted to do so.

Bashir also give Diana a lot of space to answer questions in her own way and to talk about her feelings and her ideas for the monarchy. His question 'What are you doing to effect some kind of change?' gives Diana the opportunity to present herself well by showing that she is taking action to make the monarchy more compassionate.

Most of Bashir's questions are open questions, which invite discussion. These are questions that start with 'Do you think...?' or 'Why...?' They can't be answered with a yes or no answer, so the interviewee has to give a fuller answer. Another example of this type of broad question is 'What kind of monarchy do you anticipate?'

The opposite type of question is known as a 'closed' question. Some of Bashir's questions are closed questions, which have yes or no answers. Closed answers generally don't invite a lengthy answer. (Although Diana goes beyond answering with a simple yes or no.)

Some of Bashir's questions might be thought of as leading questions. A leading question encourages the interviewee to answer a certain way. There are different reasons for an interviewer to do this. Some interviewers might want to encourage the interviewee to sound more likeable, or some interviewers might want to trap an interviewee into saying something they will regret. 'Do you think...?' might be considered a slightly leading question, as it encourages the interviewee to agree with the interviewer. 'Wouldn't that resolve matters?' encourages a 'yes' answer, but Diana does not answer this way and it is likely that she has had media training in order to notice this type of question.

There is also one question where Bashir makes a slight error and then corrects his own speech. When we analyse spoken language, we call this type of correction a 'repair'. (This is one of the terms explained in the glossary in the first topic for this unit.)

Closed question - A closed question gives the interviewee a limited range of options in answering. A closed question can usually be answered with a 'yes' or 'no' answer. Multiple choice questions are also closed questions.

Open question - An open question cannot be answered with a 'yes' or a 'no'.

Leading question - A leading question is phrased in such a way as to suggest the answer e.g. The question 'What do you think of this terrible weather?' encourages the responder to agree that the weather is terrible.

Thinking Further About Interviews

There are a few further considerations to think about when reading a transcript of an interview.

At first it may seem that interviews are simply a conversation between two people, but they are rarely natural or spontaneous. Many televised interviews will have been heavily edited before broadcast and some parts may have be re-recorded several times before the perfect 'take' is achieved. Some interviews may be partially or wholly scripted, or the interviewee may be given a list of questions beforehand. Even for a live interview, the interviewee may be given an idea of what they will be talking about once the broadcast starts. This gives the interviewee an opportunity to think about how they want to come across and to decide how to create a sense of 'voice'.

We should also remember that this is only a transcript of an interview, and that some information would've been conveyed by gesture and facial expression. In English language and literature, however, we are mostly interested in how voice is created through words.

Read Text 5.2 Jay Leno's Interview with President Obama. Answer the following questions:

1) What are your initial impressions of the opening of this dialogue?

2) Who do you think are the audience for this interview?

3) Discuss 3 or more examples of President Obama's language choices. What is the register of his speech?

4) How does this compare to Diana's choice of language?

Commentary

1) Our first impression of this dialogue is that it takes a long time for the conversation to get around to the actual subject matter. There is a very long preamble here, filled with digressions and anecdotes. The opening of the interview includes many phatic expressions, such as 'Welcome back' and 'It's good to be back'. Indeed, Obama then repeats this phrase again, as 'It is good to be back', which emphasises this point, but is also likely to be simply a polite response to the statement 'We're thrilled to have you'. The interview follows the principles of politeness with regular turn-taking and completed adjacency pairs. These polite formalities continue for a long time, and this might reflect Barack Obama's extremely important political and social position and Leno's need to appear polite and friendly.

Leno puts a lot of effort into building a rapport with the President, before he asks any questions of substance. Obama also tries to keep the dialogue light however, deflecting the more serious question 'But you're pretty competitive' by agreeing and then quickly changing the subject to 'But the day of my birthday...' This perhaps suggests that Obama does not want to talk about himself in too much detail in this interview.

2) The Tonight Show with Jay Leno was an American TV chat show, broadcast Monday-Friday in the popular late night 11.35pm timeslot. It was pre-recorded for broadcast, but filmed in front of a live audience. The regular format included comedy sketches, music and interviews with celebrities. It was designed to have as much popular appeal as possible and to appeal to a wide audience of American adults.

Viewing figures averaged at around 4 million, with peak ratings for certain episodes as high as 22million people.[7]

We can tell from the content and tone of the interview that it is intended to appeal to a wide audience. The interview is friendly, informal and relaxed. The material discussed in this extract is lightweight. After the polite opening material, the interview moves into a humorous discussion of birthdays, aging and marriage, filled with humorous anecdotes. This shows a focus on Obama as a real person and a family man, rather than concentrating on his political role.

The interview progresses to a serious political discussion with Leno's question about embassy closures. This transition is quite abrupt, although softened by 'I've got to ask you about this' which signals the change in subject matter. This reminds us that the large audience of this interview is likely to include people with different interests. Some may be regular viewers interested in general interviews with public figures, while some will have tuned in just for the interview with Obama. The challenge for Leno (and Obama) here is to maintain the interest of the whole audience.

The appeal to a wide audience is shown in the language choices made by Obama and Leno.

3) Obama's language choices here are fairly informal and colloquial. The phrase "I had a bunch of friends come over" sounds very ordinary and normal, especially in the choice of the adjective 'bunch' which is very informal and helps create the impression that the President is just an ordinary man. Obama reinforces this sense of himself as an ordinary, likeable, family man with his anecdote about a staff member's 'really cute, young son. He looked like Harry Potter.' This word 'cute' is again informal and friendly and Obama also includes a reference to popular culture in the comparison to Harry Potter, which again makes him seem more accessible.

His language choices are generally quite simple and straightforward. There are a few instances of higher level lexis such as 'transitioning' and these increase as Obama starts to talk about the embassy closures. However, the usually takes the form of select instances of higher level language used within more straightforward phrasing. An example of this is his phrase 'We had already done a lot to bolster' where 'bolster' might be seen as an example of higher level lexis, while 'done a lot' is very simple English.

This phrase also shows Obama's use of the first person plural 'we', which is very inclusive. This creates a sense of his place within a wider team of government and military officials and might also be thought to include the audience as part of America as a whole.

---

[7] https://en.wikipedia.org/wiki/The_Tonight_Show_with_Jay_Leno Accessed <23/06/2015>

When talking about the government's actions there are also select items of political jargon, such as 'threat steam', but again these are usually embedded within more usual everyday language. This clearly contrast with the higher register language that Obama would use when addressing the Senate, for example, and so shows how his language choices reflect the expected audience.

4) Diana mainly uses standard English, with select items of more colloquial speech such as 'you know'. Obama uses more colloquialisms and his overall tone is less formal. Obama therefore creates an impression of himself as one of the people to a much greater extent than Diana.

The different voices and personas of Obama and Diana can be read as a reflection of their respective positions. The American social and political system (in theory) encourages the idea that anyone can rise to a position of power or wealth regardless of their social origin. By contrast, the royal family are examples of a system of inherited wealth and status. Through select use of colloquialisms Diana makes herself appear as closer to ordinary people than the rest of the royal family, but still maintains some social distance.

Topic 9 – Speeches

Introduction

In this topic, we will look at the genre of speeches.

Aims and Objectives

- To learn about speeches
- To gain an overview of the speeches in the anthology

Speeches

There are many different kinds of speeches. Political speeches, wedding speeches, eulogies, pubic apologies (by disgraced celebrities), motivational speeches and courtroom addresses are all examples of the genre. One of the key features of all these examples is that they will be prepared in advance and will be carefully crafted in order to suit the speaker's point and purpose.

Many speeches will be intended to persuade, but they may also be written to inform, instruct or entertain. A speech will usually have a clear purpose, so the structure is often important. Like a good essay, a speech will often build up an argument and you will need to be able to trace the overall line of this argument. Speeches also ofter use literary and linguistic features. As they are carefully prepared in advance, the author of a speech will have time to consider their use of language. They may utilise rhetorical devices or metaphorical language in order to make their points more persuasively. Indeed, speech writing is considered a venerable art that dates back to ancient Greece (or beyond).

Commonly Used Rhetorical Devices in Speeches

Rhetoric is the art of discourse, or in other words, of speaking and writing effectively. Authors can use rhetorical devices to enhance the effectiveness of their appeals to their audience. Until the nineteenth century, rhetoric was widely studied and the techniques well known.

The ancient Greek philosopher Aristotle divided rhetoric into three types of appeal to the audience:

- Logos - The use of logic to appeal to the audience
- Pathos - The use of (or appeal to) the audience's emotions
- Ethos - The use of (or appeal to) a set of guiding beliefs (or ideology). The ancient Greek word 'ethos' meant 'character' and so this could also refer to the character or credibility of the speaker.

Aristotle then went on to discuss these different appeals in much more detail, but in English Language and Literature, we are more interested in the literary and linguistic techniques that might be used to enhance an author's writing style. These are some of the main forms of rhetorical device.

Repetition

Repetition is one of the most common rhetorical devices. Repetition can be used for emphasis, as repeating a word or phrase tends to either draw attention to it. It can also be used to provide a pleasing symmetrical structure that is easy on the ear.

Ancient Greek terms are used for some of the types of repetitions that might be used.

Types of Repetition:

Anaphora	Repetition of words at the start of clauses or verses
Epanalepsis	Repetition of same words at the end and start of a sentence
Epimone	Repetition of a phrase (usually a question) to stress a point
Epiphora	Repetition of the same word at the end of each clause

Parallelism

Parallelism (also known as parallel syntax) is a form of repetition in which the syntactical structure of a clause or sentence is repeated for adjacent clauses or sentences. An example would be the phrase 'I came, I saw, I conquered'. If two clauses/sentences are repeated this way, this is known as an isocolon. If three are repeated, this is called a tricolon. 'I came, I saw, I conquered' is therefore an example of a tricolon.

This technique can aid comprehension and it is easier for listeners to quickly grasp material that is delivered this way. Repeating and recapping the argument also works to embed the idea into the listener. This can therefore be a persuasive rhetorical technique.

Syntactic Reversal

A closely related technique is syntactic reversal, where the syntax of a clause /sentence is reversed in the following clause/sentence. For example: 'you can take the child out of poverty, but poverty cannot be taken out of the child'.

This can also take the form of a negative-positive restatement. This is a powerful rhetorical technique, where a phrase is first phrased negatively and then phrased positively. An example is: 'Ask not what your country can do for you, ask what you can do for your country'. This creates a strong impression on the listener.

Hyperbole

Hyperbole is deliberate over-exaggeration. It has many uses. It can be used for emphasis or to show strong feelings. It can also be used for comic effect. For example, phrases like 'It weighed a ton' or 'It was a million miles away' are meant to show how the speaker felt, rather than the actual weight or distance. Hyperbole is never intended to be taken literally.
Idioms (common colloquial phrases) are sometimes also examples of hyperbole. An example is the phrase 'I could eat a horse', which is not meant to be taken as literally true. Hyperbole is more usually associated with informal speech or writing, but can also occur in formal texts.

Litotes

Litotes is a deliberate understatement. For example, if someone says 'Sam's not the most punctual of people', this would mean that Sam is habitually late. Litotes can therefore also be compared to euphemism or might be used to sound modest. Sometimes phrases can be ambiguous and may depend on the context. For example, the expression 'not bad' could mean anything from average to excellent. 'Not bad' is also comparable to the use of double negatives.

Irony

Irony is almost impossible to define (and you should be aware of this in your own essay writing) but as a rhetorical technique it refers to a text where the surface meaning is different to the implied meaning. Irony is therefore used to emphasise the difference between a real and a perceived situation. The speaker is therefore employing an intentional contradiction to create a deliberate effect. In other words, they are saying something that they don't mean, in order to draw attention to their real meaning.

An example would be a political speech where the author said 'Students are happy that tuition fees have increased' in order to show the opposite, i.e. that students are not happy. In this way, irony can be very close to satire. Another example would be the phrase 'Of course, people are glad that there are no jobs, because it means they can spend more time watching TV and sleeping.' Here, the phrase is ironic, and might also be used to satirise the conservative attitude that connects unemployment and laziness.

Rhetorical Questions

A rhetorical question is one that is not meant to be answered. Sometimes the answer is implied (as an obvious 'yes' or 'no') and sometimes because the question is unanswerable. An example might be 'Are we content to stand by and do nothing? or 'But is there anything we can do?' These types of questions are often used in political speeches as they add emphasis and create a strong persuasive effect. In making the listener think about their own answer to the question, they make the reader think about what is being said. This helps to reinforce the message of the speech.

Figurative Language and Metaphor

Figurative language can also be used as part of a speech. This can include the use of strong imagery and powerful descriptions. Although more usually associated with fiction, strong images can also be used in non-fiction works. In a speech, they help to create an impression on the reader and add to the overall effect of the speech.

As in fiction, metaphors can also be used to add colour to descriptions. They can also be used to extend or explain an idea in a way that makes more sense for readers.

Sounds

Speeches are intended to be listened to (or watched on TV) so the way the words sound is important. Patterns of sound or rhythm in the words used can therefore create a strong impression on the reader. The main terms that you will encounter are:

- Alliteration - The repetition of the same sound at the beginning of each word in a string of words e.g. 'Peter Piper picked a peck of pickled peppers' or 'She sells sea shells on the sea shore'
- Assonance - The repetition of vowel sounds to create internal patterns of rhyming, e.g. 'Soon the moon will bloom'
- Onomatopoeia - Onomatopoeic words suggest the sound they describe. For example, 'Meow' is meant to indicate the sound a cat makes, while a wood like 'boom' represents an explosion

John F. Kennedy

John F. Kennedy was the 35th President of the United States. He was in office from January 1961 until he was assassinated in November 1963. This was a dramatic and significant period of US history that saw the beginnings of the Civil Rights movement and the continuation of the Vietnam war. It was also the era of the Cold War: a nuclear stand-off between Western Bloc (US and NATO) and Eastern Bloc (USSR and Warsaw Pact) countries. These important historical events are part of the context of this text.

This text is part of Kennedy's inaugural speech, given on January 20th, 1961. The inauguration of a new president is an opportunity for that president to set down his ideas and intentions and to explain what he intends to do while in office. The audience for the speech is therefore very wide. It includes the American people and, because of America's status, the speech would also have been broadcast worldwide to a global audience.

We can see some features of this speech which reflect its wide audience. The speech is a direct address to the listener. Each section is separated by discourse markers to show who is being addressed. These utilize the rhetorical device of anaphora. The first two paragraphs begin with 'To those' and this is then followed by variations in the form of 'To our sister republics' and 'To that world assembly'. Kennedy then finally repeats the phrasing of 'To those' at the end of this section, as he refers to America's adversaries. This use of repetition creates a sense of symmetry and balance. It may also be intended to create a sense of equality or unity between groups, each of which is given similar attention.

Structurally, these audiences have been listed in such a way as to provide a neat frame that progresses the speech forward. The importance of peace is suggested and reiterated through the paragraphs on 'sister republics', the UN and then America's adversaries. This leads neatly into the next section of the speech in which Kennedy appeals for a renewal of the 'quest for peace'.

Task

Read Text 9.1 Kennedy's Inaugural Address.

Again, the language in this section is inclusive and uses the first person plurals 'we' and 'us'. There is repetition of the phrases 'both sides' and 'so let us'. This encourages a sense of inclusivity, and even solidarity with, the USSR. As a rhetorical device this is powerful and it creates a very positive impression of Kennedy and his goal of preserving peace and creating 'a new world of law'.

These phrases then combine into 'Let both sides' which is repeated at the start of four paragraphs in another sequence of anaphora towards the end of the extract. Again, this is aimed at fostering a new spirit of co-operation between the Western and Eastern Bloc. This is enhanced by the use of asyndetic listing in 'explore the stars, conquer the deserts, eradicate disease...' . The final paragraph of this text acknowledges that this is a difficult task, but ends on a note of optimism with the phrase 'But let us begin'.

Task

Re-Read Text 9.1 Kennedy's Inaugural Address.

Find examples of the following literary and linguistic techniques:

1) Alliteration
2) Figurative language
3) Parallelism
4) Negative positive restatement

Commentary

1) Examples of alliteration include:

'colonial control'

'strongly supporting'

'break the bonds'

'mass misery'

'strengthen its shield'

'steady spread'

2) Examples of figurative language include:

'casting off the chains of poverty'

'the dark powers of destruction'

3) Examples of parallelism include:

'Let all our neighbours know... . And let every other power know...'

'both sides overburdened..., both rightly alarmed by ..., yet both racing to alter ...'

'where the strong are just, and the weak secure, and the peace preserved'

'nor will it be finished...; nor in the life of ...; nor even perhaps ... '

4) Examples of negative-positive restatement:

'We shall not always expect to find them supporting our view. But we shall always hope to find them strongly supporting their own freedom.'

'Let us never negotiate out of fear, but let us never fear to negotiate'.

Task

Read Text 9.2 Colonel Tim Collins to 1st Battalion, Royal Irish Regiment, in Iraq in 2003.

How does the audience and purpose of this text differ to the audience and purpose of Kennedy's inauguration speech? How is this reflected in the writer's language choices?

Commentary

Text 9.2 is a speech by Colonel Tim Collins to the 1st Battalion of the Royal Irish Regiment. It is a speech given to the soldiers before they go into battle. The purpose of Tim Collin's speech is to rouse the soldiers for war, but also to encourage them to act with respect towards the Iraqi people. This purpose is reflected in the phrases used and Collins refers to both the need to 'tread lightly there' but also states that, to those who want to fight them, 'we aim to please'.

In many ways, this purpose is very different to that of Kennedy's speech. Kennedy is using his inauguration speech to set out the aims he has for his presidency, which is directed towards 'the quest for peace'. Collins' speech is set within a context where war has already been declared and where he is part of an invading army, while Kennedy is seeking to avoid war. Therefore, their purposes are very different. Kennedy is urging peace while Collins is seeking to avert the worst cruelties of war.

Yet there are also some similarities of purpose here. Kennedy is not advocating passivity and he also intends to acquire weapons until 'our arms are sufficient beyond doubt'. Collins is also telling the soldiers to be prepared to fight. He uses a mixture of high register language, such as 'the enemy should be in no doubt that we are his nemesis' and more colloquial, informal phrases such as 'rock their world'. This is designed to appeal to different audiences within the Battalion, from officers to ordinary soldiers, and this use of language shows awareness of audience.

Both texts make a direct address to their audience. Kennedy is addressing a huge audience that includes people all over the world. Collins is primarily addressing the men and women of his own battalion, and his speech is aimed mainly at them. However he is also aware of the likely international audience and the presence of the press. This is shown in the content of his speech where he states several times that only those who 'choose' to die will be killed. This is an implausible statement, but is probably intended to reassure the international community in the context of a deeply unpopular and illegal war.

Both of these writers address their audiences directly, as is usual in the genre of speeches. Kennedy addresses different groups of people directly, from 'new states' to the UN, and he uses a lot of inclusive first person plurals, such as 'we' and 'us', to enforce a sense of unity. Collins also uses 'we' and 'ourselves' and this creates the sense that he is one with his men as he leads them into battle. This is the usual style for eve of battle speeches given by a military commander.

There are more instances of 'I' and 'you' in Collins speech however. He uses the second person 'you' to differentiate those who behave cruelly, saying 'you will be shunned' and this makes his point without directly suggesting that such instances are likely to occur. He uses the first person where he warns against 'over-enthusiasm in killing' saying of those who kill needlessly that 'I can assure you that they have the mark of Cain upon them'. This is a reference to the biblical story of Cain, and is one of several references to the bible in this speech and to Iraq as 'steeped in history'. Collins also refers to a more general shared culture of the military. He appeals to the regiment and its history saying that 'we will bring shame on neither our uniform nor our nation'. This is an example of Aristotle's definition of the persuasive appeal to ethos. Tim Collins is here appealing to a set of guiding values that he believes he and the soldiers share. This shows Collins' awareness of his audience and the values he has instilled in them as soldiers.

Optional Task

Imagine that you are a journalist witnessing Colonel Tim Collins give his speech.

Try to write a piece of reportage that describes the scene. Think about what Collins says, but also try to create your own sense of voice. What is your reaction to his words? What are your own feelings and attitudes?

This task is optional and you won't get a task like this in the exam. However, it will help you to think about these different genres and their features.

There is no commentary on this task.

Topic 10 – Radio Drama / Screenplay

Introduction

In this topic, we will look at the radio drama / screenplay texts.

Aims and Objectives

- To learn about the genre of radio drama and screenplay
- To gain an overview of the texts in this section

Radio Drama / Screenplay

The texts in this section are the only fictional works in the Voices anthology. Drama is a genre which is very concerned with a sense of voice. In drama, the fictional events of the narrative are conveyed mainly through dialogue. There is less opportunity for the author to convey information through description, as they would be able to do in a novel.

A screenplay is a script for TV or film, so it is a visual medium. When the screenplay is filmed, the audience will be able to see what the actors are doing, so their action and gestures can be used to add meaning. The first audience for a screenplay, however, are the producers or commissioning editors who will decide whether to select the screenplay for production. It is therefore important that a screenplay contains all the information necessary for the reader to 'see' the action in their mind's eye and to get a good sense of the characters and their voices.

Radio drama is intended to be listened to, so there is no visual action. Instead, all the information needs to be conveyed by sound. This can include sound effects (abbreviated to FX in the script). These can be used to create some atmosphere, but the main narrative will have to be communicated to the listener through dialogue.

You may think that radio drama has been superseded by television and this is true to some extent. However, it still remains popular with some audiences and BBC Radio 4 broadcast original radio dramas on a regular basis. It is in some ways a difficult genre to write for, because of its limitations.

Task

Read Text 6.2 When I Lived in Peru by Andrew Viner on pp.25-26 of your anthology.

Answer the following questions:

1) What features show you that this is a script for radio drama?

2) Who are the audience for this play?

3) Do you find this dialogue realistic?

Commentary

1) The features that show this is a radio drama include:

- Use of dramatic techniques, such as monologue
- Division into scenes
- Presence of stage directions for voice actors (OLDER, AVUNCULAR)
- Use of sound FX
- Scenes separated by FX (shows audience the beginning of a new scene)
- References to character's names (to tell the audience their identities)

2) This play was written for BBC Radio 4. BBC Radio 4 has an avowedly middle class audience, who generally consider themselves intelligent and well-educated. These plays are broadcast during the afternoon, so their likely audience includes retired people and full-time parents.

Some awareness of audience may be shown in the subject matter of this play, which seems to be a married couple's relationship. It's possible that the experience of being made redundant, or of your partner's career exceeding yours, might strike a chord with some members of the audience. The tone here is light and humorous however, as far as we can tell from this extract, this is not intended to be a serious piece. Its primary purpose is to entertain.

3) A lot of the dialogue here is very unrealistic. The author has attempted to use language from the semantic field of the IT industry in 'bug' and 'version' but the actual line 'If it's about those bugs, we'll have a new version out next week' is laughably unconvincing and it is extremely unlikely that anybody would actually speak this way in a business context. In some ways, the simplicity and predictability of the dialogue here suggests that this might be written for children, although we can tell from the content (work and relationships) that it is not. Interestingly, however, a lot of Andrew Viner's other work is for children's programs.

The dialogue here is probably intended to be light in tone, with an emphasis on comedy rather than realism. Many of the lines are meant to be funny, such as 'That's what I loved' and 'What about the stubble and drool?' and this creates a humorous tone for the piece. This suits the purpose of entertainment, and suggests that this is not intended to be a particularly serious play.

The King's Speech

The King's Speech was produced in 2010 as a very popular film, starring the actor Colin Firth. It won an Academy Award for Best Picture. It is based on the true story of King George VI and an unconventional speech therapist who helped him to overcome a speech impediment.

Task

Read the extract from The King's Speech on pp.23-24 of your anthology.

Answer the following questions:

1) Who are the audience for this film?

2) What is the purpose?

3) Is this dialogue more realistic than When I Lived in Peru? How are the characters' voices developed?

Commentary

1) The audience for this film is very wide. It would include: people looking for films to watch; people interested in film; fans of Colin Firth (or other actors in the film); students studying award winning films; people interested in the monarchy or the life of George VI; and people interested in the portrayal of speech impairments and their treatment.

2) The purpose of this film is to entertain. It also has a secondary purpose of informing the audience about the life of George VI, since it is partly based on a true story. However, despite the similar purpose, the tone and style is very different to the

3) We might argue that the dialogue here is much more realistic than in the Andrew Viner text (although this does not necessarily mean that it is totally realistic, or that realistic speech is even desirable in fiction). The short, incomplete sentences, like the opening line 'Know any jokes?', sound much more like real speech and there is a much better developed sense of character in this extract. Crucially, this sense of character is developed through the dialogue (rather than imposed in monologue), and this is reliant on a the creation of individual voices.

We get a sense of Lionel's deliberate informality here in phrases such as 'Cuppa tea?' and 'How about Bertie?' This contrasts with Bertie's formality 'No thank you' and 'I prefer Doctor'. From this extract, we can tell that part of Lionel's treatment technique is to try to get Bertie to relax and to break with tradition and form. Lionel does this by deliberate irreverence and by not bowing to Bertie's socially superior position. We see this in the way he corrects Bertie by saying 'I prefer Lionel' and 'Don't do that', in his decision to call his patient 'Bertie' (not Your Royal Highness) and in his insistence that they be as 'equals'. In this way, the author creates a strong sense of voice and identity for both characters, and we get a very good sense of the characters' relationship. This scene is very economical and we learn a lot about Bertie and Lionel within only a few lines.

Linguistic Features

There are several features to note in this extract. You will see that it most of the dialogue takes the form of questions and answers. This is similar to real-life conversation, which usually follows the pattern of adjacency pairs and turn-taking, in accordance with the principles of politeness.

The interview texts that we have studied also follow this pattern, and there is therefore some similarity between these two genres. When I Lived in Peru also follows this format, where a question leads to an answer and this progresses the conversation, such as in the exchange regarding Martin's redundancy. This process is sometimes called chaining.

In The King's Speech, however, you might note that the dialogue is at times much more closely linked. An example is the repetition of grammatical structure in the echoing of the lines 'I prefer Doctor' and the retort 'I prefer Lionel'. This creates symmetry, and in this case, humour.

You will also notice that the lines of dialogue are also generally very short. As with the example above, lines echo each other in patterns of repetition and antithesis. This technique is called stichomythia. If we compare this to When I Lived in Peru, we can see that this technique creates a much faster pace and that the dialogue in The King's Speech is succinct and snappy. The overall effect of this is more aesthetically pleasing and, in this case, also a lot more realistic.

In this way, Screenplay and Radio Drama use features of real speech in order to sound more realistic. However, you will also notice that some of the features of real speech, such as overlap or repair, are not usually used in fictional works. Other techniques, such as stichomythia, are dramatic and real people rarely speak this way in real life. Although fictional dialogue is meant to sound convincing, it is also somewhat stylised. It is not meant to sound exactly like real speech.

Vocabulary

Turn-taking - The way that, in normal conversation, a speaker waits for another person to finish speaking before taking their turn to speak.

Adjacency pairs - An adjacency pair is an example of conversational turn taking. One statement follows on from another. Such as 'How are you?' and 'I'm fine, thanks', or 'Are you cold?' answered by 'Yes, we should go indoors'.

Chaining - The process of adjacency pairs forming a conversation.
Stichomythia - A series of short lines of dialogue, featuring repetition or antithesis.

Overlap - When two speakers talk at once. Often this is accidental, for example if two people start to answer the same question.

Repair - When a speaker corrects an error of speech.

Topic 11 – Reviews

Introduction

In this topic, we will look at the review texts in the anthology

Aims and Objectives

- To learn about reviews
- To gain an overview of the two review texts in the voices anthology

Reviews

You will probably already be familiar with reviews. Reviews are short critiques of a new book, TV programme or film, and they give the author's view of the work and a recommendation as to whether readers will enjoy it or not.

The style of review might depend on the publication for which it is intended, or the personal style of the reviewer. Some reviewers take pleasure in being very harsh on the works they review and they make slating comments about them. Many people enjoy this type of criticism because it is very provocative, and this can help to increase a publication's audience and the profile of the reviewer.

Other critics attempt to be more balanced or more generous. These reviewers might want to be seen as objective, rather than opinionated, and this is again part of their personal voice. This might be particularly true of online reviewers on websites such as goodreads, who often review the works of friends or acquaintances, in exchange for a reciprocal review of their own work.

In either case, review writing has much in common with writing fiction and, conversely, with writing articles. The objective is usually for your review to be memorable and to make an impression on readers. The purpose is to inform, entertain, persuade and instruct. The reviewers opinion can be very influential and readers may buy a book or see a film based only on the opinion of a well-known reviewer. Good reviews make a huge difference to sales.

Task

Read Text 8.1 Flemmich Webb on Boxer Handsome.

Answer the following questions:

1) What do you notice about the following passage:

"Whitwham's writing is as sharp as a one-two combination".

Do you think this is effective?

2) What do you think about the author's use of quotations in this review? (Draw on your

knowledge of how to write a good answer in A-Level English Language and Literature here.)

Commentary

1) This phrase is drawn from the semantic field of boxing, which is the subject matter of Anna Whitwham's novel. Webb also follows this up with a reference to 'short, punchy sentences' in case any of his readers have missed his first reference to boxing terminology.

Clearly, Webb is trying to sound clever here, to show his own abilities as a stylist and to entertain his audience. Personally, however, I don't think this is particularly effective and to me it just sounds trite. Possibly it would've been more effective if it was more subtle, and there was only a single select use of boxing terminology. It does tell us something about Whitwham's writing style however, and the impact that this is likely to have on the reader.

Different members of his audience might regard this differently, however, and it may appeal more strongly to some readers than others. Reviewers must make personal decisions on what to write about a text, and create their own individual voice.

2) Webb uses two direct quotations from Whitwham's novel here. Both of these are quite long extracts, introduced by a colon. He doesn't make any particular comment on the language of these extracts after quoting them, and leaves them to speak for themselves.

As you know from your own writing in English Language and Literature, the best way to comment on the text is to use short quotations and to include them as part of your own sentences. You can then explore the precise language used in more detail, in order to make a more exact analysis of the author's choices. You must always comment on what you choose to quote, using analytical language such as 'this shows that...' .

> Task
>
> Read the next review text on p.32. This is Martin Hoyle's review of television drama The Bridge.
>
> Which one of these two reviews do you prefer? Why do you think this is?

Commentary

I personally prefer the second review: Martin Hoyle on The Bridge.

Hoyle's review is much shorter and sharper than Webb's sprawling piece. It gives a much better indication of the content and tone of the TV drama being reviewed. The concise sentences, such as 'Saturday is complete again: Scandinavian noir is back' are engaging and they create interest for the reader. Hoyle describes the premise, characters and themes of the drama quite succinctly. His description that 'Saturday's brace of episodes is rich with subplots...' is interesting and enticing, without bogging the review down in detail or giving away spoilers.

Webb uses a lot of positive pre-modifiers, such as 'exciting debut' and 'promising future'. Although this is a positive response to the novel, it also creates a sense of distance from the reader and the tone is more instructional. Hoyle uses a lot more verbs, such as 'we plunge into the dark world of...'. This use of the first person plural includes the reader as part of the review, and the overall effect is more engaging, exciting and dramatic.

Both authors try to capture the tone of the piece that is being reviewed, but here Hoyle is much more successful. His final phrase 'The dark is all pervasive' is a lot more powerful than Webb's more humorous attempt at capturing tone through boxing comparisons. Hoyle's review also has a more pleasing overall structure and his short final phrase also creates a nice symmetry with the short opening phrase.

In short, although both of these reviews are positive, Hoyle's review generates more interest in the subject being reviewed. In some ways, this is the best way to evaluative the success of a review, and a reviewer.

> **Task**
>
> Next time you read a weekend newspaper, read the reviews in the section for arts, culture and books. Think about the ways that the reviews are structured and the sense of voice that the authors create. The more reviews you read, the more you will get a sense of the genre. You may even like to try writing your own short review of a book, film or TV show. As you do this, think about the choices you are making and how you are trying to create a sense of voice.

Topic 12 – Articles

Introduction

In this topic, we will look at the genre of articles and the attitudes and values of different publications. We will gain an overview of the articles in the anthology.

Aims and Objectives

- To learn about articles
- To gain an overview of the two articles in the anthology

Articles

Although articles are the first genre in the anthology, we have decided to study them nearer to the end of this section, as they are in some ways the most diverse of the genres that we study in Component 1. This is because articles are the mainstay of journalism. They fill up the majority of any published material (newspaper, magazine, website), across a huge variety of different publications, all catering for slightly different (if overlapping) audiences.

One distinction that we can immediately draw is the difference between news articles, feature articles and opinion pieces. A further distinction is often made between the broadsheet and tabloid press.

News articles deal with items of immediate national and international importance. The first pages of a newspaper will deal with items of this kind. An editor will select which item/s to run on the first page and then how to select and prioritise the items for the next few pages. This decision will be based on the item's perceived relevance and importance, and on the decisions made by other newspapers.

Feature articles tend to cover less serious pressing issues, but might still consider social concerns or important areas of human interest. Opinion pieces are an expression of the author's opinions. This would often be in the form of an editorial or a column. These types of articles are usually written in a more colourful style than a news article. The author will try to engage the reader and may have a more individual voice.

The broadsheet press is called 'broadsheet' because they were traditionally printed on A1 paper and folded to A2 size. The tabloid press is printed on A2 paper and folded to a smaller A3 size. The distinction between these types of paper is often also a judgement related to their content. Broadsheets are generally thought of as a 'quality' press aimed at well-educated and professional readers. They are assumed to focus on providing information in a neutral tone, using a sophisticated vocabulary and technical terminology. Feature articles are likely to be aimed at their predicted audience. In The Telegraph, for example, a feature might be an account of a family holiday in the French countryside.

Tabloids, by contrast, are sometimes called the 'popular' or 'gutter' press and you will immediately notice that this is a judgemental and pejorative term. Tabloids are said to focus on sensational issues and to use florid language. Typical front page subjects might be defined to include grisly murders or celebrity scandals. Some features magazines that have a similar tone are magazines such as Chat or Take a Break, which deal with real-life, human interest stories of a particular kind. An example of this type of feature might be 'My sister stole my baby', or 'My step-mother was a murderer'.

You will notice that in discussing these different types of article, it is easy to make a judgement about their respective quality and this is something which is very prevalent in our society. Indeed, most publications aimed at a working-class audience are derided by middle-class commentators. Yet broadsheet publications are every bit as interested in selling copies and are not necessarily any less 'sensational' in their own way. This is, however, often less obvious and their supposedly more educated audience may not always notice the more subtle meanings in an outwardly neutral article.

This is something to be aware of in our studies of English Language. In thinking about audience, purpose and the author's adopted voice, we can start to examine how meaning is conveyed in the texts we read. This can help us to uncover the covert and hidden meanings in the language that we read every day.

Summary of British Broadsheet Newspapers

Newspaper	Political Affiliation
The Times	Centre-right, liberal
The Guardian	Left-wing, liberal
The Telegraph	Right-wing, conservative
The Independent	Economically liberal, centre-left
i	Economically liberal, centre-left
The Financial Times	Economically liberal, centrist

Most of these newspapers have a separate Sunday version, such as The Sunday Times or The Independent on Sunday. The Guardian's Sunday version is called The Observer, and it is the longest running Sunday newspaper. Sunday newspapers generally contain more features and supplements than weekday papers.

Task
Read Text 1.2 Ian Birrell: 'As gay people celebrate, the treatment of the disabled just gets worse' 1) Complete the table overleaf. 2) Is there a strong sense of voice created in this article?

	Text 1.2 Ian Birrell
Audience and purpose	
Tone	
Typographical features	
Literary and linguistic features	

Commentary

	Text 1.2 Ian Birrell
Audience and purpose	Audience: Readers of i newspaper; followers of Birrell; readers interested in disability rights Purpose: To express an opinion on a topical issue
Tone	Reflective: Birrell shows muted celebration of gay marriage, and compares this to the situation of the disabled. Sense of distance created in 'They were clearing up the confetti' and 'The ceremonies mark'. Mostly third person plural 'We should rejoice' which creates impersonal tone. Past tense creates a sense of something sad and concluded, rather than an ongoing achievement: 'It was a remarkable moment' Occasional informality 'it is great to see...'
Typographical features	This article has many typographical features associated with newspaper articles. It has a heading in a large font, and a subheading in a slightly smaller font. It is divided into columns. Paragraphs are not indented.
Literary and linguistic features	Use of alliteration for emphasis/effect 'stuck in the shadows of society' Some use of dramatic language in 'locked out of society' Juxtaposition of contrasting ideas, such as the normally positive 'rejoice' with 'jailed, mocked and used' Use of rhetorical questions, similar to speeches in '...are we content to...?' and 'So why is this happening...?' Intertextual reference to material outside of the article but not directly cited, such as

	'stories of awful abuse commonplace' and 'all these damning statistics'.

2) Is there a clear sense of voice in this article?

There is a sense of voice here and we are aware of the presence of the author and his views. However, for the most part, this article uses a formal voice, which is quite distant. The article is mainly in the first person plural, as in 'we should rejoice'. This includes both the author and reader as members of society, but the tone here feels removed. The modal verb 'should' creates a sense of obligation and even a slightly supercilious tone.

The author is present here in phrases such as 'Within my lifetime', but this is still quite muted. Overall, there is a clear sense of voice in this article, but the tone is quite distant and formal. We learn about the author's ideas and concerns, but we don't get a very strong sense of the author's personality.

Task

Read Text 1.2 Charlie Brooker 'Too much talk for one planet: why I'm reducing my word emissions'

Brooker's Voice

Charlie Brooker has a very distinctive voice. He is wry, sardonic and self-conscious, with a biting sense of humour. He has become very popular in recent years, and his articles have a large following.

In this piece, Brooker is very aware of his own voice and his own participation in worldwide culture of 'jabber'. In this article, Brooker makes readers aware of the process of writing 'for money' and of the process of reading. He also considers why we might stop reading an article in his reference to full stops as 'exits all over this building'. This is all very arch, but it is also clever and funny. Brooker's articles are always entertaining.

You can read more examples of Brooker's voice on the Guardian website at: http://www.theguardian.com/profile/charliebrooker

Task

Think about ways to compare these two articles, how are they similar and different?

Add your observations on Brooker's article to the table below:

	Text 1.2 Ian Birrell	Text 1.1 Charlie Brooker
Audience and purpose	Audience: Readers of i newspaper; followers of Birrell; readers interested in disability rights Purpose: To express an opinion on a topical issue	

Tone	Reflective: Birrell shows muted celebration of gay marriage, and compares this to the situation of the disabled. Sense of distance created in 'They were clearing up the confetti' and 'The ceremonies mark'. Mostly third person plural 'We should rejoice' which creates impersonal tone. Past tense creates a sense of something sad and concluded, rather than an ongoing achievement: 'It was a remarkable moment' Occasional informality 'it is great to see...'	
Typographical features	This article has many typographical features associated with newspaper articles. It has a heading in a large font, and a subheading in a slightly smaller font. It is divided into columns. Paragraphs are not indented.	

| Literary and linguistic features | Use of alliteration for emphasis/effect 'stuck in the shadows of society' Some use of dramatic language in 'locked out of society' Juxtaposition of contrasting ideas, such as the normally positive 'rejoice' with 'jailed, mocked and used' Use of rhetorical questions, similar to speeches in '...are we content to...?' and 'So why is this happening...?' Intertextual reference to material outside of the article but not directly cited, such as 'stories of awful abuse commonplace' and 'all these damning statistics'. | |

Commentary

These are some observations you might have made:

	Text 1.2 Ian Birrell	Text 1.1 Charlie Brooker
Audience and purpose	Audience: Readers of i newspaper; general broadsheet readers; followers of Birrell; readers interested in disability rights Purpose: To express an opinion on a topical issue	Audience: fans of Brooker; Guardian readers; general broadsheet readers Purpose: To express an opinion; to entertain; to answer the paragraph in Private Eye; to satirize social media and 'green' issues. Both these articles are written for broadsheet readers, but we can sense from the tone and content that the audience is slightly different. Birrell is writing a serious piece about rights for the disabled. Brooker is also making a comment on society, culture and online conversation. He also argues against the negative treatment of women online, which is a serious point. But the tone he adopts means that Brooker's work is more accessible, more popular and probably more widely read than Birrell's.
Tone	Reflective: Birrell shows muted celebration of gay marriage, and compares this to the situation of the disabled. Sense of distance created in 'They were clearing up the confetti' and 'The ceremonies mark'. Mostly third person plural 'We should rejoice' which creates impersonal tone. Past tense creates a sense of something sad and concluded, rather than an ongoing achievement: 'It was a remarkable moment' Occasional informality 'it is great to see...'	Sardonic, wry, self-aware. Use of irony and sarcasm. Use of humour. 'An intense flurry of activity, by which I mean four people asked me about it'. This article is funny, but the tone is not light. Short minor sentences as 'And another' used to create weight. Uses mixture of formal and informal register 'recently been overwhelmed by the sheer amount of jabber'. Direct address to the reader 'you're a human being with free will' and strong sense of author speaking to us. Frequent digressions and seeming changes of topic, although actually part of overall structure/integrated. Features combined to create very strong sense of author's voice and personality.

Typographical features	This article has many typographical features associated with newspaper articles. It has a heading in a large font, and a subheading in a slightly smaller font. It is divided into columns. Paragraphs are not indented.	Like the Birrell article, Brooker's article uses many of the typographical features of newspapers. It too has a heading in a large font and a sub-heading in a smaller font. Unlike Birrell's article, it is not arranged into columns. It has a large initial letter, which is an example of the newspaper's house style. It is a little less formal than Birrell's article. The use of hyphens - to separate clauses - creates a more informal and chatty effect.
Literary and linguistic features	Use of alliteration for emphasis/effect 'stuck in the shadows of society' Some use of dramatic language in 'locked out of society' Juxtaposition of contrasting ideas, such as the normally positive 'rejoice' with 'jailed, mocked and used' Use of rhetorical questions, similar to speeches in '...are we content to...?' and 'So why is this happening...?' Intertextual reference to material outside of the article but not directly cited, such as 'stories of awful abuse	Use of lexis of online and social media 'reader comments', 'cloud', 'blogs' 'Photoshop' 'Twitter'. Neologisms (invented words) such as 'wordstorm'. Use of hyperbole (over-exaggeration) 'everyone or the planet typing words into their computers, for ever' for both emphasis and comic effect. Use of repetition for emphasis and comic effect 'events and noise, events and noise'. Use of repetition to link paraphrase: 'I don't get it' to 'But then right now I don't "get"'. Echoed in final 'Now get out' which mirrors earlier 'exits all

	commonplace' and 'all these damning statistics'.	over this building'. Creates structural symmetry.

Topic 13 – Digital Texts

Introduction

In this topic, we will look at the digital texts in the anthology.

Aims and Objectives

- To learn about digital texts
- To gain an overview of the digital texts in the anthology

Digital Texts

In the last topic, we read an article by Charlie Brooker on the proliferation of online commentary. In this topic, we will look at some of these forms of online communication. These are blogs and podcasts.

A blog is a form of online writing, which is similar to a diary or journal. The word 'blog' began as an abbreviation for 'web log' but has since entered the English language as its own word. This word itself is therefore an example of the new language of the internet. Blogs are usually the work of a single individual, and they may be used to record the author's opinions and experiences. A blog may be quite general and deal with a range of daily activities, or it may be focussed on a specific area of activity or interest. For example, the blog in the anthology is focussed on a cycling club. A blog can also be used to raise awareness of wider issues. This might include the experience of food poverty or the problems faced by people with disabilities.

Blogs are usually separated into individual 'posts', where each post is similar to a diary entry, or similar to an article. Blogs are generally considered as a non-permanent medium, and although many sites have an archive, usually only the most recent post will be read. They are therefore in some ways pieces of fast, disposable writing. Usually the style will be informal and chatty. The author will, however, need to cultivate a close relationship with their readers. This will mean creating a strong identity and a sense of voice.

Some popular blogs are also now hosted by larger organisations, which then become more like online magazines (or zines). These publications usually contain information on a particular topic or specific subject matter. They can include blog posts by different authors, creating a multi-author blog (or MAB) or by 'staff' authors with an occasional 'guest blog'. These types of blogs will have unifying features. Like a magazine, they may even have a house style.

Digital blog texts can also include hyperlinks. Like a website, it is possible to add links to other pages into a blog article. The reader can then click these links to reach that site. This can be especially useful when the author is discussing an article in another publication, as that article can simply be linked to. Music or images can also be easily referenced. This does have the disadvantage, however, that readers can be distracted by additional material and may not return to the original blog. Good online writing is therefore often shorter and snappier than printed forms, in order to keep the reader's attention.

The presence of hyperlinks might be thought of as the main distinguishing feature of digital texts. Printed material cannot include these links in this way. When blogs are printed, the hyperlinked text is often underlined.

Most blogs also have facilities for readers to comment, and they encourage readers to do so. The interactional quality of online media is also different to that of more traditional forms of publishing, as Brooker discussed in his article above.

The impermanent, interactional and multimodal nature of online writing therefore means that reading a blog is often a quite different experience to reading a printed piece of writing. For this reason, David Chandler (2006) sees a writer's online identity as permanently 'under construction'.[8] The author can alter, change, or delete elements at will and can assemble different elements to create a sense of identity. This can create interesting, new kinds of online voices.

---

[8] David Chandler cited in Adrian Beard (Ed.) *Working with Texts: A Core Introduction to Language Analysis* (Routledge, Third Edition, 2008 p. 19

A podcast is an episode of a video or radio programme. Each programme is downloaded and can be played on a media device at a time to suit the listener (the transmission not contemporaneous like radio and TV). Most podcasts will have a theme and may try to attract regular listeners and contributors. 'Podcast' is a neologism formed from the words 'broadcast' and 'pod' for the iPod (a brand of portable digital music player).

Like blogs, podcasts can be interactional in that they will usually have accompanying sites where listeners can comment on what they have heard. It is also easy for listeners to become more involved, and they may themselves suggest topics and be interviewed by the hosts.

Podcasts are not always non-fiction and sometimes novels can be serialised as podcast novels or podcast audiobooks. Short-fiction is also popular in podcast form, especially in the horror genre or as 'real-life' ghost stories. These may use sound effects and music to enhance atmosphere and have some similarities to radio drama.

In the section on digital texts. We will be reading two texts:

- 4.1 Blog by George Scott: 'A ride of two halves...'
- 4.2 Past Masters Podcast: 'The Truth is in Here: UFOs at the National Archives'

Task

Read Text 4.1 Blog by George Scott: 'A ride of two halves...'

How does this text fit the genre of a blog post?

For this task, treat this blog post as an unseen text. Don't look up RoadCyclingUK online, and try to answer this question with reference to the text alone. Comment on the genre, audience and purpose with reference to the literary and linguistic features of the text.

Commentary

This text, 'A ride of two halves...', has many of the features that we would expect from a blog post. It is aimed at a readership who are interested in cycling and who are regular readers of the RoadCyclingUK blog. It uses the terms drawn from the semantic field of road cycling, with references to 'the front of the bunch', 'lead car' and 'ride guide'. The use of these terms without definitions shows the author's awareness of his expected audience and illustrates the way this blog is tailored to his readers. There are also lots of references to speed and distances, such as 'with 35 miles on the clock' and 55kph on a rolling road' and this will appeal to fans of road cycling.

The purpose of this text is to describe the third day of a cycling training camp in Spain. Some awareness of this is assumed by the author and the sub-heading does not really make sense unless we know that this post refers to a training camp holiday. We also need to presume that 'a four-hour loop on the flat' is an easier route than the original plan and that this has been chosen on account of 'most of the group' having 'sore legs'. This is not that clearly expressed however, and this knowledge has to be assumed by the reader from the rest of the article.

We also get the impression that this training camp is at least in part a holiday for the participants, as the programme seems to be quite flexible with time to visit cafes and for sunbathing. It is therefore possible that a further audience for this blog might be family members at home, people looking back at their holiday afterwards and people considering going on this trip next year. Therefore, another purpose of the article is to present a favourable impression of the ride.

The blog post is written in an informal and chatty style. This helps to create a sense of the author speaking directly to the reader. This is especially apparent in the phrase 'Trouble is,' which is more typical in spoken discourse than written texts. Clichés such as 'middle of nowhere' help the text to seem more accessible to readers and help the author to sound ordinary and likeable. Humour is also used to entertain, such as the repetition used in the phrase 'de-tour off our de-tour'. This also helps to create a sense of the author as a likeable, pleasant person.

There are lots of asides, separated by commas, and these are used to add additional information. This also creates the sense of the author speaking to us directly, as in the example 'with James, who had previously visited the area...'. These asides are also used to add additional material about the countryside, such as 'Mojacar receives just 200mm or rain per year' and so can also be used by the author to add a sense of place through factual information. This impression is then emphasised through the author providing further atmospheric descriptions, such as pre-modifying adjectives in the phrase 'bone-dry river bed' which creates a sense of place. Long lists of descriptors are quite popular with this author and there are several examples, the longest being 'a snaking, two-mile, car-free climb'.

We also get a sense that this article has been written at speed and this would suit the genre of a blog where posts are often written quickly and are not intended to be permanently available. As we have seen the subheading is not that well-expressed, as it is not immediately obvious why having sore legs would justify going on a four hour bike ride (rather than no bike ride!). Possibly, 'the third day of training camp' would be 'the third day of the training camp' in a more formal text and this could be an unintentional error.

The structure of the article follows the course of the day and the ride with lots of discourse markers, such as 'After a short descent' and 'We now had' to show the progression of events. This provides a clear structure to the blog post and brings it to a natural conclusion at the end of the ride/day.

Overall, this author creates a good sense of the ride in this piece. Some of the references to cycling may put off readers who are not interested in the hobby, but the author generally comes across as friendly and likeable and this sustains interest for this short piece. The tone is cheerful and upbeat, as shown in the final line 'some of the best riding of the camp so far'.

Task

Read Text 4.2: Past Masters Podcast

1) What other genre(s) does this remind you of?

2) What is Bob's tone here?

---

presented in the form of a factual programme, however, with a clear introduction (where they explain what they will be talking about today).

This podcast might also be thought of as similar to an interview in style. Bob and Jo talk to each other, using the model of spoken discourse. They take turns and they answer each other's questions.

However, there are significant differences to the interviews that we have looked at in the anthology. Instead of being used to build rapport and elicit further information, the questions here are often used aggressively. This shuts down the conversation. Bob's questions are sometimes rhetorical, such as 'Like the lights you get on aircraft?' and these close down, rather than open up the discussion. This is something that most interviewers would try to avoid.

2) Bob's tone is quite argumentative here. He begins as sceptical, saying 'I think that's very unlikely'. He asks some questions to keep the discussion going, such as 'What have you got?'. However, he becomes less open to discussion as the conversation progresses. Some of his other questions, 'What else have you got?' tend to invite argument rather than good natured debate. This question implies that not only has he dealt with Jo's evidence (despite not waiting to hear any actual examples from the files) but that he expects to be able to deal with every example the same way.

From this transcript, Bob seems fairly aggressive in his opinions. Although he softens some of his views by seeking agreement with phrases such as 'aren't they?' we also get the impression that his tone is quite harsh and uncompromising. We can't hear the way he delivers these lines, but Jo's reaction seems to suggest that it is definitive enough to knock her off her stride. Jo reacts with phrases such as 'Oh. Okay', which suggest that she was not anticipating Bob's attitude. Towards the end of the transcript Jo starts to lose coherence saying 'Well, sort of, but not -' and seems to trail off.

This suggests that this podcast has been recorded live. Jo's reaction seems genuine and non-scripted and this contrasts with the interviews that we have read. It also suggests that Jo and Bob are inexperienced with the broadcast media, and this is in keeping with the DIY ethos of podcasting. Neither of them has the skills to keep a dialogue going and their debate is not as informative or entertaining as it would be if their discussion had been developed further.

Bob could keep the conversation going by asking her, more gently perhaps, for some other UFO examples, but instead his reaction to Jo's disconcertion is victorious. His reply 'That's another mystery solved then. I'm getting good at this' makes Bob sound quite arrogant and unlikeable.

Topic 14 – Travelogue

Introduction

In this topic, we will look at the final text type in the anthology: travelogue.

Aims and Objectives

- To learn about the genre of travelogue
- To gain an overview of the texts in the anthology

Travelogue

Travelogues are texts that describe the experiences of a traveller. They are designed to create a strong sense of place, usually from the perspective of an outsider. Examples of travelogues could be printed sources, digital (multi-modal) texts, or broadcast media (such as documentaries).

Generally, people are interested in reading travelogues because they have an interest in visiting the place described, because they enjoy travel writing generally or sometimes because they are interested in the author.

Travelogues also show a wide range of styles. Some may be written in a very literary style, while some may be more journalistic. Most travel writing is intended for publication.

Task

Read Text 10.1 Sea and Sardinia by D.H. Lawrence.

Sea and Sardinia

Sea and Sardinia is a travelogue written by D.H Lawrence and first published in the autumn of 1921.

D.H. Lawrence is now considered a great author and many of his works are included in the canon of English Literature. These include his novels: The Rainbow; Women in Love; Sons and Lovers; and Lady Chatterley's Lover.

However, D.H. Lawrence's work was not appreciated during his lifetime. According to the standards of the time, much of his work was considered pornographic or 'obscene'. During the First World War, Lawrence was also viewed with suspicion due to his anti-militarist stance and his relationships with German citizens (his later wife Frieda von Richthofen was a distant relative of the 'Red Baron'). The British Government accused him of being a spy and he suffered constant harassment.

Due to the poor critical reception of his work and his unpleasant experiences during the war, Lawrence undertook what he termed a 'savage pilgrimage' and became a voluntary exile. Together with his wife Frieda, he spent the rest of his life travelling and only returned to Britain for short visits. During this time, he visited many countries, including Australia, Italy, Ceylon (now Sri Lanka), America, Mexico and the South of France.

Sea and Sardinia recounts a journey from Sicily to Sardinia that Lawrence undertook in January 1921. It has been praised for capturing the spirit of a place and people and Lawrence is often considered the finest travel writer in the English Language.

Task

Re-read the extract from Sea and Sardinia.

How does Lawrence create a sense of voice here?

Commentary

Sea and Sardinia begins in the first person with multiple direct references to the author and his actions. These are relatively mundane references to the author's activities, such as 'I slept..', 'I made haste and washed myself' and 'I went on deck'. This immediately gives a strong sense of the author's presence and we are made aware of his daily routine on board the ship.

In the second paragraph, however, the tone changes and we get a slightly different sense of voice. The exclamative 'Ah the lovely morning!' signals this transition from the everyday to the poetic. In this paragraph the audience get a different sense of Lawrence, and Lawrence's language here is powerful and beautiful, almost like a prose-poem. For example, in the phrase 'the sky all golden' he ellides the verb 'was' to create a more poetic effect and this phrase is more evocative without the verb. The imagery here is strong, as in the phrase 'the sea was glassy bright' and we get a strong visual image from this choice of language. He goes on to use the alliteration of 'long, long undulations' to convey the slow movement of the waves and he repeats the adjective 'sweet' to add emphasis and create a strong sense of his lovely morning.

Lawrence continues to use repetition of key words throughout the piece. He repeats 'sweet' again in the next paragraph in the phrase 'sweet it would be', and this patterning has a cumulative effect. He also uses 'gold' and 'golden' repeatedly and this creates a strong impression of the light. He also creates close similarities that are just short of being direct repetitions. For example the phrase 'small, quiet lonely ship' uses a string of three pre-modifying adjectives. This is then echoed in the later, shorter phrase 'Give me a little ship', which reminds the reader of his earlier desire 'to sail for ever' and reinforces his idea.

Another interesting form of repetition used by Lawrence occurs in the line 'world-lost souls, and world-lost saunter, saunter on along with them'. This is similar to the poetic technique of gradatio, where the last word of one clause becomes the first word of the next. Indeed, the overall effect of all the repetitions, echoes and patterns here is to create a rather dreamlike, hallucinatory effect and it transports the reader to share Lawrence's experience of sea and sky. His use of techniques that are perhaps more common in poetry than prose creates a powerful impression on the audience.

Lawrence has structured this text so that it moves from the ordinary, first person routine of waking up in the morning, through his evocative description of the morning at sea, and into a more general desire for the future. The descriptive paragraphs are deliberately devoid of pronouns and Lawrence phrases he sentences carefully to avoid their use, saying 'How glad to be' and 'Ah if one could'. This might be thought to include the reader and enhance their sense of being there, but without spoiling the sense of solitary enjoyment. The reader can be there himself, rather than there with Lawrence, as would have been suggested by the first person plural 'we'. Indeed, although we are aware that we are listening to Lawrence's voice, he himself is 'far, far' away.

In the final paragraph, however, we are again made aware of Lawrence's presence especially in the final lines in the gentle imperatives 'Give me', 'Hear me!' and 'let me'. We get a new sense that we are not only sailing through the sea, but also through Lawrence's thoughts. Lawrence is here stating a desire for an eternal voyage 'as long as life lasts' and we may relate this to the context of Lawrence's travels through the world as a voluntary exile and his desire not to return to England. This is shown in the rhetorical question 'Why come to anchor? There is nothing to anchor for.'

The extract closes with Lawrence's desire to 'wander aimless' as a solitary, spiritual journey. Our impression of this as readers is enhanced by the use of infinitive verb forms, such as 'to find', and the use of the present tense. This creates a sense of timelessness and of eternity, as is further suggested by his appeal to 'kind gods', possibly a reference to the gods of ancient Greece or Rome. In these last phrases, we hear Lawrence's voice speaking clearly in his direct appeal to the gods (or to the reader). This leaves the audience with a strong sense of Lawrence's presence, but our connection to the author is now deeper. We notice that we can feel more understanding and a more personal connection to him than we did from the more straightforward voice used in the beginning. This creates a sense of symmetry in this extract.

Overall, through this careful use of voice, the audience are given a sense of both a physical and an emotional journey in this piece. This creates both an awareness of Lawrence as a person seeking to escape the world, and of the timeless voice and beautiful words of Lawrence the poet.

Riding the Iron Rooster

Riding the Iron Rooster is a very different piece of travel writing. In this extract, Paul Theroux describes an evening spent in an airport hotel outside Paris.

Task

Read Text 10.2 Riding the Iron Rooster

Answer the following questions:

1) Find three examples of descriptive phrases. What do you notice about these?

2) Find two examples of reported speech

3) What impression do we get of Theroux in this text? Do you find the author sympathetic here?

Commentary

1) Some examples of descriptive phrases that you may have chosen include:

- 'simple and awful'
- 'a poky little flat'
- 'a tall grey building'
- 'a wet black morning'

These phrases are comprised of multiple adjectives. In the first example, the conjunction 'and' is used, but Theroux more commonly strings the descriptors together directly. Most of the adjectives chosen are short and quite simple. The simplicity here is what makes this description quite effective.

You will also note that the adjectives chosen for each list have the same number of syllables: i.e. *poke-y* (2 syllables) and *litt-le* (2 syllables); or *wet* (1 syllable) and *black* (1 syllable). This creates a sense of symmetry and balance.

- 'There were too many of them, and they were too close together'

Rhythm is also important in this phrase. This is an example of isocolon. The rhythm this creates is pleasing to the ear, even though the description itself is unpleasant.

- 'Brutal pavements'

This is an example of pre-modification. It is also interesting as 'brutal' is not an obvious choice of adjective for a pavement. This is therefore fairly original and it creates a strong impression.

You may also notice that all the descriptions in this text are unremittingly bleak and negative. This is intended to persuade the reader that the outskirts of Paris are grim and the cumulative effect of these descriptors is effective.

2) In this text, there are several instances of reported speech.

We hear the voices of the people on the bus with Theroux asking:

- 'Is this Paris? Is this France? Where's the Eiffel Tower?'

This creates some interest, by allowing the audience to hear other voices. The other voices also agree with Theroux (like a chorus) so the audience are encouraged to agree with his impressions of the area and to feel that his description is accurate.

We also hear the author's voice directly:

- 'I thought: No wonder!'
- 'How could houses so old look so awful?'

This also livens up the text by creating variety and gives us a more immediate sense of Theroux's voice.

3) Theroux has adopted a journalistic style here of the type common to feature articles and he is writing primarily to entertain. He attempts to be amusing, such as 'residents waited for Godot by watching television', but his jokes are often quite tasteless, such as 'seemed designed to encourage suicide'.

Overall, he is very negative and judgemental in this text. Consequently, we may get a poor impression of him as a person and find him unlikeable.

Topic 15 – Connecting and Comparing Texts

Introduction

In this topic, we will start thinking about how to connect and compare texts.

Aims and Objectives

- To start thinking about how to connect and compare texts
- To start preparing for Section A of the Component 1 exam

Section A of the Component 1 Exam

As we saw in Topic 2, the Section A exam will ask you to **compare** the ways that the writers of two texts create a sense of voice. You will be asked to compare one of the texts from the anthology to another text that you have not seen before.

In this course, we have already started learning how to compare texts. You have used comparison tables to look at the different features of texts and you have completed tasks that asked you to compare different authors and texts.

We have also structured most of the topics so that we have read the first text together and you then studied the second text more independently. Through this approach, you will have already started to learn how to approach an unseen text. We will build on this knowledge in this section to look at how to answer a question in the exam.

Writing Analytically

Writing analytically is the basis of getting a good mark in English Language and Literature. An analysis is a detailed examination and writing analytically means that you are breaking down ideas to explore how an author has constructed a text. You need to show the examiner that you have these skills.

A good way to make sure you are writing analytically is to adopt a clear structure for every paragraph. For every paragraph, follow these steps:

1) Make a clear point that directly answers the question
2) Use evidence from the text (a direct quotation or a reference to the structure of the text) to illustrate and support that point
3) Explore your example in more detail and explore the language used
4) Try to use literary or linguistic terminology
5) Use analytical phrases such as 'this shows that' or 'this suggests' in order to explain why an author has chosen to use this technique or this choice of language
6) To show evaluative thinking (for the highest levels) go on to explain why technique is effective.

Once you become confident with writing analytically, you will be able to vary this structure. In the beginning however, following these guidelines will help you to answer questions effectively.

If we look back at the Commentary on Sea and Sardinia from the previous topic, then we can look at how analytical writing works in practice.

Task

Re-read the Commentary on Sea and Sardinia from the previous topic.

This Commentary is not a 'perfect answer', but it does have features that you should try to adopt in your own writing.

On the next page is a paragraph from this commentary, where the features of analytical writing are explained.

Lawrence continues to use repetition of key words throughout the piece. He

Comment [hb1]: This first sentence makes a clear point. This paragraph will look at repetition and how this creates a sense of voice.

repeats 'sweet' again in the next paragraph in the phrase 'sweet it would be',

Comment [hb2]: This is a direct quotation from the text. It is used as an example of repetition.

and this patterning creates a cumulative effect. He also uses 'gold' and

Comment [hb3]: This is an example of analysis. It might be better to say what the cumulative effect is here i.e. repetition is used for emphasis.

'golden' repeatedly and this creates a strong impression of the light. He also

Comment [hb4]: This is the next example from the text. Again, this is an example of repetition (the focus of this paraphrase).

Comment [hb5]: This is an analytical phrase. Phrases such as 'this shows that' or 'this creates' show that the student is aware of why the author has chosen to use this technique.

creates close similarities that are just short of being direct repetitions. For

Comment [hb6]: This is a new but closely related idea. As well as the repetition of individual words, repetition can also form part of the structure of the piece.

example the phrase 'small, quiet lonely ship' uses a string of three pre-

modifying adjectives. This is then echoed in the later, shorter phrase 'Give me

Comment [hb7]: The student gives an example and uses the terminology of English Language to describe its features.

a little ship', which reminds the reader of his earlier desire 'to sail for ever' and

Comment [hb8]: This is the next example, which illustrates the repetition described earlier.

reinforces his idea.

Comment [hb9]: This is the analysis. The student examines the effect of this repetition and decides that it is intended to reinforce the idea of an eternal journey.

Analysis in the Exam

In the exam, you will need to apply your analytical skills to make a comparison of two texts. One will be a text that we have studied. The other will be an unseen text.

Approaching an Unseen Text

When you are allowed to turn over your exam paper, look at Text B in the Source Booklet. This will be one of the texts that you have already studied, so you will already be familiar with the ways in which the author has created a sense of voice. After you know which text the examiners have chosen for this year's exam paper, you can then look at Text A. This will be the unseen text.

Read the text carefully and be aware of your initial impressions. You can write on the Source Booklet, so you might like to start to underline any features of the text that you immediately notice. (However, note that any work you write on the Source Booklet won't be marked. Only work in the Answer Booklet will be marked.)

Re-read the text a second and third time. Keep thinking about the main features of the text and how they compare to the studied text. Think about the author. The author may be someone you have heard of before or s/he may be someone new to you. What impression do you get of this author from this text? Do they create a strong sense of voice? How is this sense of voice constructed?

You can now start to make a rough plan for your answer (in your Answer Booklet). Take some time to think about the ways that the two authors create their voices. How are these voices similar and different? What examples can you find? What named literary and linguistic techniques are used? Why are these voices different and how can this be explained through thinking about genre conventions and context?

From considering these questions, you will begin to construct a plan for your essay. In the next section we will look in more detail at how to do this, by considering two texts from the anthology that we have already read.

Making Comparisons

In your reading, you should have started to notice some of the features of these texts and started to make comparisons. For ease of reference, 'A ride of two halves' will be called Text A and Riding the Iron Rooster will be Text B. These are some of the features you may have noticed.

Genre

From their sections of the anthology, Text A is a blog post and Text B is a travelogue. However, both are descriptions of travel. The main difference is one of mode (digital and printed). Text A could include multi-media material, such as video of the ride, but as it doesn't do this it is really a written text. In many ways, these texts have a lot in common.

Context

Both texts are written about another country, by visitors to that country.

Text A is written by an amateur writer whose main aim is to describe the training camp that RoadCyclingUK has organised. He wants to communicate the events of the ride and show that they enjoyed the French countryside. His intention is probably to create a positive impression. This is important for friends, relatives and club members who may be at home reading about the training camp, but also for prospective attendees of the next camp, who he will want to encourage. He is probably also aware that saying positive things generally creates a more positive impression of the author and this suits this context.

Text B is a more general description of the outskirts of Paris. The author is spending a in an airport hotel outside Paris before the author takes a flight. We know from the title that the main subject of this book is the author's travels in China. The author of Text B therefore has a less direct purpose than the author of Text A and his account is more impressionistic.

Literary and Linguistic Features

The Literary and Linguistic features are the basis for your main comparative points and the evidence used to support those points. Here are some similarities and differences that you may have noticed.

- Clear narrative structure - Both texts have a clear structure and create a sense of time passing. Both use discourse markers.
- Place names - Both authors make references to places by name. This creates a strong sense of place. (Relates to genre.)
- Description -Both texts also use description to create sense of place. Text A is more factual than Text B ('200mm of rain', '35 miles', etc.) Text A does use some more descriptive phrases 'bone-dry'(cliché). Text B uses more description 'we black morning' and Text B more evocative/effective. Author likes hyphenated words, some similarity of effect. Parallel clauses 'two-mile, car-free' same as symmetrical phrases in Text B. (Relates to audience/genre/voice.)
- Negativity - Text B very negative and this creates a less favourable impression

Selecting Material

In completing this exercise, you will have noticed that there are a lot of possible comparisons that you can make between texts. We have only mentioned a fraction of the possible comparisons in the exercise above.

You won't be able to say everything about the texts in the time allowed. Exams are short, and you need to be selective in your use of material.

The best way to select material is to think about your overall argument. Try to select the material you write about so that you can form a clear argument from it. Spend some time when you plan your essay thinking about your own response to the texts. Which author do you like or dislike? Does one author come across as more likeable than the other? Does one show more literary skill?

Thinking in this way will help you to start thinking evaluatively, as well as analytically. Remember that your comparisons should inform your reading and help you to gain a deeper knowledge of both texts. It shouldn't be a formulaic exercise.

Planning an Essay

A good essay plan has an introduction that sets out the main ideas of the essay, a series of linked paragraphs that build an argument and a conclusion that sums up that argument.

Task

Using the ideas above or your own notes from the previous task, plan an essay that answers the question above.

Complete this task before reading on.

This is a basic plan for this essay, using the ideas above.

Introduction:

A good way to open your introduction is through a direct consideration of voice. This will be the main focus of your answer, so it is good to make sure you start considering voice from the beginning. What are the main similarities and differences in the author's voices?

Main points

- Both create clear sense of voice
- Both quite informal
- Different sense of people
- Refection of difference of genre, audience, purpose

Body of Essay:

One good way to structure your essay is to make comparisons first. This ensures that you are writing comparatively from the outset. You should mention the differences between the texts as they occur, but the clearest arguments mention the main areas of similarity first, and then mention more areas of difference as they move though the argument. This creates a clear sense of progression and a clear overall argument.

Para 1
- Comparison of genres
- Examples of voice

Para 2
- Comparison of context
- Examples of voice

Para 3
- Structure
- Examples

Para 4

- Place names
- Examples
- Relationship to genre

Para 5

- Use of description
- Examples

Para 6

- Negativity
- Text B unremittingly bleak. judgmental

Para 7

- Impact on voice
- Text A's author more likable

Conclusion

Summary of overall sense of voice. Consideration of how effective both writers are.

This plan will cover all the requirements of the question and moves through the texts making structured comparisons between them. The essay builds up following a clear line of argument. The direct discussion of voice is quite near the end, however, which would be a real problem if the student were to run out of time.

Writing Comparatively

Based on this essay plan, these are examples of paragraphs that two students have written. Both have strengths and weaknesses. Read the examples overleaf.

Example 1

Text A is a blog and Text B is a travelogue. Text A is written for a large

> **Comment [hb1]:** A word such as 'whereas' would be more comparative here. The conjunction 'and' is not actually comparative.

audience because it is a blog post and anyone on the internet can read

it. Text B was also written for a large audience. It was published in a

> **Comment [hb2]:** This shows some awareness of genre, but it is not very nuanced. Are all blogs widely read?

> **Comment [hb3]:** Good. This is a direct comparison.

book, so this is more sophisticated than the internet. Text A is written

> **Comment [hb4]:** This is a generalisation and it is too judgemental here. This isn't always true and the student needs to think further about genre to develop their own 'more sophisticated' response.

by an amateur author while Text B was written by a professional author.

> **Comment [hb5]:** This kind of comparison isn't wrong, but it is quite simplistic and formulaic. It doesn't really tell us anything interesting or improve our understanding of the texts.

This means that Text B is more professional.

> **Comment [hb6]:** In many ways, Text B *is* better written, but this student need to explore this further here. Without evidence this is only an unsupported generalisation. There is also repetition of the word 'professional' . It is better to avoid such repetitions where possible.

Example 2

Text A and Text B were both written for an audience and both are

intended to be read by many people. Text B is taken from a travelogue

> **Comment [hb7]:** It is good to open with a comparison, although this is perhaps a bit obvious.

published by a well-known travel writer and will have had a large

audience. Text A on the other hand would have had a smaller and more

> **Comment [hb8]:** This shows some awareness of the author. Perhaps more awareness of purpose would be illuminating. How do you know this was written for a large audience?

> **Comment [hb9]:** Good use of a comparative phrase.

select audience. Although Text A is a blog post and could be read by

anyone (for free) in practice the readers of this blog are likely to be only

the friends, family and members of the cycling club. This is reflected in

> **Comment [hb10]:** Good. This student is knows that not all blogs are the same, and this shows a more nuanced understanding of genre.

the authors choice of language.

> **Comment [hb11]:** Good. This shows awareness of the relationship between genre, audience and language and how one informs another. It also links to the next paragraph well.

Task

Following the essay plan above or using your own plan, write a comparative essay that answers the question:

Read Text A (the Blog by George Scott: 'A ride of two halves') and Text B (Riding the Iron Rooster: By Train Through China by Paul Theroux) in your anthology.

Compare the ways in which the writers create a sense of voice as they describe their experiences. In your answer you must consider linguistic and literary features, drawing upon your knowledge of genre conventions and context.

Commentary

This essay answers this question using the essay plan given above. It is designed to show how to write both comparatively and analytically.

As you read through this answer, try to do so critically. What has this student has done well? Is there anything you would change? What mark would you give this answer? Thinking about this essay critically will help you to improve your own essay writing.

Your essay will not be exactly that same as this example, but you should check that you are also using analytical phrases, and making direct references to literary and linguistic features, genre and context.

Read Text A (the Blog by George Scott: 'A ride of two halves') and Text B (Riding the Iron Rooster: By Train Through China by Paul Theroux) in your anthology.

Compare the ways in which the writers create a sense of voice as they describe their experiences. In your answer you must consider linguistic and literary features, drawing upon your knowledge of genre conventions and context.

The authors of Text A and Text B both create a strong sense of voice. These texts are interesting and engaging and we get a strong sense of the authors' personalities and personas from reading these texts. Both texts are quite informal and both deal with the theme of travel. However, they are drawn from different genres and are written for different purposes and audiences. These different genres, intentions and audiences mean that these authors have selected different voices and they present themselves in different ways.

Text A is a blog post. It was first published on the website of RoadCycling UK. Usually, blogs are written quite quickly and the content is changed frequently. This means that the author may not have spent a long time on this piece. On the other hand, Text B is part of a long travelogue that describes the author's travels in China. As part of a longer work, by a professional author, we can expect that Theroux has taken a more considered approach to writing his piece and is more conscious of his style and voice.

These authors also have different intentions in writing their pieces. Text A is a blog post by an amateur author, while Text B is written by a professional travel writer. Text A's main aim is to describe the 'best riding of the camp so far' and to create a positive impression of the training camp. However, the author of Text B is a professional travel writer, so he is most interested in conveying his impressions of his time in Paris and to do this in an entertaining, memorable and provocative way.

However, there are also many similarities between these texts. Both are descriptions of travel and both texts are written about another country, by visitors to that country. The main difference is therefore one of mode (digital and printed). Text A could include multi-media material, such as video of the ride. However, as it does not, we can also read both these pieces as primarily written texts. This is the first of many similarities between them.

Both texts are structured following a clear narrative, that covers the course of a journey. For Text A this is the course of the cycle ride, while for Text B it is a night spent on the outskirts of Paris. Both texts show this progression through a clear use of discourse markers. These include 'After a short decent', 'We now had' and 'By now we were' for Text A and 'We came to Paris', 'Then I was told' and 'It was a wet black morning'. This creates clear structure and gives a sense of time passing. This is very appropriate for these texts which both describe the writers' experiences abroad.

In keeping with their content, both texts create a strong sense of place. Both writers use the names of the places they visit. In Text A the author describes the journey through Mojacar, Bedar and Los Gallardos. In Text B, the writer mentions the Gare de l'Est' and the 'Left Bank' and the and explains some of the geography of the city, describing the local of the 'Hotel St. Jacques' in 'the fourteenth *arondissement* near the end of the Metro line' , which is 'seventeen stops' from the centre of Paris. The author of Text B is a well-known travel writer who has visited many countries and he therefore also makes comparisons between Paris and other cities, including 'London', Chicago and South Boston'. This gives his voice a sense of authority.

Both authors also add anecdotal information to increase the sense of place. For the writer of Text B this includes discovering that Samuel Beckett lives in the area and some amusing speculations on why Beckett has chosen to live 'in a poky little flat'.

By contrast, the author of Text A's anecdotes are more closely related to cycling and to his companions, such as 'James, who had previously visited the area...'. Some of the information that the author of Text A shares is informative, but has the sense of being taken from a guidebook, for example 'Mojacar receives just 200mm of rainfall a year' rather than being a personal impression.

Again, this illustrates the difference between these two texts. Text A is mainly interested in cycling and offers general information about Andalucía, while Text B is a travelogue intended to convey the writer's personal experience of the places visited. This shows the authors' awareness of their respective audiences. Readers of RoadCyclingUK are likely to be more interested in the cycling than the location (although both are important) whereas readers of travelogues can be assumed to be more interested in the place described (or the author's impressions of it).

Text B continues to explore the writer's personal impressions of the area through the choice of descriptions. He uses many short adjectives such as 'wet black morning' and 'tall grey building'. These phrases are very evocative, probably because they are so simple. They are also nicely balanced and the adjectives chosen have the same number of syllables. Generally, the sense of rhythm is an important part of Theroux's writing in this text. The phrase 'There were too many of them, and they were too close together' is an example of isocolon. The rhythm this creates is pleasing to the ear, even though the description itself is unpleasant.

Interestingly, Text B also uses a similar technique. The phrase 'two-mile, car-free climb' also uses balanced, parallel clauses to create a pleasant symmetry. This is also shown in the alliterative phrase 'beautiful and barren'. Overall, however, the description in Text A feels more basic and is less evocative overall. For example, the author uses cliché in the phrase 'bone-dry river bed'. This shows that he is not necessarily trying to impress his audience with his literary skill. His voice is more accessible than Theroux's and is more similar to natural speech.

There is some further similarity to natural speech in that both authors address the audience directly. In Text A this is shown through the phrase 'Trouble is'. In Text B through the use of comments such as 'No wonder!' and questions like 'Beckett came here for pleasure?' For both authors this creates a strong sense of voice, but these voices are different in tone.

The author of Text A uses a light-hearted and positive voice, as is shown in the phrase 'detour off our de-tour'. This creates a favourable impression of the author and suits the holiday atmosphere and tone of the piece. The author of Text B also uses humour in phrases such as 'residents waited for Godot by watching television', but his jokes are often quite tasteless, such as 'seemed designed to encourage suicide'. This creates a clear sense of voice, but this voice is more negative and pessimistic. Combined with the authors unfavourable impressions of the district and his choice of very negative descriptors, this creates a less-favourable impression of Theroux. Some readers may even find him unlikeable.

Overall, therefore, both writers create a very strong sense of voice, but how we react to these voices as readers may be very different. Through creating a sense of their individual personality, an author can either attract or alienate different members of their readership. The authors' choices therefore show their awareness of the audience, genre and purpose and reflect their intentions in writing the text. Whether we always like the voice of the author or not, we can always admire their skilful use of literary and linguistic features to convey a successful sense of voice.

Topic 15 – Preparing for the Exam

Introduction

In this topic, we will look at how to start preparing for Section A of the Component 1 exam.

Aims and Objectives

- To begin preparing for Section A of the Component 1 exam
- To collect texts to use as part of your revision

Preparing for the Exam

Although the exam is a long way away, there are many things that you can do now to help you to prepare.

Now that A-Level exams are linear (so that the exams are only held at the end of the two year course) it is very important to prepare as much as you can in advance.

Between now and the exam, try to become as familiar with the texts in the anthology as you can. You can also gain more practice at preparing for unseen texts by reading as much as possible from a range of genres. In this way, many of the skills that we have learned in this part of the course can be practised in everyday life.

Preparing the Texts

In our discussion of the anthology, we have looked at some of the main features of the texts. However, as A-Level students, you will need to go beyond the basics and to form a personal response to the texts.

Although this is the final topic in this section, your work should not stop here.

Get to know the texts in the anthology really well. Read and re-read them, and spend time exploring them in detail.

These are some issues to think about for each text:

- What is its genre and what features does this genre have? For example, think about a speech, what features might this have in common with an interview? What features does an interview share with a radio drama? What genres are most similar to blogs? What genres are most similar to podcasts? How would the text need to be altered to suit a different genre?
- What is the audience of the piece and how can we tell? How has the author crafted the text to appeal to his audience or to different sections of his audience?
- What is the author's intention? What is he trying to tell the reader? Does his point come across effectively?
- Are there contextual factors that we need to consider? Is our reaction to the text today different to how it might have been when it was originally written.
- How does the author create a sense of voice? How do they present themselves to the reader? Do you find their personality likeable or unlikeable? Does their voice change or develop?

Keep reading and thinking about the texts in the anthology. Try to analyse their features and how the authors construct a sense of voice. Do this for all the texts, especially those that we studied at the beginning of the course. You will find that you notice more now than you originally did.

Remember to make notes on your ideas, so that you can use these to revise for the exam.

Thinking about Voices in Everyday Texts

One good way to prepare for the exam is to think about voices in the texts that you read every day. Every time that you read a text, think about the sense of voice that the author creates and the techniques that s/he uses to do this. This can be applied to every text that you read.

For example, do you think that I have created a sense of voice in this course? There are areas where I have given my own opinion of the texts (rather than being studiedly neutral). Do you agree with me? Do you think that authors of course materials should have voices? Do you find my persona likeable or unlikeable?

Academic writing could also be thought of as a genre. When you write essays, do you think that you are adopting a certain kind of voice? Do you use a particular register or tone, or a particular vocabulary? For example, you will be using the terminology of English Language and making references to literary and linguistic terms. You might also use words such as 'however' and 'moreover' and these are often associated with essay writing. How would this be different if you were writing, for example, a blog post?

In this way, keep thinking about authorial voices in the texts that you read every day. Every time that you read a review of a film or a newspaper article, keep thinking about how the author has created a sense of voice.

The more familiar you become with asking analytical questions of the texts that you read, the better prepared you will be for the exam.

Task

By practising reading texts and thinking about voices, you will develop your analytical skills. From now until the exam, keep reading regularly. Read as widely as you can. For example, you should try to read at least one broadsheet newspaper every week. Vary the newspaper that you buy, so that you can get a sense of different author's voices.

You should also try to read texts from the other genres. For example, you can read reviews in newspapers, magazines or online. You can also read blog posts, or dip into memoirs or autobiographies. When you are at a library, try reading a section of a travelogue or look into a book of political speeches.

From the texts that you read, try to collect interesting examples of the voices that you find. (You could cut the page from a newspaper, or photocopy a page from a book). Keep these texts in a safe place. When you come to revise, you will have forgotten most of the content of these texts. These will therefore provide you with a bank of unseen texts to compare to those of the anthology, and you will be able to use these to practice for the exam.

(There is no commentary on this activity.)

Topic 16 – Component 1 - Section B: Drama Texts

Introduction

In this topic, we will begin our work on Section B of Component 1. We will learn what will be required in the exam and start to think about voices in drama.

Aims and Objectives

- To learn about Section B of Component 1
- To think about voices in drama
- To gain an overview of the exam requirements

Component 1 - Section B: Drama Texts

In Section B, we will still be considering voices and how they are created, but our focus will now be on a drama text. The drama text we will be studying is Arthur Miller's All My Sons.

Voices are very important in drama. In a dramatic work, most of the information will be conveyed through dialogue and this is especially true when the text is read, rather than watched in performance. Although we usually think of plays as performed, the first audience (including the actors and director) will read the text on the page, so it is important that the playwright creates a strong sense of voice from the words alone. Our focus in this section is to think about how the playwright does this.

Voices in Drama

Voices in drama are the main means for the writer to create a sense of character. Therefore, unlike our non-fiction texts where the author is creating a sense of their own voice, a dramatist is creating a sense of many different voices, each representing a distinct character.

Voices in drama have some of the qualities of real spontaneous speech and some non-realist qualities. Dramatic speech is usually intended to be a lot more significant than real speech. It includes literary techniques that are devised so that the actors words mean more than they would in an ordinary conversation. Scripted speech also doesn't usually have the fillers (e.g. 'um' or 'erm') or repairs ('oh no, I meant...') that real, spontaneous speech does.

Indeed, the speech in a play is not of the exact quality of spontaneous speech. Though many dramatists may aspire to recreate speech that sounds authentic, it is still spoken by actors who have learnt a script and who are therefore unlike speakers in normal conversation. They know what is going to happen ahead of time.

It is also possible for a playwright to create speech which is not meant to be naturalistic. For example, a character may speak in verse, or have a highly stylised form of speech which is designed to create a different, non-naturalistic effect.

In this way, voices in drama can be more complex and more interesting than we may immediately realise. In this section, we will explore how Miller creates a sense of voice for his characters.

The Format of the Exam

In Section B, you will answer one question on All My Sons. You will be given an extract from the play in the Source Booklet. You will answer the question looking at this printed extract and other parts of the play (of your own choice).

The format of the question will be:

All My Sons, Arthur Miller

Read the extract on pages [X-X] of the source booklet.

Question 2

Using this extract as a starting point, and with reference to other parts of the play, discuss how Miller develops [....]

In your answer, you must consider Miller's use of linguistic or literary features and relevant contextual factors.

Following this format, the question will ask you to look at how particular issues or themes are developed. You will need to explore this issue by making references to the use of linguistic or literary features and relevant contextual factors.

You should also notice that this question asks you to make connections between different parts of the play. You must start with the printed extract and you can then choose other parts of the play to refer to. You must make some connections between these sections and use these to inform your reading. In other words, you must look at the play as a whole, not complete two separate analyses of two separate sections.

Keep It Clean!

As you will note from the question, you will need to refer to both the printed extract and other parts of the play. You will be allowed to take your copy of All My Sons into the exam with you, so long as it is clean and completely unmarked. **Do not write anything on your copy of All My Sons.** This includes writing notes, highlighting or underlining any parts of the text. If you write anything on your copy of the play, you won't be allowed to take it into the exam with you.

Task

Using the Edexcel website, look at the Sample Assessment Materials for Section B: Drama Texts.

Read through the questions on the exam paper and make sure that you are familiar with the format of the exam.

(There is no commentary on this activity.)

Topic 17 – Arthur Miller

Introduction

In this topic, we will look at the life of Arthur Miller and at the background to All My Sons.

Aims and Objectives

- To learn about the life of Arthur Miller
- To learn about the background to All My Sons

Arthur Miller

Arthur Miller has a formidable literary reputation. Indeed, some commentators have gone so far as to call him the greatest dramatist of the twentieth century. Arthur Miller's long career was marked not just by dramatic achievement, but also an outstanding career in the public arena. He wrote novels and essays as well as plays, and was outspoken on the subject of human rights. Through these activities he managed to gain international recognition.

Arthur Miller's plays are thoroughly American, and his dramatic outlook was shaped by his experience of key moments in American history. Arthur Miller was born in 1915 to a wealthy Jewish family in New York. This decade was a time of American confidence, vitality and economic success, immediately following the First World War.

However, the boom years came to an abrupt end in 1929, the year of the Wall Street Crash. The following years brought on a Depression, and experience of both of these events (economic boom and bust) were subsequently immensely important to Arthur Miller's drama and to his thinking.

For Miller, living through the failure of the economic system in 1929 made him fundamentally re-evaluate his understanding of what was normal. Seeing poverty and hardship in New York after the crash, where before he had become used to a life of prosperity, was a huge influence on his literary output and on his human rights advocacy.

Arthur Miller wrote many successful plays in his career. Besides *All My Sons*, he is probably most famous for the play *The Crucible* which is an outspoken condemnation of tyranny and Puritanism. However, he is also famous for *Death of a Salesman*, which questions the tensions and contradictions of the American Dream. These are typical Miller themes: American values and society; and Americans and how they live. In this regard, *All My Sons* is no different.

All My Sons

By the mid 1940s, Arthur Miller was beginning to feel despondent about his literary career, and his attempts to establish a name for himself as a dramatist and writer. Although he had experienced some success in publishing a novel (which sold well), he had not had much success on the stage. Also, at around this time another famous American playwright called Tennessee Williams had just opened a production of his play, *The Glass Menagerie*, which was a huge success. This made Arthur Miller all the more resentful and concerned about his own talent.

Arthur Miller therefore wanted to find a good subject for his next play, and one that he could use to explore more of the contradictions and tensions in American society. Miller had heard a news story about a family that was torn apart when a daughter reported on her father for selling faulty machine parts to the army. Miller used this real-life story as inspiration for the play *All My Sons*, though he changed the detail of a daughter to a son, and brought in another family, whose two fortunes become linked together.

Through developing this idea, Arthur Miller wrote a play that was ultimately condemnatory of American cut-throat capitalism, and which went on to establish his stage reputation. Miller's play opened in January 1947. It had a first run of 328 performances and was a massive financial and dramatic success, and it won the Drama Critics' Circle Award. The amazing success of the play in New York really transformed Miller's life, and established him as a literary name, giving him the stage success that he had always wanted.

A central theme of the play is that of social responsibility, and the question of what we owe to the wider society. In this, Miller is asking us to think about the relationship between the individual and others. To what extent ought we to act for ourselves alone, to what extent ought we be motivated by concern for our family and to what extent for the world outside us? In this way, the play explores the ways in which our past choices impact on our current situation, and give rise to future, unforeseen consequences.

As Miller himself stated about his own technique in structuring the play:

'The structure of a play is always the story of how the birds came home to roost.'[9]

For Miller, this has always been his guiding principle in how he writes his plays, and we will certainly see this in evidence in *All My Sons*.

As this quote implies, Miller slowly builds and builds the dramatic tension that moves towards the final confrontation and outcome of the play, to prove that the past can never be forgotten, nor can it be erased. We will see in *All My Sons* a series of events that move towards the climax.

---

[9] Arthur Miller, The Shadows of the Gods, in Robert A Martin (ed.), *The Theatre Essays of Arthur Miller* (New York: Penguin Books, 1978), p.179

Task

Read All My Sons.

It is important that you do a first reading so you are aware of the overall plotting and ending. This is important — it will help you study the characters and themes as we look at the play more closely on our second and further readings.

Topic 18 – Speech Features and Characterisation

Introduction

In this topic, we will read *All My Sons* and consider the use of speech in relation to characterisation.

Aims and Objectives

- To read and analyse the speech features of *All My Sons*
- To consider how the staging and setting of *All My Sons* prepare the audience or reader for the play
- To undertake character analysis

Introduction

Now that we have set the scene for our study of the play we can now turn our attention more closely to the set text and to how Miller represents speech.

Task

Read the opening stage directions of *All My Sons*. What impression do you get of the Keller house, where the play is set, by this description? Make some notes of your ideas, and then read the comments below.

Commentary - First Impressions

The description of the stage scenery is vital for the reader of the play, because it helps to give us a mental image of the place where the play is set. For the director of the play, it is just as useful as a guide to how to set the scene, and thus how the audience come to see the play.

Whether we are readers or members of the audience, the setting of the play will invoke for us a sense of what the play is going to be about.

In this case, we read that the Keller house is neat, tidy, prosperous and well-to-do. The scene is a typical American suburb – we are supposed to think that this is a normal household with nothing unusual about it.

The two characters who are first on-stage are Joe Keller and Dr Jim Bayliss. Miller makes it clear that the first of these characters is an older man who is successful but not well educated, while the Doctor is younger and more intelligent, but with an inner sadness.

Task

Return to the start of the play, and re-read the opening dialogue as follows:

Jim: Where's your tobacco?

To:

Jim: Then it can't rain.

From this very short section, how does Miller use language to convey information about these two characters? Answer this question with reference to the text, and then read my comments below.

Commentary

Miller has already used dramatic techniques – such as the stage directions, which tell us how the characters and stage are to be presented, and how the characters are to act as well as speak – to set the tone and mood of the play.

Besides the dramatic techniques, Miller uses the speech of the two characters to tell us something about the two men on stage.

This section is an excellent example of a chain – a common feature of spontaneous speech. Jim asks a question, and Keller replies. Jim also responds to the information contained in Keller's reply – he walks over to the table. This is all a common and natural feature of spontaneous speech. Keller makes a comment himself, and Jim responds with a follow-up question of his own. Keller replies – another link in the chain – and Jim continues the pattern of question-answer, statement, question-answer by completing this with a final statement of his own.

However, his statement, unlike that of Keller's, is not a straightforward comment in the style of: 'Gonna rain tonight'. Instead, Jim's statement is a reversal of Keller's information – he states that *because* the papers say it will rain, it will not rain. In other words, he is making a light-hearted joke about the reliability of weather forecasts, and about believing what you read in the paper.

Therefore, in this very brief piece of dialogue, Miller immediately starts characterising these two men. Keller comes across as a straightforward man, one who is not quick-witted, sharp or bright. Jim Bayliss, on the other hand, is a more insightful and quick-thinking individual. This is shown in his ability to make quick-witted and light-hearted jokes which play with meaning and language.

Frank Lubey

Miller has successfully started characterising Keller and Jim Bayliss in the first six lines of dialogue – in a play, there is no time to waste since every statement made must add to the plot, setting or characterisation. Miller also uses Lubey's first entrance to do something similar. From the stage directions, we learn that he is fairly young but perhaps seems older, is 'pleasant' but also fundamentally unsure of himself. This is important information to bear in mind as we read further.

Spontaneous and Prepared Speech

Since Miller is attempting to write natural-sounding dialogue, we know that we are operating on a middle ground between fully prepared speech and fully spontaneous, natural, real-life speech. In which case, we can expect features of both in this section of *All My Sons*, and that is indeed what we find.

Spontaneous Speech

We have already noticed chaining, consisting of a series of adjacency pairs in the opening lines of dialogue. Keller and Frank also engage in turn taking, as in a real-life conversation, and in doing this they make use of adjacency pairings, also as in normal spontaneous conversation. There are many examples of this, such as:

Keller: Hello Frank. What's doin'?
Frank: Nothin'. Walking off my breakfast.

Notice that this adjacency pairing also makes use of American dialect, which tells us something further about these two characters. They seem familiar and at ease with each other, which implies that they are friends because they use this more informal way of speaking.

This greeting and response is a form of phatic utterance, the value of which is mainly to act as social glue in conversations rather than to convey any specific information. However, it is very typical of spontaneous speech.

The build-up of adjacency pairs to form chains, which make a real conversation, is an expected feature of spontaneous speech. There is a chain, or series of adjacency pairs on the subject of the weather, which leads off from Frank's walk. In turn, this also links back to Keller's prediction of rain, which is a nice thematic connection of related topics. This relation of topics is a very common feature of spontaneous speech, and Miller has produced something that sounds very realistic for a conversation, here.

Prepared Speech

Despite all the features of spontaneous speech we can find, it is still the case that these characters are **not** speaking spontaneously, because the speech of the actors who would perform *All My Sons* has been prepared for them.

After all, that is the point of acting in a play! In which case, we should be able to notice some of the features more common in prepared speech, despite Miller's desire to create authentic-sounding dialogue. Some of those features are listed below.

For example, Keller and Frank do not interrupt each other or overlap their conversations; in genuine spontaneous speech we might expect these two features to occur.

Also, unlike spontaneous speech, each word is meaningful or adds direction to the plot and characterisation. There is 'nothing wasted' in the dialogue of a play. In genuine spontaneous speech we would expect speakers to trail off far more, leave sentences incomplete and change direction in their conversation. This does not happen so much in the section we are considering.

In conclusion, it is clear that Miller has written the play with a good ear for dialogue, since we find many of the features of natural and idiosyncratic speech in the way the characters talk. However, in order for the audience or reader to follow the conversation with ease, and for plot and narrative direction to develop, it is also necessary for Miller to order the dialogue to an extent that we don't find in spontaneous speech.

Miller already knows where he wants his characters to 'go', and what messages he wants to develop in the play. As such, each line is carefully written with this in mind. No words are wasted or are without significance, since all contribute to the plot development and characterisation. This is unlike natural, spontaneous speech.

Task

Now consider the next short extract of *All My Sons*.

From:

Keller: Here's another one. Wanted – old dictionaries. High prices paid. Now what's a man going to do with an old dictionary?

To:

Keller: Well, that shows you; in my day, there was no such thing... You look at a page like this and you realize how ignorant you are. ... Psss!

As you read this extract, consider the following question:

What do the speech and actions of Keller and Frank tell you about their characters, and about the relationship between them both in this extract?

Frank and Keller

Miller has established for us that Keller is a man who is not very quick-witted or well-educated. It is very telling, for example, that he can't imagine why somebody would want to collect old dictionaries. The fact that somebody would be interested in old books, in words and language, is a foreign idea to him. It is also very telling that when Frank suggests that such a man might be a book collector, Keller's only idea is that a man would collect books in order to sell them again – as a living, rather than as a hobby, interest or pursuit.

Having intellectual pursuits, such as enjoying collecting for its own sake or for the sake of research, is therefore something that Keller finds very difficult – impossible – to comprehend.

Frank seems to be more adventurous: he tells us that when he was younger, he wanted to be a forester. This is also something that Keller finds hard to understand; in fact, he tells us that when he was young, such an occupation didn't even exist! This shows us the extent of Keller's ignorance, as do the stage directions, where he speaks with wonder as he reads the page of news.

However, his ignorance is something he also admits quite openly. This shows us that Keller is also an open and direct man – he knows he is not very well-educated, but he is not too socially embarrassed to admit this, at least in front of Frank.

The openness and informality of the language between Frank and Keller certainly suggests that they are friends. However, Frank is a much younger man than Keller, though he seems more adventurous, curious and interested in the world around him. This makes the relationship between them interesting – although Keller is older, it is Frank who is perhaps more knowledgeable and more curious about the world outside.

Topic 19 – Character Dynamics

Introduction

In this Topic, we will complete our re-reading of the end of Act One, and continue to analyse the speech the characters use.

Aims and Objectives

- To read to the end of Act One

- To consider how speech reveals the dynamics and tensions between the characters

- To consider how the speech used conveys information about the characters, such as their thoughts and feelings and inner emotional states.

- To consider how Miller builds up the key themes and events of the play

---

Task

Re-read the whole of Act One. As you do so, consider the features of both spontaneous and prepared speech that you come across in the play.

Also, continue to think about the nature of the relationships between the characters, and how this is shown both by the content of the conversation but also the way in which it is said. Make some notes of your first impressions.

Exam Focus

For the exam, you will need to know this play extremely well, because you have to comment on a section of the play which is reprinted for you on the exam paper against another section or sections of your own choice.

The best sections to choose are those which contrast with the printed extract. Often, these will be sections that contain interesting plot development or characterisation, so there is a lot you can comment on.

Since you have now read the play through at least once, you should be starting to have a good idea of the interesting parts of the play you could possibly choose.

Task

Now we'll re-read sections of Act One in more detail.

Concentrate on the section that starts:

Frank: Hey, what happened to your tree?

To:

Mother: It's not like a headache.

Try to divide this first half of Act One into shorter sections, of around the length of 20-30 lines of dialogue.

This helps you to get a hold on the order of events in the play and to think about different sections of the play.

When you have done this read my suggestions below.

Breaking up the play into short sections

It is certainly not the case that there is only ONE possible way of dividing up the play into shorter chunks. It is most useful if you complete this task yourself first since it will encourage you to think about where the important events occur.

However, you may find reading my completion of this task useful for your own interpretation of the play.

First section

Start of Act One (including all stage directions and scenery information)

To:
Keller: Well, that shows you; in my day, there was no such thing.. You look at a page like this you realize how ignorant you are. Pss!

Second section

Frank: Hey, what happened to your tree?

To:

Keller: (*to Jim*): Is he talkin' sense?

Third section

Jim: Him? He's all right. He's just completely out of his mind, that's all.

To:

Jim: (*Sue, Jim's wife, enters. She is rounding forty, an overweight woman who fears it. On seeing her Jim wryly adds.*) Except my wife, of course.

Fourth section

Sue: (*in same spirit)* Mrs Adams is on the phone, you dog.

To:

Frank: I don't know why you can't learn to turn on a simple thing like a toaster! (*He exits.*)

Fifth section

Sue: (laughing) Thomas Edison.

To:

Lydia: Sh! Sh! (*She exits, laughing.*)

Sixth section

Chris watches her off. He is thirty-two; like his father, solidly build, a listener. A man capable of immense affection and loyalty. He has a cup of coffee in one hand, part of a doughnut in the other.

To:

Bert: (*mystified, but willing)* Okay. (*He runs off stage back of arbour*).

Seventh section

Keller: (*Calling after him*) And mum's the word, Bert.

To:

Chris: You know Larry's not coming back and I know it. Why do we allow her to go on thinking that we believe with her?

Eighth section

Keller: What do you want to do, argue with her?

To:

Keller: I ignore what I gotta ignore. The girl is Larry's girl.

Ninth section

Chris: She's not Larry's girl.

To:

Keller: Now what's going to happen to Mother? Do you know? I don't! (*Pause.*)

Tenth section

Chris: All right, then, Dad.

To:

Mother *appears on the porch. She is in her early fifties, a woman of uncontrolled inspirations and an overwhelming capacity for love.*

Eleventh section

Mother: Joe?

To:

Mother *picks a few petals off the ground, stands there smelling them in her hand, then sprinkles them over plants.*

Twelfth section

Mother: No more roses. It's so funny.... everything decides to happen at the same time. This month is his birthday; his tree blows down, Annie comes. Everything that happened seems to be coming back. I was just down the cellar, and what do I stumble over? His baseball glove. I haven't seen it in a century.

To:

Mother: It's not like a headache.

Task

As you can see, the first half of Act One can be divided up into twelve shorter sections. In each of these, there is a key plot or character development.

Either using your own divisions of the first half of Act One, or my own, summarise the key events of each in terms of character and plot development and provide one example of language analysis which links with this.

When you have done this read the examples that follow.

First section

Miller establishes the difference between the characters of Keller and Jim Bayliss. Jim is a quick-witted man; Keller is slower and is not a thoughtful or intellectual man.

Language analysis: Keller's exclamation of shock or surprise at the variety of careers or hobbies that it is possible to undertake: 'Psss!'

Second section

Miller introduces one of the key symbols of the whole play: the tree. In this play, the tree is connected to the family's sense of loss for Larry, and to the character of Larry himself.

Frank: He'd been twenty-seven this month. And his tree blows down.

Language analysis: Notice the American dialect and the informality of the way in which Frank speaks. For example, he misses out 'have' in the future perfect tense – would **have** been in Standard British English. Through these two separate short statements, Miller parallels Larry's birthday this month (in August) with the blowing down of the tree. This is symbolically significant, and Miller communicates this to us by pairing these statements so closely.

Third section

In this section, Miller introduces a new character, and the first woman: Annie. This is also important; Annie was Larry's fiancée – like the tree which has now blown down, she is also a reminder that Larry is no longer here. Through the introduction of another character linked to Larry, Miller is quickly building up a picture of the two families (the Kellers and the Deevers) who have been devastated by the loss of one of 'all my sons': Larry.

Keller: Girl leaves here, a scrawny kid. Couple of years go by, she's a regular woman.

Language analysis: The passing of time is effectively conveyed in Keller's abbreviated way of speaking. Notice how he misses out the indefinite article 'a' at the start of this first statement. Also notice how he misses out a conjunction ('and') which would be expected in Standard British or American English. Compare the following rephrase into Standard American English:

A girl leaves here and she's a scrawny kid. A couple of years go by and she's a regular woman.

The impact of missing out the indefinite article 'a' and the conjunction 'and' should now be clearer. Notice also the informal and familiar lexis, such as the noun 'kid', and the informal adjective 'scrawny'. This tells us that Keller is speaking about someone for whom he has a great deal of affection.

Fourth section

In this section, Miller introduces the second female character and the first to appear on stage: Sue Bayliss. Like her husband Jim, Sue is also quick-witted and has a sense of humour. In this, she is something of contrast to Keller who is not a quick-thinking man. Miller characterises this husband and wife as alike, in order to show that there is affection and love between the two.
Sue: (*in the same spirit*) Mrs Adams is on the phone, you dog.

Sue: Don't sniff around me.

Language analysis: Sue uses a common informal metaphor, a type of idiom, to describe her husband. She characterises him as a 'dog'. Depending on context, this could either be a serious insult or light-hearted fun. It is clear that in this context, it is the latter. We know this because Sue replies *in the same spirit* as her husband. Jim has just made a wry and light-hearted, ironical comment – and Sue responds in kind. This shows us that she is just as quick thinking as her husband, and is able to join in with his verbal games.

She also proves this in her ability to follow up on her use of this idiom, and uses an imperative to her husband. She instructs him not to 'sniff' around him – and this verb choice is deliberately chosen because it recalls the idiom of the dog which she has already used, and so is intended to be witty.

Fifth section

The second female character to enter the stage is Lydia. Her entrance parallels Sue's. Jim's wife (Sue) has entered the stage, and then Frank's wife (Lydia) also enters. Just as Miller shows us how Sue and Jim are a good match, he also shows that Frank and Lydia are too. Like Sue and Jim, Frank and Lydia also share some characteristics. Miller presents Lydia as a kind-hearted and pleasant character. This is shown through her concern with Annie.

Lydia: Is she still unhappy, Joe?

Language analysis: Lydia asks a question about someone she refers to using the personal pronoun 'she'. Usually when we use a personal pronoun in this way, it is clear from context who we are speaking about. In this case, Lydia is so sure that Keller will know who she means that she doesn't need to use Annie's name.

Moreover, since she has also introduced the topic of Annie in her previous question:

Lydia: Annie get in?

Then it is clearly Annie who is on her mind.

However, Keller checks Lydia's meaning in his reply, by stating her name with a questioning intonation. The fact that Lydia did not use Annie's name in the first place shows us that she thinks it unnecessary to make it clear who she is speaking about – everybody knows that Annie is unhappy, so it must be Annie she means. This shows us the level of her empathy and concern for Annie.

Sixth section

In this section, there is some affectionate joking with one of Jim and Sue's sons, Bert Bayliss. Like the Kellers, Jim and Sue have two sons: Bert and Tommy. This parallels Chris and Larry, but since Bert and Tommy are still both young and alive, this brings the Keller's loss into an even sharper focus. It is touching that Keller jokes around with Bert in a fatherly and affectionate way, which shows his love for children and his sadness at the death of one of his sons. Chris is now Keller's only living son, and the title of Miller's play deliberately reminds us of the loss the Keller family have suffered.

Keller: Now you're talkin', Bert. Now you're on the ball. First thing you know I'm liable to make you a detective.

Language analysis: Keller jokes that Bert is a 'policeman' of the block where they live, and that he reports anything wrong to Keller. If he does this successfully, then he may even be promoted to detective! Notice the informality of the speech and the American dialect which comes through in Keller's use of 'talkin'' rather than 'talking'.

Seventh section

As you will have noticed, Miller builds up the play quickly by introducing new characters on-stage in a systematic fashion. He continues this trend in this section by introducing Chris, another key character.

In this section, a key point of tension is introduced. It becomes clear that Chris is now in love with Annie. However, if Chris marries Annie then this will make it very clear to everyone that Larry really is dead. Since this is something that the Keller family are trying not to admit to themselves, this would be too big a change for the family to handle.

Admitting to Larry's death would be particularly devastating for Keller's wife, Kate. This is the character also referred to as 'Mother'. The reference to Keller's wife also completes the systematic pairing of the spouses: we first met Keller, Jim and Frank; then we were introduced to Sue (Jim's wife), then Lydia (Frank's wife), so only Keller's wife now needs to be introduced.

Chris: One of these days, they'll all come in here and beat your brains out.

Keller: What's she going to say? Maybe we ought to tell her before she sees it.

Language analysis: Notice how effectively Miller breaks the conversational chain in the incident quoted here. There is not the adjacency pair anticipated by Chris's statement, which refers to the jokes Keller plays on the children of the neighbourhood. It is expected by this statement that Keller would reply to this by keeping to the topic. He might agree with the statement, for example, or make a parallel example of his own about the children and about the jokes he plays.

However, what we have instead is a non-sequitur. Keller makes no reference to Bert, to the games he plays with him or to the children of the neighbourhood at all. Instead, he dramatically changes the direction of the conversation by asking a question on an entirely different topic.

This question refers back to the tree. Like Lydia's question about Annie, where she assumed that Keller would know exactly who she meant, Keller assumes that his son will understand exactly what he means and who he is talking about.

This time, 'she' is not Annie. Instead, it is Kate, Keller's wife. The concern both father and son show for Kate, and for her seeing the fact that the tree has blown down, makes it clear that Larry, his death and the tree are symbolically connected in this play. The tree therefore represents Larry and his loss: it is a symbol for him.

For the tree to blow down therefore means something greater than itself, which is why both Chris and Keller fear the consequences of Kate seeing the dead tree. For Kate, it would represent the reality of Larry's death, and this is something that the family – especially Kate – are not yet ready to admit to openly.

Eighth section

Miller builds up the tension further in this section. He has established the point of disagreement between Chris and Keller – about accepting Larry's death, admitting to this openly and moving forwards – but it becomes clear that this is something that Keller is not yet able to do. The reason why he cannot yet admit to Larry's death is fundamental to the themes of Miller's play, and which will become clearer as the play progresses.

Language analysis: Unlike Keller, Chris is able to be open and honest about Larry's death. However, he is very different to Keller. Chris is in love with Annie himself, and in order to able to have a relationship with her, he has to be able to face the truth that Larry is dead and she is no longer his fiancée. Miller makes this clear in his use of direct statements. For example:

Chris: I don't want to argue with her, but it's time she realized that nobody believes Larry is alive any more.

What is also notable about this direct statement – the truth is, after all, that Larry really is dead – is Keller's reaction. Miller conveys this through a dramatic technique. Instead of openly responding to Chris's statement, Miller makes it clear that Keller is uncomfortable. He moves away from Chris, a physical separation that communicates his unwillingness to engage with him on this topic. He also looks at the ground. Since maintaining eye contact is an expected part of normal discourse, shifting one's gaze away from the person you are speaking to is an effective way to convey embarrassment and unwillingness to talk openly on a subject.

Ninth section

Miller builds the tension and the conflict that is by now very clear between Keller and Chris. Quite dramatically, father and son confront each other over the truth of Larry's death, and the necessity of being open about this, especially with Kate. It becomes clear that the Keller family made a decision to confuse the issue of Larry's death by implying that there was some chance he may not have died, and that he might yet come home.

This hope – that Larry is missing, rather than dead – is really what is sustaining Kate. However, both Chris and Keller know that it is not true. For Keller, it is possible to maintain this illusion because he is an old man and like Kate, wishes that Larry could come back. As we know, there is also another reason why he finds it so important to maintain this illusion, and his guilt about his son's death, which explains his need to deny its reality, drives the events of the play.

Chris is not like Keller. He is a young man, and he has his life ahead of him. He is also in love with Annie, now – and this is complicated because Annie was 'Larry's girl'. For Chris to live his life, which means having a relationship with Annie, and being open about Larry's death, the family have to admit this as being true. However, since both Keller and Kate are highly unwilling to do these things, Miller has effectively brought Chris into conflict with his parents over this emotional issue.

Although Miller has presented Chris as a kind and loving man, he also presents him as someone who has internal conflicts of his own. While Chris *is* loving and kind, it is also clear that he is frustrated and unhappy with the family state of affairs. This makes him human: he is not totally (and unbelievably) selfless or altruistic. He resents the fact that his relationship with Annie – which he cannot see as being wrong – is frowned upon by his parents. He resents the fact that they cannot bear to admit to Larry's death. Miller shows us his human or emotional side, when he says:

Chris: I don't know why it is, but every time I reach out for something I want, I have to pull back because other people will suffer. My whole bloody life, time after time after time.

Language analysis: The lexis choice of the phrasal verb 'reach out' and 'pull back' are telling, here. Chris presents himself as if he were grasping for something which he is then made to feel he has to withdraw from. This verb choice has the connotation of a physical action, and it makes us feel as if Chris is imprisoned or trapped – he is physically constrained from the things he wants (such as Annie). This is a powerful and vivid use of language, and is a way in which Miller conveys Chris's emotional state at this point of the play.

Tenth section

Although the conflict and tension over openly admitting to Larry's death is the biggest that exists between Keller and Chris, other conflicts also arise as a result of Keller's inability to admit to the truth, and Chris's desire to be open and move on. Because Chris feels like he is being denied the life he truly desires – with Annie, a family and a satisfying job – he no longer sees any reason for him to live close to his parents and work in the family business.

Chris's desire to leave the family business, and Keller's disbelief that Chris could contemplate such a thing, is the point of tension in this section. However, Miller has managed this build up of conflict carefully: the theme of the family business is another important part of the play, and the nature of this business and Keller's way of managing it will become all the more vital as the play progresses.

The tension between father and son reaches its climax in this section. Keller shows his frustration and anger with his son through a dramatic technique: he puts his fist up to Chris's jaw. This is a threatening gesture, and it underlines the disagreement and conflict between the two. However, Keller can also see that Chris is confused, and only wants the kinds of things that Keller also wants (and has): a home, a business, a wife and a family.

Instead of the conflict coming to violence as Keller's gesture implies, the men recognise the fact that they stand a long way apart from each other.

Keller: I don't understand you, do I?

Chris: No, you don't. I'm a pretty tough guy.

Language analysis: Miller shows us Chris's inner strength and conviction in this section. He is firm in what he wants – Annie, a job, a family and a home – and that he won't let his parents' refusal to admit to the truth stand in the way of that. It is this that Keller cannot understand – he wishes his son were able to cover up the truth like he has been doing with Kate, and also that he were not in love with Annie.

Notice Keller's question tag at the end of his statement. This emphasises the lack of understanding between the two, because the expected answer to this question tag is 'no', from Chris. Chris supplies this himself – he and Keller can at least agree on one thing. They can agree that Keller does not understand Chris, though the same could also be said in reverse.

Eleventh section

After the drama of the preceding sections since the entrance of Chris on to the stage, Miller introduces one of the remaining key characters: Kate Keller. Her entrance also serves to change the mood and tone of the conflict between Chris and Keller. Since their conflict was partly about the need to protect Kate from the truth, her entrance requires the two men to drop their argument, at least for now, and to act very differently around her. This happens as soon as she enters – Chris welcomes her and Keller politely answers her question. They do their best to show that they were not having an argument.

Mother: It's her day off, what are you crabbing about?

Language analysis: in this section, Miller shows us Kate's straightforward and loving nature, despite her sadness for Larry. She is direct and straightforward with Keller, whom she clearly loves, because she has an affectionate way of talking to him, borne from the familiarity of many years of marriage.

Kate and Keller bicker over the potatoes and the garbage, and to Kate's practical way of thinking, if Minnie the maid is not in the house then it must be Kate who does the cooking and household tasks. This straightforward willingness to do the cooking is demonstrated in her statement: It's her day off. This answers Keller's question implicitly rather than directly. Like Keller and Chris, Kate also speaks in an American dialect appropriate to her character. She uses an informal Americanism when she uses the verb 'crabbing' to describe the action of moaning.

Twelfth section

This is the final section of the first half of Act One. In this section, Miller develops the character of Kate even further. We find out some more important information: she has a pain in her head, but not like a headache. This shows us that despite her ability to carry on the day-to-day tasks, like the cooking, and her love for her husband, there is something that is deeply troubling her, and it is something which is making her restless and unhappy. As we know, this is her inability to come to terms with the death of her son.

Language analysis: Miller makes the symbolism of the play very clear for us indeed in Kate's speech, when she says:

Mother: No more roses. It's so funny.... everything decides to happen at the same time. This month is his birthday; his tree blows down; Annie comes. Everything that happened seems to be coming back. I was just down the cellar, and what do I stumble over? His baseball glove. I haven't seen it in a century.

In this telling quotation, Kate connects up all the symbols of the play so far. These are: Larry's death, his tree, Annie and the fact that this month is his birthday. Miller is clearly setting the scene for something to happen, and we can guess that this will be connected to the conflict between Chris and Keller and must therefore have a connection back to Larry's death.

Kate uses the verb 'decides'. This is important, because it is an active verb. The subject of the verb in this statement is 'everything'. This has the effect of personifying 'everything'. Normally, it is only people who make decisions, but in this way of speaking, it is as if 'everything' has made a decision – like 'everything' was a person. The impact of this is to suggest that events are happening to the Kellers as if they had no control over their direction. This is an effective way of communicating to us that the family are in the middle of events over which they have little control, and the seeds of which were already planted a long time ago, through decisions that have already been made.

If we think back to Miller's own description of how he writes drama, as being structured around the story of birds coming home to roost, then the play becomes all the more clear. Miller is showing us the inevitable unfolding of the consequences of decisions made a long time ago – the consequences of which are now entirely unavoidable and impossible for the characters to escape.

Task

Make a character study of the following: Chris, Keller, Kate, Ann, Jim, Sue, Frank and Lydia.

For each of the characters, choose 3-5 key quotes from the first half of Act One that you think really summarise them and the important issues and concerns that drive them. Draw up a list of these and include a comment as to why you think these quotes are so telling.

It is important that you complete this task as a way to build up your understanding of how Miller develops character throughout the play, and how different sections of the play show us this.

Since you will be asked to comment on how characters or themes are presented in two separate episodes of the play, it is important that you can start thinking in terms of character development now, and can see how the language characters use effectively conveys information about them to us as the audience.

When you are satisfied that you have completed this task continue to the next Topic.

Topic 20 – Speech, Characterisation and Theme

Introduction

In this Topic, we will look closely at the second half of Act One and analyse the speech, characterisation and the changing relationships between the characters. We will also consider the thematic development of the play.

Aims and Objectives

- To read to the end of Act One

- To analyse the speech of the characters and what this reveals about the power each character holds

- To study the characterisation and development of the three main characters

---

Task

Now re-read through the second half of Act One. As you do this, think about how Miller develops the characters and the themes.
Now make a list of what you think are the key themes Miller has developed in Act One so far.

When you have done this read my own list below.

Key Themes of Act One

- Actions and their consequences

- The unavoidability of the past

- The father-son relationship

- Generational conflict

- Death, bereavement and grief

- Love

- Families and responsibility

- Business and industry

Task

Now divide the second half of Act One up into shorter sections or episodes suitable for comparison, as you did in Topic 6.

Using these, and either your own section divisions for the first half of Act One or mine, pair them according to their shared connections – either in theme or character.

Bear in mind that many pairings are possible. You should try and link two sections that share a theme or tell us something important about a particular character. Use the table that follows to help you complete this task.

Section from the first half of Act One	Section from the second half of Act One	Connection: either theme or character

Once you have your pairs for the whole of Act One then continue reading below.

Examples

Here are two examples of pairs of Act One episodes that you could have chosen, and the character of theme that connects them both.

Example 1

First half of Act One	Second half of Act Two	Connection: either theme or character
Twelfth section	Keller: You don't sleep, that's why. To: Mother: He's not going to marry her.	Larry's death and the unavoidability of the past **Or:** The character of Kate Keller.

Example 2

First half of Act One	Second half of Act Two	Comparison: either theme or character
Tenth section	Keller: (*asking uncomfortably*) Chris! You – you think you know her pretty good? To: Chris: (*a little frightened*) Dad, you don't have to tell me this.	The nature of business or industry **Or:** The character of Chris Keller.

Exam Focus

In the examination, one episode or section from the play will be printed or the examination paper and you will have to choose another part of the play against which to make a comparison.

Imagine that your examination question is on the section I have identified as being the Twelfth section from the first half of Act One. In which case, the question you were asked could be similar to the following:

> Using this extract as a starting point and with reference to other parts of the play, discuss how Miller develops ideas about the past and the unavoidability of past actions and decisions.

Now imagine that your examination question is on the section I have identified as being the Tenth section from the first half of Act One. In which case, the question you might see would follow this format:

> Using this extract as a starting point and with reference to other parts of the play, discuss how Miller develops ideas about business and ethics.

Task

You now have two possible examination questions, based on the two example pairs outlined as a response to the previous task. Choose ONE of these.

Make some notes on this question. How would you answer it? What points you would make? How you would analyse the language in the sections identified?

Make sure that you apply literary and linguistic terminology and think about relevant contextual factors.

When you have done this, read my analysis of the linguistic features below.

Using this extract as a starting point and with reference to other parts of the play, discuss how Miller develops ideas about the past and the unavoidability of past actions and decisions.

- Miller builds up frequent mentions of the key symbols of the play that are connected to Larry and his death, for example: the tree blowing down; it is the month of his birth; his fiancée has returned to the neighbourhood; and his mother discovered his old baseball glove in the cellar. These all build together to indicate that events of the past – still unresolved and unexplored – are to come out into the open over the course of the play.

- Kate Keller makes a bold statement showing her inability to comprehend what is happening: 'I still don't know what brought her here.' Along with her use of the verb 'decides', this suggests to us that she is in the middle of events – as are all the characters – over which they have little control. There is a sense of inevitability to this since the characters do not understand, and thus cannot control, what is happening to them.

- Miller's stage directions show how characters such as Kate are half-aware of the truth – but are still not willing to openly admit it. For example, Kate nods ever so slightly, but it is as if she still doesn't have the courage or strength to state it openly. Her son Larry is dead and he will not be coming back. This suggests that even though the characters are in denial, they will soon be unable to maintain this illusion for any longer.

- Kate asks: 'Why then isn't she?' Her question is unusual, and the position of 'then' in the question makes it so. It strongly links it back to Chris's statement about how Annie's single status does not necessarily imply that she is still mourning Larry. This question and the way Miller presents it shows us that whereas Kate cannot see any other possibilities, Chris can. For Chris, there is a third possible solution: Annie is no longer mourning Larry and yet she is still single because she is actually also in love with Chris, just as he is with her.

- In the episode of the play which follows this one, Miller continues his theme. Kate vividly describes her traumatic dream about Larry. This helps to communicate her heightened emotional state. There are many sentences that start with a conjunction, such as 'and'. The use of short and sharp statements, for example, 'Only high up.' Or 'And suddenly he started to fall.' show that Kate is describing a painful dream. This is a very real indication to the audience that it is impossible to 'bury' traumatic events such as the death of a son – the family have tried to act like it didn't happen, and that Larry will return, Kate in particular – but Kate's mental and emotional health are beginning to suffer as a result. This shows us that it is impossible to avoid the past, and to avoid reality. Larry is dead – and trying to pretend otherwise only makes things worse.

- Chris tries to reason with his mother – 'The wind blew it down. What significance has that got?' but for Kate, the connection between Larry and the tree is too strong. Chris also begs his mother, using words such as 'please' and imperatives 'don't go through it all again'. Forceful language such as this tells us that he is trying to force her to see the truth, and to escape the grip of the past. However, the actions of the past are still too strong for Kate; she is still having highly vivid and traumatic dreams about Larry and his death, after all.

- Kate's 'headache' – her mental and emotional pain – is also a real manifestation of all the stress she is under. This dramatic technique also tells us that something is boiling very close to the surface in this family, and that tensions and conflict are soon to erupt. It is therefore inevitable that the consequences of past actions – which Keller and Kate in particular have been trying to avoid – are now going to come out into the open.

Using this extract as a starting point and with reference to other parts of the play, discuss how Miller develops ideas about business and ethics.

- The family business is a thorny issue for the Kellers. This is for many reasons: the family business is in manufacturing, and was concerned with making aeroplane parts for the Second World War. Since Larry was a pilot in this war and died in an aeroplane crash, there is a thematic connection between Larry's death and the business. The theme of guilt and complicity in Larry's death by the Kellers themselves and their business is also important for the play – and it is these themes that Miller is establishing throughout Act One.

- Chris sees the family business as a necessary evil: 'If I have to grub for money all day long at least at evening I want it beautiful. His choice of verb 'grub' is very expressive, because it implies dirt, earth, digging and worms. It therefore effectively conveys the message that earning a living is doing something shameful or dirty, like digging around in the earth. However, it is a necessary trade-off in order to able to have the 'beautiful' – a happy home and family life.

- For Keller, the family business represents his life's work, family reputation, pride and honour. These are also problematic, given what his business was about and the mistakes he made. If his only remaining son does not want to continue in the business, then it puts everything into question. It means that there is nothing left for Keller, no remaining consolation after Larry's death and no way to justify or to excuse himself and what he has done. His fear, shock and surprise are evident in: 'Tell me something, you mean you'd leave the business?' If Chris did this, then Keller would have nothing left.

- Keller's fear and anger at losing Chris from the family business, and losing a way to help him hide from his own involvement in Larry's death, are shown in his angry outburst: 'That's only for you, Chris, the whole shootin' match is for you!' This has features of spontaneous speech, such as the informal American dialect of 'shootin'. The exclamation mark makes it clear that Keller is speaking direct from the heart, and the repetition of 'for you' emphasis what Keller is passionately trying to communicate to Chris. In this, Miller is showing us the emotional side of business: while earning money may be something all families have to do, if it is linked in with relationships, loss, guilt and resentment, as it is with the Keller's family business, then it becomes far more complicated. Like the tree, the Kellers' business is not just a business – it is far more than that.

- The link between the characters' emotional and personal lives and the family business is made even clearer later on in Act One, when the character of George Deever, Annie's brother, is introduced. Keller wonders if Annie might hold something against him for the imprisonment of Annie and George's father, but his question is really about whether Annie is here to find out more information. In a subtle way, Miller is building up a picture of Keller's guilt. For example, he asks: 'I mean if she was sent here to find out something?'

- Chris's reply 'Why? What is there to find out?' Makes it clearer that Keller is harbouring a guilty secret which he is hiding from the rest of the family. Chris does not have Keller's guilt, so he cannot see why Annie would have anything to find out. Keller is guilty, so this kind of reasoning is far more natural to him, and is evidence of a guilty conscience.

- Keller's attempts to erase his own guilt and the actions of the past are represented in his desire to have a fresh 'new sign over the plant – Christopher Keller, Incorporated.' However, a change of sign over the factory is a cosmetic change. Keller is aware that it is too late to go back and change the past, and that it is impossible to wipe out or paint over his guilt and complicity in Larry's death through his business decisions – but here he is making a futile and superficial attempt to do so anyway. However, what is needed is something more fundamental: an open and honest admission of Keller's own guilt and complicity in the death of his son, Larry.

Task

Return to the pairings you made between different sections of Act One. Using the format and style of the examination questions which I have described, write out a complete list of all the possible examination questions you can think of, based on these pairings.

Here is the format of the examination question to remind you:

> Using this extract as a starting point and with reference to other parts of the play, discuss how Miller develops ...

Now choose another of these possible examination style questions, and practise planning and answer to it.

Remember, it is very important to use the tools and techniques of language analysis in your answer in order to show the examiners that you understand how meaning is conveyed through word choice, sentence structure and voice.

Task

Now look at the last few lines of dialogue in Act One, from:

Mother: I don't know. (*She speaks with warnings.*) He's a lawyer now, Joe. George is a lawyer. All these years he never even sent a postcard to Steve. Since he got back from the war, not a postcard.

To:

The end of Act One.

How has Miller built up tension over Act One, culminating in this short section of dialogue?

Make some notes in answer to this question and refer to the language used and the events of the play so far.

Topic 21 – Act Two

Introduction

In this topic, we focus on the first half of Act Two, and on how Miller continues to build the play towards its climax using the foundation he established in Act One.

Aims and Objectives

- To read the first half of Act Two

- To consider how Miller builds the play up to its climax and how he uses the themes and characterisation he established in Act One to do this

- To consider themes and characterisation

Task

Re-read the first half of Act Two, from the beginning

to:

Ann (*deeply shaken*): Don't talk like that!

Now return to the first half of Act Two and divide it into shorter episodes or sections, as we did for the first half of Act One.

When you have done this yourself continue reading the examples that follow. As you can see, I have called the Act Two sections A, B, C etc rather than First, Second, Third. This is to make them distinct from the Act One sections.

Section A

The start of Act Two

To:

Chris: Look. .. Let me know when George gets here.

Section B

Sue: Is my husband - ?

To:

Ann: Oh....

Section C

Sue: That's why I've been intending to ask you a small favour, Ann. It's something very important to me.

To:

Sue: (*Chris enters on porch, wearing shirt and tie now. She turns quickly, hearing. With a smile.*) Hello, darling. How's Mother?

Section D

Chris: I thought George came.

To:

Chris: Do you think I could forgive him if he'd done that thing?

Section E

Ann: I'm not here out of a blue sky, Chris. I turned my back on my father, if there's anything wrong here now -

To:

Keller: I don't know, everybody's gettin' so Goddam educated in this country, there'll be nobody to take away the garbage. .. it's gettin' so the only dumb ones left are the bosses.

Section F

Ann: You're not so dumb, Joe.

To:

Keller: To know you got a place.. it sweetens you.

Section G

Ann: Joe, you owe him nothing.

To:

Keller: 'Oh come on up, come on up, and comb my lady's hair-'

Section H

Chris: What's the matter? Where is he?

To:

Chris: Nobody's afraid of him here. Cut that out!

Section I

Chris: Helluva way to do; what're you sitting out there for?

To:

Chris: (*starts for George*) Kind of a remark is that?

Section J

Ann: (*breaking in, putting a restraining hand on Chris*) When did you start wearing a hat?

To:

Ann: You kissed me when I left, now you –

Section K

George: (*breathlessly*) My life turned upside down since then. I couldn't go back to work when you left.

To:

George: The court didn't know your father! But you know him. You know in your heart Joe did it.

Section L

Chris: (*whirling him around*) Lower your voice or I'll throw you out of here!

To:

Ann: (*deeply shaken*) Don't talk like that!

Task

Now review all the sections from Act One and the first half of Act Two. For each of the sections of the first half of Act Two you have identified (or you may wish to use mine, as above) identify AT LEAST one other section from anywhere in Act One which has a thematic or character link with it. Complete the following table to keep a reccrd of your pairings.

Section from the first half of Act Two	Section from anywhere in Act One	Connection: either thematic or character, or both.

Examples

Now read two examples of my own pairings, using the sections I have identified from the first half of Act Two.

Example 1

Section from the first half of Act Two	Section from anywhere in Act One	Connection
Section K	Chris: Let's drive some place.. I want to be alone with you. To: Chris: Oh Annie, Annie.. I'm going to make a fortune for you!	Morality, ethics and responsibility Or The character of Chris Keller

Example 2

Section from the first half of Act Two	Section from anywhere in Act One	Connection
Section C	Chris: He murdered twenty-one pilots. To: Keller: Look at him, he's blushin'!	The character of Ann Deever Or Morality, ethics and responsibility.

> Task
>
> Using the Section B examination question format, write out at least two possible examination questions based on your own Act Two-Act One pairs.
>
> Choose one of these questions and make some notes on how you would go about answering this question, including literary and linguistic features and relevant contextual factors.

Example Examination Questions

Using the examples above, here are two possible examination style questions:

> Using this extract as a starting point, and with reference to other parts of the play, discuss how Miller uses the character of Ann Deever to explore idealism.

Or:

> Using this extract as a starting point, and with reference to other parts of the play, discuss how Miller uses the character of Ann Deever to convey ideas about family loyalty.

In these examples, we will look at how the same character can be used to convey different ideas. This will help you to practice selecting relevant material for your answers.

Using this extract as a starting point, and with reference to other parts of the play, discuss how Miller uses the character of Ann Deever to explore idealism

This was one of the examination style questions I identified, based on my Act Two-Act One pairings given in Example 2. What follows are some notes on how to answer this question, using appropriate language analysis.

- In Section C, it is important for the characterisation of Ann that she is speaking to another woman, and that they are alone on stage. Miller's play is primarily concerned with themes that are distinctly male-orientated in the era in which they are set (1940s America). These are themes such as warfare, business and becoming a man. However, the female characters are still important in this play, and Miller provides us with a different viewpoint on them when they are not in the company of men.

- In section C, we see another side to both Sue and Ann. Ann has been generally praised by many of the other characters for being young and pretty, and pleasant company. However, Sue is not as fond of Ann as Chris, Kate and Keller are.

- Sue is very direct – she comes out with a bold statement about how she would rather Chris and Ann did not live near her. The reason is surprising – Chris's idealism is too much for Sue. She has a witty way of phrasing this:

  > Research pays twenty-five dollars a week minus laundering the hair shirt. You've got to give up your life to go into it.

  The 'hair shirt' Sue refers to is an idiom. 'Wearing a hair shirt' means to deliberately deny oneself pleasure for the sake of a higher ideal – saints used to wear an actual hair shirt because it was painful, but because they thought this suffering brought them closer to God. Sue is suggesting that Jim would have to wear a 'hair shirt' – suffer a lower income – in order to live up to his ideals of carrying out research. However, Sue makes the idiom humorous by suggesting that the metaphorical 'hair shirt' would still have to be laundered – this verb jokingly implies that the hair shirt is real!

- Sue dominates the conversation and speaks over or interrupts Ann. For example, Ann starts saying 'I don't agree with you. Chris –' but Sue interrupts. This is a feature of spontaneous speech, and is one indication that their conversation is getting more heated. This shows us her loyalty to Chris; she defends him against Sue's charges that his idealism is unrealistic, and that it has a bad effect on Jim. In this way, Miller shows us that Ann and Chris are alike: both are in love with each other, both are very loyal (Ann defends Chris here; Chris defends Ann against her father's supposed crimes).

- However, Ann does not let Sue take complete control of their conversation. She puts her own case: she also makes it clear what she thinks. For her, Chris is beyond reproach. Sue thinks that if Chris were so idealistic, he wouldn't work at his father's company still, which has a damaged reputation. However, Ann defends still Chris, which also shows her loyalty and devotion.

- Ann is also clear that she is not responsible for the hurt feelings Chris's idealism causes others 'I can't do anything about that.' For Ann, loving Chris and sharing her life with him is enough. She is less concerned with people outside her own small circle in this instance.

Using this extract as a starting point, and with reference to other parts of the play, discuss how Miller uses the character of Ann Deever to convey ideas about family loyalty.

- Ann is defensive. She is prepared to defend Joe – this shows us that she is quite firm in her belief that her father was at fault, and not Keller. Sue also hints that perhaps Ann is not as clear as her words would suggest. She asks Ann why she doesn't go and talk to other people in the neighbourhood about Joe and about what they think about the business. The fact that she doesn't suggests that she might not want to hear what they say. This could be because she would rather not think anything else other than what she has decided is the truth: her father is guilty and Joe is not.

- Ann's black-and-white sense of right and wrong has already come across in this episode in Act One. Here, Ann also shows her clear moral convictions. As soon as Larry's death was reported to her, she made firm decision that her father was guilty. It is interesting that it was her grief at Larry's death that made her turn against her father: it was therefore a highly emotional decision, rather than one made based on the evidence or facts. This suggests to us that Ann has a highly personal or emotional reason for thinking that her father is guilty and Joe is not. The fact that she strongly defends Joe to Sue also implies that this is the case – perhaps she doesn't really want to think that anything else could be the case.

- Miller contrasts Ann and Kate in this section. For Ann, the way she has dealt with the death of Larry is to blame her father for this, and to cut him out of her life. However, the way Kate has dealt with Larry's death is to convince herself that Larry might come back. She even states that Larry is 'not dead', though this is clearly not true. Larry is definitely dead.

- Both Ann and Kate's ways of dealing with the death of Larry are problematic. Ann's decision to blame her father for Larry's death makes Keller feel guilty. This is because Keller knows that it is not true; he is the guilty one. He is therefore in a tense situation – he tries to make Ann feel less bad about her father because he can see she is hurt. However, he is really speaking about himself when he asks the characters to: 'See it human, see it human.' This is a very telling phrase; the noun 'human' is used here as an adverb. Joe is asking us to take pity on people's faults and failings, and to try and understand why people make the decisions they do.

- However, Joe's attempts to ask Ann and Chris to understand people's failings do not work. This is clear when Ann says: 'Joe, let's forget it.' Ann would like to move on, like Chris – but all the characters are caught in the consequences of past events and decisions which they now have little control over. It is becoming clear that the truth about what happened will have to come out into the open.

Topic 22 – Dramatic Tension

Introduction

The aim of this topic is to read the second half of Act Two, to the end. We will consider how Miller has developed the themes and how he has built up the dramatic tension to the climax of the play in Act Three. We will also consider characterisation.

Aims and Objectives

- To read the second half of Act Two

- To consider how Miller builds the play up to its climax and how he uses the themes and characterisation he established in Act One to do this

- To consider themes and characterisation

Task

Now re-read over the second half of Act Two, from

Chris: (*sits facing George*) Tell me, George. What happened?
To:
The end of Act Two.

As with Acts One and the first half of Act Two, divide Act Two up into shorter sections or episodes.

When you have done this read my suggested divisions below. As you will see, I have kept the alphabetical listing started in the first half of Act Two.

Section L

Chris (*sits facing George*): Tell me, George. What happened?

To:

George: (to Ann) What more do you want! (*There is a sound of footsteps in the house.*)

Section M

Ann: (turns her head suddenly towards house) Someone's coming.

To:

Mother: Why didn't you give him some juice!

Section N

Ann: (defensively) I offered it to him.

To:

LYDIA *enters on porch. As soon as she sees him:*

Section O

Lydia: Hey, Georgie! Georgie! Georgie! Georgie! Georgie!

To:

Lydia: (*as she runs off*) Oh, Frank!

Section P

Mother: (*reading his thoughts*) She got pretty, heh?

To:

Mother: (to George) He never shot anybody.

Section Q

Keller: Well! Look who's here!

To:

Keller: As long as I know him, twenty-five years, the man never learned how to take the blame. You know that, George.

Section R

George: (he does) Well, I –

To:

George: You too, Joe, you're all amazingly the same. The whole atmosphere is.

Section S

Keller: Say, I ain't got time to get sick.

To:

Mother: Why isn't it possible, why isn't it possible, Chris!

Section T

George: (to Ann) Don't you understand what she's saying? She just told you to go. What are you waiting for now?

To:

Chris: And I'm his brother and he's dead, and I'm marrying his girl.

Section U

Mother: Never, never in this world!

To:

Keller: How could I kill anybody?

Section V

Chris: Dad! Dad!

To:

The end of Act Two.

Task

Now look over your section or episode divisions for the second half of Act Two. If you wish, you may use my example divisions above. For each section, find a pair from anywhere else in either Act One or Two.

Use the table below to record your pairings. Remember to look for a character of theme that they have in common.

Section in the second half of Act Two	Section from anywhere else in Act One or Two	Connection: theme or character

Task

Now look over the pairings you have made. Using the examination question format, write out as many examination style questions that you can, based on the pairs you have identified.

When you have done this continue reading below.

Exam Focus

In your exam, you will need to know the play well enough to be able to choose your own sections to act as a useful comparison against the section printed in the Source Booklet.

Therefore it is useful to keep thinking about how the different sections relate to each other. How does Miller develop his themes through the course of the play? Keep thinking of examples of literary and linguistic features which you can use to illustrate your ideas.

Task

Now return to your section divisions for Act Two. If you wish, you may use mine For each of these short sections, write a brief summary of what happens, and provide an example of language analysis.

It is important that you attempt this task yourself so you can practise the skills of language analysis.

When you have completed this task yourself read the analysis that follows.

Section A

At the end of Act One, Miller has indicated that there are secrets and tensions that lie beneath the surface of the Keller family. Since both Kate and Keller are hiding the fact that it was really Keller who was responsible for the faulty cylinders, and not Steven Deever, the arrival of George (his son) naturally causes them some tension. This is shown by the fact that Kate is acting strangely and Joe is sleeping a great deal.

Although Kate wants to see George, she also knows that doing this is dangerous because of what truths might come out. This is why she says, in a direct command to indicate her clarity of purpose:

When George goes home tell her [Annie] to go with him.

Section B

Sue enters in this section. This is a chance for Miller to reveal more about the character of Ann in particular, by having both her and Sue on stage alone together.

Ann: I don't know. I think it's mostly that whenever I need somebody to tell me the truth I've always thought of Chris. When he tells you something you know it's so. He relaxes me.

Language analysis: Here, Ann explains that Chris is a straightforward character, and this is why she loves him. In this respect, she is also like him – they are both uncompromising in their ethics, and see the world in black-and-white terms. They find it hard to understand people who don't live up to their ideals, and if they think that a person has done something wrong, then they do not find it easy to understand why. Ann also shows her trust for Chris – he 'relaxes' me. This verb is important. Perhaps Ann has been feeling tense and on-edge about something? Perhaps there is something she doesn't want to admit is true – and perhaps this is to do with her father's guilt?

Section C

Sue: Who is he [Chris] to ruin a man's [Jim's] life? Everybody knows Joe pulled a fast one to get out of jail.

Miller is building up more and more doubts and questions about Larry's death and what really happened in the Keller factory. Sue now states outright what the neighbourhood all think – that Joe was just as guilty as Steven, but Steven went to jail and Joe didn't. Sue says this to imply that Chris's father is not as idealistic and perfect as Ann would like to think – and so Chris has no right being that way, either.

Miller therefore uses the minor characters (such as Sue and Jim) to increase our doubts about the Kellers and to increase the tension as we learn more and more about what really happened when Larry died.

Section D

Chris: Do you think I could forgive him if he'd done that thing?

Miller builds the tension relentlessly. We already know that George is due to arrive – with news from his father. Ann's presence is also disturbing, since she is 'Larry's girl' but Chris is now in love with her. She threatens to unsettle Kate and Keller for this reason. Miller makes it clear that if the truth did come out – the truth about the family business – then it would wreck Chris's relationship with his father. This increases the dramatic tension a great deal, since it is also clear that the two love each other as well.

Language analysis: The bold question Chris asks is telling. Chris describes the whole incident – sending out faulty plane parts, and his father's involvement in that – as 'that thing'. This is an indirect way of speaking, using the generic noun 'thing' rather than being specific or naming it openly.
The fact that Chris does this implies that he finds it hard to describe or talk about openly, and also that he talking quickly because he is emotional. This is how Miller helps to show us his mental and emotional state at this time.

Section E

Ann's reply to Chris's heated question is very important:

I'm not here out of a blue sky, Chris. I turned my back on my father, if there's anything wrong here now –

Ann uses an interesting image. She says that she is not out of a 'blue sky'. This recalls Larry's career as a pilot, his mother's dream of him falling and his own death in a plane crash. But in this context, her image is a metaphor for the fact that she is not unaware of the past. What Ann is saying is that she knows what has happened between the two families, and she knows about their shared history and background together. She is not a complete stranger who came 'out of a blue sky'.

However, her next statement makes it all the more clear that her way of dealing with Larry's death – blaming her father and rejecting him – is all dependent on her certainty that her father really was to blame and Joe was not guilty. If anything threatens the certainty of this truth, then it will force her to confront painful questions.

There is a causal connection implied in the construction – the connective 'so' could be added between the two clauses in this sentence:

I turned my back on my father [I have blamed him and rejected him]

SO if there's anything wrong here now – [then I can't blame him any more]

If Ann's father Steven is not actually guilty, then this will be painful for Ann, because she will have to confront the fact that she blamed and rejected her father unfairly and falsely. It will also reopen the pain of Larry's death for her.

Section F

Miller shows us Keller's firm conviction that family is all that matters. For Keller, is it family bonds – to his wife and son – that matter more than anything. This is how he sees the world; as a result he thinks that parent-child relationships are also of supreme importance to other people. This is why he says:

You're in love now, Annie, but believe me, I'm older than you and I know – a daughter is a daughter, and a father is a father. And it could happen.

Keller thinks that blame and shame about the past could come between him and Chris, and Chris and Ann – because Ann's loyalties would be to her father first and foremost. In this, he thinks that Ann thinks like he would – loyalties to parents or children are the first and only thing that matters.

Because the family bond matters so much to Keller, he wants to ensure that Steven does not cause resentment when he gets out of jail. This explains his desire to bring him back into the family business – it is a seemingly kind gesture but is really a way to cover over his own guilt, shame and deception.

Section G

Keller's insistence on the important of family duty and loyalty become even clearer, here. He is made nervous in the way in which Ann has rejected her father because she thinks he is guilty. This makes him nervous because he knows that he is really the guilty one, and he fears what Chris would do if he found out. He knows that Chris is not like him – he acts in a far more idealistic fashion, like Ann. He is therefore worried, nervous and tense underneath it all, and Miller shows us this by the way he speaks.

The stage directions tell us that Keller is speaking with 'high nervousness' and is also angry. He also speaks 'as though the outburst had revealed him'. What he says - 'a father is a father' – is his own highest ideal. No matter what a father (or a son) does, a father is still a father, and so you must never reject him. The fact that Ann has turned her back on her father – and the fear that Chris could be capable of the same – is making Keller tense indeed.

Section H

Just as Sue's arrival has put Ann on edge, by giving her a hint that matters to do with the past are not all sorted, so does Jim's, in this section.

Jim also speaks directly:

You know why he's here, don't try to kid it away. There's blood in his eye; drive him somewhere and talk to him alone.

Jim knows that George – remember that he has seen his father, someone whom he hasn't seen for a long time while he is in jail – is due to arrive. This suggests that George and his father are on speaking terms, and that he will bring more information about what really happened in the factory. George also wants to take Ann back with him – and this suggests that he no longer wants Ann to be around the Kellers.

Jim is insistent that Ann drive George away so they can talk together, alone, so that George's arrival doesn't 'explode' in front of Kate. This is a vivid lexis choice to make, and it suggests the powerful emotional impact that George's arrival is certain to have.

Section I

Miller communicates a great deal about George when he arrives in this section through dramatic techniques. For example, he looks pale and he acts as if he is on edge – he is certainly tense and uptight with the truth of what he now knows. His father is innocent and Keller is really the guilty one. Miller shows the audience that George is also nervous, such as his 'forced appreciation' of the grape juice.

George's arrival certainly is explosive – he upsets the pretence that the Kellers have been trying to maintain by making it hard for the issue of Larry's death and Keller's factory to be ignored. The fact that he wants to take Ann away with him is also important – he doesn't see that there can be any connection between the Kellers and Deevers anymore. Of course, this will cause conflict – Ann and Chris are now in love, and two families have a close and shared history together.

Section J

It is clear that George's arrival is problematic by the way he speaks about his father. He says:

George: He's a little man. That's what happens to suckers, you know. It's good I went to him in time – another year there'd be nothing left but his smell.

George connects the literal and metaphorical meanings of the adjective 'little' when he suggests that his father is literally getting physically smaller in jail. However, other characters have also described George's father as a 'little' man – but meaning weak and unimportant, rather than physically small. George connects to this meaning of the adjective 'little', by suggesting that his father is also a 'sucker'. This use of an American idiom is vivid. George implies that because his father is a 'sucker', or a 'little' man, he has also been physically reduced in height. This is a graphic way to describe what his false imprisonment has done to him – and now George is sure of the truth. This is what he has come to reveal.

Section K

George arrives and makes it clear that he now thinks both he and Ann were wrong. They were wrong to cut their father out of their lives completely – and they were also wrong to blame him. Instead, he gives his father's account of what actually happened in the factory. This complements Keller's own account in Act One of what happened in the factory, when he asked everyone to 'see it human'.

George: They knew he was a liar the first time, but in the appeal they believed that rotten lie and now Joe is a big shot and your father is the patsy. Now what're you going to do? Eat his food, sleep in his bed? Answer me; what're you going to do?

Miller communicates George's emotional state in the way he speaks. For George, it is clear – if Keller allowed Deever to take the blame, then Ann can have no business marrying Chris. His shortened question shows how urgent an issue this is for him:

[Are you going to] eat his food [and] sleep in his bed?

This would be the more expected format in Standard English. However, remember that Miller is aiming to reproduce spontaneous speech and to communicate the feelings of the characters in the way they speak. George is angry, tense, nervous and emotional. This comes out in his language.

Section L

George: Everything they have is covered with blood.

This vivid phrase brings out George's sense of the Kellers' guilt. Since their business was responsible for sending out faulty parts that killed twenty-one pilots, they have blood on their hands. And since their business is how they pay for 'everything they have' then this image cuts straight to the point. The Kellers' have profited from selling faulty parts to American forces which killed American pilots.

George also recalls Ann, when he says that because Chris was such a trustworthy and straightforward man, they both believed him and the court verdict. And in Chris's opinion, his father was not guilty and Deever was the only one responsible.

Section M

This section is poignant because Miller reveals the close and affectionate relationship between Kate and George. This reminds us that before Larry's death and the business scandal, the two families were closely related – they even lived next door to each other. For example, Kate uses an affectionate diminutive 'Georgie' – a familiar and informal way of speaking.

George is touched and moved by Kate's love for him – he says that she hasn't changed. This is certainly true – the characters are still the same in their essence, but what has changed is that events have now caught up with them. It will soon not be possible for the Kellers to go on denying the truth of Joe Keller's guilt and his responsibility for the faulty parts made at his factory.

Section N

The debate in this section over whether or not Ann will leave with George is symbolic. Who Ann decides to go with represents where her loyalties lie. If she stays with Chris, then that decision represents her loyalty to Chris and the Kellers. This itself implies that she has rejected her father and her brother, and she believes in Joe's innocence, as Chris does. However, if she goes home with George, then this represents her break with Chris and the Kellers. It shows that she is still loyal to her family – and that she now doubts her father's guilt. Miller brings in this theme throughout this section and Act Two, with various questions and references made to whether or not Ann will be leaving with George. For example:

George: The train leaves at eight-thirty, Ann
Mother: You're leaving?
Chris: No, Mother, she's not –

Language analysis: George's deceptively simple statement – about the time the train leaves – means more than a mere communication of information. It implies that this is the train George will catch, and that Ann needs to come with him as well. The fact that this statement is elliptical is made all the more clear by Kate's question. She understands the intent of George's question – which is why she checks this with Ann. Since Chris loves Ann and wants her with him, he answers on Ann's behalf - because Ann herself is very confused and torn as to what she should do. She loves Chris, but she also loves her brother – and she wants him to stay longer.

Section O

This section breaks up some of the tension that George's arrival has caused, and the debate it has occasioned over whether or not Ann will leave with George. Miller reintroduces Lydia to the stage. We have already met this character and therefore know a little about her, but the purpose of her re-entrance is to show us another side of George's character.

It becomes clear through their speech that George was once in love with Lydia – but because he was drafted into fighting in the Second World War and so left the neighbourhood, she married Frank instead. She now has three children – so the sight of Lydia again reminds George of what might have been, and what he has lost.

Lydia's calls out 'Georgie' five times. This is an emphatic demonstration of her excitement at seeing George again. This shows her emotions and her love for George – like Kate, she uses this familiar diminutive of his name. George also has a familiar nickname for Lydia – he calls her 'Laughy'. This suits her – she seems to be a pleasant and good-humoured person. This makes it clear that they have a lot of affection for each other.

There is sadness in the stage directions, because Miller indicates that George is 'hurt' by the news that Lydia now has three children. He says, with a mournful tone: 'I'm beginning to realize'. He is beginning to realize that he *has* been away for a long time – and that in that time, the people he used to love are now older, have moved on and have changed. George cannot turn back the clock – he and Lydia have grown apart and they can't have a relationship. This is why he doesn't want to see her children – it would hurt too much because it would remind George of what he has lost.

Section P

Kate shows again her ability to read people's emotions and to understand other people's thoughts and feelings. Miller portrays her as an intuitive and understanding character. She can tell that Chris and Ann are in love, though she would rather they were not because Ann will always be 'Larry's girl' to her. She can also see that George is sad for seeing Lydia because he used to love her – which is why she wants to introduce him to another girl so he can forget Lydia and fall in love again.

Language analysis: the conversation between Kate, George and Chris here sums up many of the major themes of the play.

Mother: Look what happened to you because you wouldn't listen to me! I told you to marry that girl and stay out of the war!
George: She used to laugh too much.
Mother: And you didn't laugh enough. While you were getting mad about Fascism Frank was getting into her bed.
George: He won the war, Frank.
Chris: All the battles.

Like Keller, Kate's main concerns are with family first and foremost. This is why she berates George – while he was living up to ideals (fighting Fascism in the Second World War) – another man fell in love with the woman he was in love with.
As a result, he is now without a family and a wife. This is why Frank was really the one who 'won the war' – even though he didn't fight in the Second World War. The war he won was the 'war' for Lydia – the only war that really matters, in Kate and Keller's moral code.

However, for George and for Chris and Ann, living up to higher ideals is important. The question of how far you have a responsibility to wider society – to higher ideals – and how far you have a responsibility and duty to your family, is a key theme of the play.

Section Q

George shows the extent to which he is also torn, like Ann. Like Ann, he too loves the Kellers – he feels affection for Kate in particular, and he grew up with Chris and Larry. However, he has visited his father for the first time since his jail sentence, and this has shaken him. He is now increasingly convinced that it was Keller who should take responsibility – and not his father.

George: It's everything, Joe. It's his soul.

Language analysis: the use of the noun 'soul' here implies that the very root of George's father's being is sick. The injustice of his imprisonment, and the rejection of his family as a consequence, has clearly hit him hard indeed. He is therefore not so much physically sick – in his heart – but sick in his mind or essence, because he has been wronged. Moreover, this sickness has now affected George, who is troubled by it – and it will soon also affect the Kellers, because the truth of what really happened is now certain to come out into the open.

Section R

Keller can sense that George is uneasy. He knows what really happened – so he tries to regain some control of the situation. He asserts that George's father was always the kind of man to make a mistake and blame others. This unnerves George – but he still tries to reply to Keller's criticisms of his father. However, Keller interrupts him or cuts him off on more than one occasion. This is a common feature of spontaneous speech, though it is typically interpreted as a hostile way of speaking, because it implies that what the person who is speaking has to say is unimportant.

Language analysis: George finishes this section with a moving comment on how much the Kellers mean to him. This makes his emotional dilemma all the more difficult: he grew up with this family and has a great deal of affection for them. Being with them really feels like 'home'. This is shown through his happiness at being back with the Kellers again. However, George is also distressed and anxious for his father.

Section S

The mention of Keller's flu during the Second World War abruptly changes the mood and atmosphere of the play – for example, George 'stands perfectly still' while Keller speaks of this, because it refers to the night at the factory when the decision was made to send out faulty cylinders.

Kate's difficulty in remembering Keller's flu is shown by the filler 'Huhh?' This is not a word as such; it stands in for a question, but is spoken with a question intonation, as indicated by the question mark. This is another spontaneous speech feature which Miller has deliberately included. However, its purpose is really to show us that Keller's flu might be more imaginary than real. The fact that Kate has difficulty remembering this episode, as shown by her surprised question, and her sudden memory of it again, make George suspicious and nervous. This kind of behaviour implies that they are trying to cover something up – they are trying to pretend that Keller really did have flu, when in fact he did not.

The smaller episode between Kate and Frank is also poignant. Kate is trying everything to convince herself that Larry is really still alive. If he died on a day that was supposedly 'favourable', according to his horoscope, then this makes it more likely, for Kate, that he can't have died on that day. In fact, he is missing rather than dead. However, for Chris, this is more unwelcome evidence of his parents' inability to come to terms with Larry's death.

Section T

Once George hears Kate's confirmation that Keller has never been sick – and her hurried backtrack to deny this once she realises that she has revealed Keller's lie – then he is only interested in speaking to Ann.

George: Don't you understand what she's saying? She just told you to go. What are you waiting for now?

Language analysis: Here, George tries to get Ann to see the truth. He asks Ann to understand what Kate is really saying. Kate initially made it clear that Keller was never ill – which means that Keller's flu must have been a lie. In which case, it was really a cover up for Keller's own part in the decision made in the factory. This is why George interprets this as Kate telling Ann to go – although Kate never actually told Ann to go in this direct way. The fact that Kate has opened up the truth, accidentally, equals Ann's awareness that the Kellers have been lying. This is them telling Ann to go – she must choose her family now, rather than the Kellers (even including Chris) because they have been lying.

Section U

In this section, all the buried emotions and tensions that Miller has been carefully building over Act Two erupt. They do actually 'explode' – an appropriate verb choice of Jim's from earlier on. The stress that Kate has been under – made clear with her headaches and vivid dreams about Larry – all comes out, as does Keller's anger. Keller speaks hurtfully (and truthfully) to Kate, and Kate responds with a violent gesture. It becomes clear the extent to which Kate is deluding herself. She is determined to force everyone to put their lives on hold as they wait for Larry to return – forever. This means that Chris can't marry Ann, for example.

The extent of Kate's emotionally heightened state is made clear. The words come 'rolling out of her', and this choice of verb implies that she has little choice over what she is saying; that this is such a strong impulse that it is controlling her.

Kate: Till he comes; forever and ever till he comes!

This is what Kate wants most of all – Larry to return – and because she wants to believe Larry is alive so much, then everyone must wait for him. If her family are not waiting, then it means that Larry is actually dead. This is too painful for Kate to really accept at this point. However, the real reason for Kate's pain is not just the obvious – the tragic death of a son. What is really painful is Kate's awareness of Keller's guilt, and that this implicates him somehow in Larry's death.

Kate: Do you understand me now? As long as you live, that boy is alive. God does not let a son be killed by his father. Now you see, don't you? Now you see.

Miller's stage directions indicate that Kate is 'beyond control' – again showing the extreme emotions she is feeling at this time. She cannot bear to admit that Larry is dead because to do so would be to admit that Keller was somehow to blame for Larry's death – his own father. Because Keller's factory shipped out faulty plane parts, to pilots like Larry, then Keller's fraud is also tied up with the family's grief and mourning for Larry. This is a painful emotional state to bear – so Kate's way to deal with her grief and anger has been to deny that Larry is really dead. This means he must be missing rather than dead – and since he is alive, then the entire family must wait for his return.

As Chris hears his mother's outburst, and has just seen George's shock at discovering once and for all that the Kellers were lying about Keller's illness, then his own certainty is also broken. Instead of believing his father's account, he questions his father. He does this in a way which troubles Keller greatly: he is quiet and insistent, and his lack of a violent outburst of anger scares Keller even more.

Section V

Keller's distress and the extent of his own personal crisis are revealed in his broken account of what happened that night at the factory. He speaks as if he were guilty of sending out faulty parts – which confirms for the audience the truth. He no longer tries to claim his innocence, his illness or his lack of awareness of what Deever was doing at the factory.

Keller explains some of the stress that he was personally under: his earlier plea to others to 'see it human' is all the more relevant here. He wants other people to understand his own situation – and to understand his own failings and faults. He was being pressured to produce parts, which was stressful. He had a business to run and a family to support – he wanted to hand on a successful business to his sons, and he wanted to keep his business going. He knew that if he didn't, then the factory would go out of business. His voice cracks as he recounts all this – a dramatic technique that Miller uses to convey his emotions.

You lay forty years into a business and they knock you out in five minutes.

Language analysis: Keller is making a sharp contrast between 'forty years' and 'five minutes' for rhetorical effect, to increase the power of what he is trying to communicate. The clauses are paralleled – they are both structured in the same way.

You [pronoun] lay [verb] forty years [time] into a business and [link]

They [pronoun] knock you out [phrasal verb] in five minutes [time]

He is asking us to see his own dilemma – how hard it was for him to know that his business would go bust in 'five minutes' – wasting 'forty years' of work, if he didn't send out the parts that he was contracted to produce.

Chris's own emotional breakdown is just as severe as Keller's. In reply to Keller's emotional appeal to Chris, to make him understand where he was coming from, Chris makes his own response. Chris was also under a lot of stress – he fought in the Second World War himself, and he knows what it was like to watch fellow soldiers die. The fact that the faulty parts caused the death of American pilots is too painful for Chris for this reason – he himself fought in the war, and his own brother was also a pilot.

Chris: Is that as far as your mind can see, the business? What is that, the world – the business? What the hell do you mean, you did it for me? Don't you have a country? Don't you live in the world?

Chris's frequent and fast, insistent questions make it clear the extent of his own rage. Chris is unable to understand his father – and vice versa. For Chris, it is meaningless that his father was trying to create a livelihood for his son, if doing that meant killing 'kids' – kids like Chris himself.

Chris can't understand why his father doesn't understand him – why he can't see that having ideals, like fighting in a war or for a country, also matter. And why having a responsibility outside of one's own family – to other people's families and children – also matter. Chris feels that his father is unrealistically trying to exclude the world – as if only family mattered. This is behind Chris's question: don't you live in the world? This is rhetorical and sarcastic. The only possible truthful answer to a question structured like this is 'yes I do'. Chris's question therefore effectively makes the point that it is impossible to shut out the world – as his father and mother have tried to do.

Topic 23 – Act Three

Introduction

In this topic we will read the whole of Act Three. This completes our reading of *All My Sons*.

Aims and Objectives

- To read Act Three

- To consider how Miller builds the play up to its climax and how he uses the themes and characterisation he established in Act One and Act Two to do this

- To consider themes and characterisation

Task

Re-read the whole of Act Three. As you do this, pay close attention to how the play ends, and how Miller draws all of the themes together.

Act Three

Now the truth about Keller and the business scandal is out in the open, after the emotional ending of Act One. Miller uses Act Three as his chance to show how this truth affects the characters differently. He also shows how the truth of what Keller has done is too much for the family to stand, especially so given the nature of Larry's death. This builds towards the final, dramatic climax of the play.

Notice how all the events of the play have taken place over the course of one intense day and night. The play opened on a Sunday morning in August, and by the early hours of the next day (early on Monday morning) the Keller and Deever families have been torn apart by the events that have happened and the truth about Keller that has finally been revealed.

Task

The first thing to do is to divide Act Three up into smaller sections, as with Act One and Two.

Remember that these sections should be of a suitable length to use as a comparison text in your exam.

Once you have done that write a short paragraph on the key events of each section, including language analysis of your own to demonstrate how effects are created and ideas conveyed.

Act Three Sections

As with Act One and Two, here are my own section divisions. Remember, these are a suggestion only – you are free to use your own if you wish.

Section 1

The start of Act Three

To:

Jim: It occurred to me a long time ago.

Section 2

Mother: I always had the feeling that in the back of his head, Chris ....almost knew. I didn't think it would be such a shock.

To:

Mother: You can't bull yourself through this one, Joe, you better be smart now. This thing - this thing is not over yet.

Section 3

Keller: And what is she doing up there? She don't come out of the room.

To:

Keller: Forgiven! I could live on a quarter a day myself, but I got a family so I –

Section 4

Mother: Joe, Joe ... It don't excuse it that you did it for the family.

To:

Mother: I know, darling, I know.

Section 5

Ann: Why do you stay up? I'll tell you when he comes.

To:

Mother: What's enough for me? What're you talking about?

Section 6

Ann: You're hurting my wrists.

To:

Ann: Kate, dear, I'm so sorry ... I'm so sorry.

Section 7

Chris: What's the matter -?

To:

Ann: Then I will!

Section 8

Keller: What's the matter with you? I want to talk to you.
To:
Chris: I can't look at you this way, I can't look at myself!

Section 9

Mother: Give me that!
To:
Keller: I think I do. Get the car. I'll put on my jacket.

Section 10

Mother: Why are you going? You'll sleep, why are you going?
To:
The end of Act Three.

Task

Now review the section divisions you have made out of Act Three. You are free to use the section divisions presented here if you wish or to use your own.

For each section of Act Three, find at least one complementary section from either Act One or Two. Remember, you are looking for a thematic or character connection.

Use the table below to record your pairings.

Act Three section	Act One or Two section	Connection: either theme or character

Task

Now that you have read to the end of the play, review your work on the characters that you completed during your reading of Act One. You should already have some key quotes for each of the following characters: Keller, Kate, Chris, Jim, Sue, Frank, Lydia and Ann.

Now include George, as well. Find 3-5 key quotes from anywhere in the play that you think really summarises George as a character and his most important motivations.

Once you have compiled a list for George, review the lists you made for the other eight main characters. Now that you have read the whole play, you can add more quotes to your lists, including material from the rest of the play.

When you have done this continue reading the analysis that follows.

Section 1

In this section, Miller shows that Jim is an intuitive and perceptive character, just like Kate. Jim has guessed that the Kellers were hiding from the truth of Joe's involvement in the scandal – and Kate has always thought that perhaps Chris also knew, even if only subconsciously.

Miller also uses the first two sections of Act Three as a way to explore the character of Jim further.

Section 2

Here, we discover more about Jim's idealism as contrasted against his wife Sue's practicality. This is a theme already discussed from another angle in Ann and Sue's conversation.

Therefore, this is a chance for Miller to explore the same dilemma from the other side – this time we have a chance to hear Jim's side of the story. Jim really enjoys doing medical research, but it doesn't pay very well. As a result, he had to live on 'bananas and milk'. However, for Jim, having to put up with that didn't matter – he was doing what he really loved. He makes this clear: 'It was beautiful.' He was living up to his ideals – doing what he really wanted rather than just what he had to do to pay the bills.

However, Sue did not find it easy to live without Jim. He refers to her as 'she' – Jim does not name Sue in Section 2, but it is clear that he means her. Sue was worried that Jim's dedication to research meant that she would lose him; she was naturally upset. Jim made the decision to go back with her – but this sacrifice of what he really wants to do with his life means that now he lives 'in the usual darkness'. This is a striking phrase. The adjective 'usual' conveys that he thinks it is only a unique man who lives up to his ideals, and that he is not one of them. The 'usual darkness' is the day-to-day mundane way of life that most people choose, rather than having the courage to do what they really want.

This is a key theme of the play, but explored in the context of the Bayliss couple rather than the Kellers or Deevers. To what extent do we have a duty to our family, and to what extent do we have a duty to ourselves and to higher ideals?

Section 3

Keller and Kate's discussion in this section is moving. It is clear that the emotional turmoil between them has exhausted Kate and made Keller frustrated and scared. Kate's suggestion that Keller says he wants to go to prison is her only solution. It would be a way for Keller to show Chris that he was sorry for what he did – that he wanted forgiveness.

Keller however can't understand where Kate is coming from. He really doesn't understand why he would need to do this – because it is an alien thought to him. For him, family duty and loyalty are everything. He wanted to look after his family and he had to work, to run a business. This meant he had to make difficult decisions – but he doesn't see anything wrong with that. He only wants other people to 'see it human' – to try and understand the difficulty and complexity of the situation, rather than to impose an impractical and unworkable idealism. Or, as Keller would say more aptly: you can't be a Jesus in this world.

Section 4

Miller introduces a powerful piece of dramatic irony here, and in this way he sets in motion the dramatic culminating events of the play.
Keller really can't understand Chris's anger and hurt at discovering the truth about him. He says:

Keller: Nothin's bigger than that. And you're goin' to tell him, you understand? I'm his father and he's my son, and if there's something bigger than that I'll put a bullet in my head!

This threat of Keller's – which we know he lives out – therefore sets in motion the unravelling of the Keller family towards Keller's suicide at the end of the play.

Section 5

We now see the impact the revelation of the truth has had on Ann, in this section. In this way, Miller shows us how the scandal has an impact on each of the characters in turn. For Ann, it is important that she has Chris. She does not want to be alone – she is no longer 'Larry's girl' because Larry is dead. But she doesn't want her relationship with Chris to come between Chris and his parents – she knows that would only hurt them in the long run. This is why she wants Kate to be open about Larry's death – as a way to set Chris free.

But like Chris and Keller, this is another divide that separates these two characters. Ann wants Chris more than anything – but Kate wants Larry to be alive more than anything. Neither can understand each other because both are so heavily emotionally invested in Larry's death (Ann) or Larry's still being alive (Kate).

Section 6

The antagonism and separation between Ann and Kate reaches a climax of its own, here. Ann is so frustrated with Kate's inability to accept the truth of Larry's death that she finally decides – though with awareness of how emotional it will be – to show Kate the last letter Larry ever wrote.

It is at this emotional juncture that Chris then re-enters the stage after his absence. In this way, Miller quickly builds up the emotional intensity toward the dramatic climax of the play.

Section 7

The letter is a turning point. Larry's letter to Ann is something that neither Kate nor Keller have read before, but we (the audience) do not get to find out what is contained in it until later. Meanwhile, Miller shows us the impact the truth has had on Chris. He wants to find a job elsewhere – he feels he can no longer honestly work in the family business, given the nature of the scandal.

Chris accuses his parents 'you made me practical'. For Chris, being practical and sacrificing your ideals is a terrible thing. But for his mother and Keller, 'You can't be a Jesus in this world'; you have to accept the reality of the world and of difficult situations and decisions. Idealism is of no use in this case, when you have to make a living and feed a family.

Chris recalls his service in the war, and he longs for it, because honour and duty (his ideals) were real and necessary. It felt meaningful to live in this way - like really being alive, though they were aware that they might die. His realisation that the real world is messy is contained in his exclamation 'This is a zoo, a zoo!' By this, he is implying that there is no moral code, no order, no principle at work in the world. It is simply everyone out for oneself – dog eat dog. This is the idiom that Chris references indirectly with 'This is the land of the great big dogs'.

Section 8

This is Keller's entrance. We can see the emotional turmoil the truth about Keller has had on Kate, Ann and Chris. Now it is Keller's turn himself to re-enter, before the dramatic climax.

Although Keller and Chris are still very much at odds, the real reason for Chris's extreme hurt are revealed by Miller. Keller makes the point that it is not just him who acts in a 'practical' or pragmatic way. Other people also deserve jail, if he does. Chris is not so blind or uncaring that that he can't see the truth of this, but this still does not resolve anything for him.

Chris: *I* know you're no worse than most men but I thought you were better. I never saw you as a man. I saw you as my father (*Almost breaking.*) I can't look at you this way, I can't look at myself!

For exactly the reason that Keller is his father, Chris expected better of him. But for Keller, exactly because he is his father, he thinks that Chris should be able to forgive him. As Keller has said before, there is nothing that Chris could do that he wouldn't forgive – because he is his father. This shows the extent to which the two men stand opposed to each other because they think in very different ways, and have very different priorities.

Miller cleverly combines these two thoughts in Chris's statement 'I can't look at you this way, I can't look at myself!'

For Chris, to discover that his father is not the man he thought he was – a good man – is to break apart all his ideals. He can no longer look at his father – but what he also can't do is 'look at himself' or think of himself as related to a man who could do what Keller has done. For a man like Chris, who is so idealistic and driven by higher goals, the thought that his father has not lived up to ideals is unbearable.

Section 9

Finally, the letter is read out to us, the audience. This delay in revealing the contents of the letter is a way for Miller to increase the sense of anticipation and tension as we wait to discover what it says. Since Larry is dead, this is also another clever way in which to introduce the character of Larry on to the stage. In Act Three, different characters come on stage in a succession to show us how the truth of what Keller did has had an impact on them. Now, it is Larry's turn – his thoughts are recorded from just before he died.

What we find out is shocking – Larry also found the thought of Keller's fraud unbearable. Keller thought Larry was practical, like himself. But Larry was just as confused and torn as Chris over the discovery of his father's involvement.

What is even more emotionally wrecking for Keller is the suggestion in Larry's letter that it was this discovery that brought about his death.

Larry says: 'I'm going out on a mission in a few minutes. They'll probably report me missing.'

The implication is that Larry intends to go missing because he predicts this happening. He intends to die on this mission – and the reason why is because he has been torn apart by the news of his father's guilt.

Section 10

Now everything is in place for Keller's final dramatic end. Reading the letter for himself is the final straw – knowing that Larry's death was caused by his pain at discovering what Keller did is too much for Keller. His mind is made up. Keller provides the statement that also names the play:

Then what is this if it isn't telling me? Sure, he was my son. But I think to him they were all my sons. And I guess they were, I guess they were. I'll be right down.

This moment marks a change in Keller's understanding. He now sees the world as his sons see it – for Larry and for Chris, killing twenty-one pilots through the faulty parts was like killing them, his own sons. The other pilots were also his 'sons' in the sense that everybody is responsible for everybody else – the dead pilots could have just as easily been Larry or Chris.

Once Keller really sees this, then he has no choice. He lives up to his earlier statement. He has just seen that there is something bigger than the family. And now he is going to finish what he started – he goes into the house.

However, Kate does not yet fully grasp this feeling. But Chris's statement neatly summarises this:

You can be better! Once and for all you can know there's a universe of people outside and you're responsible to it, and unless you know that, you threw away your son, because that's why he died.

Larry died because he couldn't bear the knowledge of his father's own lack of responsibility to the 'universe of people outside'. The people who are 'all my sons'. In this way, Miller through Chris and Larry have extended the concept of the family and of duty. If everyone is like 'family', then you can't think that your sense of duty and responsibility stop at the front door. And because Keller did think that, he can no longer live with himself.

The play ends with Chris and Kate in an emotional wreck at the knowledge of Keller's suicide. Both are exhausted and broken by what has happened. In one short day, Miller has dramatically staged the breakdown of a normal American family, and asked us to question ourselves closely. Who are we really responsible to? Where do our duties and responsibilities end? How should we live our lives? All these are questions that Miller asks us in *All My Sons.*

Coursework Component

Topic 1 – Introducing the Coursework Component

Introduction

In this topic, we will learn about the coursework component of Edexcel A-Level English Language and Literature. We will look at what you need to do for your coursework and begin looking at our texts. We will also introduce the concepts of plagiarism and authentication.

Aims and Objectives

- To learn about the coursework component for English Language and Literature
- To gain an overview of the coursework submission process
- To learn the importance of avoiding plagiarism

Please note that the information in this Component is designed for students using CloudLearn's recommended exam centres. Students at other centres must make their own arrangements with their centre.

The Coursework Component - Investigating and Creating Texts

For the coursework component of English Language and Literature, you will be investigating and creating texts. We will study two texts (one fiction and one non-fiction) based around a theme. You will then create your own texts (one fiction and one non-fiction). You will also write a commentary on these texts, explaining your language choices.

This is a summary of the work that you will need to complete:

Assignment 1-

- One piece of creative non-fiction (such as an article)
- One piece of creative fiction (such as an additional scene for a play)

Assignment 2 -

- One analytical commentary reflecting on the two pieces of creative work that you have produced.

The total word count should be 1000-2000 words (combined) for the two creative pieces and 1000-1250 words for the commentary.

The coursework component is worth 20% of your overall A-Level.

Theme: Art, Artifice and Identity

On our course, the theme is Art, Artifice and Identity. This is the theme that links the two texts that we will be investigating.

These two texts are:

- Non-fiction - Wendy Jones *Grayson Perry: Portrait of the Artist as a Young Girl*
- Fiction - Oscar Wilde *The Importance of Being Earnest*

We will be studying these texts together, and you will then choose your own task for your coursework.

The Aims of Coursework

Coursework is the opportunity to develop your skills of original, creative writing. The purpose of completing coursework is to show that you are able to work independently, to undertake research, and to draft and re-draft a piece of work.

Some students find the idea of completing their coursework daunting at first, but the procedure is much easier than it first appears. Indeed, many students really enjoy the coursework component and find it a great opportunity to work on their own creative ideas.

Drafts

Although you need to work on your coursework independently, you will have the opportunity to have your first draft checked by your tutor.

Your tutor can look at one draft of your coursework portfolio (fiction, non-fiction and commentary) and offer you feedback and ideas for improvements. In accordance with Edexcel's examination policy, your tutor can only look at **one** draft of coursework. Please remember to allow 7-10 days for the return of written work.

Using your tutor's feedback, you will then prepare your final draft.

Coursework Deadlines

On our course, we recommend that you complete your coursework before you begin work on Component 2.

This means that you are probably beginning work on this component in the Summer between years 1 and 2 of your A-Level.

Ideally, you will aim to complete your coursework by the autumn of your final year of A-Level, so that you are ready to move onto Component 2.

What is Authentication?

Authentication is the process by which your tutor will certify that your work is your own, unaided work. Your tutor will need to have seen at least two TMAs in order to be able to authenticate your work. She will also use anti-plagiarism software to check that no material has been copied.

It is very important that your coursework is your own, unaided work. You must not copy any material that you read. Copying any material from this course, from books or from internet resources are all forms of plagiarism. **You must always use your own words to express your ideas.**

The creative nature of the coursework tasks means that you will be encouraged to develop your own ideas and to write in your own words. So long as you do this, you will not need to worry.

After your coursework has been completed, your tutor will be able to write a letter for your exam centre, in order to authenticate your work.

Submitting Coursework

Coursework must be submitted in the final year of A-Level, at the end of the two year course.

Your exam centre will have a coursework deadline for the submission of coursework. This is usually early in May, but it could be considerably earlier. Check your exam centre's coursework deadline when you register to take your exams. Make a note of this date.

Your tutor cannot remind you of deadlines, so make sure that you are well organised.

Leave plenty of time to complete your coursework before your exam centre deadline.

Unfortunately, unforeseen events can and do happen. Postal delays may occur, or coursework can be lost in the post. Allow extra time before your submission deadline, so that there is space for unforeseen events.

Enjoy your Coursework!

Coursework is an exciting opportunity to complete original pieces of creative work and to develop your own ideas. Try to enjoy your work and let your enthusiasm for language and literature shine through!

In the next topic, we will start thinking about our theme.

Topic 2 – Art, Artifice and Identity

Introduction

In this topic, we will begin exploring our chosen theme. We will then start to think about creative writing.

Aims and Objectives

- To explore the theme of Art, Artifice and Identity
- To think about the process of creative writing

Art, Artifice and Identity

The idea behind this theme is to look at ideas of art, artifice and identity. All three of these words could have multiple definitions. One of the aims of studying English Language and Literature is to think about different possible meanings and to open up new readings and new ideas.

Task

Using an online dictionary or encyclopaedia, look up the following words:

- Art
- Artifice
- Identity

Start thinking about the meanings of these words. What do they mean to you?

You might like to create some spider diagrams to explore your ideas.

We could start to think about some of the ideas behind these concepts as follows.

- Art - Art might be defined as the products of creative work, such as paintings or sculptures. or as the process behind creating these works. It could be the technical skill behind creating an object, or a particular category of imaginative or emotive works. It could also be an evaluative judgement, a process of giving a certain value to particular works, such as 'I like it, but is it Art?

- Artifice - Artifice might be clever or artful skill; ingenuity; or deception and trickery.

- Identity - Identity is our core concept of who we are. It could be our characteristics or personality, or it could be an identification with a particular group. Identity could be something that we feel we choose ourselves or something that we think is imposed on us by other people.

As you will see, these themes are very broad and you will have a lot to think about in this section of the course.

Creative Writing

This may be the first time that you have had the opportunity of writing creatively in an assessed piece of work. Although this may sound challenging, it is also a great opportunity.

You will be able to write one piece of creative non-fiction (such as an article or review) and one piece of creative fiction (such as a short story or screenplay). You will notice that these genres considerably overlap with those that we studied in Section A of Component 1. This means that you are already familiar with the features of these genres and that you are already know what you will need to do to construct a text of this form.

In this coursework component, you will be able to use your knowledge to create texts that are tailored to your audience and purpose. This is your first opportunity to develop your own skills as a writer. In this way, creative writing gives you the freedom to express some of your own ideas, and to practice writing effectively.

Working Independently

As distance learning students, you are already working independently and you will be able to continue to develop this ability in this component.

In this component, you will have more opportunity to work on the texts yourself and to develop your own ideas about them. Bringing your own responses to the texts will help you to craft an original and creative pieces of writing. It will also encourage you to think about your own reading and writing process. This will help you to write your commentary.

Keeping a Reading Diary

For this component, we will introduce the idea of a keeping a notebook or a reading diary.

A reading diary is a record of a book you are reading and your response to it. This can be a useful record of your thoughts and feelings as you work through a text. You can write down how you feel about particular sections, your observations of the author's technique, any interesting quotations, and any questions raised or unfamiliar ideas that you would like to look up.

Reading diaries can be useful as they help us to remember our initial impressions This is difficult to do once you know the whole of a story. As we can't usually remember our first thoughts about a text after we have reached the end, keeping a note of our thoughts as we read can be useful. It helps us to reflect on our reading and to be more aware of our responses to a text.

In short, it is a useful way to take notes as you read. Thinking about your reading and keeping a record of these thoughts will also help you when you come to write the commentary for your coursework.

In the next topic, we will look at our first text *Grayson Perry: Portrait of the Artist as a Young Girl.*

Task

Find a notebook that you can use as a reading diary. You will need this for the next topic.

Topic 3 – Grayson Perry: Portrait of the Artist as a Young Girl

Introduction

In this topic, we will introduce our non-fiction text - *Grayson Perry: Portrait of the Artist as a Young Girl*.

Aims and Objectives

- To learn a little about Grayson Perry and his art
- To gain an overview of *Grayson Perry: Portrait of the Artist as a Young Girl*

Portrait of the Artist as a Young Girl

The title of this book is an amusing reference to a work by James Joyce titled *A Portrait of the Artist as a Young Man*. Grayson Perry is a male artist who sometimes dresses as his female alter ego Claire, on occasion wearing a style of pretty dress archetypally associated with a young girl. This is therefore a clever and witty title that references both Grayson Perry's past and his present.

This title also draws attention to the relationship between Joyce's protagonist and Grayson Perry. Joyce's modernist novel charts the intellectual development of its protagonist Stephen Dedelus (a reference to Daedalus, a skilled artist and craftsman from Greek mythology) who learns greater self-awareness through rejection of the norms of his society. This is therefore an illuminating allusion and a very suitable title for this biography of Perry.

In this biography, Perry describes his childhood experiences and the (good and bad) events that happened to him through his childhood, his adolescence and his early twenties. It explores his difficult relationship with his family, his feelings about transvestism and sexuality, and his awakening and growth as creative artist. In many ways, it could be read as a bildungsroman (a 'coming-of-age' story).

Grayson Perry's Life and Work

Although you will be reading about Perry's life in detail, it may be useful to you to have some background information before you begin reading the text.

Grayson Perry is a ceramic artist. Many of his creative works are pots and vases. These often use strong colours, text and collaged images. Many explore the relationship between gender and society and often include autobiographical elements and themes. Perry has said that he is attracted to pottery because of "the ways artifice could be deployed to make the innocent or honest pot have a purpose and mean something".[10]

---

[10] Wilson, Andrew. *Grayson Perry: General Artist* cited in Wikipedia 'Grayson Perry'
https://en.wikipedia.org/wiki/Grayson_Perry Accessed 16/07/2015

As well as his art, Perry is also known for his transvestism. 'Transvestism' means wearing clothes associated with the opposite gender and Grayson Perry sometimes dresses as his female alter ego Claire. Claire often wears pretty, little girl dresses but has been described by Grayson as having different identities including a C19th reformer or an 'Eastern European Freedom Fighter'.[11] He collected the Turner Prize as Claire in 2003. He was awarded a CBE for Services to Contemporary Art in 2013.

Task

You may like to look at some pictures of Grayson Perry's work.

There are some pictures in the biography itself. These are printed on colour plates in the centre of the book and as black-and-white images at several points in the text. You could also look for the book Grayson Perry by Jackie Klein (Thames and Hudson, 2013). You may be able to find this in your local library.

You could even look to see if there are any exhibitions of his work that you could visit.

Voices

We have already looked at the genres of biography and autobiography and we are already familiar with these genres.

In this text, we hear Grayson Perry's voice directly. The author, Wendy Jones, tells us in the introduction that she worked from recorded conversations with the artist. However, we should note that Jones has also edited and constructed this text. For example, she will have devised the chapters and tried to make an overall whole out of the recorded conversations.

As you read the text, you might like to think about the genre and the sense of voice that is created. This will also help you to practice your ideas from Component 1.

Remember however that you don't need to study this text in detail, or to look at the literary and linguistic features. Instead, our focus here is the themes and ideas raised by the text.

---

[11]Wilson, Andrew. *Grayson Perry: General Artist* cited in Wikipedia 'Grayson Perry' https://en.wikipedia.org/wiki/Grayson_Perry Accessed 16/07/2015

You will be able to think about Grayson Perry's voice, his life and his art. You will be able to think about any similarities between his life and your own, or you may recognise similarities to the lives of people you know. In this way, your response will be personal to you.

Task

Your task now is to read the text.

Although you can read quite quickly and you don't need to study every word, you should also keep thinking about what you are reading.

Read a chapter or so at once, and take time to reflect on what you have read. Make notes in your reading diary.

These notes will be useful when you come to write your commentary.

Topic 4 – Choosing a Non-Fiction Task

Introduction

In this topic, we will look at how to choose a task for your non-fiction piece of coursework.

Aims and Objectives

- To select a task for your non-fiction piece of coursework

Choosing a Non-Fiction Task

Creative non-fiction encompasses many of the genres that we studied as part of the Voices in Speech and Writing anthology.

For your coursework, you will need to prepare a piece of creative non-fiction. Your piece should respond to our theme of Art, Artifice and Identity and to our non-fiction text: *Grayson Perry: Portrait of the Artist as a Young Girl.*

Suggested Tasks

Below is a list of suggested tasks that you might like to choose for your non-fiction piece:

1) A 'Career Overview' article for careers magazine Get Smaart on possible career paths in art

2) An article for the RA magazine exploring the inner imaginative life of the artist Grayson Perry

3) An article for the online blog of Seventeen magazine on fashion, identity and dressing up for parties

4) A Wikipedia-style article on Grayson Perry

5) An article for a magazine aimed at teenagers offering support and advice on exploring your sexuality

6) An article for Tate Etc. magazine on (an aspect of) the life and work of Grayson Perry

7) A review of *Grayson Perry: Portrait of the Artist as a Young Girl* for the 'Books' page of The Guardian (or another named newspaper of your choice)

8) An article for the non-fiction section of Teen Ink magazine that explores an aspect of Art, Artifice and Identity of your own choice

To help you choose a task from this list, we will look in a bit more detail at these choices below:

1) A 'Career Overview' article for careers magazine Get Smaart on possible career paths in art

The careers magazine Get Smaart (http://getsmaart.com/) is aimed at school leavers and students. It has information on careers and courses and is marketed as a useful resource for young people. It is produced as both an online magazine and a printed magazine (which you may have seen at your school or library).

For this task, you will need to look at the magazine and examine the layout of their 'career overview' features. Think about what you know from Grayson Perry's experience and undertake your own research. What career pathways are there for students who want to become artists? The tone of this magazine is realistic (e.g. mentioning that a career is competitive) but also encouraging.

2) An article for the RA magazine exploring the inner imaginative life of the artist Grayson Perry

The RA magazine is published four times a year for RA members. It is a well-respected art magazine that adopts an academic and scholarly tone. For an article on this subject, you could discuss the powerful imaginative life that Perry had as a child and consider how this may have influenced his life and art. How does Perry describe his games and fantasies as a child? How might this have affected his adult work? Do you think it is important for an artist to have a good imagination?

Another way to approach this might be to look at one of Grayson Perry's artworks, and look at how the images might have evolved, based on what you now know about his life experiences.

Getting the right tone for this type of article is essential. You need to be both interesting and quite formal and academic. There are articles from the RA Magazine on their website at: https://www.royalacademy.org.uk/articles/tag/ra-magazine. Use these articles to get a sense of the tone and voice you will need to adopt. This is quite a challenging task.

3) An article for the online blog of Seventeen magazine on fashion, identity and dressing up for parties

In Chapters 16, 17 and 18 Perry talks about how he and his art college friends often dressed in elaborate or outlandish costumes for parties. Think about how dressing up can be an expression of art, artifice or identity. Think about how different looks could express a different mood or personality. Could charity shop chic be a good look? Do teenagers today wear the same over-the-top clothes that they did in the 80s, or is fashion more homogenous? Could a teenage girl wear (New) New Romantic fashions today? Remember that this is a fashion magazine for teenage girls, so you will need to use a light, informal tone.

4) A Wikipedia-style article on Grayson Perry

This task would require you to summarise the biography in the form of a Wikipedia article. To research this idea, read over several different Wikipedia articles and make notes on what the headings are (e.g. Early Life, Career, Media, etc.). You will also need to consider the style and tone of the articles. What kind of voice do they use?

There is, of course, already a Wikipedia article on Grayson Perry and (at the time of writing) this draws quite heavily on material from *Portrait of the Artist as a Young Girl*. The object of this task is not to copy this article, but to create your own ideal version.

5) An article for teenagers giving advice/support on exploring your sexuality

For this task, you will first need to choose a suitable style of magazine to copy (you will need to specify this magazine in your commentary). Think about the magazines that you read regularly. Do any of these have features articles offering advice to readers? Do they list places where young people can get help and support for their concerns? What tone do they adopt? In your article, try to provide as much help and encouragement as possible. Think about how your audience might be feeling and what advice might be most helpful to them.

6) An article for Tate Etc. magazine on (an aspect of) the life and work of Grayson Perry

Tate Etc. is an art magazine inspired by the collections of the Tate galleries. The magazine prides itself on taking an original approach. You will gain a good insight into the style of this magazine by reading an edition of Tate Etc and an edition of the RA magazine (from Task 1) and seeing how these two publications differ.

For this task, you could also consider taking an idea from Task 1 (for example the way that Grayson has been inspired by images from his childhood) and then exploring this idea in a slightly different way.

7) A review of *Grayson Perry: Portrait of the Artist as a Young Girl* for the 'Books' page of The Guardian (or another named newspaper of your choice)

For this task, you will need to research the reviews in The Guardian or another broadsheet newspaper of your choice. What kind of tone do the authors adopt? Are they usually positive about the works they review, are they negative (even scathing) or do they try to give a balanced viewpoint? What are your own responses to this text? What do you think are its main strengths and weakness? Try to form your own view of the text and then frame this in the style of your chosen publication.

8) Write an article for the non-fiction section of Teen Ink magazine that explores an aspect of Art, Artifice and Identity of your own choice

Teen Ink (http://www.teenink.com/) is a magazine written by teenagers and for teenagers. It publishes a wide-range of non-fiction articles on a wide range of subjects.

Look at the site and read a selection of non-fiction articles. Many ask questions, and are framed as composition essays where the student forms a response to a social issue. (This style of essay writing is more popular in the American education system than it is in the UK, so you may not have encountered it before.)

Choose a theme for your article. It should focus on art, artifice and identity and be inspired by our non-fiction text. For example, you could write about one of the issues that Grayson Perry experienced in his childhood, such as divorce or domestic violence. How do these issues affect young people? Another possible issue to write about would be finding your own identity and gaining the courage to follow your own path.

Think about your own response to the text and the issues that you found most interesting and important during your reading. Choosing the issue that seems most important to you will be a good basis for approaching your article.

Choosing a Task

Hopefully, you will find that one of these tasks appeals to you.

If you have another task of your own that you would like to complete, please contact your tutor to discuss this.

Starting your Coursework, Researching and Making Notes

The aim of this coursework is to develop your skills as an effective writer. You will learn how to do this through writing your own non-fiction text.

Think about the genre and what you know from studying the anthology. This time you will be crafting your own piece instead of analysing a text, but many of the skills are the same. What will be the audience for your piece and how will you select your language to appeal to that audience? What is your purpose and how will you convey it effectively? Thinking about these questions and making notes on your answers will help to guide your writing (and provide material for you commentary).

Try to follow the format of your chosen genre as closely as possible. You will need to research the publication and then try to imitate its style. For example, does it use headings and sub-headings? Try to be as realistic as you can.

As you work on your piece, keep thinking about how effective your writing is. Are you expressing your ideas clearly? Is the language you are using appropriate for your audience? Keep evaluating your own work and try to write as well as you can and use the style that will most appeal to your audience.

Word Count

The word count for this part of your coursework is 1500-2000 words. This is a total word count for both pieces of creative work (one non-fiction and one fiction). Therefore you will want to think about how you intend to split the word count between these two pieces. For example, if you write an article of 1000 words for your non-fiction piece, you will have 1000 words for your creative piece.

On the other hand, if you write a review of 600 words, then you will have 1400 words for your creative piece.

For this reason, you may like to think about a few ideas now and then choose your activity for our fiction text, *The Importance of Being Earnest*. This will help you to think about how many words you will need for your second piece.

For example, if you think that you will want to write a short story for your second piece, then you will probably need more than 1000 words to do this. You should therefore choose a shorter task for your non-fiction piece.

Getting Started

If you feel inspired by one of the tasks above and you are ready to get started, then you should begin work straight away. It is a good idea to get your ideas down quickly, while you have plenty of energy and enthusiasm.

Alternatively, if you are unsure on which task you would like to choose, you may like to give it some more thought. You can complete the next section on *The Importance of Being Earnest*, and then return to your ideas for your non-fiction task. You may develop your thoughts on this theme after you have read both texts.

Remember that your coursework is your own project, and so you are free to approach it in the way that suits you best.

Have fun with your coursework and try to enjoy this opportunity to develop your style as a writer.

In the next topic, we will start looking at our fiction text: *The Importance of Being Earnest*.

Topic 5 – The Importance of Being Earnest

Introduction

In this topic we will learn a little about *The Importance of Being Earnest* and the life of Oscar Wilde.

Aims and Objectives

- To learn a little about the background of *The Importance of Being Earnest* as preparation for reading the play.

The Importance of Being Earnest

The Importance of Being Earnest premiered at the St. James Theatre, London, on Valentine's Day 1895. It received many positive reviews and played to packed houses.

Part of the play's attraction was that it was quite different to anything else that was then on the stage. Although it combines elements of Melodrama and Comedy of Manners, it is also a Farce: a kind of comedy intended solely for entertainment. Early critics found it difficult to analyse precisely because, unlike many plays shown in the West End at the time, it did not make a serious or moral point.

Indeed, *The Importance of Being Earnest* is not a realist play. The dialogue and characterisation are not realistic. It is not required to be 'truthful' but only to be artistic. Through *The Importance of Being Earnest* we are invited to believe, as Gwendolyn does, that 'style, not sincerity, is the vital thing'.

The play is subtitled 'A Trivial Comedy for Serious People' and this subtitle encapsulates Wilde's intention. Thus, although the play references serious issues of the day, such as gender relations, identity and 'double lives', it does so in a way that subverts or makes fun of the form. We can think about the issues within the play or we can enjoy it merely as art, and recognise that literature can be enjoyed purely aesthetically. It is up to us, the audience, to decide how we wish to view it.

The play is still regularly performed and enjoyed today.

Aesthetic Movement – the Aesthetic Movement was anti-realist and opposed to the didacticism and moralism of much Victorian art. The aesthetic movement instead focussed on art in its own right and on the subjective impressions received from it. The highest ideal of the aesthete was to live artistically and in the moment.

The Life of Oscar Wilde

Oscar Wilde was born into a wealthy and cultured family in Dublin, Ireland. He was an exemplary classical scholar and studied at Trinity College, Dublin and Oxford University, where he achieved a double first. In his third year, he also won the Newdigate Prize for his poem *Ravenna*.

After graduation, he made his way to London, where he wrote poetry and worked as a journalist. He also completed a lecture tour of America where he talked on the Aesthetic Movement as part of the advertising for a Gilbert and Sullivan opera. He became known for his wit and his eccentric dress and was a well-known figure in society. He was, at least to some extent, an early celebrity, famous only for being famous.

Wilde married Constance Lloyd in 1884 and they had two sons, Cyril and Vyvyan. The marriage was a love-match and the couple were, initially at least, very happy.

Wilde's family commitments encouraged him to pursue his writing more seriously. He wrote prolifically from the 1888 onwards, completing many stories, essays and children's works. His novel *The Picture of Dorian Gray* was published in 1891 but received mixed reviews, with many contemporary critics finding the subject matter distasteful.

Wilde is best-known as a playwright however and he wrote four plays: *Lady Windermere's Fan, A Woman of No Importance, An Ideal Husband* and *The Importance of Being Earnest*. Although all these plays are society comedies, *Lady Windermere's Fan, A Woman of No Importance* and *An Ideal Husband* all have serious themes and morals, as well as witty lines. Only *The Importance of Being Earnest* was intended to be a light work. Arguably it is also Wilde's best play. It was first performed in 1895.

Despite Wilde's success however, he was unhappy in his private life. He began having homosexual affairs from around 1886 and was, in many ways, leading a 'double life'. Homosexual relationships were particularly dangerous in this period as in 1885 The Criminal Law Amendment Act had criminalised all same-sex sexual activity between men. A series of events revolving around his relationship with Lord Alfred Douglas led to his being tried and convicted under this Act.

In 1895 Oscar Wilde was imprisoned for Gross Indecency. He suffered cruel and terrible treatment at the hands of the Victorian penal system, and by the time he left prison, after serving the full two years of his sentence, his health was wrecked and his sprit broken. Exiled in Paris, he died in poverty only two years later. He was only forty-six.

Oscar Wilde and Homosexuality

From the intensely homophobic 1890s onwards, the association between Wilde and 'scandal' has greatly affected the reception of his plays. Wilde's play *An Ideal Husband* was closed the day after his arrest and it is proof of the popularity of *The Importance of Being Earnest* that it continued to be performed with Oscar Wilde's name removed from the advertisements. Indeed, it was not until as late as the 1970s that Wilde's reputation as a writer fully recovered from his 'disgrace'.

However, an emphasis on Wilde's life as a gay man has altered contemporary interpretations. Indeed, an over-emphasis on Wilde's homosexual identity has lead to some ludicrous and baseless interpretations of *The Importance of Being Earnest*, such as the idea that the title is a play on the word Uraniste (questionably a Victorian slang term for a homosexual) or that Bunburying was a known term for gay sex (which it was not).

Wilde may have used autobiographical elements in the play in his reference to the cigarette cases (he himself gave cigarette cases as gifts to his same-sex partners) and even potentially in reference to the tension in Wilde's own life caused by hiding his homosexual affairs both from his wife and children and from the intensely homophobic society of the 1890s. However, *The Importance of Being Earnest* is obviously not an autobiography and these aspects of the play are often exaggerated by critics.

Be aware that these types of interpretations are themselves homophobic in that they suggest that Wilde, as a gay man, was somehow incapable of writing about anything else. He was, remember, also a married man in society, who knew quite as much about upper-class courtship rituals as anyone else of the time. *The Importance of Being Earnest* remains a play essentially about heterosexual marriage. Be very cautious of any literary criticism that you may read which suggests otherwise.

Modern Queer Theory focuses on the definition and breaking down of categories, particularly sexuality and its relationship to gender. Therefore it is possible to analyse the reaction of modern audiences to *The Importance of Being Earnest* as a play written by Oscar Wilde as a gay man. It is unacceptable, however, to consider *The Importance of Being Earnest* as a play with homosexual subtext. This view is both old-fashioned and offensive.

Therefore, when considering homosexuality and the play, remember to consider the context of reception and not the context of production.

Task

In the Voices Anthology, we read an extract from De Profundis. It may be interesting for you to re-read this text now. Wilde's attitude to art and artifice changed considerably during his time in prison.

Topic 6 – Act I (First Part)

Introduction

In this topic, we will read the first part of Act I of *The Importance of Being Earnest*. We will explore some of the sources of comedy in the play, including the dialogue, the social relationships, setting and stage business.

Aims and Objectives

- To read the first part of Act I of *The Importance of Being Earnest*
- To begin thinking about the sources of comedy in the play

Task

Read Act I of *The Importance of Being Earnest* up to the entrance of Gwendolyn and Lady Bracknell.

The First Part of Act I

The opening of the play rather brilliantly and succinctly conveys many of the play's themes.

The play begins in Algy's London flat where he is awaiting his aunt Lady Bracknell who is expected for tea. The curtain goes up on Algy playing the piano (offstage) while his servant Lane is getting the tea things ready. These opening exchanges between Algy and Lane neatly convey the tone of the play.

The first thing to note is that the dialogue is not realistic. Instead, it is comprised of **repartee**. This style of light-hearted banter is used throughout the play and Wilde's clever witticisms are one of the main sources of comedy. For example, Lane says he doesn't think it 'polite' to listen to Algy's bad piano playing while Algy insists that 'anyone can play accurately' meaning that anyone, except him, can play accurately. There are many small jokes of this type within the opening lines and these set the tone of the play. The audience has to pay close attention to the dialogue in order to catch these jokes.

The relationship between Algy and his servant Lane is also very unrealistic. Algy is unconcerned that the servants have drunk the expensive champagne and the incident merely forms the basis for a discussion on marriage. Victorian servants would have been expected to be deferential to their masters but here, although Lane is outwardly subordinate, the two speak almost as equals. The relationship between master and servant also indicates a critique of convention that will form much of the substance of the play. Algy's further comment (in his **direct address**) that the lower orders should inspire the upper classes in matters of morality is a direct contradiction of traditional Victorian thinking.

In this way, the light-hearted tone and social contexts of the play are immediately introduced to the audience.

Repartee – a style of dialogue characterised by quick-witted retorts.

Direct Address – is where an actor addresses the audience directly.

Stage Business – actions performed by an actor for dramatic or comic effect.

Setting and Staging

It is also important, when reading drama, to read the stage directions that are given by the author.

The first direction given is the description of Algy's morning room, which is 'luxuriously and artistically furnished'. Although at first sight a sparse piece of description, this stage direction actually says quite a lot.

A morning room was a daytime sitting room where a Victorian wife would go to write letters and deal with the household budget and there is therefore some potential significance to this location. The description of the luxury of the room signifies Algy's idle bachelor character while the reference to it being 'artistically furnished' can also be read as a joke in the context of Algy's bad piano playing.

It was also sometimes a feature of the British Well-Made Play that realistic domestic settings, such as parlours and drawing rooms, were the main location for the action. In these 'realistic' fictions a domestic setting was used to convey the scene's authenticity. Here, however, Wilde is clearly subverting the form. There is nothing remotely realistic about the situations or dialogue in *The Importance of Being Earnest* and the domestic morning room setting is a further play on this.

Indeed, a lot of information can be shown to the audience without the use of any dialogue at all. When staging the play, a designer might design this set, for example, in a hugely exaggerated way. They might use lots of rich fabrics, vast potted plants and excessive numbers of object d'art. The audience would then get a pretty good idea of Algy's character before he had even uttered a word.

Costume can also be used to convey character and you may like to think about the type of clothes that you imagine Algy might wear. For example, he might wear something very fashionable, stylish and over-the-top. Perhaps some striped trousers (in the style of Lupin Pooter from *Diary of a Nobody*) would be appropriate.

In this way, the words of a dramatic text are only part of the play. Actors also add to the characters through their gestures and expressions. This is known as Stage Business.

Task

With reference to the staging of the play, consider the comic effects of:

The Cucumber Sandwiches; and

The Cigarette Case.

Commentary

The Cucumber Sandwiches

The cucumber sandwiches provide an ongoing point of comedy throughout the scene. Algy insists that they are for his aunt Lady Bracknell, yet he continues eating them himself until they are all gone. Indeed, Algy's voracious appetite is a consistent source of comedy in the play. Algy also prevents Jack from eating the sandwiches and gives him bread and butter instead.

The actors and direction may further emphasise this comedic effect. For example, the director may instruct Algy to continue eating the sandwiches throughout the dialogue, perhaps even talking with his mouth full. When the stage direction reads that Algy prevents Jack from taking a sandwich, it is also possible for the actors to use physical or slapstick comedy. Algy might, for example, slap Jack's hand away and Jack might act-up the hurt caused by this.

This is therefore an additional source of comedy that can be exaggerated through the staging of the play.

The Cigarette Case

The cigarette case allows for further repartee over the matter of the reward and word play as regards the dentist's 'false impressions'. It also introduces one of the main themes of the play; the confusion over names and identities.

There is also a further comic effect in the chase scene where Jack tries to retrieve the cigarette case from Algy, which can be used to symbolise how Algy has the physical as well as the verbal 'upper hand'. The director may get the actors to physically chase each other around the room, perhaps even climbing or standing on furniture. In this way, the scene can have elements of physical comedy and even farce.

In both these examples, therefore, the comedic effect can enhanced through **Stage Business**. It is important to consider how a play will be staged when reading the text.

Topic 7 – Act I: Characterisation

Introduction

In this topic, we will begin looking at the characters in *The Importance of Being Earnest*. We will also consider how some of the social relationships and social conventions are used to comic effect.

Aims and Objective

- To read to the end of Act I.
- To consider the subversion of social conventions to comic effect.
- To begin looking at the characters of Algy, Jack, Gwendolyn and Lady Bracknell.

Act I (Second Part)

The second part of Act I, when Gwendolyn and Lady Bracknell arrive for tea uses social relationships and social conventions to comic effect.

Task

Read Act I from the entrance of Gwendolyn and Lady Bracknell through to the end of the Act.

Character and the Inversion of Social Convention as Comedy

In the latter part of Act I, a lot of the comedy comes from both character and social convention.

For example, Jack's proposal to Gwendolyn is hopelessly ineffectual. He struggles through what he is trying to say, repeating himself, until Gwendolyn takes charge of the situation. This is a reversal of the traditional gender dynamics of marriage where women were expected to take a passive role.

Lady Bracknell is a further example of this reversal of gender roles. Indeed, she is a strong and formidable woman. Her frequent and absurd statements go completely unchallenged simply because she delivers them with such absolute conviction. An example of this is her heartless attitude to Bunbury and to Jack's 'lost' parents. As well as demonstrating a very 'unfeminine' lack of compassion, it is also an example of her nature as a forceful character who no-one will argue with. We get the impression that she is also very much in charge of her own husband who, for example, is accustomed to having to 'dine upstairs' in order to suit his wife's table arrangements.

Lady Bracknell is also similarly pragmatic when it comes to the usual social and gender conventions. Victorian masculinity demanded that men be active, holding responsible jobs and taking a keen interest in matters of politics, as well as showing a strong sense of duty and moral virtue. Lady Bracknell, however, cares very little that Jack is idle and takes no interest in politics, but is scandalised by his lack of family connections. This indicates Lady Bracknell's emphasis on the importance of superficial social relations, rather than on character and ability.

Indeed, Gwendolyn further exemplifies this attitude. She is especially keen that Jack should look at her lovingly 'especially when there are other people present'. She is obsessed with a man who is called Ernest rather than a man who is earnest.

This confusion of names, identities and characteristics is used to satirise the trivialities of upper-class society.

Task

Prepare spider diagrams illustrating five characteristics each for Jack, Algy, Gwendolyn and Lady Bracknell.

Commentary

Inarticulate – Jack lacks the verbal skills to win arguments with anyone else in the play. He is particularly inarticulate as he repeats himself during his proposal to Gwendolyn. He says 'ever since I met you I have admired you more than any girl... I have ever met since... I met you'. Jack's clumsy use of words suggests his lack of social power.

Obedient – Jack, unlike Algy, usually does as he's told. For example, He eats the bread and butter when asked to by Algy. He is easily controlled by both Gwendolyn and Lady Bracknell.

Double identity / hypocrisy – Jack pretends to be Ernest in town and Jack in the country in order to conceal his bad behaviour behind another identity. He even tries to deceive Jack, his best friend. Arguably, this is more serious form of deceit than Algy's rather innocent 'Bunburying'.

Jack

Critical - He is critical of Algy's lack of seriousness, but seeming ignorant of his own.

Idle – Jack also doesn't work or have any other occupation. Yet, he does have the means to support his lifestyle. He seems to have no real interest in moral duty or politics, describing himself as a 'liberal unionist' although he is also a Justice of the Peace.

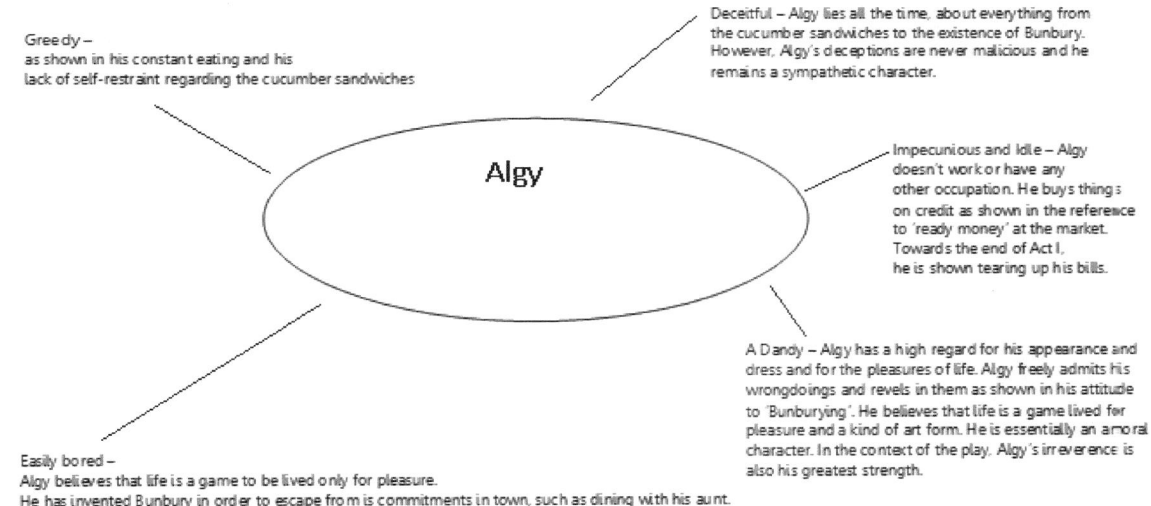

Greedy – as shown in his constant eating and his lack of self-restraint regarding the cucumber sandwiches

Deceitful – Algy lies all the time, about everything from the cucumber sandwiches to the existence of Bunbury. However, Algy's deceptions are never malicious and he remains a sympathetic character.

Impecunious and Idle – Algy doesn't work or have any other occupation. He buys things on credit as shown in the reference to 'ready money' at the market. Towards the end of Act I, he is shown tearing up his bills.

Algy

A Dandy – Algy has a high regard for his appearance and dress and for the pleasures of life. Algy freely admits his wrongdoings and revels in them as shown in his attitude to 'Bunburying'. He believes that life is a game lived for pleasure and a kind of art form. He is essentially an amoral character. In the context of the play, Algy's irreverence is also his greatest strength.

Easily bored – Algy believes that life is a game to be lived only for pleasure. He has invented Bunbury in order to escape from is commitments in town, such as dining with his aunt.

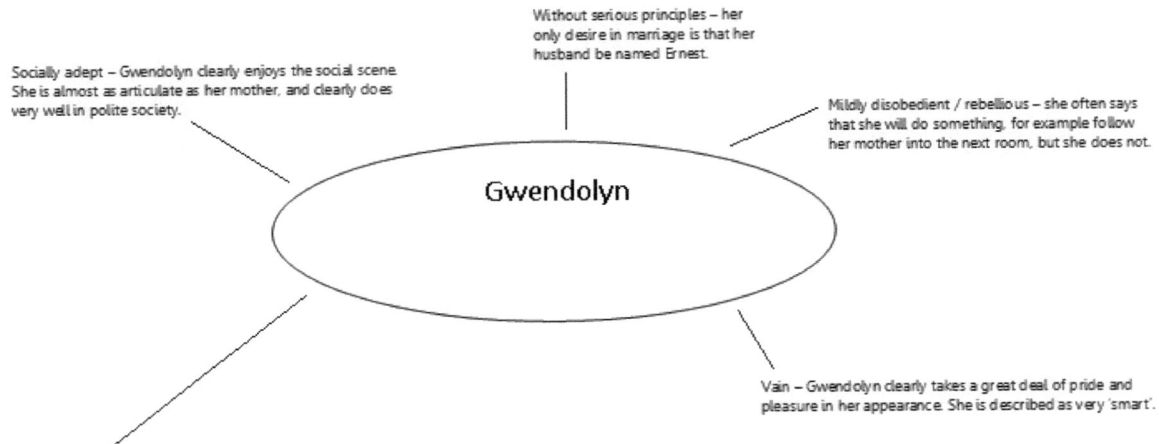

Socially adept – Gwendolyn clearly enjoys the social scene. She is almost as articulate as her mother, and clearly does very well in polite society.

Without serious principles – her only desire in marriage is that her husband be named Ernest.

Mildly disobedient / rebellious – she often says that she will do something, for example follow her mother into the next room, but she does not.

Gwendolyn

Vain – Gwendolyn clearly takes a great deal of pride and pleasure in her appearance. She is described as very 'smart'.

Potentially domineering / Likely to end up like her mother – In the way that Gwendolyn takes charge of Jack's proposal, it seems likely that she will end up controlling him just as Lady Bracknell dominates Lord Bracknell. Algy also realises this and warns Jack of it.

Articulate – Lady Bracknell's speeches are vastly longer than anyone else's. She never fails to express herself and she uses her wit to railroad her opponents into submission. This is all the more noticeable when so many of her opinions are patently absurd. One example of this is her statement that to be bred in a hand-bag "seems to me to display a contempt for the ordinary decencies of family life that reminds one of the worst excesses of the French Revolution."

Uncompassionate / Uncharitable – this can be seen in her attitude to Bunbury and in her statement that she does not 'approve of the modern sympathy with invalids'. She regards a pun as a suitable reaction to Jack relation that he has 'lost' both his parents.

Lady Bracknell

Domineering - exercises a tight control on her daughter and her husband. For example, she says 'an engagement should come on a young girl as a surprise'. She also often encourages her husband to eat upstairs to suit her table arrangements.

Powerful – Lady Bracknell is a formidable and terrible figure. Jack, her husband and even to some extent Algy and Gwendolyn seem to bow their will to hers. Jack describes her as 'a perfectly unbearable' and as a 'Gorgon.'

Snobbish - social connection is extremely important to Lady Bracknell. Although Jack's income and 'character' are quite acceptable to her, she cannot consider him marriageable because of his lack of family relations. She unkindly mocks him as being related to a parcel.

Character Summary

Overall, however, it is also important to notice that there are many overlapping characteristics between the characters in *The Importance of Being Earnest*. The word 'character' had itself a particular resonance in the Victorian period, where 'character' meant one's moral standing and was an important part of a masculine identity (as well as being a word meaning 'resume' for a servant).

In short, none of the characters in *The Importance of Being Earnest* can be said to have psychological depth. None are realistic.

Wilde himself did not use the term characters and preferred to use the term 'personalities'. Arguably, their very lack of solid character traits is one of the key features of the figures in *The Importance of Being Earnest*.

Topic 8 – Act II (First Part)

Introduction

In this topic, we will read through the first part of Act II. We will explore some of the comic themes within the first part of Act II. We will then consider the character of Cecily.

Aims and Objectives

- To read through the first part of Act II
- To explore the comic themes of the first part of Act II
- To consider the character of Cecily

Task
Read through Act II up to the point where Cecily and Algy go into the house and Miss Prism and Dr. Chasuble return.

Act II – The Garden Scene

One of the themes of the play is the difference between town and country. Traditionally in literature, the country is seen as representing rustic innocence while the town represents sophistication. Here, however, Wilde plays with this idea in keeping with the theme of lack of seriousness in the play. In Cecily's garden, the roses are every bit as artificial and cultivated as any in the town and this gives further dramatic irony to Algy's statement that Cecily is 'like a pink rose'. This emphasises the play's theme of the interaction between realism and artifice, fiction and reality and of life itself as a work of art.

Fiction and reality are contrasted throughout the play, and this theme is also brought out through Cecily and Miss Prism's discussion of fiction. Miss Prism's definition of fiction is that it should be both moralistic and tedious. She champions the three-volume novel, admitting that she herself wrote one in former times (although it was never published). Mudie was a home lending library that lent books considered suitable for women, and it seems that Miss Prism's prudish nature means that she thinks only this type of book should be read by Cecily. Indeed, the chapter of political history on 'The Fall of the Rupee' is considered by Miss Prism as too sensational for a young woman to read.

Cecily, on the other hand, craves excitement and life. She hates to study but she likes to write in her diary. The diary is made up of completely fictional events and 'usually chronicles the things that have never happened, and couldn't possibly have happened'. We may surmise that this diary is every bit as sensational as Gwendolyn's.

She seems to dislike the cause-and-effect morality of the three-volume novel when she says that she does not like happy endings and that she thinks the bad endings for a villain are 'unfair'. When she says that she considers three-volume novels to be the work of memory, she may mean either that they are selective remembrances or that they are works of memory, rather than imagination.

The realism of the three-volume novel contrasts with the artifice of Oscar Wilde's play. When Miss Prism says of her novel that 'The good ended happily, and the bad unhappily. That is what Fiction means', Wilde is inviting us to think about this statement. Even at this stage of the play, we already know that *The Importance Of Being Earnest* is unlikely to end this way.

Task

'Little Cecily' is described by Jack as 'not some silly romantic girl'. Complete a spider diagram for Cecily's character. Is she as innocent / unromantic as Jack thinks?

Commentary

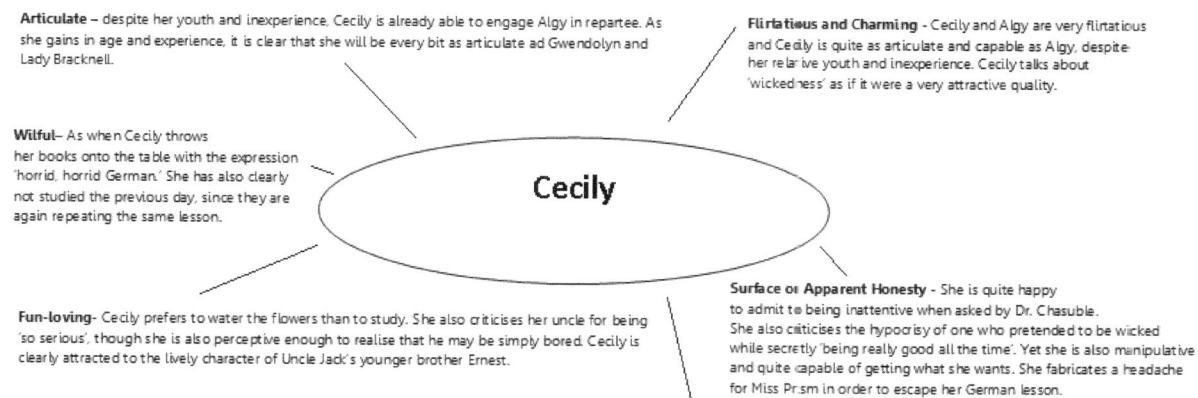

Articulate – despite her youth and inexperience, Cecily is already able to engage Algy in repartee. As she gains in age and experience, it is clear that she will be every bit as articulate ad Gwendolyn and Lady Bracknell.

Flirtatious and Charming - Cecily and Algy are very flirtatious and Cecily is quite as articulate and capable as Algy, despite her relative youth and inexperience. Cecily talks about 'wickedness' as if it were a very attractive quality.

Wilful – As when Cecily throws her books onto the table with the expression 'horrid, horrid German.' She has also clearly not studied the previous day, since they are again repeating the same lesson.

Cecily

Fun-loving - Cecily prefers to water the flowers than to study. She also criticises her uncle for being 'so serious', though she is also perceptive enough to realise that he may be simply bored. Cecily is clearly attracted to the lively character of Uncle Jack's younger brother Ernest.

Surface or Apparent Honesty - She is quite happy to admit to being inattentive when asked by Dr. Chasuble. She also criticises the hypocrisy of one who pretended to be wicked while secretly 'being really good all the time'. Yet she is also manipulative and quite capable of getting what she wants. She fabricates a headache for Miss Prism in order to escape her German lesson.

Young, Pretty and Rich – Cecily is described by Algy as a 'pink rose' and as 'the prettiest girl' he ever saw. It is her attractiveness that makes Jack unwilling to let Algy meet her in Act I. Cecily also complains that her German lesson make her plain.

Cecily

Despite Little Cecily's country location, she is clearly no country-bumpkin. She is clearly very interested in 'Ernest' despite or even because of his wickedness. Although outwardly proper, if flirtatious, she is keen to hear about his escapades as is shown in how she is 'glad to hear' of his fecklessness. She also may not even want him to change and says she has no time to reform him that afternoon, though she thinks he should try.

As we learn in the next part of Act II, Cecily is, in fact, both romantic and extremely silly. Like Gwendolyn, she has completely fallen in love with the name of Ernest. She believes she is destined to fall in love with a man she has never met and has created a completely fictitious fantasy life to this effect.

Jack is wrong.

Topic 9 – Types of Comedy in Act II

Introduction

In this topic, we will read through to the end of Act II and begin looking at some of the types of comedy which are used in this act.

Aims and Objectives

- To read Act II
- To look at examples of the different types of comedy used in this Act

---

Task

Read through to the end of Act II.

Types of Comedy in Act II

There are many different types of comedy used in Act II. We will examine some of these types of comedy below, although this is by no means an exhaustive list.

Verbal Comedy and Repartee

Wilde is known for his clever verbal comedy and sharp wit. A good example of this in Act II is the forced, polite argument between Gwendolyn and Cecily. When Gwendolyn says, for example that she doesn't like crowds, Cecily is quick to say that this must be why she lives in town.

It is important to note that the audience would need to concentrate quite hard to follow the back and forth dialogue. The audience, therefore, would need to be educated and attentive. This is a different type of audience to other popular Victorian theatrical entertainments, such as melodrama and music hall.

Comic Characters and Comic Names

Miss Prism and Dr. Chasuble are both comic characters. Our first indication of this is in their names. A chasuble is part of a priest's dress used for serious Christian rites while Miss Prism may be a pun on the word misprision, which can mean a mistake or misunderstanding, or the neglect of an official duty.

However, as with much of *The Importance of Being Earnest*, although these characters are funny, they are also used to make serious points.

In some respects, these characters can be seen to represent the twin authorities of Education and the Church, both of which are mocked through these humorous personifications. Miss Prism's teaching is unspeakably dull and her interest in the three-volume novel is conservative and old-fashioned. She is also ignorant of the classical reference to Egeria, a figure representing female wisdom and a reference which, as a Victorian governess, she should be expected to know. She also makes several other mistakes and coins a neologism 'womanthrope' for the more usual word 'misogynist'. Furthermore, she is moralistic and unsympathetic, which is shown in her repetitions of the phrase 'as a man sows so let him reap'. She is extremely callous in regard of Jack's brother's death.

The Church is also mocked through the figure of Dr. Chasuble. Chasuble uses the same sermon for every occasion, which implies that it cannot be either very interesting or very useful. He also offers unhelpful platitudes saying that Jack's brother's death may be an example of 'blessings in disguise'. Baptism, an important Christian rite, is also treated extremely lightly by both Jack and Algy. Jack asks for his Baptism to be performed 'if you have nothing better to do' and says that he will 'trot round about five'. This is a very lax arrangement for a serious Christian practice.

Stock Characters

Act II also plays with the comedic device of Stock Characters. The Stock Character called the ingénue is a young woman from the countryside who is innocent and naive. Here Wilde plays with the idea of this in the character of Cecily who, although young, is every bit as sharp witted as the more sophisticated Gwendolyn.

Farce

Farce is a comic genre characterised by stereotypical characters, physical comedy (slapstick), sexual innuendo, lots of entrances and exits, and by complex, fast-moving plotlines. Part of the definition of Farce is that it is devised solely in order to entertain and should have no 'serious' intent.

Another feature of Farce is the near-miss meetings of persons and couples who should not meet. There is an element of this in Jack's arrival, dressed in mourning, just as his 'brother' Ernest has entered the house.

There are many aspects of Farce used in *The Importance of Being Earnest.*

Misunderstanding

The main instance of comic misunderstanding in Act II comes from the impersonation of Ernest by both men in different contexts, leading to Cecily's and Gwendolyn's mistaken belief that they are both engaged to the same man.

Comedy of Manners

Comedy of Manners was a style of comedy developed by Restoration dramatists such as Wycherley and Vanbrugh. It is characterised by fast-moving verbal exchanges. Indeed, the events in a comedy of Manners take place behind what Cecily describes in Act II as 'the shallow mask of manners' and Gwendolyn and Cecily's exchange over the tea table is a direct reference to this form of drama.

In a Comedy of Manners villainous characters would often get their way through their intellect and skill at word-play. In *The Importance of Being Earnest* however, no-one is really good or bad. Neither Cecily not Gwendolyn intends or suffers any real harm from their polite animosity and they quickly become 'sisters' again as soon as the misunderstanding is resolved.

Social Satire

A Social Satire is a type of literature that is critical of society and social norms and that is written is a sarcastic or humorous tone. An example of social satire in *The Importance of Being Earnest* is Gwendolyn's comment that 'The home seems to me to be the proper sphere for the man. And certainly once a man begins to neglect his domestic duties he becomes painfully effeminate, does he not?' This is a satire on the idea of the domestic sphere as being appropriate for women. It also satirises the anxiety of conservative Victorians that masculine and feminine identities would be altered if activities (such as professional work) were undertaken by women outside of the home.

Dramatic Irony

Dramatic Irony occurs where the audience knows something that is unknown to one or more characters. An example of this occurs in Act II where the audience know that Jack's 'brother' Ernest is really Jack himself, a fact unknown to Cecily and Miss Prism.

Melodrama

There are also instances of melodrama in Act II, chiefly in the arrival of Jack dressed in full mourning regalia and lamenting the death of his brother. We will examine Melodrama further in the next topic.

Task

You may already be thinking of ideas for your creative piece of coursework. If so, make a note of any ideas as they occur to you.

Topic 10 – Act III

Introduction

In this topic, we will read the third and final act of the play. We will think about some of the types of comedy referenced in Act III.

Aims and Objectives

- To read the third and final act of *The Importance of Being Earnest*.
- To think about the types of comedy used in Act III.

Task

Read through Act III, to the end of the play.

Act III

Act III opens with the women retaining a 'dignified silence' in the house and the men eating muffins in the garden. The silence does not last long however, and when the men return to the house, sheepishly whistling, they are quickly forgiven for their transgressions. Algy honestly explains that he merely pretended to be Ernest in order to meet Cecily. Gwendolyn then asks Jack whether he invented the identity of Ernest in order to visit her and Jack allows her to believe that this is true, although she knows that this is not really the case. She is prepared to accept his untruthfulness in keeping with her attitude that style is more important than sincerity. When the men explain that they have both arranged to be Christened Ernest that afternoon, the ladies' final objection to their proposals seems resolved.

The couples' happiness is ended, however, by the arrival of Lady Bracknell. Lady Bracknell removes her objection to Algy and Cecily's union after Jack, in a comically drawn out interrogation, tells her that Cecily is worth a great deal of money. Lady Bracknell however, will still not allow her daughter to marry anyone with Jack's lack of family connections. Jack therefore withholds his permission for Cecily to get married until Lady Bracknell will consent to his marriage to Gwendolyn.

The resolution comes from the accidental reunion of Lady Bracknell and Miss Prism and the resolution of the mystery of Jack's true identity. It transpires that the hand-bag was left at Victoria Railway Station after Miss Prism confused the baby with the manuscript of a three-volume novel 'of more than usually revolting sentimentality' that she had been writing. Jack is, in fact, the son of Lady Bracknell's sister and is Algy's older brother. Miss Prism is delighted to be reunited with the hand-bag while Jack discovers that his name has really been Ernest all the time.

The play ends in a tableau where Gwendolyn and Jack, Algy and Cecily and, more surprisingly, even Miss Prism and Dr. Chasuble are all engaged to be married.

In this final act, therefore, Wilde uses several further forms of comedy to great effect.

Types of Comedy in Act III

Movement and Stage Business

The actors may be able to use aspects of movement and stage business to heighten the comedy at several points in Act III. The men's arrival, whistling nonchalantly, may be used to comic effect. Their speech 'in unison' is also comedic and introduces an element of farce, as does the hand clasping of Algy and Jack. The couples' melodramatic reuniting embrace could also be played in a comic way, as could the fact that they are written to 'separate in alarm' at the entrance of Lady Bracknell.

Jack also gets the opportunity for several comic actions in Act III. There is considerable noise and disruption as he searches for the bag. The stage directions then say he 'rushes to bookcase and tears the books out' and this may provide the actor with further opportunity for physical comedy.

The final tableaux also may be used to comic effect. The three couples may embrace dramatically but it is tempting to see the central figure as a still disapproving Lady Bracknell dominating both the centre of the stage and the couples' future lives.

Melodrama

Melodramatic plots often relied on improbable coincidences, chance meetings and recognitions. Therefore, Jack's foundling status sets up certain expectations for a Victorian audience used to viewing melodramas. This sets up the joke in Act III where Jack, upon discovering that Miss Prism left the hand-bag at Victoria Station, believes that she is his mother.

There is an inherent absurdity in Jack's production of the hand-bag and this can be enhanced through stage business. The comedy of this scene is further heightened by Miss Prism's delight in recovering the bag itself and by Jack subsequent comment that 'more is restored to you than this hand-bag' which is to be delivered in a 'pathetic voice'.

He then launches into a sentimental and melodramatic speech where he forgives her and laments the double standard that condemns women but allows men to walk away from illegitimate births. This is a quite typical sentiment in Victorian fiction and well-worthy of Wilde's clever lampooning.

A Well-Made Comedy?

In Act III, Wilde may also be critiquing certain aspects of the Well-Made Play.

The Well-Made Play was often quite tightly and cleverly plotted with many twists and turns and, here, Wilde uses these conventions to comic effect. The plot elements of the railway station and the three-volume novel come together in the final act. Structurally, this final revelation happens quickly and just before the final curtain falls, which is also similar to the structure of the Well-Made play.

Family disclosures and secret identities were also common themes of the British Well-Made Play and Wilde uses both of these in *The Importance of Being Earnest*. Document discovery was also a frequent plot device and here Wilde plays with this idea with the confusion of the baby for the three-volume novel and the public document of the army lists, which is neither the secret or hidden document usually associated with this type of revelation.

The Well-Made Play was a conservative genre that can easily be sent-up as comedy. It is possible, therefore, that Wilde is taking elements of the Well-Made Play and twisting them to comic effect.

References to Other Plays of the Period

The literary critic Kerry Powell has identified several plays from which Wilde may have derived elements of *The Importance of Being Earnest*. In Powell's work *Oscar Wilde and the Theatre of the 1890s*, she posits that the plot may have referenced a popular play titled *The Foundling* while the elements of food and drink may have been derived from the popular 1892 farce *Charley's Aunt*.[12]

Puns as Verbal Comedy – The Title of the Play

Puns are a form of verbal comedy based on word-play. There is a clever pun in Act III where Lady Bracknell, compares his lineage to a train line.

Lady Bracknell is still scandalised by her view of Jack as the product of a 'social indiscretion' at a railway station and consequently, no longer feels the need to be particularly polite to him. She plays on the word 'connection' which can mean both a family relation and a place where different railway lines converge. She then plays on the railway words origin (for the start of the line) and terminus (for the end of the line) in her phrase 'whose origin was a terminus.' This is a rather witty response on the part of Lady Bracknell, who is usually depicted as articulate but often stupid.
This pun also introduces the pun which forms both the final line and the title of the play.

This central pun revolves around the difference between the name Ernest and the word earnest, meaning sincere or serious. Jack's discovery that he is, in reality, named Ernest removes the distinction between his real and fictional personas.

---

[12] Kerry Powell 'Oscar Wilde and the Theatre of the 1890s' cited in Ruth Robbins *The Importance of Being Earnest* (York Notes Advanced, Longman, 1999).

It also works as a pun on another level, whereby Miss Prism's confusion of her novel with the baby parallels the confusion of Jack's real and fictitious identities. This also contributes to Wilde's perennial theme of life as a work of art.

Jack, in discovering that he has been, in fact, both earnest and Ernest, then finds himself in something of a paradox. Jack, of course, is anything but earnest and, unlike the amoral Algy, is actively deceitful. Indeed, Jack is almost unaware of the depths of his own untruthfulness and lack of seriousness. Jack's discovery that he has been 'speaking nothing but the truth' therefore represents a mockery of both conventional Victorian morals and the hypocrisy of the double life.

The idea of the double life is expressed in being 'Ernest in town and Jack in the Country'. Jack will therefore have to reconcile his two personalities in his marriage to Gwendolyn. That is the importance of being Ernest/Earnest.

However, it remains for the audience to decide whether the revelation of Jack's accidental truthfulness represents the first step towards the resolution of Jack's double life, or as Gwendolyn predicts, whether he is 'sure to change'.

Task

You may like to view a production of *The Importance of Being Earnest*. The play is frequently performed and you may be able to find a production in your local area.

If you cannot find any, look for film versions of the play that you can buy or rent. The 1952 version starring Dame Edith Evans is particularly well-regarded.

Try to view a production, if at all possible.

When watching the production, pay special attention to the way that Stage Business is used to enhance the comedy of the text.

There is no commentary on this task.

Topic 11 – Critical Approaches, Themes and Interpretations

Introduction

In this topic we will look at how the *The Importance of Being Earnest* was approached by contemporary critics. We will then move on to looking at the themes and interpretations of the play.

Aims and Objectives

- To gain a critical overview of the play and its themes.

Critical Approaches

The critic William Archer, in his review in *World* on the 20th February 1895, wrote of *The Importance of Being Earnest* that 'as a text for criticism, it is barren and elusive'. He added:

> What can a poor critic do with a play that raises no principle, whether of art or morals, creates its own canons and conventions, and is nothing but an absolutely wilful expression of an irrepressibly witty personality?[13]

Indeed, Wilde himself described *The Importance of Being Earnest* as 'written by a butterfly for butterflies'. Yet today's critics do not see Wilde's play as a merely frivolous piece of comedy. Indeed, the subtitle of the play is 'a trivial comedy for serious people' and there are a number of instances in which Wilde uses comedy to make serious points. An example of this is Lady Bracknell's attitude to (the fictional) Bunbury. Her conflation of illness with moral weakness is merely an exaggeration of some of the more conservative attitudes of the time and Wilde is critiquing this attitude by taking it to an absurd conclusion.

Therefore, although the play has a light and frivolous tone, that is not to say that it does not have serious themes too. Indeed, if we choose to, we can find a number of serious themes within *The Importance of Being Earnest*. We can also analyse what the characters and the play have to say about these themes.

There is a brief discussion of some of these themes and interpretations below.

---

[13] William Archer in *World* magazine, cited in Ruth Robbins, *The Importance of Being Earnest* (York Notes Advnaced, Longman, 1999).

Themes and Interpretations

Marriage

The Importance of Being Earnest includes an ongoing critique of marriage. The play begins with a discussion of marriage where, in Act I, Lane says that he has 'only been married once', and that as a 'consequence of a misunderstanding between myself and a young person'. This theme is continued in the discussion on marriage between Jack and Algy. Indeed, Algy's statement that married men who do not know Bunbury have 'a very tedious time of it' is highly critical of married life and his further idea that 'in married life three is company and two is none' seems to be a reference to the perceived benefits of infidelity.

It also seems that marriage is considered no more preferable for women than for men. This is shown in Lady Bracknell's discussion of her friend the widow Lady Harbury who is much happier now that her husband has died and now looks 'twenty years younger' and is 'living entirely for pleasure now'. Lady Bracknell's dominance over her husband is another criticism of marriage and its implicit gender and power relations.

Marriage was a hugely important social institution in Victorian Britain and these views can be seen as an express social criticism. There are many further examples of unusual attitudes to marriage throughout the play.

Gender Relations, Role Reversals and Social Inversions

The relations between men and women were of great importance during the 1890s. The situation for women was slowly changing as they were increasingly able to access higher education and were agitating for access to the professions.

There were therefore many anxieties over the place of women in society and many more conservative people had an interest in the maintenance of gender roles. *The Importance of Being Earnest* plays with these ideas in several ways. The idea of proper (and separate) spheres for men and women is referenced by Gwendolyn when she says:

> Outside the family circle, papa, I am glad to say, is entirely unknown. I think that is quite as it should be. The home seems to me to be the proper sphere for the man. And certainly once a man begins to neglect his domestic duties he becomes painfully effeminate, does he not?

Gender stereotypes of the period also required men to be active and to have a strong sense of moral and political duty. Women, by contrast, were supposed to be passive and to confine their activities to the domestic realm.

In this play, however, the men are lazy and effete, while the women, by contrast, are active. Gwendolyn is especially representative of the type of 'new woman' who would attend lectures and political meetings. She is assertive and articulate.

It is therefore significant that the female characters in the play are active and powerful while the men are almost useless. The older characters take this to its furthest conclusion with Lady Bracknell dominating the world of the characters while her husband is entirely invisible. We are lead to believe that this will also be the eventual fate of Jack and Algy. This was indeed a great fear to some in Victorian society who feared that active women would usurp the traditional role of men.

Wilde is therefore playing with these ideas of gender and role reversal within the play. Today however, we are no longer surprised by the idea of powerful women and it is not certain whether today's audiences have the same view of the comedy as those of the 1890s. This is part of the context of reception of the play.

Double Lives and Hypocrisy

The idea of the Double Life is explored through the actions of both Algy and Jack. Algy has invented a fictional friend, Bunbury, who allows him to escape from any social engagements that he does not want to attend, such as dining with his aunt.

Jack lives a double life. He is known as Jack in the country where he lives a serious and moral life taking care of his ward and being a Justice of the Peace. However, Jack also pretends to have a brother Ernest who gets into all sorts of scrapes in London, which Jack then has to bail him out of. This not only give Jack the chance to escape to the city once in a while, but he also pretends to be Ernest in London. Thus, none of his city indiscretions can possibly affect his country life and reputation.

In this way, Jack's attempt to be 'Jack in the country and Ernest in town' is much more serious that Algy's 'Bunburying'. While Algy has merely invented a friend, Jack is actually pretending to be Ernest while he is in town and uses this identity to hide his wrongdoing from those close to him. This is hypocrisy.

This core hypocrisy was a constant fear in Victorian society and double lives were seen as commonplace. Indeed, there was a great fear that many Victorian men were preoccupied with the appearance of morality rather than with the reality of living a respectable life. Indeed, the strictures of moralism may have been so severe that there was no choice but to flout the rules. Wilde plays with this idea in the characters of Jack and Algy.

Therefore, although Jack and Algy seem similar, they are crucially different in their attitude to life. Jack pretends to be moral, but sees no problem in lying to his friends and dependents. Algy, on the other hand, is amoral. Algy freely admits his wrongdoings and revels in them. He believes that life is a game lived for pleasure and a kind of art form.

Language

The play frequently explores the relationship between the words spoken and their meaning. For example, Algy states that the cucumber sandwiches are not to be eaten, before eating them all himself. He also plays with the ideas of seriousness and triviality when he says how he thinks it is 'shallow' not to take meals 'seriously'. He also mocks ideas of morality when he wants to inform Jack of the 'rules' of Bunburying. Furthermore, most of the characters lie or tell untruths and direct instructions are agreed and then ignored.

Gwendolyn in Act I, for example, says that she will follow her mother into the next room and later that she will go directly to the carriage. She does neither of these things. There is therefore a break between what is said and what is done.
Puns also illustrate some of the difficulties with language and with double meanings. Indeed, although puns are often considered a low form of wit, Wilde uses them here to great effect. The pun of the title is a good example of this.

This attitude towards and use of language illustrates the oppositions between truth and deception, reality and fiction, artifice and nature and triviality versus earnestness. It therefore both reflects and forms a key theme of the play.

Morality, Art and Life

Fiction is a recurring motif throughout *The Importance of Being Earnest* and most of the characters have a complex understanding of the relationship between fiction and reality. Indeed, this relationship between fiction and reality is given an additional dimension by the theatrical experience and by the audience's knowledge that they are watching characters being played by actors.

Within the play, Algy has created a fictitious invalid friend Bunbury, while Cecily writes entirely fictional events into her diary. Gwendolyn also writes a diary, which she describes as 'sensational', and uses it to prove that her engagement is real, as if writing something down yourself can make it true. Jack has also created a fictional persona, Ernest, who he pretends is his brother. He also uses props when he dresses in deep mourning, expressing a theatrical understanding of fiction.

Yet, whilst Algy and Cecily's deceptions are good-natured, Jack and Gwendolyn are more serious and hypocritical. Jack pretends to be moral and virtuous when he is nothing of the kind, while Gwendolyn is slightly pretentious and affected. Wilde uses these characters to represent the inherent discrepancies between fiction and real-life, honesty, respectability and morality.

Algy and Cecily, on the other hand, know that their behaviours are fictional and that their attitudes are trivial. They appreciate life as art and as fiction. They are, at least, honest about their own dishonesty. Thus, in many ways Algy, a completely amoral character, is the most moral character in the play.

Task

Think about our theme of Art, Artifice and Identity. How does Wilde express ideas relating to this theme?

Spend a short time thinking about the play and how it explores these ideas.

We will look at generating coursework tasks in the next topic.

Topic 12 – Generating Coursework Ideas for *Earnest*

Introduction

In this topic, we will consider some ideas which you may like to use for your creative coursework piece.

Aims and Objectives

- To choose your task for your creative coursework piece on *The Importance of Being Earnest*

Creative Coursework Ideas

For your piece of creative fiction, you can explore one of the genres of fictional writing. These genres include short stories, screenplays, radio drama or fictionalised diary entries.

You will also be able to explore your own ideas about Art, Artifice and Identity.

Suggested Tasks for Coursework

This is a list of some suggested tasks for your creative fiction piece:

- A short story or scene from a screenplay about a Victorian or modern man living a double life. This piece could be serious or comic.

- A fictional diary entry or an extract from a memoir by Jack, explaining how his life in the country and town differs and how he feels about these differences. To write this piece, you will need to try and capture a sense of Jack's voice.

- One or more of the letters between Cecily and Algernon (as Earnest). Remember that Cecily has written these letters herself. You will need to create a sense of her voice.

- A diary entry by Cecily, in which she describes her fictional relationship with Ernest. Again, you will need to create a sense of her voice.

- One of Gwendolyn's 'sensational' diary entries.

- An extract from Miss Prism's novel that looks at an aspect of art, artifice and identity.

- A letter from Bunbury, writing about his latest illness and asking Algy to visit him. Algy would have written this letter himself, in order to escape a dinner with Lady Bracknell.

- A short story, short radio drama or screenplay about Algy, Cecily, Jack and Gwendolyn 10 years into the future. (This would be about 1910). How do they get on now? Have they changed? This would likely be a comic piece and you should try to capture the voices of the characters.

- A short story with the title The Shallow Mask of Manners. This piece could be comic or serious.

- A short story about a young Victorian woman looking for a husband

Hopefully, one of these ideas should appeal to you.

If you have your own idea for a coursework task, please contact your tutor to discuss this.

Word Limits

Some of these tasks will require more words than others. For example, a short story will need more words than a diary entry or letter. Remember that the total word limit is 2000 words for both your fiction and non-fiction piece, so you will need to balance the word count between your two pieces.

Task

Start to think about which task you would like to complete for your fiction piece. Make notes on your ideas and record your thought processes. Also, make a note of any websites that you visit in order to research your ideas.

These notes will be helpful for your commentary.

Topic 13 – How to Write a Commentary

Introduction

In this topic, we will look at how to write a commentary. You will also need to include a bibliography as part of your coursework portfolio and we will look at how to format a bibliography correctly.

Aims and Objectives

- To look at the requirements for the Assignment 2 Commentary
- To learn how to format a bibliography

Writing a Commentary

As we saw at the beginning of this component, the two coursework pieces (one fiction and one non-fiction) are called Assignment 1. Assignment 2 is the accompanying commentary. The word limit for the commentary is 1000-1250 words.

The idea of the commentary is to encourage you to reflect on your own work and the decisions that you have made in your creative pieces.

You should write about both of your pieces together, rather than looking at one and then the other. Ideally, you will use an integrated approach that considers both of your creative pieces throughout.

Your commentary should include:

- An introduction that explains your theme and states that the stimulus texts are Wendy Jones *Grayson Perry: Portrait of the Artist as a Young Girl* and Oscar Wilde *The Importance of Being Earnest*. Your introduction should also explain the tasks that you have chosen and say why you have chosen these tasks. How do they relate to the texts and theme?

- An analysis of key features of the stimulus texts and how these features have influenced your own writing.

- A discussion of genre, audience and purpose.

- A discussion of form, structure and language.

- An analysis of the literary and linguistic feature that you have used and why you have chosen to use these features. What effect were you trying to create?

- You should also try to finally sum up your ideas in a conclusion. Your conclusion should explore the overall relationship between the stimulus texts and the tasks you have chosen.

According to Edexcel, some things to **avoid** doing in your commentary are:

- Avoid giving long explanations of your research
- Avoid using long quotations from the stimulus texts
- Avoid self-evaluation e.g. 'I think my tasks have been very successful' [14]

Although it may sound difficult to write a commentary at first, it is actually quite straightforward. Keep thinking about your own ideas and the decisions that you made while you were writing your creative pieces. The aim is to explain this decision-making process to the examiner, so that you can show how your studies of language and literature have helped you to develop your own skills as a writer.

You will find that your reading diary will be very helpful to you as you complete your commentary. It will help you to remember your initial reactions to the text. You will also find it useful to look over the notes that you made as you worked through the texts and developed your ideas for your tasks.

---

[14] The Edexcel Getting Started Guide for AS and A-Level English Language and Literature at:
http://qualifications.pearson.com/en/qualifications/edexcel-a-levels/english-language-and-literature-2015.coursematerials.html#filterQuery=Pearson-UK:Category%2FTeaching-and-learning-materials

Bibliography

You coursework portfolio should also include a bibliography. Your bibliography doesn't need to be extensive, but you must cite every relevant text that you have used.

You should include the references in the following format:

Bibliography

Core Texts

Jones, Wendy. *Grayson Perry: Portrait of the Artist as a Young Girl*. Vintage 2007
Wilde, Oscar. *The Importance of Being Earnest*. Oxford University Press 2015

Wider Reading and Research

Wilde, Oscar. *De Profundis, The Ballad of Reading Gaol & Others*. Wordsworth Classics 1999

Websites

https://en.wikipedia.org/wiki/Oscar_Wilde
https://en.wikipedia.org/wiki/Grayson_Perry

Copy this format exactly for your bibliography. Include your bibliography as a separate page after your commentary.

Task

You are now ready to complete your creative fiction and non-fiction coursework tasks and write your commentary.

When you have completed the first draft of your coursework tasks, you can get feedback on your draft from your tutor. Your tutor can only comment on one draft of your coursework, so make sure that you are happy with your work before you send it for feedback.

Please email your complete coursework portfolio to your tutor as a Word document or Rich Text File, and please remember to allow 7-10 days for the return of written work.

Component 2:

Varieties in Language and Literature

Topic 1 – Component 2: Varieties in Language and Literature

Introduction

In this topic, we will look at the requirements of Component 2. We will then begin to look at some of the features of prose.

Aims and Objectives

- To learn about Component 2
- To understand some of the features of prose

Component 2: Varieties in Language and Literature

Component 2 is focussed on how different writers explore similar themes. In our course, we will be looking the theme of Encounters. We will be investigating this theme across both fiction and non-fiction prose works.

Overview

The Component 2 exam lasts for two and a half hours. It has two sections.

In Section A, you will write a critical evaluation of a previously unseen text. This text will be linked to our theme of Encounters.

In Section B, you will answer one comparative essay question on *Wuthering Heights* and *The Bloody Chamber*. You will be able to take clean (unmarked) copies of these texts into the exam with you.

All of the texts that we will be studying in this component will be prose texts.

What is Prose?

Prose is usually defined as written or spoken language, in its ordinary form, without metrical structure.[15] In other words, prose is generally considered to be any text (written or spoken) other than poetry (poetry usually has a 'metrical structure' or rhythm). This is therefore a broad and all-encompassing genre that can include literary texts (for example, novels and short stories) and non-literary texts (such as newspaper articles, textbooks and travelogues).

Prose works have a grammatical structure and are written as sentences and paragraphs. Beyond this, however, there is a great deal of flexibility and writers approach prose in many different ways. There are a huge number of possible linguistic and literary techniques that can be used in prose and we will be looking at some of these as we work through this component.

Features of Literary Prose Works

In this component, we will be studying one novel (*Wuthering Heights*) and one collection of short stories (*The Bloody Chamber*). These are works of fiction.

Fiction is not the same as real-life. It sounds obvious but it is really important to grasp this difference. The world that the author creates is completely artificial and the author therefore has complete control over the events and their representation. Nothing in a novel is accidental. Everything is (or should be) deliberately controlled.

Thus, the author has to make large numbers of decisions about where and how to begin the story, how to develop it, and finally, how to end it. Some of these decisions will be intended to create drama, or they can be used to draw the reader's attention towards certain points, or to create a certain mood. Other decisions will be related to what the author is trying to say, sometimes called the ideology, purpose or destination of the novel. Authors, therefore, have to structure their stories carefully.

---

[15] Oxford Dictionaries <http://www.oxforddictionaries.com/definition/english/prose> Consulted 27/05/2015

In this way, when creating fictional worlds, authors will make lots of decisions about structure and technique. There are many different features of fictional narratives. These can include: the author's choice of point of view (also known as focalisation); choice of setting; use of time and sequence; characterisation; voices and dialogue; mood and atmosphere; use of motifs and metaphors; and the use of symbolism and allegory.

Authors of literary texts therefore use a wide range of stylistic and literary techniques to convey their intended meanings. Each of these techniques will be chosen to create a certain effect. We will look at some of these techniques in detail as we examine our set texts *Wuthering Heights* and *The Bloody Chamber*.

Features of Non-Literary Prose Works

We have already seen a number of non-literary prose works in Component 1. The types of texts that we considered (articles, blogs, interviews, travelogues, etc.) are all forms of prose. As we have seen, each of these forms has its own genre conventions. There are many linguistic and stylistic features that authors can draw upon in their construction of non-literary works. We will begin thinking further about these in Topic 3.

Thinking about Prose and its Features

The flexibility of prose allows authors considerable freedom in their choice of technique and this leads to a wide range of possible effects. When reading any prose text, it is therefore important to keep thinking about the author and his or her intentions. Keep asking yourself questions about the author's choices. Why has the author chosen to use this technique? What effect is s/he trying to create? Is it successful? What impression does the reader receive? Answering these questions will help you to think analytically about the techniques that authors use and to take a critical and evaluative approach to literary and linguistic features.

Prose has sometimes been seen as a mundane, ordinary form of writing and, indeed, one of the secondary meanings of 'prose' in the OED is 'plain or dull writing'[16]. Samuel Taylor Coleridge once joked that novice poets should know the "definitions of prose and poetry; that is, prose,— words in their best order; poetry,— the best words in their best order".[17] However, as we explore our chosen texts, we might begin to think differently! The astonishing variety and flexibility of prose means that it can be used in many, various, creative ways. In this component, we will learn more about this form of writing as we explore this diverse genre further.

Task

Look at the Edexcel A-Level English Language and Literature Specification on the Edexcel website and make sure that you are familiar with the requirements for Component 2.

There is no commentary on this activity.

---

[16] http://www.oxforddictionaries.com/definition/english/prose
[17] Samuel Taylor Coleridge cited Wikipedia 'Prose' <http://en.wikipedia.org/wiki/Prose> Accessed 27/05/2015

Topic 2 – Encounters

Introduction

In this topic, we will begin thinking about Encounters.

Aims and Objectives

- To start thinking about Encounters

Exploring a Theme

In this component, all the texts that we study will be linked by the theme of Encounters.

A theme can be used to make connections between texts. It can allow us to look at how authors use similar themes in different texts. In this component, the theme should be interpreted loosely and broadly and, as we shall see in this topic, there are many kinds of encounters.

Before we proceed with our study of prose, it is therefore worth considering this theme further.

What do we mean by Encounters?

Task

Using one or more dictionaries, look up the word 'Encounter'.

Write down some of the definitions you find.

(There is no commentary on this activity.)

From this activity, you will notice that the word 'encounter' can have many definitions. It can be a noun or a verb.

As a noun, encounter can mean:

1) An sudden or unexpected meeting with someone or something

2) A confrontation

3) A military conflict or battle

4) A sports match

As a verb, encounter can mean:

1) to meet with (someone or something)

2) to come across (someone or something)

3) to struggle against difficulties

4) to engage (a person or animal; an enemy) in conflict

Task

Next, using the definitions you have found, start making a list of some of the words associated with encounters. Here are some to get you started:

- unexpected
- meeting
- hostile
- sudden

(It is important that you start to think about these words and their connotations for yourself, so there is no commentary on this activity.)

Types of Encounters

The more we start to think about it, the more types of encounters there are.

Some types of encounters might include:

- meeting someone for the first time
- a new or unexpected situation
- running into a friend you haven't seen for a long time
- seeing your ex-boyfriend with a new girlfriend
- falling in love for the first time (encountering love as an emotion)
- a football match or a game of chess
- turning over an exam paper and encountering the questions
- finding a treasure or a mysterious object
- a close encounter (with aliens?)

Some of these encounters might be lucky or happy, some might be frightening, some might be challenging, some might be sad or cause complicated or ambivalent feelings.

These reactions might not always be the same for all people. For example, one writer might be glad to run into an old friend, while for another it might remind them of a difficult or unhappy time in their life. A football match could be an exciting Saturday afternoon out, or a scary experience playing for a new team or against a rival school. Even an encounter with aliens could be frightening and unexpected, or could confirm years of UFO research!

In this way, we can see that any encounter can be different in different circumstances. The different ways that we might feel about encounters can be expressed by writers in different ways, and the language that they use will create different impressions on the reader and guide their response.

As we read through each text, we will see that distinct types of encounters, and our various responses to them, can be used to link together and explore diverse literary or non-literary texts.

Task

Before we move onto looking at prose non-fiction, it will be useful to brainstorm a few more ideas about encounters. A good way to do this is to use a spider diagram. Use a large piece of paper and write down everything that you can think of that follows on from the word 'Encounter'. Spider diagrams can promote creative thought and help us to see new connections between ideas. You can also use wiggly or curved lines, or different coloured pens, to help boost your creativity.

Here is an example:

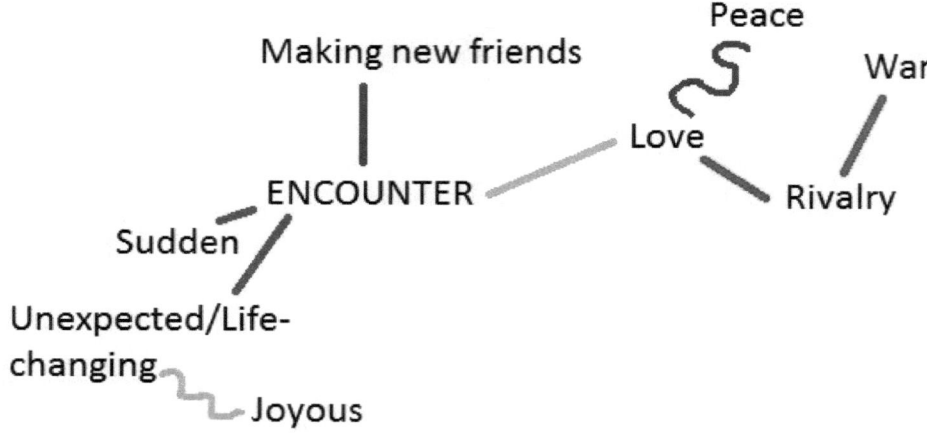

This should be a personal response to the idea of 'Encounters', so there is no commentary on this activity.

Topic 3 – Introducing Section A

Introduction

In this topic, we will look at the requirements of Section A of the Component 2 exam.

Aims and Objectives

- To learn about Section A of the exam

Section A

In Section A, you will answer one compulsory question on the theme of Encounters.

This question will ask you to write a critical evaluation of an unseen text. The unseen text will be printed in the source booklet which accompanies the exam paper. (The exam paper and source booklet will be on your desk at the start the exam.)

The question will be in the format:

Encounters

Read Text [X] on Page [X] of the source booklet

Question 3

Critically evaluate how [Author] conveys [subject of unseen text].

In your answer, you must comment on linguistic and literary features and relevant contextual factors.

The question will be worth 20 marks.

Unseen Texts

In Section A, you will be commenting on an unseen text. This may sound daunting at first, but it is actually very similar to the task that we have prepared for in Component 1. Indeed, we have already practised a lot of the skills that you will need for this section.

The main difference is that, for Section A of Component 2, you will be focussing more on the themes and issues raised by the unseen text, rather than the way that the author creates a sense of voice.

The unseen text will also not necessarily be drawn from C20th and C21st century resources, and you may receive a text from an earlier time period.

We will be looking at unseen texts in more detail in the next topic.

What Are The Examiners Looking For?

In your answer, you will need to show:

- a knowledge of genre conventions
- an appreciation of linguistic and literary techniques
- an awareness of how the writer's sense of audience informs the text
- a knowledge of the attitudes and values displayed by the writer
- an awareness of the context of the text

Task

Download the A-Level Sample Assessment Materials from the Edexcel website.

Spend some time looking over Section A of the exam paper for Component 2: Varieties in Language and Literature. Read the texts that are printed in the accompanying source booklet. You will notice that there is a section for each of the different themes. Remember that we will only be looking at Encounters.

You may not feel ready to answer the questions yet, but this activity will help you to become familiar with the style of the exam paper, so that you know what to expect in the exam.

When you feel that you are familiar with the style of the exam, you can move onto the next topic.

(There is no commentary on this activity.)

Topic 4 – Revising Our Work On Unseen Texts

Introduction

In this topic, we will revise our earlier work on unseen texts.

Aims and Objectives

- To revise the work on unseen texts that we have already done as part of Component 1.

Reading Unseen Texts

In Component 1, we looked at how to study an unseen text from one of the listed genres. We also examined how a sense of voice can be conveyed using literary and linguistic techniques.

The skills we will need for this unit are very similar.

Texts and Genres

You are already familiar with a number of genres. These include:

- Articles
- Autobiography/biography
- Diary/memoir
- Blog posts
- Interview transcript
- Radio script/screenplay
- Reportage
- Review
- Speech
- Travelogue

You may receive any of these types of texts in the Component 2 exam, as well as other possible forms, such as letters or obituaries.

Audience

You will also need to consider the audience of the text. As we have seen, the expected audience will affect the writer's choices. For example, we would generally expect that an academic paper would be written using a much higher/more specialized register than a magazine article.

Purpose

Closely related to both audience and genre, is the idea of purpose. Writers will always have particular intentions when they begin writing. Sometimes these purposes are classified as: to persuade; to inform; to instruct; or to entertain. (You may have come across these distinctions at GCSE.) However, there is considerable overlap between these purposes, and texts are often written for more than one reason.

For example, a newspaper article might be written to inform the newspaper's readers of a particular newsworthy event, for example a recent government announcement of a change of policy. This article could therefore be written to inform. However, it might also be written to persuade the audience to a particular view, depending on whether the journalist (and their editor) agree with this change of policy or not.

A review of a new film will also be written for several purposes. It might be written to entertain, but will also attempt to persuade the audience to the writer's view of the film.

Context

The context is everything that happens around a text. This will include a wide range of factors and can be everything from the historical period in which a text is written to the author's own personal circumstances.

Another way of thinking about context is as all the factors that affect how the audience will consume a text. For example, a text that gives a very conventional or commonplace view will usually be relatively uncontroversial. A text that gives a unusual viewpoint may be challenged by readers.

Again, this will depend on the audience. The Telegraph is a newspaper that promotes conservative views, so a left-wing viewpoint is likely to prove controversial for its readership. In the opposite way, a Marxist literary journal would expect its authors and readers to share that viewpoint and would find the conservative ideas expressed in The Telegraph distasteful.

Often there is a difference between the context of production and the context of reception, especially for historical texts. The way that a text would have been read when it was first written and the way it is read today can often be very different, because of a change in cultural ideas, attitudes and values.

Attitudes and Values

We all have particular attitudes and values, whether we always realise it or not. These attitudes are usually the result of the environment around us, such as our social class, culture and upbringing.

Sometimes a writer will expressly argue towards a particularly cultural, social or religious viewpoint. This will usually be when the writer is trying to persuade the audience to their view. At other times, these attitudes will be more subtle and may not be immediately obvious. As readers, however, it will be our job to look carefully at what the writer says and at what this says about them.

A writer may not always be aware of these attitudes and values within their own work. We sometimes call these unconscious biases.

Putting It All Together

In this way, the genre, audience, purpose and context will all affect the choices that a writer makes when constructing a text.

In other words, none of these aspects of a text should be looked at in isolation. Instead, we need to use our knowledge of different genres, audiences, purposes and contexts to look at how and why the writer has written the text in this way.

For example, we know that a blog post will usually be written in a less formal style than a broadsheet news article. We know that the blog writer will choose to write in this style because it suits their likely audience (online surfers, who may not spend a long time reading the blog) and purpose (probably primarily to entertain). The tone is therefore likely to be chatty and personal and use an informal register.

The next stage is to look in a lot more detail at how the writer creates this effect. We know what the writer's purpose is, but how do we know this and how can we prove it to somebody else? How does the writer create a sense of voice?

We need to consider how the choices that a writer makes are shown through the use of literary and linguistic features.

Revision

This is a good opportunity to revise your notes from Component 1.

Begin by looking at the glossary list of literary and linguistic features that you made in Component 1.

You will also find it useful to briefly revise your notes from the unseen texts in Component 1.

Remember that the more you read and revise the same material, the better you will be able to remember the information.

Topic 5 – Reading a Text and Using a Framework

Introduction

In this topic, we will begin practising unseen texts. We will learn how to use the ideas of purpose, audience and context as a framework for the initial reading of an unseen text.

Aims and Objectives

- To begin practising unseen texts

Reading a Text and Using a Framework

In the last topic we looked at how genre, audience, purpose and context work together and how a consideration of these can influence a writer's choices.

One way to explore this further is to use these categories to guide your analysis. You can approach an unseen text by first thinking about these categories and what they can tell us about the text. This can provide a framework which will help you to know how to approach an unseen text in the exam. You can think of a framework as a series of questions:

1) What is the genre of the text? (e.g. letter, travelogue, etc.)
2) Who is the intended audience? (e.g. a personal friend, readers of a travel guide, etc.)
3) What is the purpose of the text? (e.g. to inform a friend of the birth of a baby, to persuade readers to holiday in a particular destination, etc.)
4) Are there relevant contextual factors? (e.g. what is the relationship between the friends? Have they seen each other recently or have they been apart for a long time? Does the correspondent already have children or not? Do they both share the same socio-cultural background?)
5) What are the values or attitudes of the writer? (e.g. What is the travelogue writer's attitude to the country he is visiting? Is he critical of any aspects of the culture or political situation?

However, remember that there are lots of connections between genre, audience, purpose and context. Try not to think of them as a checklist of points to answer separately, but rather to look at how the author's awareness of these issues shapes the way that they write. We are aiming to explore at how the author constructs their text, with reference to the linguistic and literary features that they use.

We will now begin to apply this to an unseen text. Remember that all the texts in this component will be based on the theme of Encounters.

Task

Read the extract on the following page.

Answer the question below.

What is the genre, audience, purpose and context of the article? Find 5 examples of how this is reflected in the writers' choices.

Are there any values or attitudes to be aware of here?

Random encounter

From Wikipedia, the free encyclopedia

This article is about the feature in role-playing games. For other uses, see Random Encounter.

A **random encounter** is a feature commonly used in various role-playing games whereby encounters with non-player character (NPC) enemies or other dangers occur sporadically and at random. In general, random encounters are used to simulate the challenges associated with being in a hazardous environment—such as a monster-infested wilderness or dungeon—with uncertain frequency of occurrence and makeup (as opposed to a "placed" encounter). Frequent random encounters are common in games like *Dragon Quest*, *Legend of Legaia*, *Pokémon* and the *Final Fantasy* series

Role-playing games

Random encounters—sometimes called *wandering monsters*—were a feature of Dungeons & Dragons from its beginnings in the 1970s, and persist in that game and its offshoots to this day. Random encounters are usually determined by the gamemaster by rolling dice against a *random encounter table*. The tables are usually based on terrain (and/or time/weather), and have a chance for differing encounters with different numbers or types of creatures. The results may be modified by other tables, such as whether the encounter is friendly, neutral or hostile. GMs are often encouraged to make their own tables. Specific adventures often have specific tables for locations, like a temple's hallways.

Wandering monsters are often used to wear down player characters and force them to use up consumable resources, such as hit points, magic spells and healing potions, as a way of punishing spending too much time in a dangerous area

Video games

Random encounters were incorporated into early role-playing video games and have been common throughout the genre.[2][3][4] Placed and random encounters were both used in 1981s *Wizardry*[5] and by the mid-1980s, random encounters made up the bulk of battles in genre-defining games such as *Dragon Warrior*,[1] *Final Fantasy*, and *The Bard's Tale*.[6] Random encounters happen when the player is traversing the game world (often through the use of a "world map" or overworld). Most often, the player encounters enemies to battle, but occasionally friendly or neutral characters can appear, with whom the player might interact differently than with enemies. Random encounters are random in the respect that players cannot anticipate the exact moment of encounter or what will be encountered, as the occurrence of the event is based on factors such as programmed probabilities; Pseudo-random number generators create the sequence of numbers used to determine if an encounter will happen. The form and frequency can vary depending on a number of factors, such as where the player is located in the game world and the statistics of the player character. In some games, items can be found to increase or decrease the frequency of random encounters, even to eliminate them outright, or increase the odds of having a particular encounter.

Random encounters have become less popular in video games with the passage of time, as gamers often complain that they are annoying, repetitive or discouraging to exploration. The *Final Fantasy* and *Tales* series have abandoned random encounter systems with successive games, while relatively newer franchises such as the *Chrono* series and *Kingdom Hearts* have never used them.

A more commonly used tactic in later RPGs (used in *Final Fantasy XII*, *Radiata Stories*, *Fallout 1* and *2*, *Legend of Legaia* and all *Kingdom Hearts* games) is to set a finite number of enemies in a given area. This cuts down on grinding and does not discourage exploration to the same extent. A similar approach is spawning, where monsters always (re)appear at the same location, as seen in *Chrono Trigger*[9] and most of *Dragon Quest IX*.[10][11] Both approaches give players the opportunity to anticipate, evade, or select encounters.

Commentary

Genre: This is an extract is taken from Wikipedia and the genre is an encyclopaedia article.

Purpose: The purpose is to inform, giving factual information on random encounters (with monsters) in video and role-playing games.

Audience: The audience can be taken to be general readers who are interested in this subject matter. These might be gamers or aficionados of role playing games, as well as people using the encyclopaedia to look up an unfamiliar term or who stumble upon the article after following various random links.

Context: Wikipedia articles are usually created and maintained by a large number of volunteers, so there isn't one, single author. Contributors believe in the importance and value of community projects, such as Wikipedia. Some people are critical of this form of encyclopaedia, because they consider the community format less academically rigorous than that of printed encyclopaedias. However, contributors will usually try to provide clear citations for their information and adopt a deliberately scholarly tone, possibly in answer to this criticism.

How does this affect the writers' choices?

As the text is an encyclopaedia article written to inform it uses a fairly authoritative tone and Standard English of a formal register. For example, the first paragraph uses a fairly sophisticated vocabulary and formal lexis, including words such as 'whereby', 'occur', 'sporadically', 'hazardous', 'occurrence' etc. In the second paragraph, there are compound-complex sentences with co-ordination and subordination (dependent clauses), for example, 'The results may be modified by other tables, such as whether the encounter is friendly, neutral or hostile'. Most of the sentences in the article are fairly long, and this creates a more formal register and an academic tone.

In keeping with the informational purpose, there is plenty of factual evidence provided, with lots of examples drawn from different games. This is structured fairly historically, with the structure of the article giving a sense of progression by charting games from the 1970s onwards. As the audience are assumed to be general readers with no expert knowledge, the more technical terminology (such as 'overworld' and 'pseudo-random number generator') has hyperlinks which allow the reader to look up the articles for these unfamiliar terms. This is a useful feature of online text , which is not available to printed books, and is thus specific to this genre. There is a one instance where certain knowledge is assumed, however, and the term GM is used for gamesmaster without this being explained.

Values and attitudes

Due to the context and sometimes controversy surrounding editable encyclopedias, Wikipedia contributors usually try to adopt a scholarly approach and an academic tone. Naturally, the author or authors will still have their own biases, however.

This article to some extent creates the impression that random encounters are no longer desirable in games as they 'discourage exploration'. The article states that random encounters are not included in newer game franchises, implying that they are outdated. However, this opinion is carefully qualified by use of the phrase 'gamers often complain that' and the tone of the article is studiedly neutral throughout.

Topic 6 – Identifying Literary and Linguistic Features

Introduction

In this topic, we will start to identify some of the literary and linguistic features that occur in a text.

Aims and Objectives

- To start identifying literary and linguistic features in unseen texts

Identifying Literary and Linguistic Features

The next stage in examining an unseen text (after you have considered the genre, audience, purpose, context, attitudes and values) is to start identifying some of the literary and linguistic features in the text.

As we saw in Component 1, most authors will use a variety of features as part of their writing. In Component 1, we were mainly interested in how these features were used to create a sense of voice. In this component, we are interested in how authors convey their thoughts and feelings. Exploring the ways that authors use literary techniques can help us to understand how they have created a text. As you read a text, think about how the author has used each particular techniques to create a certain impression. Keep thinking about what the author is trying to show the reader and how s/he tries to influence the reader's opinion of a particular encounter.

In Component 2, you may also get an unseen text drawn from an earlier time period than we have looked at before. In this topic, we will be looking at a nineteenth century text by the author Charles Dickens.

In the next task, we will practice identifying some of the literary and linguistic features in this text. Remember that you need to do more than just list these features, however. You need to keep thinking about why the author has used these features and what effect they create.

Task

The text below is adapted from a Christmas article by the nineteenth century author Charles Dickens. It was first published as 'Christmas Festivities' in a weekly newspaper called Bell's Life in London in December 1835. It was then re-published as 'A Christmas Dinner' in Sketches by Boz in 1836. In this text, the author describes several encounters between members of a family.

As you read through the text, underline the literary and linguistic features that you come across.

For each feature that you identify, try to analyse the effect that it creates. Why has the author chosen to use this particular technique?

Note:

For our purposes, I have slighted edited the original essay to make it shorter. Even so, this text is considerably longer than the one you will get in the exam. This is to allow you to gain extra practice at identifying literary and linguistic features. If you want to, you can see the complete text as it would have appeared in 1836 at this website:

http://www.bl.uk/collection-items/a-christmas-dinner-from-charles-dickenss-sketches-by-boz

A Christmas Dinner

The Christmas family-party that we mean, is not a mere assemblage of relations, got up at a week or two's notice, originating this year, having no family precedent in the last, and not likely to be repeated in the next. No. It is an annual gathering of all the accessible members of the family, young or old, rich or poor; and all the children look forward to it, for two months beforehand, in a fever of anticipation. Formerly, it was held at grandpapa's; but grandpapa getting old, and grandmamma getting old too, and rather infirm, they have given up house-keeping, and domesticated themselves with uncle George; so, the party always takes place at uncle George's house, but grandmamma sends in most of the good things, and grandpapa always WILL toddle down, all the way to Newgate-market, to buy the turkey, which he engages a porter to bring home behind him in triumph, always insisting on the man's being rewarded with a glass of spirits, over and above his hire, to drink 'a merry Christmas and a happy new year' to aunt George. As to grandmamma, she is very secret and mysterious for two or three days beforehand, but not sufficiently so, to prevent rumours getting afloat that she has purchased a beautiful new cap with pink ribbons for each of the servants, together with sundry books, and pen-knives, and pencil-cases, for the younger branches; to say nothing of divers secret additions to the order originally given by aunt George at the pastry-cook's, such as another dozen of mince- pies for the dinner, and a large plum-cake for the children.

...

But all these diversions are nothing to the subsequent excitement when grandmamma in a high cap, and slate-coloured silk gown; and grandpapa with a beautifully plaited shirt-frill, and white neckerchief; seat themselves on one side of the drawing-room fire, with uncle George's children and little cousins innumerable, seated in the front, waiting the arrival of the expected visitors. Suddenly a hackney-coach is heard to stop, and uncle George, who has been looking out of the window, exclaims 'Here's Jane!' on which the children rush to the door, and helter-skelter down- stairs; and uncle Robert and aunt Jane, and the dear little baby, and the nurse, and the whole party, are ushered up-stairs amidst tumultuous shouts of 'Oh, my!' from the children, and frequently repeated warnings not to hurt baby from the nurse. And grandpapa takes the child, and grandmamma kisses her daughter, and the confusion of this first entry has scarcely subsided, when some other aunts and uncles with more cousins arrive, and the grown-up cousins flirt with each other, and so do the little cousins too, for that matter, and nothing is to be heard but a confused din of talking, laughing, and merriment.

A hesitating double knock at the street-door, heard during a momentary pause in the conversation, excites a general inquiry of 'Who's that?' and two or three children, who have been standing at the window, announce in a low voice, that it's 'poor aunt Margaret.' Upon which, aunt George leaves the room to welcome the new-comer; and grandmamma draws herself up, rather stiff and stately; for Margaret married a poor man without her consent, and poverty not being a sufficiently weighty punishment for her offence, has been discarded by her friends, and debarred the society of her dearest relatives. But Christmas has come round, and the unkind feelings that have struggled against better dispositions during the year, have melted away before its genial influence, like half-formed ice beneath the morning sun. It is not difficult in a moment of angry feeling for a parent to denounce a disobedient child; but, to banish her at a period of general good- will and hilarity, from the hearth, round which she has sat on so many anniversaries of the same day, expanding by slow degrees from infancy to girlhood, and then bursting, almost imperceptibly, into a woman, is widely different. The air of conscious rectitude, and cold forgiveness, which the old lady has assumed, sits ill upon her; and when the poor girl is led in by her sister, pale in looks and broken in hope - not from poverty, for that she could bear, but from the consciousness of undeserved neglect, and unmerited unkindness - it is easy to see how much of it is assumed. A momentary pause succeeds; the girl breaks suddenly from her sister and throws herself, sobbing, on her mother's neck. The father steps hastily forward, and takes her husband's hand. Friends crowd round to offer their hearty congratulations, and happiness and harmony again prevail.

As to the dinner, it's perfectly delightful - nothing goes wrong, and everybody is in the very best of spirits, and disposed to please and be pleased.

...

And thus the evening passes, in a strain of rational good-will and cheerfulness, doing more to awaken the sympathies of every member of the party in behalf of his neighbour, and to perpetuate their good feeling during the ensuing year, than half the homilies that have ever been written, by half the Divines that have ever lived.

Commentary

In the annotated version of the text given below, we have identified some of the linguistic and literary features. The comments in red analyse the effects that these features are intended to create. Note how we have used analytical phrases such as 'this creates a sense of' in order to explore these features.

In your own answer you may not have identified the exact same features that we have identified here, and you may not have always come to the same conclusion. This is absolutely fine, so long as your use of terminology is accurate and your ideas are logical and well-supported by the evidence you have selected from the text. There is plenty of space for individual interpretation in English Language and Literature.

The most important learning outcome here is to make sure that you are thinking about the way that the author uses literary or linguistic features and that you are analysing the effects that these techniques create.

The Christmas family-party that we mean, is not a mere assemblage of

relations, got up at a week or two's notice, originating this year, having

no family precedent in the last, and not likely to be repeated in the next.

No. It is an annual gathering of all the accessible members of the family,

young or old, rich or poor; and all the children look forward to it, for two

months beforehand, in a fever of anticipation. Formerly, it was held at

grandpapa's; but grandpapa getting old, and grandmamma getting old

too, and rather infirm, they have given up house-keeping, and

domesticated themselves with uncle George; so, the party always takes

place at uncle George's house, but grandmamma sends in most of the

Comment [hb1]: C19th writing frequently used very long and complex sentences with multiple subordinate clauses. Also note the sophisticated, high level vocabulary, using lexis such as 'assemblage' and 'originating'. This writing style may seem quite affected and pretentious to us as modern readers, but it would have been quite a commonly used, educated style at this time. This magazine was aimed at a middle-class audience.

Comment [hb2]: Minor sentence used to add interest and break up long sentences surrounding it.

Comment [hb3]: The annual nature of this Christmas celebration is important to the speaker here. He mentions it several times because he is trying to evoke a sense of tradition.

Comment [hb4]: This is an unusual use of a qualifier here. Only those who are 'accessible' are included, presumably only those who live nearby. There is no obvious reason not to just say 'all the members of the family' here unless Dickens is attempting some alliteration on annual, all and accessible. However, this seems to contradict the later inclusivity of 'young or old, rich or poor'.

Comment [hb5]: Mixture of syndetic and asyndetic listing, creates sense of completeness.

Comment [hb6]: An evocative phrase used to add interest and excitement. Although usually associated with illness, 'fever' has positive connotations here.

Comment [hb7]: This is a very long sentence and semi-colons are used here to separate the clauses and break this sentence up a bit. The length of this sentence creates a sense of the speaker's train of thought running on and on, and this creates an informal, chatty style. There is a strong sense that we are being told a story by someone we know, rather than reading a feature article.

good things, and grandpapa always WILL toddle down, all the way to

Newgate-market, to buy the turkey, which he engages a porter to bring

home behind him in triumph, always insisting on the man's being

rewarded with a glass of spirits, over and above his hire, to drink 'a merry

Christmas and a happy new year' to aunt George. As to grandmamma,

she is very secret and mysterious for two or three days beforehand, but

not sufficiently so, to prevent rumours getting afloat that she has

purchased a beautiful new cap with pink ribbons for each of the servants,

together with sundry books, and pen-knives, and pencil-cases, for the

younger branches; to say nothing of divers secret additions to the order

originally given by aunt George at the pastry-cook's, such as another

> **Comment [hb8]:** This is a vague statement that that works effectively here because it allows the reader to imagine what these good things might be, and to insert their own preferences. The same effect could not be achieved by listing items here, even if there was sufficient space.

> **Comment [hb9]:** Frequent repetition of 'always', helps to create the sense of annual event.

> **Comment [hb10]:** Capital letters used for emphasis. This is perhaps a typographical alternative to italics, which are more commonly used for this purpose today.

> **Comment [hb11]:** This creates a sense of a procession, a parade and a glorious victory. It creates a sense of ceremony. This is obviously overblown (since it is not difficult to buy a turkey).

> **Comment [hb12]:** The use of the imperative here suggests some pomposity on the part of grandpapa.

> **Comment [hb13]:** Creates a sense of intrigue.

> **Comment [hb14]:** There are lots of adjectives used here and this is a much more specific description than the 'sundry books' (an oddly uniform description to be used by a professional writer). Dickens was known as a social reformer and it may be that he is trying to emphasise the importance of buying nice gifts for one's servants here. We might note however, that the servants themselves are not differentiated and each receives the same gift.

> **Comment [hb15]:** Younger branches here is a metaphorical reference to the idea of the family tree.

> **Comment [hb16]:** The modern spelling would be 'diverse'.

> **Comment [hb17]:** This creates sense of mystery, although this is perhaps later deflated by specifying these items as mince pies and plum cake.

dozen of mince- pies for the dinner, and a large plum-cake for the

children.

...

But all these diversions are nothing to the subsequent excitement when

grandmamma in a high cap, and slate-coloured silk gown; and grandpapa

with a beautifully plaited shirt-frill, and white neckerchief; seat

themselves on one side of the drawing-room fire, with uncle George's

children and little cousins innumerable, seated in the front, waiting the

arrival of the expected visitors. Suddenly a hackney-coach is heard to

stop, and uncle George, who has been looking out of the window,

exclaims 'Here's Jane!' on which the children rush to the door, and helter-

skelter down- stairs; and uncle Robert and aunt Jane, and the dear little

baby, and the nurse, and the whole party, are ushered up-stairs amidst

tumultuous shouts of 'Oh, my!' from the children, and frequently repeated

Comment [hb18]: The impression here is of excess.

Comment [hb19]: Again, this adjective implies grandmamma's generosity.

Comment [hb20]: This creates a sense of mounting excitement, leading to Christmas day itself.

Comment [hb21]: Dickens uses the alliteration of slate and silk here to suggest the smooth, shiny qualities of silk itself. This contributes to a sense of opulence.

Comment [hb22]: We can notice here that this whole article is written in the present tense. This creates a sense of ongoing action and contributes to the idea of an unchanging tradition.

Comment [hb23]: This is clearly an impossible exaggeration, but it creates the impression of a large family.

Comment [hb24]: Again, there is a strong sense of building excitement in this section.

Comment [hb25]: 'Suddenly' is used to create an abrupt transition from the time of waiting.

Comment [hb26]: This verb suggests excitement.

Comment [hb27]: The use of this short speech within the text creates a sense of liveliness as we hear the voice of the character.

Comment [hb28]: This is a nicely evocative phrase where 'helter-skelter' is used as a verb to suggest the fast, erratic movement of the children to the door. (A helter skelter is a twisting, spiral slide.)

Comment [hb29]: The use of syndetic listing to emphasise that a large number of people are arriving and meeting.

Comment [hb30]: This creates a sense of loud and lively environment. Again, the reported speech is short, and fits into the prose. It gives a sense of voice without creating much interruption to the flow of the narrative.

warnings not to hurt baby from the nurse. And grandpapa takes the child,

and grandmamma kisses her daughter, and the confusion of this first

entry has scarcely subsided, when some other aunts and uncles with

more cousins arrive, and the grown-up cousins flirt with each other, and

so do the little cousins too, for that matter, and nothing is to be heard but

a confused din of talking, laughing, and merriment.

A hesitating double knock at the street-door, heard during a momentary

pause in the conversation, excites a general inquiry of 'Who's that?' and

two or three children, who have been standing at the window, announce

in a low voice, that it's 'poor aunt Margaret.' Upon which, aunt George

leaves the room to welcome the new-comer; and grandmamma draws

herself up, rather stiff and stately; for Margaret married a poor man

without her consent, and poverty not being a sufficiently weighty

punishment for her offence, has been discarded by her friends, and

debarred the society of her dearest relatives. But Christmas has come

round, and the unkind feelings that have struggled against better

---

Comment [hb31]: Again, the repetitions of 'and' here creates the sense that a lot is happening as more people arrive and the family share the joy of meeting.

Comment [hb32]: Although 'din' is usually a negative word, this creates a sense of excitement and of family members talking happily over each other.

Comment [hb33]: This is a necessary detail to explain how such a sound could be heard amid the general frivolity. However, it does interrupt the flow of the narrative and prevents the creation of any suspense here.

Comment [hb34]: This suggests a sombre tone, in contrast to the children's previous ebullience.

Comment [hb35]: This adjective tells us that there is some backstory here and that aunt Margaret is in some way unfortunate.

Comment [hb36]: The alliteration here is used to create an impression of grandmamma as rather austere here. We remember that she was earlier associated with the sibilant sounds of slate and silk.

Comment [hb37]: During the Victorian period, daughter's were generally expected to marry according to their parents' wishes. You could be ostracised and socially isolated if you chose to marry outside your social class and without the approval of your parents.

Comment [hb38]: The alliteration of discarded, debarred and dearest is used here to emphasise these words and to create a list-like impression.

dispositions during the year, have melted away before its genial influence,

like half-formed ice beneath the morning sun. It is not difficult in a

moment of angry feeling for a parent to denounce a disobedient child;

but, to banish her at a period of general good- will and hilarity, from the

hearth, round which she has sat on so many anniversaries of the same

day, expanding by slow degrees from infancy to girlhood, and then

bursting, almost imperceptibly, into a woman, is widely different. The air

of conscious rectitude, and cold forgiveness, which the old lady has

assumed, sits ill upon her; and when the poor girl is led in by her sister,

pale in looks and broken in hope - not from poverty, for that she could

bear, but from the consciousness of undeserved neglect, and unmerited

unkindness - it is easy to see how much of it is assumed. A momentary

pause succeeds; the girl breaks suddenly from her sister and throws

herself, sobbing, on her mother's neck. The father steps hastily forward,

and takes her husband's hand. Friends crowd round to offer their hearty

congratulations, and happiness and harmony again prevail.

Comment [hb39]: This tells us the attitudes and ideals of the author. Here, Dickens is advocating that a 'discarded' daughter should be re-introduced to her family and that Christmas is a time for such reconciliations. He phrases this idea using the simile of 'half-formed ice beneath the morning sun' to suggest that the family are only 'half-frozen' and that the hostilities can melt away. Dickens is a very sentimental writer, but this would have appealed to his audience. His ideas might have been considered progressive during his time.

Comment [hb40]: This is another repetition of the d sound used above, linking this to the previous list.

Comment [hb41]: Again, Dickens refers to the idea of family tradition here. His earlier idea of Christmas as a time of continuity is used here to justify the inclusion of the daughter.

Comment [hb42]: This is slightly contradictory. Burst suggests a sudden movement, and it is difficult to see how it could happen imperceptibly.

Comment [hb43]: Here, Dickens is telling us that, contrary to appearances, grandmamma is ready to forgive.

Comment [hb44]: Again, alliteration is used here for emphasis (although we might also get the impression that Dickens simply likes using it and that it is part of his authorial style).

Comment [hb45]: This is a dramatic moment of reconciliation. Emotional moments of this type were often illustrated in popular magazines of this format.

Comment [hb46]: This phrase transitions the reader from the emotive reintegration of the daughter into her family back to the frivolity of the Christmas celebrations.

As to the dinner, it's perfectly delightful - nothing goes wrong, and everybody is in the very best of spirits, and disposed to please and be pleased.

Comment [hb47]: This phrase confirms that everything is back to normal and that the Christmas festivities can continue. It is a light-hearted phrase that contrasts to the intensity of the last paragraph.

...

And thus the evening passes, in a strain of rational good-will and cheerfulness, doing more to awaken the sympathies of every member of the party in behalf of his neighbour, and to perpetuate their good feeling during the ensuing year, than half the homilies that have ever been written, by half the Divines that have ever lived.

Comment [hb48]: Strain is used here to mean type or quality. However, it is an unusual word choice here, as it might also be though t to suggest a trying or difficult circumstance.

Task

If you would like to look at more examples of unseen texts for this activity, there are some available on the Edexcel website at: http://qualifications.pearson.com/en/qualifications/edexcel-a-levels/english-language-and-literature-2015.coursematerials.html#filterQuery=Pearson-UK:Category%2FTeaching-and-learning-materials

Scroll down to the section titled Schemes of Work and download the zipped folder containing examples of unseen non-fiction texts. First, read through the un-annotated example texts (called Resource A un-annotated). Try to identify some of the linguistic and literary features, as we did in the task above.

You can then read the answers provided by Edexcel (called Resource A annotated) and see how many of the same features you identified.

Don't worry if your answer is not exactly the same, but you should be working along similar lines. Remember to keeping thinking about the effect that each technique creates for the reader.

We will be looking at Encounters in our course, but you can also look at the example texts from the other themes if you want to gain more practice of looking at literary and linguistic features.

(There is no commentary on this activity.)

Topic 7 – Answering an Exam Question

Introduction

In this topic, we will look at how to answer an exam question on an unseen text.

Aims and Objectives

- To learn how to answer an exam question on an unseen text

Answering an Exam Question

In the previous topics, we have looked at the genre, purpose, audience, context, attitudes and values of texts. We have also practised identifying the linguistic and literary features of an unseen text. The next stage is to learn how to use these skills to answer an exam question.

The exam question will take the form:

Encounters

Read Text [X] on Page [X] of the source booklet

Question 3

Critically evaluate how [Author] conveys [subject of unseen text].

In your answer, you must comment on linguistic and literary features and relevant contextual factors.

Critical Evaluation

You will notice that you are asked to 'critically evaluate' the unseen text. Unlike Component 1, this is not a comparison exercise.

In this exam, a critical evaluation should be in the form of an essay with a short introduction and conclusion.

Your essay should be written in sentences and paragraphs. Every paragraph should make a clear point, and this point should be supported by evidence from the text. This evidence could be an example of a literary or linguistic feature, or it could be a discussion of contextual factors.

Importantly, an essay should also have an overall point of view or argument. It is difficult to construct an argument around a text that you haven't seen before, but there are good techniques to use that will help you to do this.

Approaching the Text

In the exam, take at least 15 minutes to read over the text. Read and re-read it several times.

Think carefully about the text. What is it about? What is the author trying to say?

Next, start to think about the genre, audience, purpose, context and attitudes and values of the text. Who was the text written for? How can you tell? How has the author used language to appeal to his audience?

By thinking about these questions, you should start to recognise some of the features of the text. Keep thinking about the author and what s/he is trying to achieve. As you read through the text, do you notice any particular literary or linguistic features? What effect do these features create?

You can write on the source booklet, so you may find it helpful to underline some of the literary and linguistic features as you come across them. This will help you to remember features that you want to comment on when you plan your essay.

(However, remember that all of your answers must be written in the answer booklet. No other work will be marked by the examiner.)

You can also begin to jot down ideas. What is the author's purpose here? Are you getting a sense of any particular attitudes and values? Is the text informed by a specific context? What is the author trying to say?

Thinking about the purpose of the text and what the author is trying to say will help you to form the overall argument for your essay.

Planning Your Answer

Once you have begun to get a sense of the author's intentions in writing the text, you can begin to plan your answer. You can use the author's intentions to guide your argument. Think of your answer as filling out the detail to support this overall argument.

In the exam, you should spend about 5-10 minutes planning what you want to say. One of the most effective ways to plan an essay is to use a small spider diagram. Spider diagrams promote creative thought and help you to summarise complex ideas quickly.

In planning your answer, start to think about the main points that you want to make in your essay and the evidence from the text that you will use to support these ideas.

Prioritise features from the text according to their importance. You won't have time to write about everything you notice, so decide which features are the most noticeable, the most important and which fit your argument best.

Select short examples from the text. Write about less, but say more. Really look at the language used in detail. Think about specific words and phrases. Try to apply linguistic terminology if you can.

Look for areas of overlap or ideas that you can group together. For example, if there are several examples of a particular literary technique, such as alliteration, group these together. You can write about them at the same time, even if one is at the end and one is at the beginning of the text.

Start to look for links and connections between different points. Links between different ideas can be used to join paragraphs together and will help to build your argument towards its conclusion.

Overall, as you plan, try to create some overall shape for your answer. Think of your first paragraph as an opening, and then try to work form and develop your ideas from there. Like the texts you are reading, your essay should also have a purpose. You are trying to persuade to the examiner to agree with your analysis by making clear points and providing evidence.

Writing your Essay

A Strong Introduction

You can use your introduction to summarise your ideas and your overall argument.

First, think about the overall content of the text. What is it about? This is material you can use for your introduction. You can open by summarising the text. State the genre, audience and purpose of the text. You can then briefly summarise the content in one or two sentences. Say what the author's purpose is in writing the text. Remember that considering the author's purpose will give you an overall shape to your answer.

The Body of the Essay

The body of your essay should be separated into paragraphs. Every paragraph should make a clear point and provide evidence of that point. The paragraphs should be linked together, so that the ideas flow naturally from one to the next.

The Conclusion

Your conclusion should be derived from your argument, but should also go on to discuss wider issues. Start by summarising some of the ideas from your essay and reiterate your main, overall argument. You can then go on to perhaps explain the wider significance of the text discussed. This might include wider contextual factors, or explore some of the attitudes and values of the writer, possibly in a critical way.

Mistakes to Avoid

When writing an essay on an unseen text, there are a few mistakes to avoid:

- Don't describe the content of the text in detail i.e. don't "tell the story". If you summarise the content in a single brief sentence as part of your introduction, you won't be tempted to repeat this information later on.
- Don't write about one feature after another i.e. don't write a paragraph on audience, a paragraph on purpose, etc. This approach is cumbersome and it doesn't analyse the text as a whole. In short, if you approach the features of the text separately, your answer won't be sophisticated enough for the top levels at A-Level. Instead, try to form an integrated answer.
- Don't go through the text writing about every literary and linguistic feature in order. You won't have time to do this and you won't be able to say very much about each feature. Instead, try to write about select examples from the text and write about them in detail. You can also try to group similar ideas together. This will save time and help you to construct an overall argument.

Practising an Unseen Text

You are now ready to start practising writing a critical evaluation. In the following task, we will work through an example together, so that you can see how to work through an unseen text. We will complete this example slowly, and you do not need to work under exam conditions.

Task

On the next page, there is an exam-style question and an accompanying text.

Read the text several times and start to think about it. You may like to underline some of the linguistic and literary features.

Think about the author's purpose in writing this text. What is he trying to say? What evidence can you find for this purpose?

Encounters

Read Text A on the next page

Question 1

Critically evaluate how the author conveys the encounter with escaped zoo animals.

In your answer, you must comment on linguistic and literary features and relevant contextual factors.

Fearful Accident!
Four Lives Lost.

A Full and Particular Account of a most dreadful circumstance which happened on Tuesday the 18th February instant, in consequence of the escape, from Wombwell's Menagerie, of the celebrated Lion, Wallace, and a large Tigress, by which melancholy accident, Four Human Beings were destroyed ! ! !

A melancholy accident occurred at Wombwell's Menagerie, in consequence of the lion, Wallace, and a large tigress escaping from the caravan at Worksworth, on Tuesday night last, on the way to Newhaven fair. It appears that the drivers were putting the vans into the yard of the White Lion Inn, when a carriage, laden with timber, came in contact with the one in which the celebrated lion Wallace, who contended with and defeated the dogs at Warwick, and a very large tigress, were kept, and staved in the whole side of the vehicle. Every pains possible were taken to prevent the beasts obtaining their liberty, by repairing the van as well as circumstances would permit, and by closing the gates of the yard ; but in the course of the night, the beasts, being by nature restless, by some means removed one of the broken pannels, and succeeded in making their escape by the back yard into the fields, where the tigress attacked a number of sheep, and killed three. The lion, finding himself at liberty, was by no means idle, but falling in with some cows belonging to Mr Wilson, killed one, and severely wounded two others. The bleating of sheep, the lowing of the cows, and the roaring of the lion, aroused the keepers and several of the inhabitants, when instant pursuit was made by the whole body in order to kill, or, if possible, to retake them. They first discovered the lion about three or four fields distant, feeding on the cow which had fallen a victim to his unresistible fury. They immediately fronted him as well as their fears would admit, and several shots were fired, though contrary to the orders of the keeper, by which the lion was severely wounded. The infuriated animal suddenly rushed upon a man who was at some distance from him, and before assistance could be rendered, he unfortunately killed him. He then dashed into a cow-shed, where, by the well-known voice of the keepers, and their able management, he was secured, and lodged in a place of safety without further mischief. The party then went in pursuit of the tigress, which had taken another direction, and had fallen in with some persons going to work at the brickfields.

...persons going to work at the brickfields.

The animal attacked a woman with a child in her arms, and a boy of about 11 years of age, all of whom were killed before assistance arrived. On the party coming up they were horror-struck at the spectacle. Every exertion was made to secure the animal, but it was not before she was so dangerously wounded as not to be expected to recover, that that object could be effected. On the following day an inquest was held, when, after a patient investigation, a verdict of Accidental Death was returned, deodand £10 on the beasts. Too much praise cannot be given to Mr Wombwell on the promptness he displayed on hearing the melancholy accident. He expressed the utmost concern, ordered the funerals of the sufferers to take place at his expense, and promised to make good all damages arising from the melancholy event.—*Northampton Herald.*

The following paragraph...

About the text: This text is originally from a local newspaper, the Northampton Herald, in 1835. It was later reprinted as part of a broadside (a single page of reprinted articles) and this is taken from that source. This is why the newspaper is named at the end of the article. The journalist is anonymous.

Vocabulary:

Menagerie - A collection of animals. George Wombwell owned and operated a travelling menagerie, which was something across between a zoo and a circus.

deodand - This technically means forfeited to the Crown (i.e. confiscated) but, in practice, it meant a fine.

defeated the dogs at Warwick - This is a reference to a cruel spectator sport where dogs were made to fight against exotic animals.

Commentary

Here is a list of some of the literary and linguistic features that you may have noticed and the effects that they create:

- Large font draws attention to title. Short phrases that grab attention e.g. 'fearful accident!' and 'four lives lost'. Long preamble explaining events also in large font, but designed to interest reader. Excessive use of three exclamation marks.
- Narrative, story-telling style: 'they first discovered', 'they came upon', etc. Tone of excitement: 'The infuriated animal suddenly rushed'. Some scene-setting that might be more usual in fiction 'The bleating of sheep, the lowing of cows...' used to enhance interest and sense of story.
- Lots of adjectives used to suggest the tragic nature of the events: 'fearful' , 'dreadful' , 'melancholy', 'destroyed', 'horror-struck'. However, the overall sense here is excessive and melodramatic, possibly even slightly gothic.
- Careful and deliberate protection of Wombwell from any blame for the incident. Emphasis on 'Every possible pains were taken' and 'Too much praise cannot be given to Mr. Wombwell'. This may seem unnecessarily forgiving and seems to suggest that the author wants no trouble from a wealthy man and is taking some trouble to rehabilitate his character and business. We might even wonder if the author has been paid to do this.

The author's purpose here is to inform readers of this local incident. However, there is also a strong sense of this article being written to entertain. There seems to be a secondary purpose to absolve Wombwell from any allegations of wrongdoing.

Task

Following the advice given earlier in this topic, create an essay plan for a critical evaluation of this text.

Commentary - An Example Essay Plan

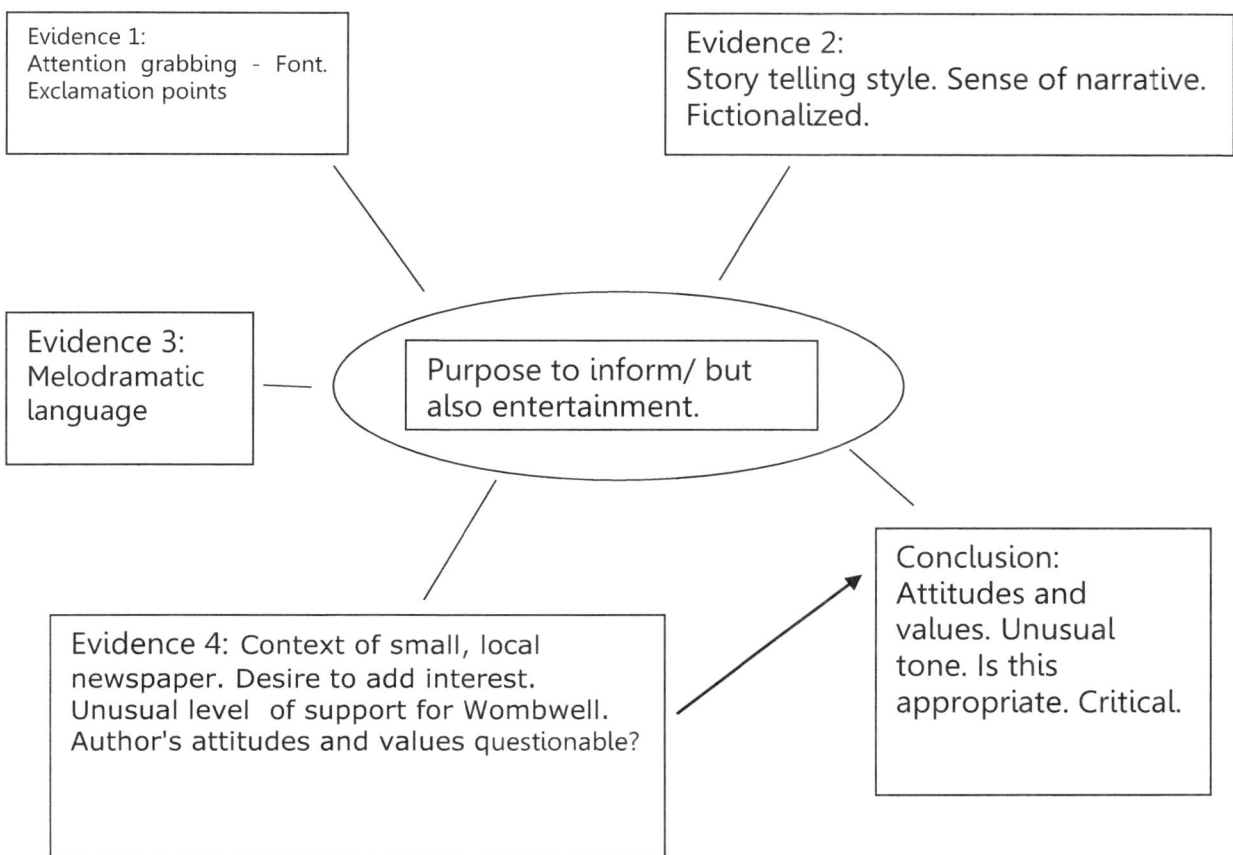

Evidence 1:
Attention grabbing - Font. Exclamation points

Evidence 2:
Story telling style. Sense of narrative. Fictionalized.

Evidence 3:
Melodramatic language

Purpose to inform/ but also entertainment.

Evidence 4: Context of small, local newspaper. Desire to add interest. Unusual level of support for Wombwell. Author's attitudes and values questionable?

Conclusion:
Attitudes and values. Unusual tone. Is this appropriate. Critical.

Task

Using your own plan, or the example plan given above, write a full answer to this exam-style question.

Commentary

This is an example of an essay that you could have written in response to this question. Your own answer is likely to be different. As with all the commentaries in this course, this is only an example of what you could have written.

As you read this answer, think about its strengths and weaknesses.

There is a fuller commentary below.

This 1835 article from a local newspaper, the Northampton Herald, is superficially written to inform readers of a terrible accident that occurred when a lion and a tiger escaped from a travelling menagerie and killed several people before being recaptured. However, we will note from the salacious tone of the article, that it is also written to entertain readers. It might be suggested that local newspaper journalists rarely have an incident as strange and unusual as this to write about, and so this author has chosen to extract maximum interest here in order to engage readers. The journalist capitalises on the bizarre circumstances of these events in order to write a highly entertaining piece that is likely to amuse, rather than horrify, readers.

We can immediately see the attention grabbing way that the article has been written from the large font and short headline sentences used to open the article. These short minor sentences 'Fearful accident!' and 'Four lives lost' are brief and attention grabbing. They have more impact because of the absence of any particles or verbs. The use of an exclamation mark after 'Fearful accident!' creates a sense of urgency and importance. However, the use of three exclamation marks after 'destroyed' seems excessive. If anything, this actually seems to lighten the mood of the article.

For an article, this text is quite narrative in tone. It is told in the style of a story, describing events as they occur. This is shown in phrases such as 'they first discovered' and 'they came upon'. The tone is often one of excitement, and the language used is colourful and immediate. This is shown in the sentence 'The infuriated animal suddenly rushed' where the adjective 'infuriated' adds a sense of the lion's rage and creates some alliteration on the 'in' in infuriated and 'an' in animal. Together with the verb 'rushed' this helps to create a sense of the animal speeding towards them. There are also some descriptive, scene-setting phrases, such as 'The bleating of sheep, the lowing of cows...' which are used to enhance interest and sense of story. Description of this type is much more usual in fiction than in news reporting, and its presence here helps to create a strong sense of narrative.

The author's use of language, however, is not always appropriate. The deaths of several people are not an obviously amusing subject matter, and the author has been careful not to treat these deaths too lightly. Although the author has made some attempt to give weight to these sad events by using adjectives such as 'fearful', 'dreadful' and 'melancholy', the overall effect of this is excessive and melodramatic. The lexical field here might even be thought of slightly gothic in tone, as if the author is trying to utilise forms from popular fiction. Indeed, in the phrase 'horror-struck by the spectacle', it seems likely that 'spectacle' is the operative word. We get a sense that the author, despite his surface disavowals, is actually both enjoying the tragedy and trying to make it as engaging as possible. This also shows that this article has been highly fictionalized, and the effect on the reader is more like that of reading fiction than journalism.

There are some areas, however, where the author is aware that he is writing about real-life events rather than fiction. Throughout the article, he is very careful not to offend Mr. Wombwell, the owner of the escaped animals. He carefully shields him from blame, emphasising that 'Every possible pains were taken' to avoid their escape and stating that 'Too much praise cannot be given to Mr. Wombwell'. This may seem unusually forgiving when we consider that four people were killed in this accident and that two of them were small children. Today, we might question this whether it is appropriate to keep animals in small, travelling cages at all as this does not seem very humane. Another author might use this event to suggest that keeping animals in travelling zoos is dangerous and cruel and should be avoided. However, the author of this article does not question this practice and seems to find no fault with it.

We may imagine that the author of this piece, as a local rather than a national journalist, does not experience events as bizarre as this very often and that he has tried to exploit the opportunity to write an engaging article here. However, we might also ask whether this is very appropriate, given the nature of this subject matter. On the one hand, this article is very successful. It is amusing, entertaining, exciting and well-written. On the other hand, however, the actual content is quite sad and the event described would have been very traumatic for the people involved.

In conclusion, the author's style, tone and language choices attempt to fictionalize the events he describes. This may be intended to make the entertainment value that he draws from this story more acceptable and less noticeable to readers. However, these events are not fictional, but refer to a real-life accident in which four people were killed. We might expect that a modern author would treat an event like this with a lot more seriousness and respect.

This is a full commentary on the above essay. Note the comments in red detail the strengths and weaknesses of this essay.

This 1835 article from a local newspaper, the Northampton Herald, is superficially written to inform readers of a terrible accident that occurred when a lion and a tiger escaped from a travelling menagerie and killed several people before being recaptured. However, we will note from the salacious tone of the article, that it is also written to entertain readers. It might be suggested that local newspaper journalists rarely have an incident as strange and unusual as this to write about, and so this author has chosen to extract maximum interest here in order to engage readers. The journalist capitalises on the bizarre circumstances of these events in order to write a highly entertaining piece that is likely to amuse, rather than horrify, readers.

We can immediately see the attention grabbing way that the article has been written from the large font and short headline sentences used to open the article. These short minor sentences 'Fearful accident!' and 'Four lives lost' are brief and attention grabbing. They have more impact because of the absence of any particles or verbs. The use of an exclamation mark after 'Fearful accident!' creates a sense of urgency and importance. However, the use of three exclamation marks after 'destroyed' seems excessive. If anything, this actually seems to lighten the mood of the article.

For an article, this text is quite narrative in tone. It is told in the style of a story, describing events as they occur. This is shown in phrases such as 'they first discovered' and 'they came upon'. The tone is often one of excitement, and the language used is colourful and immediate. This is shown in the sentence 'The infuriated animal suddenly rushed' where the adjective 'infuriated' adds a sense of the lion's rage and creates some alliteration on the 'in' in infuriated and 'an' in animal. Together with the verb 'rushed' this helps to create a sense of the animal speeding towards them. There are also some descriptive, scene-setting phrases, such as 'The bleating of sheep, the lowing of cows...' which are used to enhance interest and sense of story. Description of this type is much more usual in fiction than in news reporting, and its presence here helps to create a strong sense of narrative.

Comment [hb1]: A good opening that shows an immediate awareness of context.

Comment [hb2]: Good. This hints that a deeper meaning will be explored and builds interest in the argument put forward.

Comment [hb3]: Awareness of purpose.

Comment [hb4]: This is a good summary of the content. You don't need to explain the content of the article in more detail than this.

Comment [hb5]: Good linking of purpose and tone.

Comment [hb6]: This might sound a bit dismissive of local paper journalists, but it is an effective way of exploring how genre and context can affect the author's choice of style.

Comment [hb7]: Good use of terminology, well integrated into the discussion.

Comment [hb8]: A good use of direct quotation, included as part of the student's own sentence.

Comment [hb9]: repetition of attention grabbing is stylistically poor. A new, different phrase could've been used here.

Comment [hb10]: Good awareness of parts of speech and their effects.

Comment [hb11]: Good awareness of punctuation and its effects.

Comment [hb12]: There is some attempt to link these paragraphs together through repetition of 'article' but this is not wholly effective.

Comment [hb13]: Good use of analytical language and short, direct quotations.

Comment [hb14]: There is some good, detailed analysis of language here. Note the way the student has selected a short phrase, but analysed it in detail to draw out its meaning fully.

Comment [hb15]: This is a good sentence which both shows awareness of genre conventions and sets up the coming argument.

The author's use of language, however, is not always appropriate. The deaths of several people are not an obviously amusing subject matter, and the author has been careful not to treat these deaths too lightly. Although the author has made some attempt to give weight to these sad events by using adjectives such as 'fearful', 'dreadful' and 'melancholy', the overall effect of this is excessive and melodramatic. The lexical field here might even be thought of slightly gothic in tone, as if the author is trying to utilise forms from popular fiction. Indeed, in the phrase 'horror-struck by the spectacle', it seems likely that 'spectacle' is the operative word. We get a sense that the author, despite his surface disavowals, is actually both enjoying the tragedy and trying to make it as engaging as possible. This also shows that this article has been highly fictionalized, and the effect on the reader is more like that of reading fiction than journalism.

There are some areas, however, where the author is aware that he is writing about real-life events rather than fiction. Throughout the article, he is very careful not to offend Mr. Wombwell, the owner of the escaped animals. He carefully shields him from blame, emphasising that 'Every possible pains were taken' to avoid their escape and stating that 'Too much praise cannot be given to Mr. Wombwell'. This may seem unusually forgiving when we consider that four people were killed in this accident and that two of them were small children. Today, we might question this whether it is appropriate to keep animals in small, travelling cages at all as this does not seem very humane. Another author might use this event to suggest that keeping animals in travelling zoos is dangerous and cruel and should be avoided. However, the author of this article does not question this practice and seems to find no fault with it.

We may imagine that the author of this piece, as a local rather than a national journalist, does not experience events as bizarre as this very often and that he has tried to exploit the opportunity to write an engaging article here. However, we might also ask whether this is very appropriate, given the nature of this subject matter. On the one hand, this article is very successful. It is amusing, entertaining, exciting and well-written. On the other hand,

Comment [hb16]: There is an attempt to link these paragraphs through discussion of language, but it is not a completely natural link. It does set up a debate 'however' and this adds interest.

Comment [hb17]: Good. Consideration of author's intentions.

Comment [hb18]: Good awareness of the effects of language. Also note that although we are usually interested in the author's intentions, this effect may not be what the author intended. This shows a critical approach to the text.

Comment [hb19]: Awareness of linguistic terminology.

Comment [hb20]: Good awareness of the effects of language, style and tone on the reader.

Comment [hb21]: This is, again, a slightly awkward transition between paragraphs.

Comment [hb22]: Good. Although a generalisation, this shows awareness of how attitudes have changed over time.

Comment [hb23]: Good summary of the author's attitudes and values.

Comment [hb24]: Good awareness of the author's context.

Comment [hb25]: This sets up some debate and leads up to the final conclusion.

however, the actual content is quite sad and the event described would have been very traumatic for the people involved.

In conclusion, the author's style, tone and language choices attempt to fictionalize the events he describes. This

> **Comment [hb26]:** This is a good summary of the essay's overall argument.

may be intended to make the entertainment value that he draws from this story more acceptable and less noticeable to readers. However, these events are not fictional, but refer to a real-life accident in which four people were killed. We might expect that a modern author would treat an event like this with a lot more seriousness and respect.

> **Comment [hb27]:** This is dubious, as many modern journalists would be exactly as exploitative as this, if not more so. However, this student has broadened out the issue successfully in order to make a more wide reaching point about the nature of journalism.

This is a good answer to this question and this student has done well here. This essay has a strong overall argument and this overall argument progresses clearly through the essay. The framework ideas of genre, purpose, context, attitudes and values are well explored and are used to make meaningful comments on the article as a whole.

The student identifies and explores some the literary and linguistic features and this is well integrated and forms part of the development of the overall argument. She chooses select examples in order to analyse the language used in detail. There are appropriate references to linguistic terminology that enhance the argument and show the student's understanding of the author's technique. There is a strong awareness of context throughout.

There are a few areas for development. This student could work on linking these paragraphs together more neatly. If you look back at the essay plan, can you see that this might always have been a problem with this choice of material?

Revising Unseen Texts

In this topic, we have had extensive practice of answering an exam question on an unseen text.

The exam may seem a long way away at the moment, but it is important to keep practising your skills in reading unseen texts between now and the exam. The more you can practice your skills, the easier you will find the exam.

One good way to practice your critical reading skills is to read a newspaper at least every week, and if possible, every day. You can vary the newspaper that you read, so that you can get a sense of different styles of publication.

As part of your reading, keep a look out for any articles you find that describe 'encounters' of any kind. Keep thinking about how different authors describe different types of encounters.

You will notice that this revision technique is similar to the suggested revision technique for practising unseen texts in Component 1. It is therefore doubly useful as revision practice. It is important to get used to reading as much as possible and to practice your skills on real-life examples of English language.

Now that we have completed our work on unseen texts, we can move onto the second part of Component 2.

Task

When you come to revise for the exam, you may want some additional unseen texts to practice on. It is a good idea, therefore, to start collecting some now.

Try to get in the habit of reading at least one newspaper a week. As you undertake your weekly reading, collect examples of any articles that describe 'encounters'.

You can also collect examples from other sources, such as magazines, TV guides and advertisements.

By the time you come to revise, you will have forgotten the content of these articles and you will be able to use them as unseen text practice.

(There is no commentary on this activity.)

Topic 8 – Introducing Section B: Prose Fiction and Other Genres

Introduction

In this topic, we will look at the requirements of Section B of the exam.

Aims and Objectives

- To learn about Section B of the exam

Section B: Prose Fiction and Other Genres

In Section B of the exam, you will answer an essay question with reference to two texts. The two texts that we will be studying for this section are:

Anchor Text:
Emily Bronte – *Wuthering Heights*

Other Text:
Angela Carter – *The Bloody Chamber*

As with Section A, the theme is Encounters.

Form of Exam Question

In this exam, the question will be in the form:

Answer this question with reference to the TWO texts that you have studied from the list below.

Wuthering Heights

The Bloody Chamber

Question [X]

Evaluate the effectiveness of the methods used by the writers of your two studied texts to present encounters that [...].

In your response you must consider the use of linguistic and literary features, connections across texts and relevant contextual factors.

How to Answer the Question

Similarly to other questions in A-Level English Language and Literature, in this question you are asked to specifically comment on three aspects of the texts

- Linguistic and literary features
- Relevant contextual factors
- Connections across texts

We have already looked at how to analyse linguistic and literary features, and how to think about relevant contextual factors.

For this question, you will also need to look at connections across texts. This means that you will need to think about the links between the two texts. This is not a straightforward comparison and you don't need to use a comparative structure for your essay. Instead, think about how connections between the texts can be used to learn more about each text individually. Think about how our knowledge of the texts is increased by looking at both texts against each other. What does one text teach us about both? You can then use these ideas to help you evaluate the effectiveness of the authors' techniques.

This is a slightly different style of question to those that we have encountered so far. However, with practice, you will find that this style of question allows for a flexible, interesting and sophisticated response.

In the next topic, we will start studying our first text: *Wuthering Heights*.

Task

The best way to learn the requirements of the exam is to look at past exam papers. These are available on the Edexcel website.

Have a look at these exam papers. You will not be able to answer the questions yet, but you should familiarise yourself with what you will need to do in the exam.

There is no commentary on this activity.

Topic 9 – *Wuthering Heights*

Introduction

In this topic, we will begin our study of *Wuthering Heights*. This is the anchor text for Section B of the exam. Again, we will be focusing on the theme of Encounters.

Aims and Objectives

- To gain an introduction to *Wuthering Heights*
- To learn about Emily Bronte and her place in the Bronte family
- To consider the setting of the novel

An Introduction to *Wuthering Heights*

Wuthering Heights is a tale of passion, desire, love, hate, violence, revenge and loss.

It is a dark, complex, and sometimes violent novel, which has attracted a large number of different interpretations. Indeed, many of its early readers were shocked by its uncertain morality. In 1870, the Bradford Mechanics Institute described it as a 'very wicked book'[18] and Graham's Lady Magazine wrote 'It is a compound of vulgar depravity and unnatural horrors'.[19] Early nineteenth century readers expected an author to have a clear moral standpoint and to use the events of their novels to argue that particular view. Wuthering Heights does not do this. Instead, we, as readers, are invited to make up our own minds as to how we should interpret the characters and events. It is this multiplicity of readings that makes the novel so interesting to study.

There are many different kinds of encounters between different characters. Some of these encounters are humorous, some are loving, some are violent and some are kind. Conflicts over class, family, religion, property and propriety occur throughout the novel. These conflicts are not always satisfactorily resolved.

---

[18]As cited in Patsy Stoneman 'Introduction' in Emily Bronte *Wuthering Heights* (Oxford World Classics, 2008) p. viii

[19] Graham's Lady Magazine cited 'Wuthering Heights' Wikipedia 09/12/2014

The novel revolves around Cathy and Heathcliff, whose intense relationship forms the centre of the novel. The story involves the intertwining of two families (the Earnshaws and the Lintons) and two houses (Wuthering Heights and Thrushcross Grange). Deeply rooted in the social, cultural and physical environment of West Yorkshire, it is the setting of the novel that readers often find most memorable.

This Yorkshire setting was inspired by Emily's Bronte's life in the parsonage at Haworth in the West Riding.

The Bronte Family

Emily Bronte came from a very imaginative family. From an early age, she and her siblings would make up their own stories set in complex fictional worlds. Reading, writing and storytelling were the children's main interests and occupations. All three of the Bronte sisters went on to become authors.

Some critics have speculated that this rich imaginative life may have stemmed from the Bronte family's sadness and relative isolation. Their father Patrick Bronte was an Anglican clergyman and the family lived in the parsonage at Haworth. Close to the wild moorland and overlooking the graveyard, this location inspired much of their later creative work.

To some extent, the family were socially isolated within the village. Too well educated to be considered working class and not wealthy enough to be considered middle class, the family suffered from a marginal and uncertain status. Sadly, their mother died in 1821 and was tragically followed by the eldest Bronte children, Maria and Elizabeth, who died of tuberculosis in 1825. This left four remaining children Charlotte, Branwell, Emily and Anne.

Economic uncertainties plagued the family. Branwell found it difficult to find and keep a job and there were few career opportunities for the sisters. As educated women, their main option was teaching and they each found work as school teachers in boarding schools, a very demanding position. Emily's job in a school at Law Hill required working 17 hours a day and she returned to Haworth, exhausted, within 18 months. Emily thereafter remained at Haworth where she felt most comfortable, acting as housekeeper to the family.

Charlotte and Anne continued working as both schoolteachers and governesses and the family planned one day to open their own school. Charlotte also came up with a new idea to increase their income and decided that they might attempt to publish their poetry. A book of the sister's collected verse was published in 1846 using the male pseudonyms of Curer, Ellis and Acton Bell. Unfortunately, it attracted little attention and only a few copies were sold.

Undeterred, the Brontes then turned their attention to the more commercial practice of novel writing and all three of the sisters published novels in 1847. Curer Bell (Charlotte) published Jane Eyre, Ellis (Emily) published Wuthering Heights and Acton (Anne) published Agnes Grey. Jane Eyre was a particular success and it was republished the following year under Charlotte's real name. This paved the way for Emily and Anne to also publish under their own names, although Emily, who was an extremely private person and valued her anonymity, may not have been pleased by this development. Despite Emily's reticence, however, the Brontes became one the most significant literary families of the nineteenth century.

Emily Bronte

Little is known about Emily Bronte. She was reserved and solitary and she had few contacts outside of her family. Consequently, unlike most authors, she wrote few letters and information about her is therefore rare. Most of what is known about her comes from her sister Charlotte, who is also known to be a less than reliable source of information.

Emily died only a year after the publication of Wuthering Heights, probably from tuberculosis. Despite her failing health, she refused to rest or seek treatment and insisted on continuing with her housekeeping tasks until the day she died. From all accounts, she was a brave and strong-willed woman. Describing her death, Charlotte wrote of her immense strength:

I have seen nothing like it; but, indeed, I have never seen her parallel in anything. Stronger than a man, simpler than a child, her nature stood alone.[20]

She died at home in Haworth in 1848.

One thing that is known for certain about Emily Bronte is that she loved nature. One of her favourite activities was to walk alone on the moors.

Setting

One of the most memorable aspects of *Wuthering Heights* is its setting. Set within the striking landscape of the Yorkshire moors, the locations of the novel are much more than just background; they are a central part of the characterization and symbolism of the novel.

Terminology

Characterisation - Characterisation is the process by which an author conveys character. In Wuthering Heights, locations are themselves symbolic of character.

Symbolism - Symbolism is the process where an aspect of novel can illustrate a wider theme. For example, Thrushcross Grange is a physical house, but is also symbolic of the civilised lives of the higher classes.

Pathetic Fallacy - Pathetic Fallacy is a literary term for the use of weather conditions or landscapes to reflect the characters' emotions or illustrate the themes of a novel.

The Sublime - The Sublime produces a sense of awe. It was a C18th concept (associated with Edmund Burke) which identified particular landscapes, such as the vast mountain ranges of the Alps, with a aura of the great and infinite. The sublime therefore provokes a sense of terror in its audience, but this is a pleasurable kind of terror. It is a concept associated with strong feelings, that is often juxtaposed with the Enlightenment values of restraint and rationality.

---

[20] Charlotte Bronte cited by Rod Megham in *Penguin Critical Studies: Wuthering Heights* (Penguin, London, 1989) p.11

There are three main settings in the novel.

Wuthering Heights

Wuthering Heights is a farmhouse. It is set in a high, isolated location. The building is dark with narrow windows and it is full of hidden corners and recesses. The name 'Wuthering' suggests the weathering action of the wind and emphasises the barren situation.

Thrushcross Grange

Thrushcross Grange is a fine house, surrounded by gardens. It is a place of refinement and culture. It is frequently associated with light and fine decorations, such as the candelabra that Cathy and Heathcliff first see on their first visit to the Grange. It is thus a structural opposite to Wuthering Heights.

The Moors

There is actually surprisingly little direct description in *Wuthering Heights* and yet the dominant image the reader retains is of the wild and desolate landscape of the moors; a location as bleak as it is beautiful.

Task

The setting of Wuthering Heights was inspired by the Pennine moors around Haworth in West Yorkshire.

Using an online search engine, find some images of this moorland landscape. These will give you a sense of the landscape of the novel.

If you are lucky enough to live in Yorkshire, you may like to take a day-trip to the area.

There is no commentary on this activity.

Topic 10 – Chapter One

Introduction

In this topic, we will begin reading *Wuthering Heights*.

Aims and Objectives

- To read the first chapter of Wuthering Heights
- To think about Lockwood's role as narrator
- To consider some of the similarities between Lockwood and Heathcliff

Beginnings

Wuthering Heights starts with the arrival of Lockwood in Yorkshire. Lockwood has rented Thrushcross Grange from Heathcliff and in this chapter he describes how he goes to meet his landlord for the first time.

The novel begins in 1801, at the start of a new century.

> Task
>
> Read Chapter One of Wuthering Heights.

Lockwood's Role as Narrator

Lockwood is the first narrator of Wuthering Heights. He begins his narrative almost as a diary entry and his narrative style is self-conscious and literary. As an educated and cultured man, Lockwood's role as narrator is to guide the reader into the novel. He appears as the representative of the civilised world of the city, who leads us into the strange and impassioned environment of the Heights. His curiosity mirrors our own.

However, we soon notice that Lockwood is not quite as he seems. There is a real discrepancy between what Lockwood says and does. Lockwood first claims to be unsociable, yet he makes a great effort to visit his landlord uninvited. He speaks excessively politely, but his thoughts are often unkind and the tone of his narrative is often sarcastic. When he 'charitably conjectures' there is nothing whatsoever that is charitable about it. We learn that Lockwood is in fact fleeing society for a time after gaining a reputation for 'heartlessness', and his vacillating behaviour towards the young woman at the seaside further illustrates the difference between Lockwood's words and his actions. There is something fundamentally disingenuous about Lockwood, although he may not himself be aware of this.

Lockwood is very keen to read elements of his own assumed personality into Heathcliff's conduct, even though we, as readers, can see little basis for this. When Heathcliff doesn't open the gate for Lockwood, it makes Lockwood only more determined to go in. Lockwood believes that Heathcliff's misanthropy is merely an affectation, and that Heathcliff is merely 'exaggeratedly reserved'. As readers, we can tell that Heathcliff has no interest in entertaining his tenant and that his brusqueness is absolutely genuine.

Bronte makes us aware of this aspect of Lockwood's character when he notes that 'I bestow my own attributes over-liberally on him'. Yet Lockwood generally seems determined to find in Heathcliff something of a kindred spirit. Lockwood seems to think of this similarity as a mutual sense of civility and reserve, but it is more likely to be the existence of barely repressed violence.

In any case, these obvious inaccuracies in Lockwood's reporting of events lead us to doubt his reliability as a narrator and to question his judgements. Far from reassuring the reader, Lockwood's insincerity actually adds a note of disquiet to the narrative.

Heathcliff and Lockwood

Lockwood and Heathcliff at first seem to be polar opposites. Lockwood represents culture and civility, while Heathcliff represents a wilder and more natural state of being. This is shown in the language that they use.

Lockwood's style is highly literary and his sentences use a sophisticated vocabulary and are highly artificial. When Lockwood introduces himself it is 'to express the hope that I have not inconvenienced you by my perseverance in soliciting the occupation of Thrushcross Grange' and this sentence, with its many circumlocutions, borders on the ridiculous.

Heathcliff is far more direct. Although he is 'in speech and manners a gentleman' and can answer Lockwood using the same forms of sophisticated speech, he is generally far more brief. He speaks only when it is necessary and many of his questions are short and to the point, with no extraneous words, such as "Not bitten, are you?" As Heathcliff relaxes, Lockwood tells us that his speech becomes more informal 'chipping off his pronouns and auxiliary verbs'.

As we look closer, however, we see that there are similarities between Lockwood and Heathcliff.

Indeed, Lockwood's affected and civilised language is only a veneer over a much baser and more unpleasant character. Even though Heathcliff tells him not to annoy the dogs, he spends the few minutes he has alone pulling faces at them. He goads the dogs until they attack him, then responds with surprise and with violence, beating them with a poker.

Heathcliff is pleased by Lockwood's violence and seems to warm to Lockwood after he threatens to 'set my signet' on any dog that bites him. We can see from this that both men share a propensity towards violence and the enjoyment of violence.
We could therefore argue that Heathcliff and Lockwood are parallels, rather than opposites.

Task

Using a dictionary, look up the meaning of the word penetralium. What is the significance of Lockwood using this word here?

Commentary

'Pentralia' are the inner rooms of a house or temple. Pentralium is a singular form of this plural noun that was commonly used in the eighteenth and nineteenth centuries. It is a Latinate word (from Latin) and is a fairly obscure architectural term that only classically educated people would recognise.

In using this word, Lockwood shows off his erudition and emphasises his status as a member of civilised society. He aims to present himself as a cultured and well-educated man, and to elevate the status of the house.

However, this description of Wuthering Heights seems strange and jarring. Indeed, pentralium is an incongruous word that does not suit a crumbling farmhouse. As readers, we notice this odd word and this draws attention to Lockwood and his narration. In this way, Bronte is telling us more about Lockwood. Lockwood's use of inappropriate vocabulary exposes him as showy, false, and oblivious to the reality of a situation.

Topic 11 – Chapter Two

Introduction

In this topic, we will read Chapter Two of *Wuthering Heights* and consider the significance of the encounters in this chapter.

Aims and Objectives

- To read Chapter Two
- To examine some of the encounters in Chapter Two and to consider their significance

Chapter Two

Despite knowing that Heathcliff does not want him to visit again, Lockwood decides to play a second visit to Wuthering Heights. Once there, he has a variety of unusual and amusing encounters.

Task

Read Chapter Two of *Wuthering Heights*.

Encounters

Lockwood is completely unprepared for the environment of the Heights and has no idea of how to respond to it. He is used to the civilised, social world where people are unfailingly polite and courteous, while Wuthering Heights is a working farmhouse, and a place where many of the normal social conventions are not adhered to.

Lockwood's lack of experience causes him to make a series of embarrassing blunders. First, he refers to Mrs. Heathcliff as the lady of the house and is surprised that she does not offer him a warmer welcome. He misunderstands all the relationships between the characters, thinking first that Mrs. Heathcliff is Heathcliff's wife, then that she is Hareton's wife, and that Hareton is Heathcliff's son.

More fundamentally, he misunderstands many of the inhabitants' attitudes as well as their relationships. Lockwood doesn't understand their misery and he cannot believe that the 'universal scowl they wore was their every day countenance'. His description of Mrs Heathcliff as a 'beneficent fairy' is singularly inappropriate for such an unhappy woman. Hareton he dismisses as 'repulsive' and laughs at him 'internally', even though Hareton has shown him more consideration than the rest of the family.

He expects a genteel and civilised home and 'a pleasant family circle' and he cannot at first reconcile himself to the realities of the Heights. Amusingly, he mistakes a heap of dead rabbits for a cushion of pet cats, again showing his lack of familiarity with a working farm. His own expectations and the way that custom has moulded his own 'tastes and ideas' is responsible for the many mistakes that he makes.

As Lockwood becomes more exasperated, he loses patience with his host. He stops thinking so positively of Heathcliff and begins to think that Heathcliff has 'a genuine bad nature'. He even thinks that Joseph's insult towards Mrs Heathcliff is intended for him.

Finally, he runs off, takes a lantern and, after being knocked down by the dogs, his rage causes him to get a nosebleed, much to Heathcliff and Hareton's amusement. As Zillah (the housekeeper) splashes freezing water over his bleeding face, Lockwood realises he has no choice but to spend the night at Wuthering Heights.

Speech in the Text

Wuthering Heights is set in Yorkshire and the working class characters typically speak in a broad Yorkshire dialect. Joseph's speech has been written phonetically, in order to convey the way his words sound. This is a way for an author to convey speech realistically and to create a strong sense of character and place. It is a effective way to create a clear sense of voice.

Interestingly, in the second edition of *Wuthering Heights*, Emily's sister Charlotte Bronte considerably edited Joseph's dialect to make it more readable. This has been seen by some literary critics as part of Charlotte's aim of civilising *Wuthering Heights* in order to make it more palatable for a middle-class audience. Most modern editions, however, have returned to Emily Bronte's original spellings.

Glossary

dahn – down

rahnd - round

un war – and worse

a nowt – a nothing

aght – out

shoo - she

If you find Joseph's speech difficult to read, then you may like to try reading it out loud, as the sounds of the words will help you to understand their meaning. Many editions of the novel also come with notes at the back, containing 'translations' of Joseph's dialect.

Task

1) In the table below, tick which characteristics best suit Lockwood or Heathcliff.

	Interior	Exterior	Culture	Nature	Civilised	Wild
Lockwood						
Heathcliff						

2) Think of some similarities of character shown by the two men in this chapter.

3) Lockwood fails to understand life at the Heights. What do you think that Bronte is suggesting by this?

Commentary

1)

	Interior	Exterior	Culture	Nature	Civilised	Wild
Lockwood	√		√		√	
Heathcliff		√		√		√

2) In Chapter Two, as in Chapter One, both Heathcliff and Lockwood are shown to have volatile and violent natures. Like Heathcliff, Lockwood is quick to anger. When he thinks that Joseph has insulted him, his immediate thought is of 'kicking him out the door'. Lockwood is impulsive and irrational. Considering himself insulted by Heathcliff's refusal to let him sleep alone and unsupervised, Lockwood's immediate and ill-thought out desire is to escape. Joseph's lantern is 'seized unceremoniously'. He then describes himself as 'trembling with wrath' until his anger causes him to have a nosebleed.

3) Lockwood's inability to understand life at the Heights suggests that the reader should not judge the inhabitants according to the usual standards of polite society. From this, it seems that Bronte is suggesting that the civilised world cannot comprehend life at the Heights and that we, as readers, should also try to evaluate their world on its own terms. By understanding Lockwood as a deeply artificial character who represses (only partly successfully) his naturally violent inclinations, we are encouraged to recognise and evaluate the divide between culture and nature.

We might argue that Bronte encourages us to view the lives of the inhabitants of Wuthering Heights as a wild, passionate existence, deeply rooted in the natural environment. It is an existence far removed from the artificial culture represented by Lockwood. This has important implications for our overall interpretation of the novel.

Topic 12 – Ghostly Encounters

Introduction

In this topic, we will read Chapter Three of Wuthering Heights. We will think about the use of elements of the gothic genre in the novel and consider the significance of dreams and ghosts.

Aims and Objectives

- To read Chapter Three of Wuthering Heights.
- To gain an overview of the gothic genre and its application to the novel
- To appreciate the significance of dreams and ghosts in the novel

Chapter Three

In this chapter, Lockwood goes to sleep in a strange room where he is plagued by weird dreams.

Task
Read Chapter Three.

Wuthering Heights and the Gothic Genre

The opening of this chapter may feel familiar to you. Many ghost stories and works of gothic fiction include a scene where a housekeeper leads a guest through a maze of dark, winding corridors to spend the night in a room that has been closed up for years. Because this form of story is familiar to us, when we learn that no-one ever sleeps in this room, we suspect that it may be because it is haunted. In this way, Bronte leads us to expect a haunting of some kind. This means that, when Lockwood dreams of Cathy, we immediately feel that she is a real ghost. Unlike Lockwood, we do not think that this is merely a dream.

This chapter has many features of the gothic genre, and these give us an insight into some of the ways that we might read and interpret Wuthering Heights. The gothic genre is a literary form that is deeply concerned with the supernatural, with intense human emotions and with the relationship between good and evil.

Features of the Gothic

Gothic writing also tends to make use of particular devices, some of which are present in this chapter. References to dreams, for example, are a common feature of gothic writing.

Bronte's references to the gothic are almost certainly intentional. Therefore, we must ask ourselves why she has chosen to draw attention to this genre and what she is trying to say.

The Gothic Genre and the Violence in *Wuthering Heights*

The gothic genre also has further significance here. It seems likely that this mode of expression is well suited to the intensity of emotion displayed in the world of *Wuthering Heights*. The gothic genre's exploration of good and evil is also evident within the novel, which asks profound questions about human behaviour and challenges conventional morality.

The intensities of gothic fiction are also shown in the violence of this chapter. Lockwood responds to Cathy's ghost with extreme violence. We are told how he 'pulled its wrist on to the broken pane, and rubbed it to and fro till the blood ran down'. The violence of this (committed against a child) is quite shocking, even by modern standards. Indeed, it is likely that Bronte intends to shock.

Violence is an important and persistent feature of the world of *Wuthering Heights*; in Lockwood's first dream, we are shown how even a sermon-meeting descends into violence. This illustrates the importance of the themes of tolerance, anger, self-control and violence. Through these themes, Bronte raises important questions about human behaviour.

Dreams

Dreams are often used in gothic fiction. In this chapter, Lockwood has two dreams.

In the first dream, he imagines that he is listening to a sermon by a preacher called Jabes Branderham. The text of the sermon is Seventy Times Seven and the First of the Seventy First. This is a reference to the Gospel of Matthew, Chapter 18. Emily Bronte (and most nineteenth century readers) would have been very familiar with the Bible and would have understood the significance of this.

In this Biblical passage, Jesus tells his disciples that they should forgive a sin not only 7 times, but 70 x 7 times. This is usually interpreted to mean that sins should be forgiven infinitely. However, in the dream Lockwood forgives Branderham literally 490 times before he feels he has been patient for long enough. He forgives the sins in each of the 70 groups of 7, but at the 1st sin of the 71st (group of 7), he becomes enraged. He has therefore committed the sin of the First of the Seventy First, which is the failure to forgive.[21]

It may be that Bronte is therefore asking complex questions about how much suffering we should tolerate and whether it is possible to forgive infinitely. The literary critic Andrew Marsh see this as part of a pattern of absolutes and limitations within the novel. In this very interesting theory, Marsh sees the novel as an exploration of the tension between the limited and the limitless.[22]

We can also conclude from this (as Marsh does) that dreams have symbolic power in the novel. Bronte has clearly put considerable effort into creating Lockwood's dreams and the themes that they explore are significant and meaningful for the wider story.

In the second dream, we return to gothic imagery with Lockwood's encounter with Cathy's ghost. In this dream, 'the intense horror of nightmare came over me' and this wonderfully gothic phrase sets up our expectations for what is about to occur.

Ghosts

We have already discussed how the conventions of the gothic genre lead us to expect a haunting. There are also other ways that Bronte prepares us for the reality of the supernatural.

---

[21] See discussion in Andrew Marsh *Analysing Texts Series - Emily Bronte: Wuthering Heights* (Palgrave Macmillan, 1999) p.137
[22] Andrew Marsh *Analysing Texts Series - Emily Bronte: Wuthering Heights* p. 154

At the beginning of the chapter, we are told how the letters of Catherine's names, carved into the windowsill, 'started from the dark, as vivid as spectres'. This use of 'spectre' as a simile makes us immediately think of ghosts. This is also what later happens, as Cathy's ghostly face literally appears in the darkness outside the window, and her name takes on a quasi-physical form. This symmetry is further emphasised in the way that Lockwood describes how 'the air swarmed with Catherines'. The verb 'swarm' is then repeated when Lockwood describes the room as 'swarming with ghosts and goblins!' The repetition of this verb therefore strongly suggests that the ghost is Catherine, and therefore that the ghost is real.

Lockwood also recalls how the graveyard soil 'is said to answer all the purposes of embalming' and this creates a mildly grisly image and makes us think of the life of the body (as well as the ghost or the soul) after death. Again, this creates the sense of gothic horror and of the fantastic that allows us to believe in the reality of Cathy's ghost when she appears.

Knowing that Lockwood's vision of Cathy at Wuthering Heights is more than a dream means that we cannot dismiss this haunting as easily as Lockwood does. The supernatural elements of *Wuthering Heights* are important and they bring a new level of meaning to the novel. In short, this is much more than a story about property and propriety. It is a story of a love powerful enough to transcend death.

Ambiguity

Not all readers, however, would agree with the interpretation that I have presented here.

Many readers have not been convinced that the ghosts in Wuthering Heights are presented as real. Some feel that Bronte is deliberately ambiguous, so as to allow readers to make their own decision as to whether the ghosts are real or not.

This raises the possibility of a different interpretation. If the ghosts exist only in the minds of the characters, then this could change how we understand the novel. Instead of being a story of a powerful love, it could become a story of intense emotions leading to madness. This reading of the novel has a greater focus on the absolute, limited, 'real' world, and less focus on the limitless, boundless 'other' world: the world of the 'other'.

It is important to realise that not all readers agree and that English Literature is full of different possible interpretations. Considering and weighing the value of these different interpretations is an important part of studying English. Whether the ghosts are real or not is therefore a decision that every reader should make for themselves.

Task

Think about your own reactions to this chapter. Find evidence for and against the idea that the Bronte wants us to believe that Cathy's ghost is real.

What is your opinion?

Commentary

Evidence for Ghosts in Chapter 3	Evidence against Ghosts in Chapter 3
The use of elements of the gothic genre to signal the presence of the fantastic.	Elements of both dreams taken from narrated events, therefore, like most dreams, they could simply be based on Lockwood's recent experience. Bronte carefully sets this up so as to allow for this possible reading.
Repetition of verb 'swarm' creates sense that ghost is Catherine.	Lockwood is asleep i.e. this is clearly a dream (not a waking sighting of a ghost).
Lockwood's observation that the use of the name Linton adds veracity. As he says 'why did I think of *Linton*? I had read *Earnshaw* twenty times for Linton.'	Lockwood is tired/ill and in an emotional state.
Lockwood's belief that room haunted and his insistence that ghostly encounter was real. As usual, he cannot interpret what he has seen, but he can relate it to the reader accurately.	Lockwood is convinced the ghost is real, but he is frequently wrong in his perceptions.
Heathcliff also believes the ghost is real and reacts with grief.	The pane of glass is not broken.

I would argue that Bronte presents the ghosts in Wuthering Heights as real, and this is an important part of my interpretation of the novel. I believe that she uses the gothic genre, a mode of writing in which the fantastic is possible, to alert readers to the real presence of the supernatural.

I also believe that she supplies significant details in order to support this interpretation. For example, as even Lockwood notes, if his dream had been based on nothing but the names on the sill, then he would've been more likely to think the ghosts name was Earnshaw than Linton. These are the sort of details that an author would use in a ghost story to convince the reader of its veracity, and I believe that Bronte is using these details here for the same reason.

In short, I think that Bronte wants us to believe that Cathy's ghost is real, and that this should form an important part of how we read *Wuthering Heights*.

Topic 13 – Nelly Dean
Introduction

In this topic, we will read Chapter Four. We will then look at the role of Nelly Dean as the second narrator of *Wuthering Heights*.

Aims and Objectives

- To read Chapter Four
- To consider the role of Nelly Dean as narrator

Chapter Four

Lockwood has returned to Thrushcross Grange. He is feeling feverish and in need of company and he persuades Nelly Dean, the housekeeper, to tell him about his landlord and the others who live at Wuthering Heights.

Task

Read Chapter Four.

Nelly Dean

In this chapter, Nelly Dean takes over from Lockwood as narrator.

Nelly's narratorial style is quite different to that of Lockwood. Lockwood uses a literary style, with a sophisticated vocabulary. By contrast, Nelly's tale draws on an oral tradition of storytelling.

Nelly's style as narrator is much less formal than Lockwood's. She reminds us that she is a participant in the events that she narrates and refers to her own presence in the story with statements such as 'it seemed a long while to us all'. She uses phrases such as 'one fine summer morning' and 'well, the conclusion was that…' which sound chatty and remind us that she is telling this story, rather than writing it down.

She also takes care to keep Lockwood's interest. The chapter ends with Nelly's description of how, in her opinion that Heathcliff was not vindictive, she was 'deceived, completely'. This creates interest in the reader and draws them into the story, encouraging them to read on.

However Nelly, like Lockwood, is also an unreliable narrator. Although she was present at the events she narrates, as readers we may not always agree with her interpretation of events. Indeed, readers of the novel have often debated Nelly's role. Charlotte Bronte's 1850 *Preface* to the novel described Nelly as 'a specimen of true benevolence and homely fidelity'[23]. Yet, we might question how far her actions, particularly her desire to conceal and manipulate, actually cause many of the unfortunate events.

As you read the novel, try to keep in mind that there are different views of Nelly's character and consider her presentation of the story and her role in the events she relates.

Embedded Narratives – Power and Narration

Having two different narrators, both of which are unreliable, is an unusual narrative device. In *Wuthering Heights*, Lockwood's narrative forms a frame for Nelly's story. In this way, Nelly's story can be said to be embedded within Lockwood's. This is sometimes described as a Chinese Box structure, where one narrative is placed within another. As we read on, we will also read letters from other characters, which are also included within the main narratives. Interestingly, Anne Bronte also used a similar device (the diaries of a women, included within the letters of a man) in *The Tenant of Wildfell Hall.*

There is some suggestion that class and gender are therefore important here. In the past, only educated men have been able to write books as novelists. Meanwhile women were more likely to tell stories in the home, for example in the form of fairytales told while completing domestic work, such as spinning. These two different traditions are illustrated in *Wuthering Heights* by Lockwood and Nelly as different types of narrators.

---

[23] Charlotte Bronte Preface to the 1850 edition of Wuthering Heights, cited in Rod Mengham Penguin Critical Studies: Wuthering Heights (Penguin, 1989)

Nelly is a servant, but she occupies a social niche somewhere above the other servants, although still below the family. As she says in this chapter, she was raised alongside Cathy and Hindley and played with them as children. She sees herself almost as part of the Earnshaw family. Her position might therefore be seen as lonely and isolated and she is connected and yet disconnected from the family.

This is shown in her language. Nelly uses Standard English, not the Yorkshire dialect that Joseph and Zillah, the other servants in the novel, use. This reflects her social position. Like Heathcliff, she is an outsider.

We might argue that despite her lowly status, Nelly is able to obtain power through her narration of events. Through stories, both the narrative that she tells Lockwood and the information she conceals from others, Nelly is able to advance her own interests. In this way, Emily Bronte is clearly making a complex point about women and power here, and our conflicting sense of Nelly as both a sympathetic and an unsympathetic character therefore contributes to the uncertainties of the novel.

Task

In this chapter, Nelly explains the relationships between the people who live at Wuthering Heights. From what we learn, complete a family tree for the characters that we have encountered.

Commentary

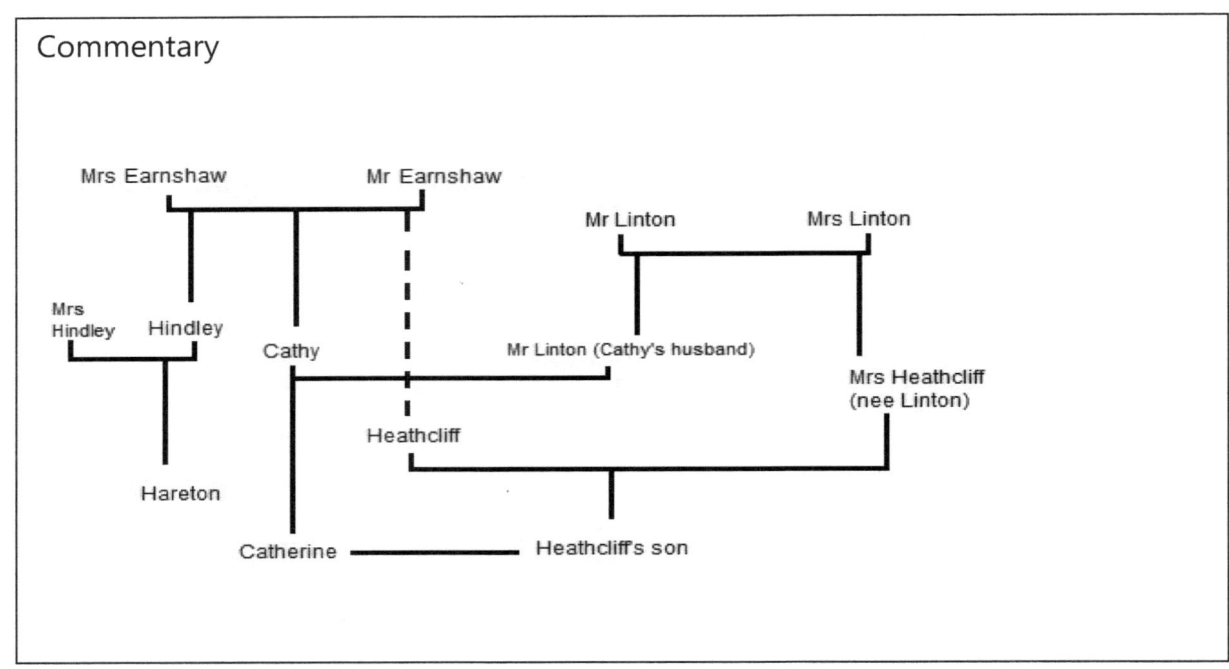

Topic 14 – Chapters Five and Six
Introduction

In this topic, we will read Chapters Five and Six. We will think about the characters of Hindley, Heathcliff and Cathy and what we learn about their childhoods. We will then think about the characters of Edgar and Isabella and what we learn about them in Chapter Six.

Aims and Objectives

- To read Chapters Five and Six
- To think about the characters of Hindley, Heathcliff and Cathy
- To think about the characters of Edgar and Isabella

Chapters Five and Six

In these chapters, Nelly continues to tell Lockwood the story of the Heights. She recalls the childhoods spent at the Heights and gives us some information on the characters in the novel. She also introduces Edgar and Isabella at Thrushcross Grange.

Task
Read Chapters Five and Six.

Characterisation

Characters in texts are not 'real' people, but are instead constructed by an author. However, to give them a sense of reality, each character will have their own distinct personality traits. The way that an author creates this sense of character is called characterisation.

Characterisation can be direct or indirect. Direct characterisation is when we are told something about a character directly.

For example, in Chapter Five, Nelly tells us a lot about Cathy directly. For example, Nelly tells us that Cathy was always 'in mischief' but that 'I believe she meant no harm'. This is therefore shown to be Nelly's opinion as narrator and we are therefore able to use our own judgement as to whether to agree or disagree. In this way, if a narrator tells us something about a character, then we may or may not take them at face value, depending on how reliable they are as a narrator.

Indirect characterisation is when we infer information about the characters from what they say or do. This may sometimes conflict with what we are told about the character by the narrator. When Heathcliff says 'Don't you cant, Nelly' we might be tempted to agree with him. Nelly might be determined to present Cathy and Heathcliff as rebellious, naughty children, but we might agree that their treatment also seems at times deeply unjust and that Nelly is often unreasonable. As Heathcliff points out, Edgar and Isabella are hardly 'good' children.

By telling us about the characters through these different methods, Bronte allows us to get to know them as people. In this way, we gain a deeper understanding of the characters. We get a sense of them as complex, nuanced and sometime ambiguous and we are allowed to form our own interpretations of their lives and personalities.

Task

When answering a question in English literature, you will need to find quotations from the text to support your view.

1) From what you have read of the novel so far, find three examples that illustrate the characters of the following:

Hindley

Catherine

Heathcliff

2) What do we learn about Edgar and Isabella in Chapter Six? What impression do we get of them as characters?

---

1) From what you have read of the novel so far, find three examples that illustrate the characters of the following:

Hindley

Hindley is an ambiguous character. He can be proud and cold. He despises Heathcliff because he seems to have replaced Hindley (as the eldest son) in his father's affections and has become 'bitter with brooding over these injuries'. This is shown in his 'manifestations of scorn' towards Heathcliff, especially the incident where he throws a weight at Heathcliff and pushes him under a horse. As soon as he inherits the Heights, 'Hindley became tyrannical'. He has Heathcliff's education curtailed and insists that he do manual work on the farm.

We learn that as a child Hindley was sensitive and possibly artistic. This shown in his choice of a violin as a gift. However, the gift is symbolically smashed by Heathcliff's arrival. From this point onwards, we sense that Hindley has become miserable and bitter and that he seeks revenge on Heathcliff. However, we sometimes also see his softer side, such as in his affection for his wife. We get the impression that, if Earnshaw had not brought Heathcliff to the Heights, Hindley would have grown up to be a very different man.

Catherine

Catherine is described as lively girl whose 'spirits were always at a high-water mark, her tongue always going'. She enjoys conflict and Nelly tells us that 'she was never so happy as when we were all scolding her at once, and she defying us with her bold, saucy look, and her ready words.' This also shows us that she is quick-witted and bright, and that she enjoys bettering Joseph and her father in verbal arguments.

Although she is 'too mischievous and wayward for a favourite', Nelly has a great affection for her. Nelly describes here as 'a wild, wick, slip she was, but she had the bonniest eye, and sweetest smile and lightest foot in the parish'.

Catherine is also stoic. We learn that, after being bitten by a dog, 'She did not yell out - no!' She shows no fear and encourages Heathcliff to go on without her. This shows great bravery and physical courage.

Heathcliff

Nelly tells us that Heathcliff is a 'sullen, patient child; hardened perhaps to ill-treatment'. We are told that Heathcliff is able to endure Hindley's treatment of him, because he knows the influence that he has over Mr. Earnshaw.

Certainly, Heathcliff uses this knowledge to blackmail Hindley into giving him his colt. He makes this request directly and straightforwardly, saying 'if you won't I shall tell your father of the three thrashings you've given me this week'. He persists despite

Hindley's further violence and this shows the young Heathcliff's determination. Nelly also tells us how she was 'surprised to see how coolly the child gathered himself up' after being pushed under the horse. Again, this shows Heathcliff's self-control and strength of character.

We also learn of his absolute devotion to Cathy. He will not leave Thrushcross Grange and watches until she seems happy to stay there. He explains that 'if Catherine had wished to return, I intended shattering their great glass panes to a million fragments, unless they let her out.' This shows the unique bond between Cathy and Heathcliff and the separation they impose between themselves and the rest of the world. It also shows the violent and dramatic nature of Heathcliff's love.

2) What do we learn about Edgar and Isabella in Chapter Six? What impression do we get of them as characters?

Our first impression of Edgar and Isabella is not very favourable. When we first see them, they are both in a tantrum of tears with Isabella 'shrieking as if witches were running red hot needles into her'. We learn that they have been fighting over who would get to pet a dog and that, in the process, they have nearly pulled the pet apart. Despite their lives of comfort and luxury, they have violent and selfish temperaments.

From this, we get the impression that the children are spoilt and cruel. Isabella seems particularly so when she describes Heathcliff as a 'Frightful thing!' and says that he should be put in the cellar. This shows a judgemental and intolerant attitude and a total lack of compassion.

Edgar seems to be shy and we are told that he hangs back looking at Cathy. We might also get the impression from this that he is immediately smitten with her, an idea echoed in Heathcliff's view that she is 'immeasurably superior' to 'everybody on earth'.

Topic 15 – Chapter Seven: Heathcliff and Cathy

Introduction

In this topic, we will read Chapter Seven. We will explore Heathcliff and Cathy's encounter with the Lintons and the impact that this has on their relationship.

Aims and Objectives

- To read Chapter Seven
- To think about the relationship between Heathcliff and Cathy

Chapter Seven

We saw in the last topic how Cathy and Heathcliff have been separated by Cathy's sojourn at Thrushcross Grange and how this is symbolically shown by Heathcliff viewing Cathy through the window.

After he returns home, Hindley Earnshaw is furious. He is reproached by Mr. Linton and moved to reassess the attitude he has taken to the children. He vows that Heathcliff will be dismissed if he speaks to Cathy again.

Mrs. Earnshaw also agrees to try and curb Cathy's wild ways. Interestingly, Nelly tells us that she accomplishes this with art, since 'with force she would have found it impossible'. Indeed, in Chapter Seven we see that Cathy is much changed.

In this topic, we will look further at Cathy and Heathcliff's relationship and how their separation increases in Chapter Seven.

Task

Read Chapter Seven.

The Encounter at Thrushcross Grange

Heathcliff leaves Cathy at Thrushcross Grange, being 'as merry as she could be' with the Lintons.

This brush with the world of the Grange shows the stark divide between the wild and natural world of Wuthering Heights and the civilised and cultured lives of those at Thrushcross Grange.

This encounter therefore serves to illustrate the difference in social class and station between Heathcliff and Cathy.

The Separation of Cathy and Heathcliff

When Catherine returns from the Grange, she has become a young lady. Far removed from her tomboy youth, she is now unable to interact with the environment of the Heights. When the dogs come to greet her 'she dare hardly touch them' and she cannot hug Nelly because she has been making Christmas cake and is covered in flour. These images of restraint are a sharp contrast with her previously boisterous character.

Heathcliff, by contrast, has become even wilder and dirtier since Catherine has been at the Grange. We are told that Nelly can only persuade him to wash once a week and that he has not washed his clothes in three months.

Catherine greats him with the line:

> Why how very black and cross you look! and how - how funny and grim! But that's because I'm used to Edgar and Isabella Linton.

The conflict between them is therefore presented, symbolically, as one of colour. Heathcliff's clothes are repeatedly described as black (with dirt) while Cathy is wearing a white silk dress. This description may also have a racial aspect, as we are told that Heathcliff has a darker skin tone than Catherine.

The main difference here, however, is one of class. Heathcliff is beginning to realise that he is not of Cathy's class and this is beginning to come between them. Heathcliff has seen that, at the Grange, he and Cathy were not considered as equals. He notes that 'she was a young lady and they made a distinction between her treatment and mine'. This class difference is further emphasised by Hindley's decision to treat Heathcliff as a servant, a situation that has become even more pronounced in Cathy's absence.

From Heathcliff's viewpoint, Cathy has changed. She is now 'used' to the more genteel company of the Lintons, and he feels not only betrayed but excluded.

This is also shown in Heathcliff's description of the Grange from Chapter Six. His first view of the drawing room takes place through the window. He says:

> ah it was beautiful! - a splendid place carpeted with crimson, and crimson-covered chairs and tables, and a pure white ceiling bordered by gold, a
> shower of glass-drops hanging in silver chains from the centre, and shimmering with little soft tapers.

This description is powerful and it tells us how strongly Heathcliff is attracted by this beautiful room. Bronte's description creates a sense of opulence. The syndetic listing (the use of conjunction 'and' to keep joining the elements together) creates a sense of abundance, and even excess. There is an emphasis on rich colours. 'Crimson' is repeated for emphasis and the adjective 'white' is pre-modified with 'pure' to heighten the impression of luxury, and create an association with cleanliness.

We know that Heathcliff finds this beautiful, not only because he describes it as such, but also because this description has such an important place in his narrative. He has never seen anything like this before. We know that he is describing a chandelier from his evocative description of the 'glass-drops' but Heathcliff does not know this word. His appreciation of the room is therefore quite affecting and we too might be moved by his fine sense of beauty.

This is especially poignant because we, as readers, know that although Cathy can move inside the Grange, Heathcliff cannot. Where once both children stood on a flower pot, looking inside, now only Heathcliff remains as an outsider. His position is thus doubly lonely, and we can certainly sympathise with his feelings in this chapter.

Heathcliff's Pride

As Heathcliff becomes more aware of his social inferiority, he becomes prouder and more defiant. Worst of all, Cathy fails to understand his feelings and continues to expect things to be the same as they were before she went away. Nelly shows some sensitivity to this. She offers to help Heathcliff clean up so that he and Cathy can sit together on Christmas Eve. Again, however, Heathcliff is defiant and he will not accept this help.

The next day, Heathcliff has changed his mind. He tells Nelly that 'I'm going to be good' and he now seems determined to change to meet Cathy. In his conversation with Nelly, we hear many of Heathcliff's insecurities. We learn how Heathcliff wishes he were more like Edgar Linton. Heathcliff defines this in terms of appearance, manners and money. He wishes for 'light hair and a fair skin, to be dressed and behaved as well, and had a chance of being as rich as he will be!'

Nelly offers him some sensible advice. She explains that not everything about Edgar is desirable, and that he is actually quite weak and spoilt. She advises Heathcliff to make the best of himself and cautions against gaining 'the expression of a vicious cur' that 'hates all the world...for what it suffers'. In some ways, this is quite perceptive on Nelly's part, since this is exactly what Heathcliff's experience of the world has been like so far. In showing some sympathy and kindness towards Heathcliff's feelings, she actually manages to get him to feel more confident and handsome.

Yet some of her advice is perhaps less sound. Despite her exhortation that 'Proud people breed sorrows for themselves' she also counsels Heathcliff to believe himself a 'prince in disguise'. Arguably, this does nothing to reconcile Heathcliff to his situation, and may even exacerbate his feelings of pride and hurt.

Heathcliff's pride comes to the fore again when Hindley orders him to remain upstairs while the Linton's are present. Following on from Nelly's pep talk, Heathcliff is especially angered by this. Edgar Linton's thoughtless and cruel comments are the final straw. As readers, we may rejoice a little when Heathcliff throws hot apple sauce in Edgar's spiteful face. Yet again, however, the consequences for Heathcliff are severe. At the end of this chapter, we hear how Heathcliff vows to have his revenge on Hindley. He says that:

I don't care how long I wait, if I can only do it at last. I hope that he will not die before I do!

Heathcliff believes he will find 'satisfaction' though getting revenge on Hindley. It is starting to become his overriding motivation. His comment that 'while I'm thinking of that [his revenge], I don't feel pain' is deeply sad. From this, we get a real insight into Heathcliff's future character.

Catherine

At first reading, Catherine seems a little selfish and unfeeling in this chapter. As Nelly says:

> How lightly she dismisses her old playmates troubles. I could not have imagined her to be so selfish.

Yet, following from Nelly's words, Catherine immediately bursts into tears and Nelly observes that 'she was in purgatory throughout the day'. This observation seems apt, as Cathy is indeed caught between two worlds. She knows that she is of a higher social class than Heathcliff and she enjoys the company of the Lintons. Yet, she is also much wilder and more robust than they are and she treats their tears and tantrums 'contemptuously'.

When Heathcliff throws the apple sauce at Edgar 'Cathy stood by confounded, blushing for all'. This shows that, like Heathcliff, she is also in a difficult and isolated position.

We will look at this further in the next topic.

Task

At the end of this chapter, we are brought back to the present day and we hear the voices of Nelly and Lockwood. What is the significance of this?

Commentary

This section at the end of the chapter reminds us that we are hearing a story, as told by Nelly to Lockwood. This draws attention to the process of narration. Bronte usually does this for a reason.

Here, we will note that Lockwood displays a rather patronising attitude to Nelly and her story. He says he is only interested in the characters 'more or less'. He also claims that the insularity of the neighbourhood means that the story has drawn more of Nelly's attention than it otherwise would have, the same way that 'a spider in a dungeon' attracts the focussed attention of a prisoner. He claims that there is something 'more in earnest' about this, because a sincere attachment to a few people seems preferable to a superficial or frivolous attachment to many people and to many different experiences.

However, this seems another example of Lockwood's misreading. This story seems important to us precisely because it has deep and powerful themes. There is something of universal human conflict in the story of Cathy and Heathcliff. Once again, we suspect that Lockwood has missed the point of Nelly's story.

Nelly, on the other hand, has no difficulty in understand Lockwood's convoluted analogy. She has acquired knowledge from reading and she tells us that 'You could not open a book in this library that I have not looked into, and got something out of also'. But she also tells Lockwood that her education consists of more than book-learning and says that 'I have undergone sharp discipline which has taught me wisdom'. For all his sophistication, we are reminded that it is Nelly who is better placed to understand the significance of the events at the Heights. This story itself therefore becomes a sort of education for Lockwood.

In this way, this brief section brings out many of the difference between the two narrators and exemplifies some of the themes and contrasts of the novel.

Topic 16 – Chapter Eight

Introduction

In this topic, we will look at the events of Chapter Eight. We will then look at the changing relationships of the three main characters.

Aims and Objectives

- To read Chapter Eight
- To explore the changing relationships of the characters

Chapter Eight

In this chapter, there are several changes at the Heights.

We learn a little more about the characters of Heathcliff, Cathy and Edgar. We also see the changing relationships of these three main characters.

Task

Read Chapter Eight of *Wuthering Heights*.

Write a paragraph on each of the main characters: Heathcliff, Cathy and Edgar. Use at least 3 examples from the text for each character and try to explore their changing personalities.

Commentary

Heathcliff

Heathcliff has changed in this chapter. We learn from Nelly that he has 'lost the benefit of his early education' and that he has had to abandon his studies and his former social level. Hard work, disappointment and ill treatment has left him bitter and morose. He had also physically changed and has 'acquired a slouching gait, and ignoble look'. In being rejected by the world, he has himself turned his back upon it Nelly tells us that 'he contrived to convey an impression of inward and outward repulsiveness' and suggests that he now takes 'a grim pleasure' in being disliked and avoided. His 'savage sullenness and ferocity' increases and Nelly even goes so far as to say that there is something 'diabolical' about him.

Edgar

Edgar is also growing up and he has become handsome. When Nelly shows Lockwood his portrait, we are told how he is 'a sweet picture'. He is described as 'soft-featured' with large eyes and curling hair. Adjectives such as 'sweet' and 'amiable' would never be applied to Heathcliff and the two men are both physically and temperamentally very different.

Edgar does not have the bravery or resilience of Heathcliff. We are told that he had 'a terror of Earnshaw's reputation and shrunk from encountering him'. He therefore avoids the Heights, even though Nelly tells us that he is actually treated politely by Hindley. Indeed, Edgar remains sensitive and, although he is now a man, he cannot hide his feelings. Following Cathy's violence he is described as 'pale and with a quivering lip'. However, we also learn that his devotion to Cathy is real and that he is in love with her.

Cathy

In this chapter, we gain further insight into Cathy's difficult position. We learn how she is still caught between the Grange and the Heights. Nelly tells us that the politeness that is adopted at Thrushcross Grange would only be 'laughed at' in Wuthering Heights and so Cathy is forced to 'adopt a double character without exactly intending to deceive anyone'.

Cathy is still strong willed and has become 'a haughty, headstrong creature!' and Nelly criticises her pride and arrogance. Some readers have suggested that Nelly may actually be jealous of Cathy's looks and the attention she receives. Nelly admits that 'I own I did not like her' and says that 'I've had many a laugh at her perplexities and untold troubles'. This may strike us as surprisingly unsympathetic, and even cruel, especially since Nelly has more or less taken the position of mother to Cathy.

Nelly, however, is determined to see Cathy as stubborn and difficult. Nelly's judgement that 'she will be sick, only to grieve us' is particularly unfair as Cathy's distress seems real and serious. As readers we may see Cathy's violence and deceit as a response to her difficult position and as a reflection of her inner turmoil. Nelly, however, refuses to help or respond to this difficult situation.

Cathy, Heathcliff and Edgar - The Central Conflict

In this chapter, we also learn of the changing relationship between Cathy and Heathcliff and between Cathy and Edgar.

Heathcliff and Cathy have remained close, despite their altered statuses. We learn from Nelly that Heathcliff 'kept his hold on her affections unalterably'. Heathcliff equally still dotes on Cathy and wants her to spend time with him. We learn that he has been marking the days of an almanac with a cross or a dot to say when she has spent the evening with him and when she has been with Edgar.

Indeed, Cathy tries to keep Edgar away from Wuthering Heights because she does not want to cause friction between the two men. She expects Heathcliff to be working in the field when Edgar arrives and she then lies to say that both Edgar and Isabella are coming, when in fact she knows that it is Edgar alone who is expected. Since they both dislike and criticise the other, she is forced to 'half coincide' with such criticisms. This is a very difficult position and means that she cannot spend time with both men at once. When Heathcliff complains that she is spending more time with Edgar she is therefore angry and agitated, as is shown in the harshness of her response that 'it is no company at all when people know nothing and say nothing'.

In this way, we can see the conflict between the two men and the two lifestyles that they represent. This is the essential love triangle: the central conflict of the novel. Heathcliff's education has been stunted and he cannot provide the civilised conversation that she looks for in Edgar. Heathcliff's value to Cathy is of a different form. It is something she finds difficult to express directly but it is more potent than her relationship with Edgar, who has not made an 'equally deep' impression on her. Many critics have therefore read the conflict between the two men in symbolic terms as the conflict between nature vs. culture, spirituality vs. material comfort, or passion vs. social status.

This dichotomy also reflects the essential conflict within Cathy herself. She may want to be polite and civilised, but her nature is wild and passionate. Taming her nature does not come easily to her. We see this at the end of Chapter Eight when her rage leads her to pinch and slap Nelly, to lie about it, and finally to box Edgar round the ears.

Edgar is shocked by this violence but, paradoxically perhaps, it actually ends up bringing them closer together. In this outpouring of emotion, Cathy shows a more genuine image of herself and is able to be more honest about her nature. The two admit their connection to each other and Edgar reveals his love.

The metaphor that Bronte (via Nelly) first uses for this is interesting however. She describes how Edgar, looking back at the house, 'possessed the power to depart, as much as a cat possesses the power to leave a mouse half-killed, or a bird half-eaten'. Although it is Edgar who Nelly describes as 'doomed', this metaphor leaves a strong impression on the reader. This image is violent and dark and it equates Edgar with the cat and Cathy as the mouse or bird. This is interesting and gives us much pause for thought, as we shall see later in the novel.

Topic 17 – Chapter Nine

Introduction

In this topic, we will read Chapter Nine. This is a significant turning point in the novel.

Aims and Objectives

- To read Chapter Nine
- To practice skills of language analysis

Chapter Nine

Task
Read Chapter Nine

In this chapter, Hindley has become extremely violent. He threatens Nelly with a knife and is abusive to his son Hareton. In a dramatic episode, Hareton's life is saved by Heathcliff, who catches the infant after Hindley drops him over the banisters.

Instead of taking his revenge on Hindley, Heathcliff has saved his son's life. According to Nelly, this gives him a feeling of the 'intensest anguish'.

While Nelly is calming Hareton, Cathy comes in to speak to her. At first, neither of them realise that Heathcliff is listening.

Cathy tells Nelly that Edgar Linton has asked her to marry him. She has accepted his proposal, yet says that 'in my soul, and in my heart, I'm convinced I'm wrong'.

This has been an impossible decision and Cathy seeks Nelly's advice. Nelly quizzes her as to her feelings for Edgar and for Heathcliff.

Cathy and Edgar

Nelly asks Cathy her reasons for marrying Edgar. She tells her that it is because he is 'handsome, and pleasant', 'young and cheerful' and, most importantly of all, he will be rich and inherit the Grange. Cathy wants this status and power and to be 'the greatest woman of the neighbourhood'. She knows that Edgar loves her, and she says that she loves him. It is worth examining her words in detail. She says:

> I love the ground under his feet, and the air over his head, and everything he touches, and every word he says - I love all his looks, and all his actions, and him entirely, and altogether. There now!

However, we might notice that this description feels insincere. Most of these things are not actually parts of Edgar, but are only loosely connected with him. For example, 'the ground under his feet, and the air over his head' are things that surround Edgar, but are not part of him. The repetition of 'all' also seems excessive and it further implies that she is being disingenuous, since no-one could really claim to love every action that another person undertakes (and this is not something that she would ever say about Heathcliff). Her claim to love 'him entirely, and altogether' has the superficial quality of an inferior romantic novel and her final exclamatory comment 'There now!' seems to show that this description of her love is designed only to satisfy Nelly.

We get the sense that she does love Linton in some ways, but that this love is of a pale and conventional kind.

Cathy and Heathcliff

Cathy's love for Heathcliff is described in entirely different and vastly more powerful terms. Cathy describes Heathcliff as 'more myself than I am' and 'my own being'. This describes a complex and unusual feeling. It is far from the commonplace, saccharine sentiments that she has used for Linton.

She goes on to say that 'I *am* Heathcliff' and that 'he's always, always in my mind'. This repetition adds emphasis and sincerity. Again, the way that she describes Heathcliff suggests an intense and dependant love. She needs Heathcliff in a way that she could never need Linton.

Cathy makes a clear comparison between the types of love that she feels for the two men when she says:

> My love for Linton is like the foliage in the woods. Time will change it, I'm well aware, as winter changes the trees - my love for Heathcliff resembles the eternal rocks beneath - a source of little visible delight but necessary.

This simile makes a comparison between Linton and the changing leaves, which change colour, die and fall off the trees in winter. It is beautiful, perhaps, but also superficial. On the other hand, her love for Heathcliff is hard and unchanging.

In a further comparison, she describes Edgar as like 'moonbeams' and 'frost' and Heathcliff as like 'lightning' and 'fire'. This creates the impression that Edgar is cold, beautiful and possibly distant. Heathcliff, on the other hand, is made of heat and passion.

Her relationship with Heathcliff provides her with a sense of wholeness. They are two parts of one and they are both the same. As Cathy describes it 'whatever our souls are made of, his and mine are the same'.

Cathy's Dream

Cathy's dream gives us an insight into her feelings. She describes how she was in heaven but that it 'didn't seem to be my home'. Instead, she cries until 'the angels were so angry that they flung me out' and she is returned to the moors above the Heights. Once back at the Heights, she 'woke sobbing for joy'.

Dreams are used several times in this novel and they have an important symbolic meaning. Thrushcross Grange is often described as a kind of heaven, where heaven is a civilised palace of gold and white, and is also associated with polite society and civilisation. This could never be Cathy's heaven. She craves the wilderness, the freedom and the oneness with nature that she finds on the moors.

In a fascinating study Gilbert and Gubar describe Cathy's heaven as a reversal of Milton's model of the Fall.[24] If the Grange represents a heaven, it is a traditional and hierarchical heaven. The freedom the Heathcliff find on the moors is a freedom from the rigid hierarchical society that imprison them within set roles. It is a freedom to be themselves.

Dreams are given great significance in the novel because they allow Bronte to explore ideas in symbolic terms. As Cathy says, she cannot explain her feelings 'distinctly' but says that 'I'll give you a feeling of how I feel'. In many ways, this is more powerful than a simple relation of her thoughts, because it relies on the reader forming their own understanding of the dream's meaning and making their own connections. Literary critics, especially of the psychoanalytic school, are particularly interested in symbolic readings of Wuthering Heights.

We will also notice that this dream of Cathy's has a further significance; it relates to Lockwood's dream in Chapter 3. We know that Lockwood has seen Cathy's ghost as a 'waif' outlawed on the moors and hoping to come in and to be reunited with Heathcliff. Cathy's dream gives us an explanation for this. It suggests that she has not gone to heaven, but that she seeks her own freedom on the land above Wuthering Heights.

This interpretation is further supported by Cathy's statement that 'If all else perished, and *he* remained, I should still continue to be'. The ghost that Lockwood sees confirms that this is true and gives weight to the existence and significance of ghosts in the novel.

Cathy's Choice

As readers, we can tell that this is a heartbreaking decision for Cathy. She craves the power, wealth and independence that marriage to Edgar will bring and she fears that, if she were to marry Heathcliff, 'we should be beggars'. For Victorian women, a good

---

[24] Sandra M. Gilbert and Susan Gubar *The Madwoman in the Attic* p. 255

marriage was essential for financial security, so this choice is more than understandable in the context of the time.

Many critics have therefore read this choice as a choice between the demands of society and the authentic self. Though Cathy wants to marry Heathcliff, social pressures force her to choose Edgar. Heathcliff does not have any family or any social position, and therefore to marry him would 'degrade' Cathy. In this way, she is forced to abandon her real self and her authentic desires and to bow her will to that of society.

Other critics, however, have seen it as a choice between two sides of her own personality. She desires power, and sees Edgar as a means to obtain it. Part of her might be seen to enjoy the attention she receives at the Grange, while another part loves the freedom of scampering on the moors. These two selves are represented in the choice of lovers. They are also shown in the names carved on the windowsill; 'Catherine Heathcliff' and 'Catherine Linton' are the two possible identities that she could adopt. Gilbert and Gubar see this as a difficulty in forming a stable identity that all women experience. They contend that 'Just as triumphant self discovery is the ultimate goal of the male *Bildungsroman*, anxious self-denial, Bronte suggests, is the ultimate product of female education.' If we cannot know our own names, they argue, how can we know who we are?[25]

It is also possible, that Cathy does not see these two identities in exclusive terms. She does not understand that to choose Edgar means to give up Heathcliff. Her desperate exclamatives 'Oh that's not what I intend - that's not what I mean!' show us that she cannot bear to be separated from Heathcliff, or perhaps from the part of herself that he represents. This also gives us another possible interpretation of her words that 'He is more myself than I am'. She could mean that Heathcliff has the freedom to be himself, and to be whole and natural, in a way that Cathy does not.

Her real search, perhaps, is to find that illusive wholeness which she has in childhood, but has lost in the process of growing up and becoming a young lady.

As readers, we can tell the significance and importance of this decision and we can empathise with the strong feelings that it evokes in Cathy. Nelly, however, is ignorant of this. She seems almost determined to see Cathy as 'a wicked, unprincipled girl' and makes no effort to understand her position.

---

[25] Sandra M. Gilbert and Susan Gubar 'Looking Oppositely: Emily Bronte's Bible of Hell' in *The Madwoman in the Attic: The Woman Writer and the Nineteenth-Century Literary Imagination* (Yale Nota Bene, Second Edition, 2000) p. 276

Task

Re-read the beginning of this encounter between Nelly and Cathy.

Read from 'I went into the kitchen' to 'less sulkily'.

Explore how Bronte presents this encounter. What literary and linguistic techniques can you identify?

I went into the kitchen, and sat down to lull my little lamb to sleep. Heathcliff, as I thought, walked

> **Comment [hb1]:** This use of alliteration creates a lullaby sound.

through to the barn. It turned out afterwards that he only got as far as the other side the settle, when

he flung himself on a bench by the wall, removed from the fire and remained silent.

> **Comment [hb2]:** Bronte tells us that Heathcliff is listening from the outset. This is an instance of dramatic irony, as the reader knows more than the characters. Although it might be more dramatic if we found out that Heathcliff was listening when Cathy does, this method means that we pay more attention to Cathy's words, and that we are also considering Heathcliff's viewpoint. This therefore creates sympathy for Heathcliff.

I was rocking Hareton on my knee, and humming a song that began,—

> **Comment [hb3]:** This verb illustrates Heathcliff's distress and anger. He has saved Hareton and lost a chance at revenge.

It was far in the night, and the bairnies grat,

The mither beneath the mools heard that,

> **Comment [hb4]:** This song refers to a folk belief that deceased mothers will come back to care for their infants. There is some irony here, as we know that by the end of this chapter even Nelly will have left Hareton. It also reminds us that Cathy has no mother, and that she seeks Nelly's advice as a mother-figure.

when Miss Cathy, who had listened to the hubbub from her room, put her head in, and whispered,—

'Are you alone, Nelly?'

> **Comment [hb5]:** This tells us that what Cathy has to say is a secret. This whets the reader's curiosity.

'Yes, Miss,' I replied.

She entered and approached the hearth. I, supposing she was going to say something, looked up. The

> **Comment [hb6]:** This creates a strong sense of narrative and creates interest in what will happen next.

expression of her face seemed disturbed and anxious. Her lips were half asunder, as if she meant to

> **Comment [hb7]:** This is an interesting verb choice. It suggests that Nelly refuses to admit that Cathy could be genuinely anxious or disturbed. It shows that she is determined to see her distress as an act.

speak, and she drew a breath; but it escaped in a sigh instead of a sentence. I resumed my song; not

> **Comment [hb8]:** Despite Nelly's lack of sympathy this image actually creates a sense of vulnerability and draws the reader's sympathy.

having forgotten her recent behaviour.

> **Comment [hb9]:** The repetition of s sounds here creates the sound of the sign. This is called sibilance.

'Where's Heathcliff?' she said, interrupting me.

> **Comment [hb10]:** Nelly is still angry about the pinch and slap she received earlier, and about Cathy's unladylike behaviour in front of Linton.

'About his work in the stable,' was my answer.

> **Comment [hb11]:** This presents Cathy as rude. However, we should also note that it is Nelly who resumed her song, instead of waiting for Cathy to speak. Nelly is, after all, Cathy's servant and Cathy might expect her attention.

> **Comment [hb12]:** This short and perfunctory response shows Nelly's coldness towards Cathy.

He did not contradict me; perhaps he had fallen into a doze. There followed another long pause,

during which I perceived a drop or two trickle from Catherine's cheek to the flags. Is she sorry for

her shameful conduct?—I asked myself. That will be a novelty: but she may come to the point—as

she will—I sha'n't help her! No, she felt small trouble regarding any subject, save her own concerns.

'Oh, dear!' she cried at last. 'I'm very unhappy!'

'A pity,' observed I. 'You're hard to please; so many friends and so few cares, and can't make

yourself content!'

'Nelly, will you keep a secret for me?' she pursued, kneeling down by me, and lifting her winsome

eyes to my face with that sort of look which turns off bad temper, even when one has all the right in

the world to indulge it.

'Is it worth keeping?' I inquired, less sulkily.

Comment [hb13]: This is very unlikely to be true, and Nelly must realise this. It is more likely that Heathcliff, hearing Cathy come in, wants to eavesdrop on what she has to say. Why Nelly says this is therefore unclear, and it is one of her many attempts to obfuscate the situation.

Comment [hb14]: Nelly sees that Cathy is crying, but remains unmoved by it. The verb 'perceived' is Latinate and flowery and it shows the distance that Nelly feels towards Cathy's sorrow.

Comment [hb15]: This minimises Cathy's sadness. 'A drop or two' suggests that she is only crying a little bit and 'trickle' suggests only a slight flow of water. Her next statement that Cathy's tears fall to the flags, however, contradicts this and shows that she is crying quite a lot more than 'trickle' suggests.

Comment [hb16]: This is a very uncharitable view from Nelly. Indeed, Cathy's decision of who to marry would be important in anyone's eyes.

Comment [hb17]: These two exclamatives are both short and simple statements. These short sentences make a bigger impact as they are surrounded by Nelly's longer phrases. This shows us that Cathy's appeal is sincere and direct.

Comment [hb18]: Again, this is very unsympathetic and it is a very unrealistic appraisal of Cathy's situation. In her isolated and chaotic life at the Heights, Cathy has neither 'many friends' nor 'few cares'.

Comment [hb19]: This presents Cathy as rather manipulative. 'Winsome' particularly suggests an attempt to 'win' Nelly over.

Comment [hb20]: This sounds self-righteous, and even a little bitter.

Comment [hb21]: 'Inquired' is another Latinate word, and it is less immediate than the more usual 'asked'. This shows that Nelly is trying not to get too interested in Cathy's cares.

Comment [hb22]: This shows us that Nelly has been persuaded by Cathy's appeal, however. She is probably curious.

Heathcliff's Absence

Heathcliff overhears Cathy's speech, up until the point where she says 'it would degrade me to marry Heathcliff'. He does not hear her say how much she loves him. 'Degrade' is a powerful word and this humiliation causes Heathcliff to leave the Heights.

That night there is a terrific thunderstorm, which symbolises the dramatic events of this chapter. A tree falls near the house and knocks down part of the east chimney. This destruction can be seen a representing the changes that have occurred in this chapter. It could even be read as nature's revenge against Cathy's decision to marry Edgar.

After standing in the rain calling for Heathcliff, Cathy catches a fever and becomes 'dangerously ill'. We also know from Kenneth, the doctor, that she must be prevented from throwing herself down the stairs or 'out of the window'. From this we realise that she is in despair, and has become suicidally depressed.

We also learn more about Nelly's character in this chapter. Although Nelly sees Heathcliff go and realises that he has overheard their conversation, she does not tell Cathy until it is too late to go after him. Her motives are unclear, and possibly she underestimates the seriousness of the situation. However, this is another instance of her personal decision-making, and the way her choices change the course of events. We also told that she has allowed Cathy sit up all night in the cold, a circumstance that causes Cathy to become ill.

Even after Cathy has recovered, Nelly shows a shocking lack of sympathy for her feelings. She even admits to responding to Cathy's moods by viciously laying the blame for Heathcliff's disappearance on Cathy 'where indeed it belonged, as she well knew'. Aside from the fact that we could just as easily blame Nelly for failing to alert Cathy to Heathcliff's presence, this is an action which shows an astonishing lack of compassion.

At the end of this chapter, Edgar has married Cathy and she has moved to Thrushcross Grange, and Nelly has gone with her, somewhat against her will. Symbolically, perhaps, Cathy's fever also kills Mr. and Mrs. Linton, who also therefore become victims of Cathy and Heathcliff's uncivilised passion.

Topic 18 – Heathcliff's Return

Introduction

In this topic, we will read Chapters Ten and Eleven. We will think about the relationship between Heathcliff and Isabella and about the importance of economic status in C19th society.

Aims and Objectives

- To read Chapters Ten and Eleven
- To think about the relationship between Heathcliff and Isabella
- To consider the importance of economic status

Heathcliff's Return

Task

Read Chapters 10 and 11 of *Wuthering Heights*.

In this section, Heathcliff has returned to Wuthering Heights to live with Hindley. His whereabouts for the past three years is a mystery, but he has returned as a handsome, educated and wealthy man.

Edgar and Cathy have been living quietly together in a situation of domestic affection. Heathcliff's return throws this into chaos. This is immediately apparent in Cathy's response to him. His return transforms their quiet sitting room scene with Cathy becoming so lively and emotional that Edgar tells her 'there is no need to be frantic'. This shows the power of Cathy's desire to see Heathcliff and shows us how much she has missed him.

However, it is not only Cathy's emotional wellbeing that is thrown into disarray by Heathcliff's return.

Isabella and Heathcliff

In Chapters Ten and Eleven, we see that Isabella has become infatuated with Heathcliff. One explanation for this is that, since Isabella's life has been fairly secluded and bookish, she has come to see Heathcliff as a romantic, Byronic hero. Cathy tries to disabuse her of this notion, telling her that 'he's not a rough diamond...he's a fierce, pitiless, wolfish man'. However, raised on literature, Isabella sees Heathcliff in far more positive terms and she is unwilling to relinquish this belief. She is determined to believe that Heathcliff has 'an honourable soul'.

Heathcliff does not love Isabella, but he starts to realise that marrying her will help him to gain revenge on Edgar. He is also aware that, if Cathy and Edgar have no male heirs, Isabella will inherit Thrushcross Grange. Marriage to Isabella is therefore also a path to increased economic status. Once Cathy makes him aware of Isabella's infatuation, Heathcliff decides to act on it.

There is also the possibility that he intends to make Cathy jealous. This interpretation is suggested when Heathcliff tells Cathy that 'I'm not *your* husband, *you* needn't be jealous of me!' This strongly suggests that he does want to make her jealous, especially as it is followed up by Heathcliff's statement that Cathy has treated him 'infernally' and that he wants revenge on the world. He claims that if he thought Cathy really wanted him to marry Isabella 'I'd cut my throat!'.

What is most shocking, however, is the violence with which Heathcliff threatens Isabella at the end of Chapter 10. After Isabella has left the room, Heathcliff says that he would rip out her fingernails if she ever used them against him. He then threatens to paint rainbow-coloured bruises on her 'mawkish, waxen face' and to turn her 'blue eyes black, every day or two'. This vivid imagery is powerful and disturbing and we get a real sense of Heathcliff's violence here. Certainly, there is nothing of Isabella's romantic hero in him in this scene. As so often in *Wuthering Heights*, love has become deeply associated with violence.

Economic Status

For women in the C19th, marriage was the main route to social advancement and a good marriage was essential for economic security. Cathy is aware of this in her choice of Edgar over Heathcliff. Edgar has money, status and a comfortable house. The young Heathcliff had none of these things and to marry Heathcliff would have been a choice of passion over security.

Heathcliff, as a marginalised character without family or inheritance, therefore also seeks to increase his economic status. This has lead some critics to see Heathcliff as a feminised character, despite his overt masculinity.[26] For these critics, Heathcliff is an outsider, while Edgar represents patriarchy: the settled hierarchy of male property ownership. Although Heathcliff has acquired wealth while he has been away, he still lacks family or connections. He does not, in fact, even have a family name.

---

[26] Sandra M. Gilbert and Susan Gubar *The Madwoman in the Attic: The Woman Writer and the Nineteenth Century Literary Imagination* (Yale Nota Bene, Second Edition, 2000) p. 277

The Lintons are above the Earnshaws in the social hierarchy, and so for Cathy to marry Edgar is a step up the social ladder. Conversely, for Isabella to marry Heathcliff would be a significant step down. As Nelly points out, it is unlikely that Mr. Linton would agree to their match. Cathy seems to think that Edgar will agree to anything that she suggests, and she says that if Heathcliff truly wanted to marry Isabella, then she would have let Isabella 'fall into his trap'.

However, we might imagine that Edgar would have other ideas. It is indeed possible that this would be the 'something of equal consequence to both sides' which would come between Cathy and Edgar. As Nelly points out, their domestic happiness is built on Edgar's willingness to compromise on small issues. Now that Heathcliff has returned, much bigger disagreements have returned with him.

Task

Think about the following quotations. What is their significance?

1) "Isabella swears that the love Edgar has for me is nothing to that she entertains for you"

2) "You are welcome to torture me to death for your own amusement, only, allow me to amuse myself a little in the same style"

3) "Cathy, this lamb of yours threatens like a bull!"

4) "I'll try to break their hearts by breaking my own."

5) "Your cold blood cannot be worked into a fever - your veins are full of ice water - mine are boiling, and the sight of such chillness makes them dance!"

6) "Will you give up Heathcliff hereafter or will you give up me? It is impossible for you to be *my* friend and *his* at the same time; and I absolutely *require* to know which you choose."

Commentary

1) "Isabella swears that the love Edgar has for me is nothing to that she entertains for you"

This is not, in fact, what Isabella said, and Cathy presumably knows this. What Isabella actually said is that "I love him more than ever you loved Edgar" and this might indeed be true.

This reversal is therefore intended to hide Cathy's ambiguous feelings for Edgar, and she sanitises them into the less controversial statement that Edgar loves her. This means that she does not need to discuss Edgar in front of Heathcliff or address her real feelings for either man.

Cathy's true feelings for Edgar are uncertain, but it is likely that they are a much gentler attraction than that which either woman feels for Heathcliff. Although Isabella is clearly infatuated, this is a powerful emotion and her feelings for Heathcliff are real. Cathy dismisses Isabella's love as something which she 'entertains' as if on a whim. Yet we might suspect that, however, misguided, Isabella's feelings should not be underestimated.

2) "You are welcome to torture me to death for your own amusement, only, allow me to amuse myself a little in the same style"

Here, Heathcliff compares himself to a slave who has been ground down. He shows a clear awareness of social patterns when he explains that those who are oppressed by tyrants are more likely to oppress those beneath them than rise up against their oppressor. He is threatening to make Isabella miserable as Cathy has made him miserable.

Yet in his twisted devotion to Cathy, Heathcliff welcomes her tortures. He will accept any cruelty, even if inflicted only for her 'amusement'. This is another violent and brutal vision of love.

Such images of hell, torment, torture, devils and lost souls recur frequently in Heathcliff and Cathy's dialogue. This contributes to the sense that there can be no peace and no heaven for Cathy and Heathcliff unless they are together. In this way, the supernatural becomes a powerful set of imagery that guides and enriches our interpretation of the text.

3) "Cathy, this lamb of yours threatens like a bull!"

A lot of Heathcliff's speech is formed of short exclamatives that are nonetheless perceptive and revealing. Edgar is often described as docile and gentle, like an innocent lamb. Heathcliff suggests that it is this version of Edgar that Cathy wants to possess and expects her to have the upper hand in their relationship. Using Cathy's name and calling Edgar 'this lamb of yours' draws attention to her role as his wife and as owner of her husband, almost as though he were a pet. Notice that 'lamb' is a metaphor, a direct comparison, whereas 'bull' is a simile. Edgar threatens 'like a bull' , but he is not a bull. Here, Heathcliff laughing at Edgar and involving Cathy in his joke.

Cathy goes further, however, and compares her husband to another animal, 'a sucking leveret', which is a defenceless, baby hare. This is even more insulting, as it lack the religious association of lambs with innocence and goodness. A leveret is merely weak, and 'sucking' is used to emphasis Edgar's childishness and immaturity. Animal imagery is used throughout *Wuthering Heights* and in many different ways. Here, Cathy and Heathcliff's animal comparisons serve to insult, belittle and infantilise Edgar. It is no wonder that he responds violently to their combined attack.

Although Edgar is shown as weak and fearful he is not as powerless as Heathcliff and Cathy seem to think. He strikes Heathcliff a blow in the throat which 'would have levelled a slighter man'. He also has the weight of his property behind him, and he can call upon his servants to forcibly eject Heathcliff from his house.

4) "I'll try to break their hearts by breaking my own."

Cathy cannot face the choice between Edgar and Heathcliff and she resents being made to choose between them. Her response is one of self-destruction. She intends to make herself ill in order to punish them and make them feel guilty.

In many ways, this strikes us as a very childish and petty way to deal with this situation. Certainly Nelly is not sympathetic and sees this as one of Cathy's 'senseless, wicked rages'. However, Nelly consistently underestimates the strength of Cathy's feelings and her ability to control her feelings and behaviour is debateable. Feminist critics have sometimes read this self-destructive behaviour as a legitimate feminine response to being in a position of powerlessness. With limited choices and limited agency, there is little else that Catherine can do to express her distress and effect change.

5) "Your cold blood cannot be worked into a fever - your veins are full of ice water - mine are boiling, and the sight of such chillness makes them dance!"

Cathy sees herself and Edgar as extremes of temperature and temperament. Where she is fire, Edgar is frozen. She is further angered by his seeming coldness, and this only increases her fiery passions.

This use of polar opposites to describe character and emotions is part of a wider set of symmetries within the novel. We are often encouraged to also view characters and events as opposites, mirrors or parallels of each other, and this can create deeper, complex and more nuanced readings.

6) "Will you give up Heathcliff hereafter or will you give up me? It is impossible for you to be *my* friend and *his* at the same time; and I absolutely *require* to know which you choose."

Edgar now asks the question that Cathy has been fearing. The confrontation with Heathcliff has brought their triangle to a point and they can no longer continue as they have been. Edgar forces Cathy to choose between him and Heathcliff. Whoever she chooses, she will have to give the other up. This is an agonising choice which Cathy is unable to make.

The phrasing of this statement is also very interesting. We might note that the language is extremely formal. The word 'hereafter' has the tone of a legal document, and it reminds us that Edgar is a Magistrate. The phrase 'I absolutely *require* to know which you choose" is also incredibly restrained and sounds very artificial, given the important of the question. The verb *'require'*, which is also given italics for extra emphasis, seems particularly formal in this situation. It has a Latinate sound and is more associated with formal written requests than direct questions. Although there is force behind Edgar words, this shows that he is uncomfortable with having to ask this question, and with expressing his feelings.

The word 'friend' is also an interesting choice here. Linton does not appeal to Cathy as his wife or lover, but as his friend. This perhaps shows that Edgar is remembering their relationship as children and thinking back to the time of Cathy's original choice between Edgar and Heathcliff. It might also be a way to minimise their marriage or distance himself from his feelings.
Cathy views Edgar as dispassionate and cold, and it is likely that this phrasing will only increase this impression. As readers, however, we might interpret this as the composure of a Victorian gentleman, rather than coldness, and assume that Edgar is distancing himself from his own emotions to maintain some decorum.

This wording therefore also shows us Edgar's character, and draws attention to the kind of man he is and the world he represents. It encourages us to view Edgar as a symbol for the bourgeois values of politeness, marriage and domestic affection. This leads to a particular interpretation of Wuthering Heights as a novel about the conflict between passionate nature and civilised culture, where Heathcliff and Edgar become embodiments of these different ideals.

Topic 19 – Chapter Twelve

Introduction

In this topic, we will read Chapter Twelve. We will consider the role of Nelly in progressing the plot and we will look at the symbolic significance of Cathy's illness.

Aims and Objectives

- To read Chapter Twelve
- To consider Nelly's role in this chapter
- To think about the use of symbolism in the description of Cathy's illness

Chapter Twelve

In this chapter, Catherine's illness worsens and Isabella's relationship with Heathcliff intensifies.

Task

Read Chapter Twelve.

Catherine's Illness

In Chapter Twelve, we learn that Catherine's illness has become serious. She has locked herself up in her room and she has been fasting for three days. This is a very dangerous thing to do, especially since she is pregnant.

Cathy wants Edgar to come and see her. When she says:

> No, I'll not die - he'd be glad - he does not love me at all - he would never miss me!'

This tells us that she loves her husband, or at least that she wants his attention. She is now in a desperate state.

However, despite her 'ghastly countenance and strange exaggerated manner' Nelly continues to believe that Cathy is not really ill. She imagines that Cathy 'acted a part of her disorder'. Again, Nelly does not understand Cathy. Indeed, although her behaviour seems melodramatic, her feelings are very real.

Nelly's Role in Chapter Twelve

Instead of offering her help or support, Nelly worsens Cathy's feelings by telling her that Linton is spending time quietly reading books, while she is 'dying'. Even through Nelly knows that this is not true, she persists in telling Cathy this, even when Cathy asks her for the truth, telling her to 'Take care'.

As well as underestimating the severity of her fever, Nelly believes that Cathy can be won round with rational argument. It takes her quite a while to realise that 'it was vain to argue against her insanity'.

It is more luck than judgement that brings Linton's arrival at the exact moment when Nelly is trying to prevent Cathy from jumping out the window. Linton is shocked by her appearance. This forces Nelly to lie to him and to tell him that 'we couldn't inform you of her state, as we were not aware of it ourselves, but it is nothing'. This contradictory statement does not convince Edgar, who admonishes her for keeping his wife's illness from him. As he tells Nelly 'It was heartless!'

This is not the only information that Nelly conceals in this chapter, however. While Catherine is ill, Nelly discovers that Isabella has eloped with Heathcliff. Far from raising the alarm while there is still time to catch them, she instead waits until the morning before doing anything at all, even though she knows that this will give them time to get away.

Her motives for doing this are entirely self-interested. She fears being the one to 'unfold the business to my master' and thus create further commotion. Since she has just been reprimanded by Linton, she does not want to provoke further anger from him and she is worried that she might get sacked if she does so. She then justifies this to herself as it being in Linton's own best interest, which it clearly isn't. Her actual reason is her desire to avoid 'the pain of being the first proclaimant' of their elopement. In this way, the secrets Nelly keeps and the way she manipulates the characters cause the events of the narrative to progress.

It is perhaps with some justification that Cathy calls Nelly a 'hidden enemy' in this chapter.

Fever, Feathers and Folklore

In her fevered state, Cathy seems to have come to an understanding of Nelly's behaviour towards her. She comments that 'I begin to fancy that you don't like me' and she then relates a vision of Nelly as a old witch, 'gathering elf-bolts to hurt our heifers'. Elf-bolts are flint arrow heads from prehistoric times, which were reputed to have been fired at cattle by elves and fairies. This shows that Cathy is seeing Nelly as a enemy, an old hag who wishes her family harm. It also uses the qualities of fantasy, especially folk tales and superstitions, in order to explain these feelings. This is another example of Bronte using indirect and symbolic images to explore Cathy's feelings.

A further instance of this type of symbolism occurs in the handfuls of wild bird's feathers that Cathy tears from her pillow. The pigeon feathers are a reference to a superstition that the a person would have a difficult and protracted death if the bedding contained pigeon feathers.[27] The lapwings' feathers lead Cathy into an anecdote about her and Heathcliff's childhood. Her reference to Heathcliff setting a trap for lapwings, leading to the starvation of their chicks, shows perhaps that he was always cruel. It also shows Cathy's ability to tame him, as 'I made him promise never to shoot a lapwing after that, and he didn't'.

In this way, the references to bird feathers are a reference to Cathy and Heathcliff's childhood and a symbol of the natural and of the wild and uncivilised. The feathers contained inside of the pillow can be seen as both dead and tamed. The dead birds' feathers therefore link to the themes of freedom and imprisonment of this chapter.

We should also notice that Cathy continues thinking about her life as a child throughout what we might call her 'mad scene'.[28] Presumably the reference to 'our heifers' that we discussed above also means that it is the Earnshaw family she is identifying with, as they are yeoman farmers who keep cattle. (The Linton's only collect rents from tenant farmers.)

This therefore shows that Cathy is seeing herself as Catherine Earnshaw. She imagines that she is back in Wuthering Heights, and she imagines that she sees the furniture of her old room, including the 'black press'. Consequently, she is amazed and terrified by her reflection. We might guess that this is because she expected to see her younger self reflected, and doesn't recognise the women she has become. This is also illustrated in her statement to Nelly that she has been 'wrenched from the Heights' and 'converted at a stroke into Mrs. Linton, the lady of Thrushcross Grange'. This therefore shows us Cathy's inner turmoil and loss of identity.

The separation from Heathcliff, 'my all in all', has caused for Cathy a profound a loss of selfhood. She tells Nelly that 'I wish I were a girl again, half savage and hardy, and free.' Eventually, in her delirium, she starts to imagine that she is talking to Heathcliff. In her vision, the way to meet him 'must pass by Gimmerton Kirk' and she laments how slow he is in joining her. This speech is powerful and macabre. Her statement that 'I won't rest until you are with me...I never will' reminds us again of her ghost on the moors.

There are several elements of the gothic genre in this chapter. These include fearful dreams, ghostly faces, the clock striking twelve, a 'piercing shriek' and the fear that the room is haunted. The prose style used here is also contains gothic flourishes, such as in the phrase 'trembling and bewildered, she held me fast, but the horror eventually passed'. These effects are clearly intended to create an eerie sense of irrationality and of the fantastic. This use of the tropes of the gothic makes this scene more effective. Bronte's use of these familiar ways of conveying the unfamiliar, helps to draw attention to Cathy's isolation and the disintegration of her identity.

---

[27] Steve Roud *Penguin Guide to the Superstitions of Britain and Ireland* (Penguin, 2003) p.359
[28] Some critics have seen a similarity between this scene and Ophelia courting flowers during her mad scene in Hamlet.

In this way, the 'strange ideas and illusions' that Cathy experiences in her dream state have a potent effect on the reader.

These symbols can also be read in different ways, according to different literary critics, and can therefore be used to support different interpretations. For example, a psychoanalytic critic might read this chapter by considering the role of dreams, symbolism, identity and the self. Meanwhile, a Marxist critic might emphasise the conflict between nature and culture and the social pressures on Cathy that are caused by becoming 'the lady of Thrushcross Grange'. A feminist critic, on the other hand, might see Cathy's madness as a result of her imprisonment in her marriage to Edgar. A feminist critic might also think about how illness could be used by oppressed women as a strategy to exert power and consider the references to this in Victorian fiction.

Thus, different critical approaches can be used individually, or in combination, to produce interesting and individual readings of the text.

Task

Is Nelly the only character who behaves selfishly in this chapter?

What is your opinion of Edgar Linton's behaviour?

Commentary

It is not only Nelly who acts with self-interest in this chapter, and Linton cannot be thought of as blameless in Cathy's decline. He knows that she is an emotional person, who has previously suffered similar illnesses, and yet he makes no effort to check on her or to comfort her. This is the meaning of Dr. Kenneth's question 'Mr. Linton will be sorry?' As he tells Nelly, he had warned Edgar to be careful of Cathy's health, and he has not done so.

Cathy is also aware of this abandonment by her husband and by the time Edgar comes to her she tells him that 'I am past wanting you'. This is a strong and evocative phrase and, in her 'angry animation', it seems that Cathy wants to be free, out on the moors and even into her grave. We can read this symbolically as meaning that she now feels trapped in her marriage to Edgar and that she wants to escape its narrow confines.

Edgar's attitude to Isabella is also cold and harsh. At the end of the chapter, he says that he will not make any attempt to overtake her or to find her. He explains this by saying that he has not disowned her but that 'she has disowned me'. This seems unfeeling and unsympathetic, especially considering what Edgar knows of Heathcliff's character. It is not the attitude of duty and Christian charity with which Edgar Linton is usually associated.

Topic 20 – Chapter Thirteen and Fourteen

Introduction

In this topic, we will read Chapters Thirteen and Fourteen. We will think about the use of narrators and voices, and the contrasts between different characters.

Aims and Objectives

- To read Chapters Thirteen and Fourteen
- To think about the use of voices in the text
- To think about what we learn from the contrasts between different characters

Chapters Thirteen and Fourteen

In the last chapter, we saw that Isabella has eloped with Heathcliff and that Cathy is ill with a brain fever.

Task
Read Chapters 13 and 14.

In these chapters, we learn more about life at Wuthering Heights. As we might expect, conditions at the Heights have considerably deteriorated as Hindley's madness, and Heathcliff's exploitation, has increased.

Isabella now bitterly regrets her decision to marry Heathcliff. She is now trapped living with Hindley, Heathcliff, Hareton and Joseph in an environment which, especially to her genteel sensibilities, seems to resemble hell. For Isabella, 'The single pleasure I can imagine is to die, or to see him dead!'

Isabella's Letter

Isabella's letter gives us a powerful insight into her mental state. It is one of several examples where we hear a voice of one of the characters directly. Like Cathy's diary in Chapter Three, through Isabella's letter we hear her own voice within the narrative.

This is a useful storytelling device as it allows Bronte to relate events that Nelly was not witness to. More than this, however, it also creates greater sympathy for Isabella, a character who we may not otherwise understand.

It is also part of the complex structure of the novel, which uses several different voices and frames. By choosing to write the novel in this way, Bronte draws attention to the different narrators and their different opinions of the events. The critic John K. Mathison has argued that this structure forces the reader 'into an active participation in the book'.[29] Through this technique, the reader is encouraged to think about the characters and to form their own opinion.

By reading Isabella's voice we get a very different impression of her than we do from Nelly. This is one of the many contrasts that Bronte makes us think about.

Heathcliff and Edgar

Another notable distinction that we can draw in this chapter is that between the behaviour of Heathcliff and Edgar.

Edgar has abandoned Isabella to her fate. Despite her obvious difficulties, he will have nothing further to do with her. Although a man of his position would be scandalised by his sister's elopement, his response nonetheless seems cold and cruel.

Edgar is usually read as a representative of patriarchal, polite society. We can therefore consider and debate what Bronte is saying here. Is she suggesting that the privileges of domestic affection are applied only to women who are good and well behaved, and that male, patriarchal society is cruel and unforgiving of women who fall outside of their sanctioned roles?

Isabella has committed the ultimate offence against property and propriety. Therefore Edgar states that 'we are eternally divided'.

By contrast, we learn in Chapter Fourteen that Heathcliff would never leave Cathy. His devotion is strong and unwavering. It is also selfless and, unlike Edgar, there is no suggestion that Heathcliff wants to own Cathy or control who she could see. He insists that 'I never would have banished him from her society, as long as she desired his.'

This forms a clear contrast with Edgar's affections, which are shown as petty and jealous, since he will not even deign to rescue his sister from a tyrant. Heathcliff further

---

[29] John K. Mathison 'Nelly Dean and the Power of Wuthering Heights' in *Nineteenth Century Fiction*, 1956 cited Claire Steele *Wuthering Heights: York Notes Advanced*, (Pearson Education, 2012) p.74

claims that if Edgar 'loved with all the powers of his puny being, he couldn't love as much in eighty years, as I could in a day'.

Indeed, depth of love that Heathcliff feels for Cathy is brought to the fore in this chapter. However, the other side of this passionate nature is again one of violence. Heathcliff's hatred for Edgar is also deep and profound and in a vivid phrase he describes how, as soon as Catherine has disregarded him 'I would have torn his heart out and drank his blood!'

Task

1) References to hell run through these two chapters. Find and discuss three examples.

2) What is the significance of the violence against Isabella's dog in this chapter?

Commentary

1) In these two chapters, there are many references to hell. Most of these equate Heathcliff with hell or the devil. In her letter, Isabella asks "Is Mr. Heathcliff a man? If so, is he mad? And if not, is he a devil?" Through asking this question, Isabella draws attention to Heathcliff's strange and terrifying nature. Indeed, many readers have questioned Heathcliff's nature as mad, bad or evil.

Hindley also refers to Heathcliff using references to hell. In a powerful statement, he says that "Oh, damnation!...hell shall have his soul! It will be ten times blacker with that guest than ever it was before!" In this phrase, he describes Heathcliff's soul as unusually evil, using the alliterative and hyperbolic phrase 'ten times blacker'. Hindley suggests that Heathcliff takes a certain enjoyment in his devilry, which we know to be true. However, this also suggests a certain loneliness or isolation, through comparing Heathcliff to one of the lost souls in hell.

Heathcliff also sees himself as a lost soul. He tells us that without Catherine, "Two words would comprehend my future, *death* and *hell* - existence, after losing her, would be hell." This echoes the other characters' description of him as a devil in hell. However, it also goes some way to explaining it. We might interpret his words to mean that his evil behaviour is a result of his separation from his love; that without Catherine he is a shade, a lost soul or a demon.

2) The hanging of Isabella's dog on a bridle hook seems symbolic. 'Bridle' (meaning the headpiece used to control a horse) is a homophone of 'Bridal' (meaning related to a bride of newly married couple). This is therefore a sort of pun, which draws attention to the way that Heathcliff will control Isabella. This is an example of Bronte's clever use of language.

Topic 20 – Volume II, Chapters I and II

Introduction

In this topic, we will read Chapters I and II of the second volume. We will look at the powerful themes of love and death and the role that these play in the novel.

Aims and Objectives

- To read chapters I and II
- To think about the themes of love and death

Volume II - A Note on the Text

From this point on, we will be numbering the chapters in roman numerals, to distinguish them from the chapters in Volume I.

We will also be using 'Cathy' to refer to the older Catherine Linton (nee Earnshaw) and 'Catherine' to refer to her daughter. This is a convention that many academics follow.

In your own essays, you must also be careful to make sure that you are clear which Catherine you are writing about, so that the examiner can follow your argument.

Task

To read Chapters I and II.

The Death of Cathy

In this chapter, Cathy is dying. We notice that Nelly is already describing her in terms that suggest an otherworldly or ghostly appearance. Dressed in a white dress, we hear that she has an 'unearthly beauty' and that she already seems to 'gaze beyond'. More prosaically, Nelly also tells us that she is 'stamped as one doomed to decay'.

Task

Re-read the section from:

'Mrs Linton bent forward' to 'had her grasped in his arms'.

Identify some of the literary and linguistic features that you find.

Mrs. Linton bent forward, and listened breathlessly. The minute after a step traversed the hall; the

> **Comment [hb1]:** This creates a strong sense of anticipation.

> **Comment [hb2]:** This builds narrative tension. The length of this sentence also adds further to this tension. As readers, we are waiting, expectantly, for Heathcliff's arrival, but we are delayed by Nelly's thoughts.

open house was too tempting for Heathcliff to resist walking in: most likely he supposed that I was

inclined to shirk my promise, and so resolved to trust to his own audacity. With straining eagerness

> **Comment [hb3]:** This is not an unrealistic expectation of Nelly's behaviour. This confirms our impression that Heathcliff is fairly astute.

> **Comment [hb4]:** This use of the present participle 'straining' also creates a sense of tension.

Catherine gazed towards the entrance of her chamber. He did not hit the right room directly: she

> **Comment [hb5]:** This verb is wistful and romantic.

> **Comment [hb6]:** This is a more complex way of saying 'door'. This again helps to draw out the narrative. It also sounds weighty and portentous and may help to create an enhanced sense of the importance of this meeting. It also has some overtones of medieval romance.

motioned me to admit him, but he found it out ere I could reach the door, and in a stride or two was

> **Comment [hb7]:** Again, this creates a strong sense of anticipation. We imagine Catherine waiting and listening as Heathcliff tries several doors.

> **Comment [hb8]:** This is quite an archaic use of language. It may also be intended to create a sense of the medieval romance.

at her side, and had her grasped in his arms.

> **Comment [hb9]:** This creates a strong impression of Heathcliff's powerful masculinity.

> **Comment [hb10]:** 'Grasped' is a very possessive verb. We get a strong sense of Heathcliff's power and desire here.

Heathcliff sees the change in Cathy and they both know that they are meeting for the last time. Their speech is powerful and impassioned. Both speak of their separation as unbearable. Cathy wishes that she could hold onto Heathcliff 'till we were both dead'. For Heathcliff, separation is the 'torments of hell'. He cannot even bring himself to use the word 'die', saying 'What kind of living will it be when you - Oh God!' These images of death, hell and suffering show the depths of their anguish and pain.

Task

Re-read the section from:

'Do come to me Heathcliff' to 'in great perplexity'.

Identify some of the literary and linguistic features that you find.

In her eagerness she rose and supported herself on the arm of the chair. At that earnest appeal he

> **Comment [hb1]:** This is a detailed image that creates a strong visual impression of this scene for the reader. This draws us in and helps us to see this scene in our mind's eye.

turned to her, looking absolutely desperate. His eyes wide, and wet at last, flashed fiercely on her;

> **Comment [hb2]:** Heathcliff is now crying, or close to it. This phrasing also creates alliteration between 'wide' and 'wet' which builds narrative momentum. As the lover's come together, the speed of the narrative picks up.

his breast heaved convulsively. An instant they held asunder, and then how they met I hardly saw

> **Comment [hb3]:** Another use of alliteration to show the force with which Heathcliff looks at Cathy. These are not Edgar's 'dove's eyes'.

> **Comment [hb4]:** This creates a strong sense of passion and romance. It would've been more original at the time of Bronte's writing.

but Catherine made a spring, and he caught her, and they were locked in an embrace from which

> **Comment [hb5]:** This is a dramatic pause. There is a very visual quality to Bronte's writing in this section. We see the actions of the character's clearly.

> **Comment [hb6]:** This might be intended to create a slight sense of mystery, or to show the speed with which they embrace.

thought my mistress would never be released alive: in fact, to my eyes, she seemed directly

> **Comment [hb7]:** The verbs 'spring' and 'caught' are dynamic and this creates a vivid sense of the action of this scene.

> **Comment [hb8]:** This shows how closely and tightly they hold each other. 'Locked' also suggests imprisonment, although the sense of it here is very different to that in Chapter 12, and it may suggest permanence. It may also suggest the idea of two halves fitting together, like a lock and a key.

insensible. He flung himself into the nearest seat, and on my approaching hurriedly to ascertain if

> **Comment [hb9]:** This echoes Cathy and Heathcliff's own desire to be together until death.

> **Comment [hb10]:** Again, this creates a strong sense of movement.

she had fainted, he gnashed at me, and foamed like a mad dog, and gathered her to him with greedy

> **Comment [hb11]:** These comparators suggest something animalistic in Heathcliff's passion.

> **Comment [hb12]:** The g sound of gathered is repeated in 'greedy'. This enhances the sense of Cathy being drawn towards Heathcliff.

jealousy. I did not feel as if I were in the company of a creature of my own species: it appeared that

> **Comment [hb13]:** This reminds us of how Heathcliff has longed to have Cathy to himself and to take her from Linton.

> **Comment [hb14]:** Again, this compares Heathcliff to an animal.

he would not understand, though I spoke to him; so I stood off, and held my tongue, in great

> **Comment [hb15]:** Nelly cannot understand the heights of this passion. Like the reader, she can only look on from the outside.

perplexity.

Heathcliff and Cathy's final meeting is full of both love and recrimination. In their embrace, they realise what they have had and lost. Heathcliff's words '*Why* did you betray your own heart, Cathy?' show that he realises how she has loved him all this time. He now blames her for leaving him and accuses her of killing herself by marrying Linton.

Eventually, they fall silent and cry together, 'washed by each other's tears'. The verb 'washed' suggests cleansing, and in the Christian religion (remembering that Emily Bronte's father was a clergyman), it also suggests spiritual purification. From this, we we get a sense that their anger has now abated, at least to some extent and that this final embrace shows their reconciliation.

This section could be considered one of the most powerful, passionate and romantic passages in all of English literature.

Nelly's Callousness

Nelly, however, is pre-occupied with her own position, and cares little for the reunion of the lovers. At the sounds of Linton's return, she is distraught. Her statement '"She's fainted or dead", I thought, "so much the better"' is extremely cold. It is clear that Nelly cares much more about herself than she does about Cathy. This is also shown when she says that Heathcliff staying is the 'most diabolical thing you ever did', since it is likely to get her fired. Considering the many terrible things that Heathcliff has done (especially his treatment of Isabella) then this statement is nothing short of ludicrous and only shows the depths of Nelly's selfishness.

She also lies to Heathcliff to get rid of him. She tells him that Cathy is better, when she is actually 'all bewildered'. She then tells us that looks quickly into the room and then leaves after 'ascertaining that what I said was apparently true'. This sentence is full of obfuscation. As Nelly well knows, Cathy will not recover. It is cruel of her to suggest to Heathcliff otherwise. Again, this decision is motivated only by her self-interest. Heathcliff, however, is perfectly aware of the truth of the situation.

Heathcliff's Reaction to Cathy's Death

Heathcliff is waiting for Nelly 'leant against an old ash tree' and we are told that he is so still that two birds are hopping around his feet. This image allies him with nature and with the natural world.

Although he is physically still, however, he is clearly in torment. He holds 'a silent combat with his inward agony' and trembles with grief. Finally, his grief explodes in 'a sudden paroxysm of ungovernable passion'. Again, Nelly describes something animal in his passion. He howls and is described as 'a savage beast getting goaded to death with knives and spears'. In death, as in life, there is nothing civilised or mild in his and Cathy's relationship.

Nelly tries to present Cathy's death as gentle and peaceful, but Heathcliff will not accept this image. He will not believe that she is at rest and longs for her to haunt him. His desire is that Cathy 'Be with me always - take any form - drive me mad!" and this again reminds the reader of her ghostly return. He describes her as 'my life' and as 'my soul'. He equates life without her to hell and to 'this abyss where I cannot find you'. These are powerful and moving words that have a considerable effect on the reader.

Cathy's Grave

Nelly makes an effort to tell us (via Lockwood) that, while watching Cathy's body, she felt 'an assurance of the endless and shadowless hereafter' and this reminds us of the traditional Christian beliefs that Nelly embodies. However, even she cannot be completely certain that Catherine is at peace. This echoes Catherine's own fears that she could not be happy in heaven and Lockwood describes this belief as 'something heterodox' or, in other words, as something outside of conventional Christian thought.

Cathy is finally buried at the edge of the kirkyard in a wild area 'where the wall is so low that heath and bilberry plants have climbed over it from the moor'. This spiritually positions her somewhere between the conventional Christianity represented by the Church and the oneness with nature symbolised by the moors. This illustrates her character. It may also suggest something about Bronte's own 'heterodox' approach to spirituality.

Topic 21 – Chapter III: Isabella, Hindley and Heathcliff

Introduction

In this topic, we will read Chapters III and IV. We will then look at the confrontation between Isabella, Hindley and Heathcliff. We will then consider the role of violence in the novel.

Aims and Objectives

- To read Chapters III
- To consider the role of violence in the novel

Chapter III

In this chapter, Isabella returns to the Grange with a dramatic story to tell.

Task

Read Chapter III.

Violence

We have seen before how violence is a central theme of Wuthering Heights. The extremes of emotion associated with these characters' wild and passionate natures often overspill into physical violence.

In this chapter, Isabella, Hindley and Heathcliff all show their violent side. In dramatic episode, the relations between Hindley, Heathcliff and Isabella reach a climax. Hindley is less drunk than usual and decides to lock Heathcliff out of the Heights. Heathcliff eventually manages to seize Hindley's weapon, and in a scene reminiscent of Lockwood dream of the ghostly Cathy, the knife slices Hindley's wrist. Heathcliff is then able to enter through the window and attack Hindley.

Therefore, although Heathcliff is frequently referred to as a devil or a 'fiend' (and this is especially so in this chapter), he is certainly not the only character to exhibit violent tendencies. This shows that violence is a perennial part of life in the novel. But where does this violence originate and what is Bronte suggesting about its source?

Both Hindley and Heathcliff have experienced violence from childhood. There is a strong suggestion that Heathcliff's character has been formed from the harsh life that he has suffered. Hindley, too, has experienced displacement from his father's affections and the loss of his wife.

Yet, this wildness does not only exist at the Heights, it exists at the Grange as well, albeit in a different form. When we first see Isabella and Edgar, they have been arguing over a pet dog, almost tearing the dog to pieces in the process. Cathy is then attacked by a bull dog, since old Mr. Linton thinks that she and Heathcliff are trying to steal their rents. Thus, we see that not only is violence a hidden or suppressed part of genteel life, civilised life is actually supported by hidden brutality. The guard dog represents the force that lies behind civilised authority.

Isabella and Violence

In this way, violence is part of the sophisticated and civilised lives of the Grange, just as much as it is part of the wilder life at the Heights. Violence is shown to exist in women as well as men, and Bronte never draws the superficial gender distinction that women are less violent than men.

Indeed, this violent streak is certainly present in Isabella. Despite her role as a representative of the genteel young lady, in this chapter, she is every bit as wild as any other character.

Isabella explains that her violent feelings are the result of her treatment by Heathcliff. In a long passage which is worth quoting at length, she says:

> I gave him my heart and he took it and pinched it to death; and flung it back to me - people feel with their hearts, Ellen, and since he has destroyed mine, I have not power to feel for him, and I would not, though he groaned from this to his dying day, and wept tears of blood for Catherine!

This tells us a great deal about sympathy and empathy. Isabella has suffered greatly at Heathcliff's hands and she claims that she can no longer feel anything for him, however much he hurts. Nelly's constant exhortations to 'Be more charitable' are also therefore interesting. Nelly represents the ideals of Christianity. Her ideals are the way that human beings should behave, but Isabella is here reflecting on the way that people really do behave and their reasons for doing so. Isabella's statement that 'I'm afraid, Ellen, you'll set me down as really wicked - but you don't know all so don't judge!' is very apt. Bronte has created a world here that was strange and alien to readers. There are no easy moral answers.

Bronte's Views

What Bronte seems to be saying about violence is complex and interesting. It would be straightforward and possibly simplistic to suggest that violence begets violence. As Hindley tells Heathcliff "Treachery and violence are a just return for treachery and violence!"

There is nothing in Wuthering Heights to contradict this view, but Bronte's argument seems to be more nuanced than this. Violence, she seems to be suggesting, is a part of life and a natural response to strong emotions. It is an intrinsic part of our animalistic natures.

She might even be suggesting that this form of natural violence is more honest than that shown at the Grange. There may even be something slightly false about the behaviour that Isabella exhibits in this scene. Although Isabella says that 'I wouldn't have aided or abetted an attempt on even *his* life, for anything', she actually wants Hindley to kill Heathcliff and so she also takes no action whatsoever to prevent it. If Hindley had succeeded, she could not be considered legally culpable. However, we might wonder whether or not she could really be absolved of all moral responsibility? Is she adhering to a sense of morality than is superficially correct, but somehow disingenuous? What does this suggest about her character, and about civilised society more generally? This is an idea that Bronte encourages us to think about, rather than to take at face value.

In this way, as with so many aspects of this deep and complex novel, the reader is left to make up their own mind about the events and their significance. As Nelly says, with some irony:

> But you'll not want to hear my moralising, Mr. Lockwood: you'll judge as well as I can, or you'll think you will, and that's the same.

The many ambiguities of the novel, including the structure through dual narrators, are intended to make the reader ask questions. We have to bring our own ideas to our reading, however problematic that may be.

Task

As Isabella runs out of the house, she sees Hareton 'hanging a litter of puppies from a chair-back in the doorway'.

What is your interpretation of this?

Commentary

Situated in this chapter, this is a further example of the violence at the grange.

However, unlike the Heathcliff's hanging of Isabella's dog, there is no malice in Hareton's hanging of the puppies. It is simply practical. Wuthering Heights is a working farm, and there is no space for pets.

This is therefore a different presentation of violence in this chapter, which again shows the complexity of Bronte's ideas. The juxtaposition of these different examples of violence encourages the reader to ask questions of the novel.

Task

This task is simply to think and reflect on the powerful themes of Wuthering Heights.

Thinking about the novel, and forming your own personal response to it, is an important part of studying English. It is useful to take time, at regular intervals. to think about the important issues that the novel raises. Remember that you don't have to agree with my views, and that you should bring your own ideas to the text. You may also like to take a few notes to record your thoughts.

As this is a personal response, there is no commentary on this activity.

Topic 22 – Chapter IV: Young Catherine

Introduction

In this topic, we will read Chapter IV. We will then look at the character of young Catherine.

Aims and Objectives

- To read Chapters IV
- To consider the character of young Catherine

Task

Read Chapter IV.

Young Catherine

In this chapter, we learn a little about young Catherine. We are told that she is 'a sweet little girl' but that she also has something of a rebellious or 'saucy' nature. Nelly is very fond of young Catherine and speaks very highly of her.

At the beginning of the chapter, there is a long description of Catherine. We can look at this extract in full:

> She was the most winning thing that ever brought sunshine into a desolate house - a real beauty in face - with the Earnshaws' handsome dark eyes, but the Lintons' fair skin, and small features, and yellow curling hair. Her spirit was high, though not rough, and qualified by a heart sensitive and lively to excess in its affections. That capacity for intense attachments reminded me of her mother; still she did not resemble her; for she could be soft and mild as a dove, and she had a gentle voice, and pensive expression: her anger was never furious; her love never fierce; it was deep and tender.

In this passage, we are told that Catherine has some of the physical attributes of the Earnshaws and some of the Lintons. She is therefore shown to be a blend of the characteristics of her parents, Edgar and Cathy. This is shown to be a matter of personality as well as physical appearance, and it has some symbolic significance.

We are told that she has a gentle voice and pensive expression, and these are attributes of Edgar. She also has the high spirit and intense affection of Cathy. However, her strong emotions are tempered by the more reflective nature of the Lintons. In short, she has combined the positive qualities of both parents into a well-balanced whole.

We might wonder whether some of this praise is for Lockwood's benefit, since Nelly is hoping that he will marry Catherine and rescue her from the Heights. However, we know that Nelly's affection for Catherine is genuine and she describes her childhood years as 'the happiest of my life'.

Some of the similarities between Catherine and her parents further suggest a system of parallels between the characters of the novel. In giving the same name to both heroines, Bronte emphasises both the similarities and differences between them.

We might therefore be able to read the younger Catherine as a daughter who has risen above the flaws of her mother. We might even be tempted to see this as a second chance for a romantic resolution, and the possibility of a happier life for her daughter.

Task

What do you think is the symbolic significance of Penistone Craggs?

Commentary

Penistone Crags has a symbolic significance. Catherine's journey there represents the more rebellious side of her character. Her life is fairly sheltered, and she longs for new experiences. As she says 'But I know the park, and, I don't know those'. They therefore represent the exciting and the unknown.

The Craggs also represent a high, towering place. Freudian readings of literary texts often suggest that such places have a phallic significance and represent male dominance. In a Freudian reading, a desire to reach the Craggs may therefore also symbolically represent a desire for more power and independence, which are traditionally masculine attributes.

Feminist critics have seen a number of examples of women desiring power throughout *Wuthering Heights*. If the gifts that the children ask Mr. Earnshaw to bring them from Liverpool are symbolic, then the older Cathy's desire for a whip illustrates her desire for power and autonomy. Similarly, Isabella looks at Hindley's pistol with 'covetousness' thinking 'How powerful I should be possessing such an instrument!' Both a gun and a whip can also be read as phallic symbols. According to Gilbert and Gubar, these are not symbols, as Freud would suggest, of the penis itself, but rather of the desire for power.[30]

It is possible to read the same symbolic significance into Penistone Craggs and the hazel switch that young Catherine uses to jump her horse out of the limitations of the park.

---

[30] Sandra M. Gilbert and Susan Gubar *The Madwoman in the Attic: The Woman Writer and the Nineteenth Century Literary Imagination* (Yale Nota Bene, Second Edition, 2000) p.264 and p.272

Topic 23 – Linton Heathcliff

Introduction

In this topic, we will read Chapters V - IX. We will think about the character of Linton Heathcliff.

Aims and Objectives

- To read Chapters V - IX
- To learn about Linton Heathcliff

Linton Heathcliff

At the end of the last topic, we looked briefly at the idea of parallels. You may therefore like to think about the arrival of Linton as a parallel for the arrival of Heathcliff from Liverpool. This parallel also draws attention to the very different characters of Linton and his father.

In this topic, we will be reading a longer section of five chapters, so that we can look at the character of Linton Heathcliff.

Task

Read chapters V, VI, VII, VIII and IX.

Think about the character of Linton and make a note of any significant quotations.

Characterisation

Linton Heathcliff is frequently described in terms of his appearance. He is 'a pale, delicate, effeminate boy' with 'a sickly peevishness'. This is not a flattering description and Linton is a stark contrast to Heathcliff's vigorous masculinity.

According to Victorian ideals, men and boys were expected to be strong and hardy. Indeed, illness itself was often feminised. This has lead some critics to discuss Linton's 'feminine' character as an example of the complex gender dynamics of the novel, where biological sex does not always equate to gendered social position.

Linton's 'weak' constitution might also have suggested to Victorian readers a weak moral character. Nelly describes him as 'selfish and disagreeable' and it is difficult to argue against this view. Linton is repeatedly described as immature and babyish. He is described as 'a whelp' and 'a pet' and a 'puling chicken' These animal metaphors are used to convey the sense that he is pathetic and helpless.

However, we may also feel very sorry for Linton. Heathcliff regards him as nothing but a piece of property, and even Nelly quickly abandons him. When Nelly says that 'I began to dislike, more than to compassionate, Linton, and to excuse his father, in some measure, for holding him cheap' then we may find this statement shocking. Linton is treated harshly by all those around him, and although they themselves realise that they are contributing to his bad qualities, they still seem unable to help him.

Yet, there is also a sense in which Linton himself drives people away. This 'fretful, ailing charge' is tiresome and trying and, like most of the character, we too may find it difficult to put up with his constant tearful demands. In short, there is very little to like about Linton Heathcliff, and we are more ready to feel pity than sympathy for him.

Indeed, although we are supposed to make our own judgements about Linton, rather than relying on that of the narrators, most readers will find him an unsympathetic character. This must be considered as part of Bronte's design for the novel. Arguably, she may be suggesting that Linton's failure to take action to improve his own physical condition or situation is his major failing. He lacks the self-improving sprit of the more robust characters. This strength and independence of was a quality that Victorian culture also often prized and that Emily Bronte herself displayed to a striking extent.

If Catherine therefore represents the best qualities of her parents, then Linton may represent the worst qualities of his. He combines Heathcliff's manipulative and sometimes petty nature with the petulance and feebleness of the Lintons.

Catherine and Linton

Catherine, however, goes to some trouble in maintaining her relationship with Linton. She seems determined to see the best in him.

Again, this has a parallel in the earlier story, and it echoes Isabella's desire to see Heathcliff as a romantic hero.

Catherine, however, seems to apply more balanced judgement than Isabella. This is in keeping with her inheritance of the good qualities of both the Earnshaws and Lintons.

We also see this dual character in her behaviour towards Linton. She is rebellious in continuing to see Linton, and she hides her correspondence from Nelly. However, she is also gentle and tender towards him, and she treats him with great affection.
In the same way that her high spirits drew her to seek out Penistone Craggs and to meet Hareton at the Heights, some readers have thought that it is her rebellious nature that draws her closer to Linton. Other readers, however, would argue that her persistence owes as much to her sense of love and charity as to her sense of rebellion.

In this reading, it is her more moral qualities of kindness and sympathy that lead her to become embroiled in Heathcliff's revenge. This is an aspect of the novel that you could think about and debate.

Boundaries

Some literary critics have drawn particular attention to the episode in Chapter VIII where Catherine climbs down from the wall of Thrushcross Park to retrieve her hat, and is then unable to climb back up. It is while in this area, outside of the safety of her father's property, that she meets Heathcliff and hears of Linton's illness. This therefore illustrates her vulnerability and gives the boundary of the park an additional symbolic meaning.

The literary critic Rod Mengham is particularly interested in the role of borders and boundaries in the novel. As he points out, many significant events take place over, through or across symbolic boundaries. Windows are a particularly important as a recurrent motif. Lockwood's encounter with Cathy's ghost, Cathy and Heathcliff's first visit to the Grange, and Heathcliff's fight with Hindley all take place through windows.[31]

This is an interesting recurrent device and it is worth thinking about the many kinds of borders and boundaries in the novel. This can help us to think about the many ways of crossing or transgressing categories, such as class, gender, or even the boundary between life and death. It also helps to illuminate some of the structural symmetries and parallels of the novel.

Task

Linton is very different to Catherine's other cousin Hareton.

Find five examples of the appearance and characters of Hareton and Linton that explore the differences between them.

---

[31] See Rod Mengham *Penguin Critical Studies: Wuthering Heights* (Penguin, 1989) p. 95

Commentary

Here are some examples that you may have found:

Hareton	Linton
'a great strong lad of eighteen'	'whey-faced whining wretch!'
'a well-made, athletic youth, good-looking in features, and stout and healthy'	'Linton's looks were very languid, and his form extremely slight; but there was a grace in his manner that mitigated those defects and rendered him not unpleasing.'
'fearless nature'	'a faint-hearted creature'
'gold put to the use of paving stones'	'tin polished to ape a service of silver'
'he was never taught to read or write'	'I've engaged a tutor, also, to come three times a week, from twenty miles distance, to teach him what he pleases to learn.'

These examples explore some of the differences between the cousins. From this, you can start to think about Heathcliff's effect on the lives of his two 'sons'.

Topic 24 – Chapters X - XII: Deceit

Introduction

In this topic, we will read Chapters X, XI and XII. We will think about the events of these chapters and how they link to the themes of the novel.

Aims and Objectives

- To read Chapters X, XI and XII
- To think about the effects of deceit in *Wuthering Heights*

Deceit

In these chapters, you will notice that the characters are keeping pieces of information secret from each other.

This contributes to the unfortunate turn taken by events and allows Heathcliff to progress in his scheme for revenge.

Task

Read Chapters X, XI and XII.

In Chapter X, Nelly realises that Catherine has been visiting Wuthering Heights while she has been ill. Catherine confesses that this was partly because she wanted to know what was happening to Linton, and partly out of a sense of duty. She feels torn between two obligations. By her logic, telling her father will only upset him, and not going to the Heights will upset Linton. Catherine therefore begs Nelly not to tell her father, saying 'It will be very heartless if you do.'

Nelly says that she will think it over, but immediately goes to tell Edgar. She leaves out the content of their discussions, and Linton's poor state of health, even though this was one of Catherine's main motives for visiting him. Edgar therefore bans Catherine from visiting the Heights.

In Chapter XI, Edgar begins to wonder what will happen to Catherine after he dies. He wonders whether Linton would be a good husband to her. Nelly seems to give him quite accurate advice that, 'he is scarcely likely to reach manhood'. But although she says that Catherine marrying him would be a 'misfortune', she also says that 'he would not be beyond her control, unless she were extremely foolish and indulgent'. On the one hand, this seems a fairly sensible assessment of Linton, but on the other, it is not really enough information for Edgar.

Edgar still does not appreciate the state of Linton's ill-health. His bloody coughing fit in the last chapter suggests that he has consumption and that he might not live very long. Heathcliff is now supervising Linton's letter writing and the idea that he is 'riding and walking on the moors' is false. Heathcliff also seeks a marriage between the Catherine and Linton for his own nefarious reasons, and he is more than prepared to lie and manipulate to get it.

Heathcliff instructs Linton to pretend to be well, even though he is now becoming seriously ill. Interestingly, Catherine notices this when she says that 'It's just as if it were a task he was compelled to perform - this interview - for fear his father should scold him'. We know that Heathcliff would do more than 'scold' however, and we realise that 'the imaginary voice' that Linton hears is actually Heathcliff's. Catherine does not fully understand this and she does not know how to interpret this situation.

Nelly, on the other hand, realises that Linton is very ill. However, she does not pass this knowledge on to Edgar.

Catherine is also unaware of Edgar's own state of ill-health. She believes that now he is able to walk in the garden, he is getting better. Again, Nelly knows that this is not true.

In this way, Bronte creates a complex pattern whereby different characters have access to different information.

Deceit in *Wuthering Heights*

In *Wuthering Heights*, and especially in Volume II of the novel, the characters frequently attempt to deceive each other.

Often their motives are 'good' in the sense that they are trying to avoid causing distress to others. However, even these positive aims actually lead to further confusion and allow Heathcliff's revenge to take shape. As the proverb suggests 'the road to hell is paved with good intentions'.

At the end of Chapter XII, Nelly tells us that when Edgar asks about the meeting with Linton, she 'threw little light on his enquiries, for I hardly knew what to hide, and what to reveal'. She therefore suggests that, had she known how to present their meeting, she would have done so. This indirectly reveals that Nelly is habitually accustomed to bending the truth in order to create a particular impression or to further a particular outcome.

This causes us as readers to question, not only her narration, but also her intentions and the influence she has on events.

Catherine is particularly susceptible to this disinformation.

Catherine is not aware of Heathcliff powers of manipulation. She hasn't been told the history of her family, and so she doesn't understand Heathcliff's motivations or the depth of his desire for revenge. Bronte may therefore be suggesting that Catherine's innocence and goodness allows her to be deceived. Or that her caregivers, in trying to protect her, have actually left her in a vulnerable position.

Wuthering Heights is often classified as a gothic novel. Interestingly, another gothic author, Ann Radcliffe, wrote a novel called *The Mysteries of Udolpho* in which the heroine Emily St. Aubert has led an overprotected life and therefore her lack of experience and education mean that she is unable to interpret the designs of her evil uncle. Like Catherine, she must rely on her inner strength and resourcefulness to make sense of her situation.

Task

How has Hareton been deceived? What do we learn about his character in Chapter X?

Commentary

Hareton has also been deceived. Heathcliff has manipulated him for his own ends and has more or less cheated him out of his position. As Hindley's son, Hareton would have inherited Wuthering Heights, except that Heathcliff became mortgagee of the house and land by lending money to Hindley for gambling. He has since kept Hareton in ignorance and servility.

Hareton, however, retains the social position of being an Earnshaw. In Chapter X, he tells Cathy, with some trepidation, that he is learning to read. He tells her that 'I can read yon, nah' and he now knows that the name above the front door is his own. Thus learning to read is symbolic of Hareton's realisation of his social position, and the beginnings of his desire to take his place in the household.

This is the source of his argument with Linton. He is now starting to realise that he, as Hindley's son, should be in charge at the Heights, and he resents Linton taking his place. Joseph encourages his new attitude saying '*He* knaws - Aye, he knaws, as weel as Aw do, who sud be t'maister yonder'.

Heathcliff sees Hareton's position as an outsider as a parallel to his own childhood and claims 'I can sympathise with all his feelings, having felt them myself'. However, Hareton is not like Heathcliff. Although, he is starting to realise that he has been lied to and manipulated by Heathcliff, he does not seek revenge. Indeed, Hareton's feelings about the Heights are complicated by the fact that he loves Heathcliff, as Heathcliff is the only person who has shown him kindness.

Hareton's views of the world are changing, however, and Heathcliff's attempt to keep Hareton in eternal 'coarseness and ignorance' might not be as effective as he thinks.

Topic 25 – Chapters XIII and XIV: Imprisonment

Introduction

In this topic, we will read Chapters XIII and XIV. We will look at the theme of imprisonment. We will then consider the role of the law in the novel.

Aims and Objectives

- To read Chapters XIII and XIV

- To think about the theme of imprisonment

- To consider the role of the law in the novel

Task

Read Chapters XIII and XIV.

Imprisoned!

In this section, Nelly and Catherine are held prisoner at the Heights for five days. This is a strange and frightening turn of events, and this is a very dramatic point in the novel.

Imprisonment is a recurrent theme in *Wuthering Heights.* At different times and for different characters both the Grange and the Heights are a kind of prison. We are reminded of Catherine's comment in Chapter IX that 'The Grange is not a prison, Ellen, and you are not my jailer'. Here, Catherine finds her genteel existence at the Grange constraining and she feels limited by the demands of family and society.

In Chapter XIII, Linton, by contrast, is forbidden re-entry to the Heights unless he is accompanied by Catherine. Heathcliff plans to keep Catherine imprisoned until she can be married to Linton.

Even after their marriage ceremony, Catherine is still kept locked up in Linton's bedroom (until she is eventually able to escape). This also recalls her mother's self-imprisonment in her bedroom in order to keep away from Edgar.

This can be read as a suggestion that marriage itself is a kind of prison, especially for women.

Property and Propriety

Heathcliff is manipulating these events in order to gain property. He seeks possession of Thrushcross Grange so that he can become a gentleman. This would be the fulfilment of his ambitions, as it would place him at the level of Edgar. In his mind, this will answer Cathy's demand and make him worthy of marriage to her.

Heathcliff's slightly convoluted plan requires that Linton live longer than Edgar, in order to inherit Thrushcross Grange when he dies. The Grange will then be passed to Heathcliff (by Linton's Will) at Linton's death.

Some critics have praised Bronte's knowledge of the Victorian legal system and some have said that she knew little about it. As one Victorian critic of *Wuthering Heights* noted, in this period, forced marriages were already illegal. However, in the wild world of the Heights, it may be that this would make little difference. As Nelly says 'There's law in the land, thank God, there is! though we *be* in an out-of-the-way place.'

This comment suggests that Bronte was well-aware of the law. The marriage between Catherine and Linton is therefore mainly a plot point that puts Catherine under Heathcliff's control.

We could debate whether or not the legal situation in *Wuthering Heights* is fully realistic, but this is not the most important issue. Many critics have instead decided to read the situation as a reflection of Bronte's impressions of the legal system and as evidence of her feminist political stance. In this way, both Marxist and feminist critics have interpreted *Wuthering Heights* as a searing indictment of the class divisions and gender inequality of Victorian society.

Certainly, the impression that Bronte creates here is of a legal system that is easily manipulated and that often acts to oppress women and deny their agency and oppose their interests. However, as with so much of the novel, nothing in *Wuthering Heights* is given to a simplistic or straightforward interpretation.

In *Wuthering Heights* we see the law being manipulated by Heathcliff to his own ends. He uses his wealth and influence unscrupulously. We learn that Mr. Green the solicitor has 'sold himself to Mr. Heathcliff'. He delays arriving at the Grange until it is too late to set up a trust to protect Catherine's interests.

However, we might also wonder why Edgar has left it so late to make these provisions. Knowing that he was ill, he could have made appropriate legal arrangements long ago. Some of the reason may be that he expects Catherine to marry Linton and therefore to be able to remain in the Grange as Linton's wife. As Nelly says, he is 'ignorant how nearly he and his nephew would quit the world together'.

This ignorance is, however, Nelly's fault. If she has taken more trouble to inform him of Linton's ill-health, Edgar would've been better placed to devise and defeat Heathcliff's plans.

Once again, we see that it is a complex mixture of circumstances that leads to the events described in the novel. In this way, *Wuthering Heights* can be interpreted in many different ways, to many different purposes, and in accordance with many critical schools.

Task

Find three examples of Nelly's untruths in this section.

Commentary

Nelly is less than honest several times in this section. These include:

'Catherine, we would have fain deluded yet'.

'I said Heathcliff forced me to go in, which was not quite true; I uttered as little as possible against Linton; nor did I describe all his father's brutal conduct - my intentions being to add no bitterness, if I could help it, to his already overflowing cup.'

'imploring her to say she should be happy with young Heathcliff. She stared, but soon comprehending why I counselled her to offer the falsehood. she assured me she would not complain.'

It is for the reader to decide whether or not these lies are justified and to consider the effect that they have on the story.

Another interesting observation of Nelly's in Chapter XIII is:

'I seated myself in a chair, and rocked, to and fro, passing harsh judgement on my many derelictions of duty; from which, it struck me then, all the misfortunes of all my employers sprang. It was not the case, in reality, I am aware; but it was, in my imagination, that dismal night, and I thought Heathcliff himself less guilty than I.'

There is some over-exaggeration on Nelly's part here. The repetition of 'all' in 'all the misfortunes of all my employers' is clearly excessive and therefore serves to suggest the opposite: that Nelly is not and cannot be responsible for all the troubles of the novel. Similarly, she is clearly not as guilty as Heathcliff and this makes her guilt appear maudlin. This can be seen as a device that Nelly uses to create sympathy for herself. Although she knows that she has told some untruths, she wants Lockwood, her immediate audience, to sympathise with her.

Yet we might also notice that Nelly is quite quick to forgive herself here, and we might wonder how far her culpability is really only in her 'imagination'.

Again, this is a question for the reader to determine.

Topic 26 – Chapter XV

Introduction

In this topic, we will read Chapter XV. We will examine the events of this chapter and then practice our skills of linguistic and literary analysis.

Aims and Objectives

- To read Chapter XV
- To gain an overview of this chapter
- To practice skills of linguistic and literary analysis

Chapter XV

In this chapter, Heathcliff comes to collect Catherine from the Grange, to bring her back to Wuthering Heights. He also tells Nelly about an incident that happened to him the previous night.

Task

Read Chapter XV.

Catherine, Heathcliff and Linton

Catherine vents some of her rage against Heathcliff when he comes to take her from the Grange. She won't be cowed by him and she shows no fear. Though Nelly says that her words are delivered 'with a kind of dreary triumph' and to 'draw pleasure from the griefs of her enemies'. Yet, much of what she says about Heathcliff seems quite astute. When she says that 'your cruelty rises from your greater misery' we might agree that this is true. Her question to Heathcliff that he is 'Lonely, like the devil, and envious like him?' also seems accurate and very perceptive.

In this way, although she obviously cannot like Heathcliff, she does offer some understanding of his character and his sufferings, perhaps more so than any other character. This can be read as showing some generosity of spirit. Catherine also gives a generous, forgiving response to Linton when she says:

> "I know he has a bad nature", said Catherine; "he's your son. But I'm glad I've a better to forgive it; and I know he loves me and for that reason I love him."

In this way, some critics have read Catherine as a representative of Christian values in the novel.

However, we might also notice that she seems to be deluded as regards Linton here; it seems very unlikely that he loves her (or anyone) in any meaningful way. Indeed, we could argue that Catherine has chosen to make her own storybook romance with Linton, in the same way that Isabella was determined to see Heathcliff as a romantic figure. This could therefore be read as part of a pattern of artificial and inauthentic relationships within the novel.

This is therefore a counterpoint to Heathcliff's authentic relationship with Cathy.

Cathy's Corpse

Heathcliff tells Nelly that when Edgar grave was being dug, he managed to gain access to Cathy's corpse. He was able to see her face which 'is hers yet', meaning it is still recognisable. He pulls away the side panel of her coffin, and bribes the sexton to lay him next to her when he is dead, so that their bodies can rot together.

In some ways, this is quite grim, and in others, quite beautiful, and how we respond might depend on our own squeamishness. Some readers have considered this chapter a sign of Heathcliff's insanity, others have seen it as evidence of Bronte's belief in ghosts and their significance in the novel.

Ghosts

Ghosts are a major theme of this chapter.

In describing his effect on Linton, Heathcliff describes his 'presence' as having 'as potent an effect on his nerves as a ghost' . This also fits with Catherine's statement that he is as lonely as the devil. He also says that, if his body is with Cathy then there will be 'a better chance of keeping me underground' after his death. This emphasises Heathcliff's isolation and his role as a quasi-supernatural figure.

Heathcliff also presents his own belief that ghosts 'can, and do exist, among us!' This exclamative helps to convey his sense of certainty. He has good reason for believing this. In the following task, we will look at his encounter with Cathy's ghost.

Task

Re-read the section from 'The day she was buried' to 'on the earth'.

Identify some of the linguistic and literary features in this section and analyse the effects that they create.

The day she was buried, there came a fall of snow. In the evening I went to the churchyard.

It blew bleak as winter—all round was solitary. I didn't fear that her fool of a husband would wander

up the den so late; and no one else had business to bring them there.

Being alone, and conscious two yards of loose earth was the sole barrier between us, I said

to myself—

"I'll have her in my arms again! If she be cold, I'll think it is this north wind that chills *me*;

and if she be motionless, it is sleep."

I got a spade from the tool-house, and began to delve with all my might—it scraped the

coffin; I fell to work with my hands; the wood commenced cracking about the screws; I was on the

point of attaining my object, when it seemed that I heard a sigh from someone above, close at the

edge of the grave, and bending down. "If I can only get this off," I muttered, "I wish they may shovel

in the earth over us both!" and I wrenched at it more desperately still. There was another sigh, close

at my ear. I appeared to feel the warm breath of it displacing the sleet-laden wind. I knew no living

thing in flesh and blood was by; but, as certainly as you perceive the approach to some substantial

body in the dark, though it cannot be discerned, so certainly I felt that Cathy was there: not under

me, but on the earth.

Comment [hb1]: This seems symbolic. The snow reflects Heathcliff's loneliness without Cathy. Also, note the pleasing symmetry of the two clauses in the sentence. This creates a sense of balance.

Comment [hb2]: This use of alliteration gives us a sense of the harshness of the wind.

Comment [hb3]: This use of Yorkshire dialect gives us a sense of Heathcliff's voice.
We might notice that Heathcliff often uses a mixture of Yorkshire dialect terms with a more sophisticated vocabulary. This reflects his uncertain social position.

Comment [hb4]: This ignores or minimises the barrier between life and death. We could argue that, for Heathcliff, this doesn't exist. This is a recurrent theme of the novel.

Comment [hb5]: This is an unusual phrasing to modern ears. It is further evidence of working class Yorkshire dialect.

Comment [hb6]: This section builds up narrative tension. We know that something will happen once he reaches the coffin.

Comment [hb7]: This use of alliteration creates the sound of the wood breaking.

Comment [hb8]: This sentence uses a very sophisticated vocabulary, and is evidence of Heathcliff's intelligence and the education he has gained.

Comment [hb9]: The phrase 'it seemed' is often used in supernatural fiction to denote a sense of uncertainly. The narrator isn't sure what he actually perceived.

Comment [hb10]: The repetition of s sounds in this sentence creates the sound of a sigh. This is called sibilance.

Comment [hb11]: This inclusion of Heathcliff's mutterings shows us his anger and desperation at the time. He is so obsessed, he doesn't care if he gets caught in this illegal act.

Comment [hb12]: This shorter sentence is positioned among several longer sentences. This draws attention to this phrase and gives it more impact.

Comment [hb13]: 'I appeared' also creates a sense of uncertainty. It is also a slightly unusual phrasing, in that it suggests that Heathcliff is being observed from outside. This could be intended to suggest the presence of a ghost.

Comment [hb14]: Heathcliff is telling us that he was certain he felt Cathy's presence. He uses a lot of sophisticated vocabulary in this sentence, such as 'perceive', 'approach', 'substantial' and 'discerned'. This shows he is an educated man, and thus lends weight to a statement which might be disbelieved.

Heathcliff and Cathy's Ghost

In this chapter, we may start to gain more insight and sympathy for Heathcliff's character.

We learn that his perception of events is different to that of the other characters. When he describes his encounter with Hindley and Isabella, we notice how unimportant it is to him. From Isabella's account, we got the impression that this was a very significant incident for all parties, but Heathcliff dismisses it in two lines as 'I remember, that accursed Earnshaw and my wife opposed my entrance. I remember stopping to kick the breath out of him, and then hurrying up-stairs'. We learn that Heathcliff's main intention here was to try to see Cathy's ghost, and we get a completely different view of his confrontation with Hindley and Isabella.

This helps us to understand Heathcliff's very different pre-occupations and motivations and we begin to appreciate the sheer power of his connection to Cathy. We start to understand his desperate torment when he feels her near him and yet cannot see her. We are moved by statements such as 'I ought to have sweat blood then, from the anguish of my yearning'.

In this way, this chapter gives us considerable insight into the strange mix of contentment and torment that characterises their relationship. Both are characterised as devils who suffer from an infernal, 'intolerable torture' in their separation from each other.

The force of their love, and its ability to transcend death, provides the true narrative power of this novel.

Topic 27 – Chapters XVI and XVII

Introduction

In this topic, we will read Chapters XVI and XVII. We will think about the theme of education, reading and books.

Aims and Objectives

- To read Chapters XVI and XVII
- To consider the role of education, reading and books in the novel

Chapters XVI and XVII

In this section, we are approaching the present time. Past and present intersect as Lockwood enters the narrative again.

> Task
>
> Read Chapters XVI and XVII.

In this section, Linton dies and leaves Catherine a widow. She owns no property and remains trapped in Wuthering Heights under Heathcliff's sufferance. Nelly desires to get her out of this situation, and the only way that she can think to achieve this is for Catherine to marry again. As we know, she hopes that Lockwood will marry her and free her from the Heights. This has been a large part of her purpose in telling Lockwood her story.

In Chapter XVII, Lockwood again takes over as narrator. Interestingly, Lockwood now seems to have revised his opinion of Catherine. He tells us that 'She's a beauty, it is true, but not an angel.' Indeed, Lockwood's assessment of the situation seems more accurate on this visit to the Heights. He is aware of her 'aspect of abstracted sadness'. This phrase still uses the long, literary terms that are typical of Lockwood, but it is an accurate assessment. He also seems to have become kinder. He tells us that he remembers 'Mrs Dean's anecdote' and therefore tries to improve Catherine's opinion of Hareton's attempts at reading. This might suggest that Lockwood has learned something from Nelly's story.

Education, Reading and Books

Education is one of the main themes of this section. However, Bronte's attitude to it seems ambiguous.

Throughout the novel, books and other documents are used to bring the story forward and to give us direct access to character's thoughts and voices. Letters are used to further the plot, as through the correspondence between Catherine and Linton. Wills and legal documents are also important, such as the Fee Tail that grants Thrushcross Grange to male heirs or the Will that Heathcliff gets Linton to sign. Some of these uses of reading and writing are therefore positive and beneficial, while others are negative and capable of corruption. In Bronte's novel, it seems that there is nothing intrinsically good or bad in education and books themselves, therefore, but rather in the use to which they are put.

For Hareton, his lack of education has been a sign of his loss of social status, just as the denial of education was a punishment for Heathcliff himself. For Hareton, therefore, learning to read is a symbol for his wider aims for advancement and self-improvement.

As Lockwood observes, Hareton is moved to improve his education by Catherine's presence. When he wants to hear her read in Chapter XVI, she mistakes this for pretend kindness, but his desire is genuine. The fact that it is Catherine's favourite works of literature that he is learning to read also shows the secret esteem he holds for her. Books again become symbolic when Hareton throws them onto the fire. In doing this, he is also consigning his hopes of advancement and of being with Catherine to the flames.

Lockwood is himself keen to show off his own education and his gifts at word play. He describes Hareton to Catherine as 'not *envious* but *emulous*'. This is not particularly clever, but it clearly appeals to Lockwood's literary sensibilities and he seems to think that it will impress Catherine. However, her lack of a response shows that it does not have this effect.

There is a strong impression here, therefore, that education is different to intelligence. Hareton has always been intelligent. Several different characters comment on his intelligence, with Heathcliff saying that 'he's no fool' and Nelly saying that he was every bit as bright as Catherine as a child. Overall, we might argue that intelligence, including emotional awareness and powers of perception, are prized by Bronte in a way that book learning (which can be put to different purposes) is not.

Task

'What a realisation of something more romantic than a fairy tale would it have been for Mrs. Linton Heathcliff, had she and I struck up an attachment'

What does this tell us about Lockwood?

Commentary

This tells us that Lockwood is still preoccupied with fiction and with fictional narratives. Imagining that ending up with him would be 'more romantic that a fairy tale' shows that he is still thinking of Catherine's life in fictional terms. Although he has learned more and has adjusted his expectations based on the story he has heard, he still seems to regard it with no more weight than he would an average novel.

We recall his earlier comment 'Why not have up Mrs. Dean to finish her tale?' within which he classes Heathcliff as a 'hero' and Cathy as 'heroine'. There is therefore some sense that Lockwood is distanced from the story of the Heights and is somewhat unmoved even by this great tale of love and revenge.

There is certainly some arrogance in casting himself in the role of handsome prince, but this is also the role that he has been given in Nelly's story. However, Lockwood's actual interest in Catherine seems slight to non-existent. In fact, he has never made any attempt to court Catherine. When he gave her Nelly's letter, he was 'fearful lest it should be imagined a missive of my own' and he seems to fear the social embarrassment of courting a woman's attention.

Furthermore, when Catherine shows little interest in him or in dining with him, he consoles himself that 'she probably cannot appreciate a better class of people'. This shows that he is arrogant enough to expect her attention, but that he is also made embarrassed and uncomfortable by the idea of a relationship.

At the beginning of the novel, Lockwood told us a story about how he was attracted to a girl he met at the seaside, but that he was afraid to pursue the attraction as soon as she returned his attention. This suggest to us Lockwood's desire to see all women as romantic figures, only so long as they are distant. We might argue that Lockwood's ideas of romance remain the fictional and unattainable ideals of courtly love. He seems to prefer the fictional world of romance and fairy tale, rather than the real world.

In this way, Bronte therefore uses Lockwood to draw attention to the relationship between the real and the fictional, and to our own reaction to this story as readers.

Topic 28 – Chapters XVIII and XIX: Hareton and Catherine

Introduction

In this topic, we will read Chapters XVIII and XIX. We will then look at the relationship between Hareton and Catherine.

Aims and Objectives

- To read Chapters XVIII and XIX
- To think about the relationship between Hareton and Catherine

Chapters XVIII and XIX

Lockwood now returns to the Heights.

Although he takes great pains to tell us that he is only 'unexpectedly' in the neighbourhood of the Heights, and visits the Grange only on 'a sudden impulse', the fact that he tells us this twice creates the impression that his return is entirely intentional. He is drawn back into the mysterious and passionate world of the Heights.

Task

Read Chapters XVIII and XIX.

In this section, we learn that much has changed in Lockwood's absence. Heathcliff is dead, Nelly has returned to the Heights, and Hareton and Catherine have become close.

Hareton and Catherine

Again, reading is used as a symbol for Hareton's increasing socialisation. Catherine now feels guilty that she has put Hareton off education, and tries to 'remedy the injury'. Nelly tells us that Hareton is 'obstinate as a mule' at first, and refuses to practice his reading. This is an interesting use of an animal simile by Nelly, as it echoes Catherine's own criticism that Hareton is like 'a dog' or a 'cart-horse' with a 'blank, dreary mind'.

After Catherine and Hareton have a heart-to-heart in the kitchen, Catherine starts to realise that she has been proud and haughty. Through the gift of a book, she manages to persuade Hareton to give her another chance. As he opens his present, 'all his rudeness and all his surly harshness deserted him' and he begins the road to civilisation. We learn that 'their intimacy, once commenced, grew rapidly'.
Nelly now tells us that she is pleased that Lockwood did not try to start a relationship with Catherine. She tells us that 'the Crown of my wishes will be the union of those two'.

Domestic Affection

It is a scene of domestic affection between Hareton and Catherine that Lockwood witnesses through the window. As we see, Hareton and Catherine are now more than friends. Hareton is handsome, clean and well-dressed and he is learning to read under Catherine's playful tuition.

Consequently, the atmosphere of the Heights has also changed. We see this in the symbolic replacement of Joseph's blackcurrant bushes with flowers from the Grange. The blackcurrant trees represent the old Heights; they are useful and practical (as fruit trees) and they are also thorny and twisted. Their replacement with flowers, which are pretty and ornamental, rather than useful, therefore symbolises the civilising influence of the Grange and the triumph of culture over nature.

We should also note the increasing references to Hareton as Earnshaw in this section. Instead of the more natural and animal name 'Hareton' he is now known by his family name. This draws attention to his lineage and reminds us that he is the heir to Wuthering Heights. It therefore emphasises his increased status and his role as a civilised landowner.

In this way, many critics have seen the relationship between Catherine and Hareton as one in which Hareton is tamed by Catherine. Other readers, however, have seen this as a more reciprocal arrangement, since 'each had so much of novelty to feel and learn'. If Hareton learns the skills of domestic life from Catherine, and the skills of reading, then she learns how to feel and experience a world outside of gentility and literature. It is therefore possible to read their union as a blend of nature and culture, creating an ideal balance.

We might notice, however, that in Bronte's ideal of a domestic vision, Catherine seems to have the upper hand. When Hareton looks up from his reading lesson, he receives 'a smart slap on the cheek' for his 'inattention'. Though he is also rewarded with kisses for his good behaviour, it does seem that this is not a wholly conventional Victorian relationship. Our final indication of this is in the word that Hareton is learning.

Interestingly, the word that Hareton is learning to read is 'contrary'. This is an important choice, since it seems to draw attention to both Hareton's obstinacy and Catherine's haughty and naughty streak. Contrary also means opposite or 'diametrically opposed' and this also draws our attention back to all the contradictions, parallels and symmetries of the novel.

Symmetry

This scene between Hareton and Catherine, in which reading together is followed by 'late rambles' on the moor, also has a parallel with Heathcliff and Cathy. Cathy and Heathcliff's early education, far from being peaceable, is rather a kind of punishment whereby Joseph forces them to read tedious religious texts and to memorise genealogies.   In Cathy's diary, which Lockwood reads in Chapter 3, Cathy describes how she throws a copy of 'Th' Helmet uh' Salvation' into a dog kennel. She is then writing her account of this in the margins of a book, when Heathcliff persuades her to join him in a 'scamper on moors'.

The similarities and differences between these two situations seems to create a structural symmetry that frames beginning and end of the novel. It encourages us to see the parallels between the characters and their situations, and to form our interpretation based on this symmetry.

Many critics, including Megham and Kermode[32], have noted the significance of the name that Lockwood reads engraved on Cathy's window-ledge:

Catherine Earnshaw - Heathcliff - Linton

As well as showing Cathy's internal conflict in choosing between the two men, this can also be read to show a structural pattern in the characters' lives. Read forwards, this shows the life of Cathy, who begins her life as an Earnshaw and ends it as a Linton. In reverse, it shows the life of her daughter Catherine, who is born a Linton and eventually marries an Earnshaw.

This has lead many critics to read the novel as showing how the second generation have resolved the mistakes of the first. The authentic union between Cathy and Heathcliff is thwarted by the demands of civilised society, but the union of Catherine and Hareton completes this halted process.

In some further sense, we could even read both Hareton and Catherine as elements of Cathy's divided personality. In this way, as Nelly observes 'their eyes are precisely similar, and they are those of Catherine Earnshaw'. We could even, therefore, read their union as the achievement of Cathy's wholeness.

Though Heathcliff has sought to take his revenge on this second generation of Earnshaws and Lintons, they have instead triumphed.

For Heathcliff this is 'a poor conclusion'. We will look at this further in the next topic.

---

[32] See Rod Mengham *Penguin Critical Studies: Wuthering Heights* (Penguin, 1989) p. 86 and Frank Kermode (1987) cited in *York Notes Advanced: Wuthering Heights* (York Press, Person, 2012) p.14

Topic 29 – Chapter XX

Introduction

In this topic, we will read the final chapter of Wuthering Heights. We will then consider the ending of the novel and its significance.

Aims and Objectives

- To read Chapter XX
- To consider the ending of the novel

Chapter XX

In the previous topic, we looked at how the union of Hareton and Cathy can be seen as rectifying the mistakes of the earlier generation. In this topic, we will consider how far the ending of the novel actually challenges the ideal of domestic bliss.

Task

Read the Chapter XX of Wuthering Heights.

In the final chapter of the novel, we learn how Heathcliff died.

In some ways, it is an unusual to structure the novel in this way. We might expect the novel to end with the union of Catherine and Hareton, perhaps when Lockwood sees them reading together.

The way that the final chapter focuses on Heathcliff draws attention to his life and death. We also note that Heathcliff's death mirrors Cathy's. He doesn't eat, he is feverish and he dies by the open window. This therefore brings the focus of the novel back to the first couple: Heathcliff and Cathy.

Some readers have felt that this undermines the romantic resolution provided by the partnership between Hareton and Catherine. Far from having a conventional happy ending, Wuthering Heights ends on a note of doubt and fear.

Task

This chapter again raises the presence of spirits.

Make some notes on the significance of the supernatural in this final chapter. When you have finished, read the section below.

A Ghostly Encounter?

The presence of the supernatural in *Wuthering Heights* raises complex questions about the nature of heaven and the final destination of the soul.

Once again, in this final chapter, we are again offered the image of Heathcliff as more devil than man. Heathcliff's death certainly has elements of the gothic and macabre. The window is open and 'his face and throat were washed with rain'. His cause of death is also unknown and it 'perplexed' Kenneth, the doctor. At his death, Joseph claims that the devil has carried him off and Nelly herself claims that 'His eyes met mine so keen and fierce, I started; and then, he seemed to smile.' Since he was already dead, this is a rather frightening image.

As readers, however, we have more information than Nelly does. Heathcliff dies by the open window where (unlike Nelly) we know that Lockwood saw the ghost of young Cathy. The verb 'washed' suggests that he is now cleansed in a way that is reminiscent of the Christian practice of Baptism, but with additional sense of this cleansing being such as to make him one with nature. It also reminds us of how Cathy and Heathcliff were washed in each others' tears at their final meeting. We might imagine, therefore, that it is not the devil that has claimed Heathcliff, but rather Cathy's ghost. His hand still resting on the window sill suggests that he has finally seen her and let her in, and that this is the reason for his unexplained death and his final smile.

This idea is given further support by the young shepherd boy's sighting of 'Heathcliff and a woman, yonder'. This account is presented so as to be fairly convincing, since both the boy and his sheep are afraid to approach too near to the supernatural figures.

As in all ghost stories, the weight of evidence is important here. In this section, Bronte offers multiple sightings of the couple. Nelly references numerous 'Idle tales' and she says that Joseph has seen the children's ghosts looking out of a window. Despite her own reluctance to believe, she also talks of her fear of being alone in 'this grim house'.

Cumulatively, this is intended to provide enough evidence of Cathy and Heathcliff's ghosts to persuade the reader that 'he *walks*'. It therefore seems likely that Bronte wants to present these ghosts as real. The significance of this is interesting.

Heaven and Hell

Throughout the novel, there are profound discussions about the nature of heaven and hell and about the existence of life after death. When Heathcliff says that he is close to 'my heaven' he implies that there is more than one, and this also echoes Cathy's dream of being cast out of heaven and back to the Heights. Although Nelly is firm in her belief that 'the dead are at peace', the sighting of the lovers' ghosts on the moors challenges the conventional Christian view of heaven.

Lockwood's role here, as a stand-in for the reader, is therefore interesting. Lockwood's final comment at first seems to be a reassurance, but it is actually a question. As he wonders 'how any one could ever imagine unquiet slumbers for the sleepers in that quiet earth', he makes the reader imagine this exact situation and so encourages the idea that Cathy and Heathcliff are, indeed, ghosts.

We remember that Lockwood himself has actually encountered the ghost of Cathy before. He may perhaps go to see their graves to satisfy himself that all is quiet, but the wind 'breathing' in the grass is reminiscent of Cathy's ghost breathing in Heathcliff's ear in Chapter XV. We may therefore feel that, far from convincing us that peace and normality is restored, Lockwood's account actually suggests a final encounter with Heathcliff and Cathy's ghosts.

Their ghosts are not frightening to us, however. In fact, we might find this image rather romantic.

In completing the novel in this way, Bronte may be offering her own vision of heaven as one of wholeness, completeness and oneness with nature.

Bronte's own attitude remains ambiguous, but we, as readers, can make up our own minds about whether this is true and what it might mean.

Task

You have now completed reading Wuthering Heights.

Take a little time to think about the meaning of the novel for you. In the next topic, we will look at some critical interpretations.

Topic 30 – Themes and Interpretations

Introduction

In this final topic on *Wuthering Heights*, we will consider some of the themes and interpretations of the novel.

Aims and Objectives

- To think about some of the themes of the novel
- To consider different interpretations

Themes and Interpretations

As we have read Wuthering Heights, we have thought about some of the major themes of the novel. There are more themes that we might consider, however.

These themes include:

- Love
- Revenge
- Wealth
- Class
- Property
- Family
- Marriage
- Heaven and hell
- Nature and culture
- Education and books
- Food and eating
- Ghosts and goblins

Considering these themes for yourself will help you to come to your own interpretation and understanding of the novel. Remember that reflecting on what you read and thinking about its significance is an important part of studying English.

You may like to make some notes on each of these themes, either now or as part of your revision.

As you consider the novel's themes, you may decide that some are more important than others. You may start to feel that Bronte is emphasising particular issues, or that certain aspects of the novel predominate. Deciding on which aspects of the novel seem most important to you is the basis of forming a personal interpretation of *Wuthering Heights*.

Interpretation and Critical Approaches

Prioritising certain themes can lead a reader towards a particular interpretation of the novel. For example, if you think that the themes of wealth, property and class are the most significant, then this could lead you towards a Marxist interpretation. On the other hand, if you think that the use of symbolism is very important, then this could lead you towards a psychoanalytic approach.

In this way, many literary critics follow a particular school of critical thought. Some of these are briefly summarised in the table below:

Critical Approach	Description
Marxist	Prioritises considerations of economics and class. Looks at how ideology underpins society.
Feminist	Emphasises the role of women and the effects of patriarchy. Later feminist works look at the construction of gender (masculinities and femininities) as a cultural category.
Psychoanalytic	Focuses on symbolic readings of texts, based on the works of Sigmund Freud. The symbolism discussed is predominately sexual symbolism. Emphasis on dreams.
Deconstructionist	Argues that there is no single, 'right' way to read a text. Instead, contradictions and multiple meanings are embraced.

Using Critical Views

You may like to use some of these critical approaches to enhance your own essay writing and to help you form overall arguments.

In the exam, it's unlikely that you will be able to remember quotes from named literary critics. However, you will be able to mention general schools of criticism. For example, if the exam question asked you to consider Bronte's presentation of encounters between men and women, then you might like to mention feminist views of the novel.

You can discuss critical views using phrases such as:

- *A Feminist critic might argue that …*
- *In this way, some critics have suggested*
- *One interpretation of this is … Another interpretation would be …*

You can also discuss your personal interpretation of the novel:

- *My reading of this is …*

In this way, using critical approaches can enhance your reading and improve your essay writing. We will look further at how to answer exam questions at the end of this component.

Further Reading

Wuthering Heights is an extremely complex and dense novel and we have barely scratched its surface here. If you would like to learn more about the novel and its many interpretations, the following textbooks will be of interest to you:

- Claire Steele *Wuthering Heights: York Notes for AS & A2* (York Press, Pearson, 2012)

- Andrew Green, *Phillip Allen Literature Guides for A-Level. Wuthering Heights* (Hodder Education, 2010

- Nicholas Marsh *Analysing Texts - Emily Bronte: Wuthering Heights* (Palgrave Macmillan, 1999)

- Rod Mengham *Penguin Critical Studies: Wuthering Heignts* (Penguin, 1989)

- Ed. Linda H. Peterson *Wuthering Heights: Case Studies in Contemporary Criticism* (Bedford St.Martin's, 1992)
  (This volume contains the full text of the novel, together with several examples of essays drawn from different schools of criticism. It is therefore a useful survey of critical approaches.)

Next, we will move onto our second text: Angela Carter's *The Bloody Chamber.*

Topic 31 – Introduction to *The Bloody Chamber*

Introduction

In this topic, we will begin our work on Angela Carter's *The Bloody Chamber*. We will try to gain an overview of the text and its relationship to the fairy tale and to the Gothic genre.

Aims and Objectives

- To gain an introductory overview of *The Bloody Chamber*

The Bloody Chamber

The Bloody Chamber was first published in 1979 and has been a popular text for study in colleges and universities ever since. It is a varied collection of stories which are often enigmatic and deliberately ambiguous. It rewards close reading and re-reading.

It would be easy to describe the collection as feminist re-tellings of fairy tales, but they are far more complex than that. Indeed, Carter's style and approach is never easy and her re-interpretations of the fairy tale tradition are challenging and exciting. They are also joyously fantastical, dense with allusion, full of powerful visual imagery and beautifully written. They are a feat of creativity and a feast for the imagination.

Angela Carter and Fairy Tales

Many of the tales that Carter uses for her re-workings were first collected by Charles Perrault as *Histoires Ou Contes Du Temps Passé* in 1697 and Carter translated this collection of tales in 1977.

However, the tales in *The Bloody Chamber* are not straightforward feminist versions of the traditional stories and should not be read as such. Instead, Carter uses the form of the fairy tale as a basis for her discussion of contemporary concerns and she brings many new ideas and imaginative concepts into her re-tellings. As Carter herself described:

> My intention was not to do "versions"… but to extract the latent content from the traditional stories and to use it as the beginnings of new stories.'[33]

Carter's main interest in this collection can be said to be the relationships between men and women and, although they are not merely feminist re-tellings, the stories are used to explore heterosexual romantic relationships in such as way as to question the gender roles and stereotypes inherent in the original fairy tales on which they are based.

---

[33] Angela Carter cited in Helen Simpson 'Introduction' to *The Bloody Chamber* (Vintage, 2006, Kindle Edition) Loc 61

The use of the fairy tale as a vehicle for the discussion of gender was not popular with all feminist critics, however. Patricia Dunker, writing in 1984, believed that the original sexism of the fairy tale was too powerful to overcome and that as 'the carrier of ideology, proves too complex and pervasive to avoid'.[34] However, this seems to ignore the critical re-evaluation that Carter makes of the original tales and more recent critics have taken a more positive attitude to Carter's ambitious and ambiguous re-workings. Indeed, many other feminist writers have also used fairy tales to explore ideas of gender and relationships. Margaret Atwood's 'Bluebeard's Egg' is a good example.

Carter was powerfully drawn to the fairy tale tradition and it is important to note that only 'The Bloody Chamber' and 'The Tiger's Bride' were written specifically for this collection. The other tales were revisions of earlier pieces. The fairy tale was a form that Carter returned to many times.

Angela Carter and the Gothic

As well as drawing from the fairy tale tradition, *The Bloody Chamber* can be seen to include many elements of the gothic. The locations of castle and forest are particularly gothic and the castle setting, with its towers, tunnels and secret rooms, is used more than once in *The Bloody Chamber*. Extremes of winter weather also add atmosphere to many of Carter's tales. Carter uses a particularly gothic tone and atmosphere in 'The Bloody Chamber' and 'The Lady of the House of Love'.

Carter also uses Gothic themes. Her primary concerns of love, sex and death, and their interrelationship, is the thematic basis of many gothic novels. The corrupting power of wealth, the female heroine as a victim of masculine machinations and the violence of sexuality are all themes that have been used by gothic writers since the C18th and her choice of character types can also be considered as gothic. Her use of gothic forms and symbols is carried through into the very language of the tales themselves and her complex use of ornamental language, including metaphor and allusion, is particularly gothic.

Indeed, Carter confessed to having a particular love of the gothic and she wrote in her afterward to Fireworks (1974) that she was drawn to:

> Gothic tales, cruel tales, tales of wonder, tales of terror, fabulous narratives that deal directly with the imagery of the unconscious.[35]

It is this love of the strange, the fantastical and the symbolic that really shines in *The Bloody Chamber*. Like other gothic works, her writing is occasionally shocking and always interesting.

---

[34] Patricia Dunker 'Re-Imagining the Fairy Tales: Angela Carter's Bloody Chamber' cited in Steve Roberts *The Bloody Chamber York Notes Advanced* (York Press, 2008) p. 106

[35] Angela Carter cited in Helen Simpson 'Introduction' to *The Bloody Chamber* (Vintage, 2006, Kindle Edition) Loc 52

Critical Approaches

Carter was both a socialist and a feminist and the stories in *The Bloody Chamber* utilise some of these political themes. Carter also uses elements of psychoanalysis, to which she often takes a playful approach. Thus it is possible to use Marxist, feminist or psychoanalytic critical theory in an analysis of *The Bloody Chamber*. However, unlike many of the earlier writers, who lived before these theories existed, Carter knowingly explores and plays with critical theory. It is therefore important to note that Carter's use of many tropes is entirely deliberate.

Interpretations

Carter's writing is often deliberately ambiguous. She was aware that there was more than one possible reading of her work and she allowed and encouraged this possibility. In this way, her work can be said to be postmodern and even deconstructionist.

It is important, therefore, for each of her readers to make up their own minds about what her work means, or perhaps more accurately, what it means for them. Consider the interpretations of critics, but also bring you own ideas to the text.

I have offered some possible interpretations of the stories here, but remember that these are only some of many potential readings.

Reading the Collection

Although the tales in *The Bloody Chamber* are individual stories, it is also important to think about the collection as a whole.

For example, there are many elements which are repeated in more than one story. The bestial, predatory male and the ineffectual father both occur in more than one story. Indeed, class and gender are themes which are returned to throughout.

Another important recurring idea is the notion of change and transformation. In many of the stories, one or more characters change in significant ways. The idea that human beings can change is central to Carter's positive political philosophy and how Carter presents these different changes gives us insight into how we should read *The Bloody Chamber*.

As well as considering the themes of the stories, remember to consider how Carter achieves her effects. Think about the narrative perspective and point of view of the stories, the use of time, and the use of character and character types.

As you read through, you should also begin thinking about the many encounters that occur throughout the stories. Start making some connections between these encounters and those that occur in *Wuthering Heights*. Take notes on these encounters as you find them, and try to record your immediate impressions. This will help you to form your own personal response to the texts.

Task

If you do not already know the stories, read the fairy tales of 'Bluebeard', 'Beauty and the Beast', 'Puss-in-Boots', 'Sleeping Beauty' and 'Red Riding Hood'.

They are widely available online or as a free ebook.

Topic 32 – 'The Bloody Chamber'

Introduction

In this topic, we will read through the title story in the collection. We will then consider the main themes of the story and some of the gothic elements and encounter in the tale.

Aims and Objectives

- To read 'The Bloody Chamber'
- To consider the main themes of the story
- To consider the gothic elements that Carter uses in the tale

'The Bloody Chamber'

'The Bloody Chamber' is the title story of *The Bloody Chamber*. It is the first and the longest short story in the collection. It is based on the fairy tale of 'Bluebeard'. However, the moral that Carter draws in this tale is quite different.

Task

Read 'The Bloody Chamber'.

An Alternative Bluebeard

'Bluebeard' is a story warning of the danger of curiosity. 'The Bloody Chamber' follows the original tale quite closely. The most noticeable difference to the original tale is that, instead of being rescued by her brothers, it is the narrator's mother who rescues her. Her entrance is dramatic and romantic, riding a black horse through the waves, with her skirts pulled up to her waist.

Indeed, the mother of 'The Bloody Chamber' is a positive figure. Unlike the other parents of *The Bloody Chamber* (and of fairy tales in general), who often encourage their children into unsuitable marriages, the narrator's mother questions and seems to want to dissuade her daughter from this marriage. Indeed, we are told that she herself married for love and she represents the wisdom of an older woman. She is also bold, adventurous and 'indomitable'. She performs a positive, active female role within the story.

The most important aspect of the rescue by her mother may be that it proves the narrator has not 'ceased to be her child in becoming his wife', thus representing the continuity of familial relationships after marriage. This challenges the traditional concept of marriage as removing a young woman from her family, transferred from a father to a husband.

The Marquis

In many ways, The Marquis can be seen as Carter's version of a gothic villain. He has very little character and no humanity. He remains a mystery to the narrator who searches his castle at least partly in order to learn more about her husband. His 'waxen face' is a 'perfectly smooth' mask and even at the point of orgasm, the narrator is uncertain whether she has seen behind this mask. Indeed, he has no name and is known only by his title of Marquis.

The Marquis is a predator and is repeatedly described in bestial terms. He is 'leonine' with a 'dark mane'. This identification between man and beast is made absolute when the narrator's mother shoots him as she would shoot a man-eating tiger.

Closely related to the idea of his bestiality is the idea of his consumption. The narrator notes his 'carnal avarice' and how he 'bought me' with the opal ring. He enjoys collecting and purchasing, as is shown in his collection of erotic art works. Thus, money and sex are related for the Marquis. Both are about possession and power.

The ultimate image of this power is his murder of his wives and his preservation of their dead bodies. That his wives have themselves allowed, or even enjoyed, this fate is shown in the way his strangled wife's 'dead lips smiled'. This illustrates the way that the Marquis's power is given willingly to him by his wives and this remains one of the most disturbing aspects of the story.

Marriage and Sexuality

In many ways, 'The Bloody Chamber' is about the developing sexuality of a young woman. It is also, however, in part a parody of a type of erotic literature that deals with that theme. The train that carries them though the night with its 'great pistons ceaselessly thrusting' is a humorous look at the sexual imagery often used in literature and film.

However, after this point, 'The Bloody Chamber' becomes a serious look at the theme of sexual attraction and particularly of masochistic desire in women. The name of the Marquis is further intended by Carter to evoke the Marquis de Sade.

Indeed, the narrator's feelings for her husband are complex. She does not tell her mother that she loves the Marquis but rather that 'I'm sure I want to marry him'. She seems to be attracted to his masculinity, his physical bulk and particularly his 'opulent male scent'. She also knows, at least to some extent, the sadistic nature of his desire. He shows her one of his erotic (or pornographic) art works before their marriage and she enjoys his kiss with 'teeth in it and a rasp of beard'.

This sexual curiosity and masochistic attraction means that the narrator can be seen as a willing accomplice in her 'corruption'. Controversially, she is aroused by the way that the Marquis views her. This is expressed clearly in the phrase 'when I had first seen my flesh in his eyes, I was aghast to find myself stirring'. But it is a 'strange, impersonal arousal'. As she watches herself 'impaled' in the mirrors, she is utterly detached and this emphasises the violence of their 'one-sided struggle'.

The idea that she might enjoy a debasing sexual relationship is further expressed in her disturbing realisation that the Marquis might recognise in her 'a rare talent for corruption'. Her desire for the Marquis is, indeed, a combination of attraction and repulsion. This is further reflected in the 'certain queasy craving' that she feels for him. In this way, many of the traditional feminist arguments are complicated by the narrator's perceived complicity in the sadistic desire of the Marquis.

In many feminist arguments of the time, it was traditional to emphasise 'patriarchy' and the way that women were effectively bought and sold into marriage as a kind of sexual slavery. Carter also reflects upon this idea of marriage as an often negative condition for women. This is illustrated through the suggestive repetitions of language. At the beginning, the narrator journeys into the 'unguessable country of marriage', but the 'kingdom of the unimaginable' that she finds is the bloody chamber itself.

However, it is significant that, in this story, the narrator has chosen this marriage and Carter's exploration of the sexual dynamics of the Marquis and the narrator is more complex and nuanced than many of the feminist presentations of the time. Indeed, her exploration of female masochistic desire, and her interpretation of de Sade in general, proved extremely unpopular amongst many feminists. The idea that women 'enjoy' being dominated was very controversial during the 1970s, and it remains so today.

However, it is important to notice that the narrative perspective of this story is the narrator looking back on the feelings of her younger self. Although she denies that she was naive, the reader may feel differently. Indeed, the narrator mistakes the Marquis's lust for love and is, in many ways, herself one of the foolish virgins of his gallery, underprepared for marriage. Certainly, she has been profoundly altered by her experience.

Carter's final comment that the indelible mark on the narrator's forehead represents her 'shame' is also ambiguous. Does it mean that the narrator regrets her foray into masochistic desire? Is Carter suggesting that this aspect of the narrator's sexuality, or the sexuality of women in general, can or can't be changed?

Female Sexuality and the Male Gaze

Feminist critics of the 1970s often discussed the concept of the male gaze. This theory was described by art critic John Berger in his book and TV show *Ways of Seeing* (1972). In this text, he discusses how art is usually created by men for men and represents male idealisations of women. This theory inspired much discussion amongst feminists, including the idea that women can internalise this male perspective and may see themselves as men see them.

The narrator of 'The Bloody Chamber' sees herself as an object of male desire in this way. When she looks at herself in the mirrors, she sees herself as the Marquis does. More controversially, she seems to enjoy seeing herself in this way, as she is 'reborn in his unreflective eyes', a statement with more than one possible interpretation. Along with the idea of sexual submission, the idea of women enjoying and absorbing the male gaze was another controversial idea amongst feminists at the time.

The fact that the piano tuner is blind therefore takes on further significance. Through her relationship with a male who cannot see her, Carter may be suggesting that the narrator has rid herself of the male gaze. It may further be suggested that this may then allow her to escape the dangers of submissive desire.

The concept of the male gaze (and the female response to it) is a major theme of Carter's work and there are many references to it in *The Bloody Chamber*. You may like to broaden these ideas to think about encounters more generally.

Wealth

As well as engaging with feminist ideas, Carter was also a socialist and she was interested in the importance of economic conditions. The Marquis represents the social hierarchy of the past and, in 'The Bloody Chamber', wealth is shown to have a corrupting influence. The vast wealth of the Marquis allows him to indulge in his cruel desires. The narrator also describes how she 'had never been vain until I met him'.

Indeed, the corruption is described as inherited through the Marquis' family along with the great wealth. There is an ironical humour to the piano tuner's surprise that a man 'so rich; so well born' could be a killer. Significantly, it is only through giving the money away to charity that the narrator, her mother and the piano tuner are able to live 'happily ever after' in any sense of the phrase.

However, the lush and sensuous way in which she describes the physical surroundings and material goods can be seen as illustrating their attractions for the characters (and the reader). However, Carter has occasionally received censure from critics who believe that the delight she takes in such descriptions can undermine her political messages.

Curiosity

Curiosity, and its dangers and enticements, is a key theme of gothic writing. This type of forbidden encounter is a staple of dark fiction. It is often true, in a gothic tale or a modern horror movie, that despite knowing that there will be nothing good on the other side, the protagonist will open the door anyway.

The scene in 'The Bloody Chamber' where the narrator approaches the door to the locked room is quite perfectly gothic. The narrator approaches the door with a taper in hand. She walks down a 'long winding corridor' as if into the 'viscera of the castle'. She the walls are hung with heavy tapestries and the narrator's footsteps and breathing are emphasised.

Carter clearly has a lot of fun with this description. The taper is only necessary, for example, because the electricity does not extend that far. Even the door 'creaked slowly back'. In the narrator's search for her husband's soul, she will find that this dark heart of the castle is indeed full of blood.

Thus, the peril of curiosity is the theme of the original Bluebeard story and it is also a major theme of 'The Bloody Chamber'. Carter, however, exposes and explores some of the assumptions of the original tale. Indeed, Bluebeard is a rather strange fairy tale and Carter draws attention to this strangeness. She highlights the gendered nature of the narrative, as is shown in the erotic drawing which is titled 'Reproof of curiosity'.

Interestingly, and a little disturbingly, the blind piano tuner compares the narrator's act of curious disobedience to that of Eve in the Bible story of the Garden of Eden. In this story, Eve was tempted by a serpent to eat the forbidden fruit of the Tree of the Knowledge of Good and Evil. The story has had profound implications for the cultural representation of women in Christian societies.

Carter's attitude to this idea of 'Eve' is ambiguous and it is interesting that Carter uses it here. She may be critiquing the association of female 'disobedience' and 'evil'. She may also be drawing attention to the gendering of curiosity as female, or to the manifest unfairness of blaming someone for doing something that you intended them to do.

Certainly, the narrator denies her own fault vehemently. She sees the events almost as fate or destiny and as inevitable. She compares the situation to the 'clockwork tableaux of Bluebeard' with all the characters trapped in their pre-ordained roles. Fate or destiny is also a gothic theme and Carter returns to the idea of automatons throughout *The Bloody Chamber* and in her novels.

This also raises further questions about the role of the Marquis. When the narrator returns with the bloodied key, he is in 'despair'. The narrator recognises his 'atrocious loneliness' and he too seems stuck in a role. However, he is not wholly reluctant for the role and instead displays a 'sombre delirium' and a 'terrible, guilty joy' and this contrasts him with the protagonist of 'The Lady of the House of Love' later in the collection. Thus, it is important to note that Carter's fiction explores how men, as well as women, are forced into predetermined roles.

Task

List some of the gothic elements expressed in 'The Bloody Chamber'.

Commentary

These are some of the gothic elements in 'The Bloody Chamber' that you may have listed:

- Isolated location of an ancestral castle by the sea
- Winding corridors which the Heroine traverses with a lighted taper
- The Bloody Chamber itself (a torture chamber complete with dead bodies and skulls)
- A Gothic villain (arguably)
- Set in the past
- Class, power and the aristocracy
- Religious significance in the story of Adam and Eve
- Vampires, staking and sexuality
- Themes of curiosity and fate

Topic 33 – 'The Courtship of Mr Lyon' and 'The Tiger's Bride'

Introduction

In this topic, we will compare 'The Courtship of Mr Lyon' and 'The Tiger's Bride', particularly looking at the representations of gender stereotypes and the concept of the Other.

Aims and Objectives

- To read through 'The Courtship of Mr Lyon' and 'The Tiger's Bride'
- To compare the ideas of gender explored in the stories and the concept of the Other

---

Task

Read through 'The Courtship of Mr Lyon' and 'The Tiger's Bride'.

'The Courtship of Mr Lyon' and 'The Tiger's Bride'

Both of these stories are versions of the fairy tale 'Beauty and the Beast'. 'The Courtship of Mr Lyon' is a fairly straightforward re-telling of the tale, where Beauty's love transforms the Beast into a man. 'The Tiger's Bride', however, has a quite different ending. Carter, therefore, is using these different permutations of the same story to explore ideas about gender and sexuality.

Indeed, Carter invites us to compare these two tellings through her repetition of phrases. For example, at the beginning of 'The Tiger's Bride', the narrator makes a reference to the lion lying down with the lamb, which seems to be a direct reminder of the previous story.

There are also many further repetitions of motif and these illustrate important themes of the stories. For example, unlike Beauty who longs for a perfect white rose, the heroine of 'The Tiger's Bride' rips up the white rose that she receives from the La Bestia. These comparisons therefore suggest that Beauty is a weaker and more passive figure than the heroine of 'The Tiger's Bride'.

This idea of self and action is carried through to structure of the stories themselves. The heroine of 'The Tiger's Bride' is the first person narrator of her own story. Beauty's tale is told for her. Significantly, therefore, we can begin to understand how Carter wants us to interpret and compare these stories through the characters of their respective protagonists.

Beauty (Miss Lamb)

Beauty is a 'lovely girl' who is constantly defined in terms of her symbolic whiteness and purity. She longs for the gift of a white rose and she is compared to the light of the snow and to a bolt of bridal satin by the omniscient narrator. We are told how 'she felt herself to be, Miss Lamb, spotless, sacrificial', a phrasing that really emphases her passivity. Indeed, Miss Lamb agrees to live at the Beast's enchanted mansion, despite her reluctance 'because her father wanted her to do so'.

The phrase 'Do not think she had no will of her own' is ambiguous because, in many ways, that is exactly what the reader will think and the explanation and that 'she was possessed by a sense of obligation to an unusual degree' and that she loved her father is a less than satisfactory reason for her behaviour. The fact that, in this explanation, her sense of obligation comes before her love seems further to suggest her adoption of a traditional feminine, passive role.

The Beast's mansion is also a highly gendered environment. Beauty spends her days in 'pastel-coloured idleness'. She is provided with equipment for embroidery and she walks in the garden. She is also expected to carry out specific domestic roles, such as pouring the coffee for the Beast.

Most disconcertingly, perhaps, from a feminist perspective, we are told that she enjoys this lifestyle, despite her expectations. She likes the 'enchantment of that bright, sad, pretty place'. There may be an implied criticism of the traditional fairy tales themselves here. In the placating 'courtly and elegant' fairy tales of transformation that she reads, Beauty acquires a model for her situation.

Her feelings about the Beast also seem ambiguous. She enjoys their conversations but she is repulsed by his otherness which she finds 'almost intolerable'. Yet, without him she feels free but also experiences 'desolating emptiness'. Indeed, though she loses her fear of him, she still cannot 'bring herself to touch him of her own free will', a disturbing phrase that also suggests something unpleasantly involuntary in the way she allows the beast to kiss her hands. She does not return to the Beast in the spring as she promised.

But, we might ask, why should she? Far from being the selfish behaviour that is presented, Beauty seems entirely justified in living her own life in London. Beauty has no obligation to the Beast and his melodramatic pining for her seems little more than emotional blackmail.

Indeed, her return to the beast, her sudden love for him, and his transformation into a man seems a little forced and unlikely. The idea that her self-sacrifice tames his bestial nature and that spring comes to the garden with their love is a very traditional ending that is unlikely to satisfy the modern reader of this collection.
Is Carter using this deliberately, therefore, to emphasise the artificiality of the endings of these 'courtly and elegant French fairy tales'?

The Tiger's Bride

From the start of the tale the narrator is a less passive figure than Beauty. Although she too is lost to a beast, she watches the proceedings with a 'furious cynicism'. Indeed, she understands her father's addiction but she is deeply angered at his 'human carelessness'; this is a very different response to the self-annihilating love of Beauty.

The narrator remains assertive as she meets Milord. She refuses to allow him to see her naked, not because she is ashamed of her body but because she is a 'proud girl', aware of both the insignificance and the enormity of what he asks.

Eventually therefore, he makes himself vulnerable first, showing her his beastliness. She is deeply impressed by the tiger. She describes this encounter in violent terms as her 'breast ripped apart' by the magnificent sight of him. After she and the tiger view each other naked she felt 'I was at liberty for the first time in my life.' In many ways, she finds kinship with the beast by acknowledging that 'The lamb must learn to run with the tigers'.

She therefore decides to reject her 'imitative life amongst men', wondering if she can send the simulacra back to her father in her place. In this way, both the narrator and the tiger each abandon their artificial lives. The simian servant abandons his livery and even her sable turns into a pack of rats.

As the house itself begins to collapse with the sound of his purring, the tiger licks the skin from the narrator to reveal 'my beautiful fur'. In this final, beautiful image, Carter seems to be suggesting that men and women can find equality and love through casting off the 'skins of a life in the world'.

The Ineffectual Father Figure

Both of the girls' fathers are presented as ineffectual, particularly in the traditionally masculine role of financial management. The father in 'The Tiger's Bride' is presented as self-pitying and weak. Losing his daughter to La Bestia in a hand of cards is particularly offensive, and this error is horribly compounded by his insistence on her blood-smeared forgiveness.

Indeed, although Beauty's father seems slightly better on the surface, there are suggestions that their poverty is also caused by his financial mismanagement and his later purchase of expensive goods and hotel rooms 'on credit' does not bode well. Beauty's father may have stolen the rose, 'Because he loved his daughter', but, arguably it is his desire for the Beast's financial backing that makes him ask her to stay.

Therefore, despite their professed love, both effectively sell their daughters.

The Beast as the Other

Mr Lyon is described in such a way as to emphasise his beastliness, most notably when he leaves the room 'on all fours'. He is very much a lion in a brocade jacket. Mr Lyon is always depicted as Other to Beauty and his 'strangeness made her shiver'. Indeed, she is never able to accept his Otherness and he eventually becomes the same as her.

His point of view is not used in the story and Beauty only guesses at his intentions and feelings. This makes it difficult for us to understand or appreciate his motivations and his final pining for her seems more pathetic than romantic. At the end, he becomes a human man, but this feels somewhat artificial and unsatisfactory.

The Beast of 'The Tiger's Bride' hides his beastliness much more fastidiously than Mr Lyon. He wears concealing clothing, a wig and a mask and he hides his beast's smell with the excessive use of perfume and incense. His pretence is much more disconcerting and frightening than the revelation of his bestiality is and the narrator states how the 'artificial mask of his face appals me' and how she does not think she can 'bear the sight of him'. His artificiality is further emphasised in his employment of simulacra, such as the clockwork maid.

Yet, the narrator of 'The Tiger's Bride' is able to understand and sympathise with his Otherness. She relates it directly to her own Otherness as a woman, and here Carter makes a deliberate link between femininity and monstrosity, a theme which is often explored by feminist literary critics.

Indeed, although 'nothing about him reminded me of humanity', in many ways, the tiger is not Other at all. Unlike many male characters in *The Bloody Chamber*, he shows genuine emotion. Although they become diamond earrings, his tears are real and 'very heavy'. After they have seen each other naked, she accepts the gift of these teardrop earrings. It is significant that these are the last thing to melt away into the narrator's 'beautiful fur' and, in this way, the tiger and his bride are able to find companionship, love and freedom in the recognition of their mutual Otherness.

Task

How does Carter use the motifs of the rose and the mirror in 'The Courtship of Mr Lyon' and 'The Tiger's Bride'?

Commentary

The Rose

In The Courtship of Mr Lyon, the white rose is a symbol of Beauty's innocence and perfection. When she sends the bouquet of roses to the Beast, therefore, she is symbolically replacing her innocent naivety with the unnatural excesses of her life in the city. The death of these roses in the Beast's room represents her dereliction of duty and therefore, the 'death' of her perfect femininity.

In The Tiger's Bride, however, the narrator takes a much less feminine attitude towards flowers. When she is sent a bouquet by La Bestia, she is deeply offended and criticises the notion that 'a gift of flowers would reconcile a woman to any humiliation'.

When her father asks for one as a gift of forgiveness, she pricks her finger on it and he receives it 'all smeared with blood'. This makes a connection between a male association of femininity and flowers that she does not endorse. Indeed, she later throws the bouquet out of the carriage, which echoes her earlier tearing up of a white rose given to her by La Bestia.

The Mirror

Beauty's admiration of herself in mirrors is used to show that she has become vain and selfish. It is said that she 'smiled at herself in mirrors a little too often' and she has acquired a hard veneer of 'invincible prettiness'. She is put into a 'trance' by her glamorous reflection that breaks when she remembers the Beast.

What the Tiger's bride sees in the mirror is altogether less pleasing, however. She watches her own 'impassivity' as she is lost in a card game, seeing the cards unfold 'A queen, a king, an ace'.

Later, the clockwork maidservant's shows her what her father is doing through a magic mirror, and she is able to witness his self-pitying behaviour, reckless spending and drunkenness. In the same mirror she then sees herself as 'haggard' and then as 'hollow eyed'.

In some ways, the clockwork servant is also presented as a mirror and resembles the narrator with her nut brown curls. She is the simulacra of the narrator, who could easily fulfil the automatic functions of being her father's daughter.

Therefore, although it is less explicit in this story, this use of mirrors again seems to reference the idea of the male gaze in the 'Eyes that watch you take no account of your existence'.

Topic 34 – 'Puss-in-Boots'

Introduction

In this topic, we will read the story of 'Puss-in-Boots'. We will then consider the perspective of Puss as a male narrator.

Aims and Objectives

- To read through 'Puss-in-Boots'
- To consider the use of Puss as a male narrator

'Puss-in-Boots'

'Puss-in-Boots' is the only comic tale in the collection. It seems to draw on the traditions of the Commedia dell'arte far more than it does upon the gothic tradition. Yet many of Carter's usual themes are displayed here, especially the consideration of gender roles.

Task

Read 'Puss-in-Boots'.

What do you think of Puss-in-Boots, the narrator of this tale? Why has Carter chosen to tell the story in this way?

Commentary

Puss is amusing but not terribly likeable. His arrogance is palpable from the beginning of the tale when he describes himself as a 'fine marmalade cat' and as 'a ginger tom and proud of it'. He is motivated solely by self-interest and by his fears of his master 'ruining them both'. Both Puss and his master are as 'proud as the devil'.

Furthermore, where Puss is proud he is also deluded. This is shown in his opinion of his 'fine, musical voice' which the townspeople appreciate with a 'deluge' of 'freshest water, vegetables hardly spoiled' and shoes. He also takes credit for the plans which the female tabby both devises and carries out, deigning to 'congratulate her ingenuity with a few affectionate cuffs round the head'.

Puss is the only masculine narrator in the collection. Therefore, through his sidelining of Tabby's contribution to the success of the plan, it may be that Carter is suggesting that women's contribution can be marginalised within male narratives.

Yet it is also notable that both the female characters also get what they want. The tabby is free of the miserly household where she was 'kept on short commons for the sake of the mousing', and the young woman is rid of her 'lubbery' husband.

Through the success of the plan, we can therefore see how women are often active participants in the events that affect them, whether that contribution is formally recognised or not. In other words, women are not always the passive victims of patriarchy than some feminists have suggested. Through using a male voice for this story, Carter is able to explore these themes through narrative structure.

Topic 35– 'The Erl-King'

Introduction

In this topic, we will read the complex story 'The Erl-King'. We will look at the use of narrative perspective in the text. We will then think about some of the themes discussed in the story.

Aims and Objectives

- To read 'The Erl-King'
- To think about the use of an unusual narrative perspective
- To think about some of the themes used in the text

'The Erl-King'

'The Erl-King' is written in a beautiful, poetic, hallucinatory prose. It is a very strange and haunting story, perhaps the most complex in the collection.

Task

Read 'The Erl-King'.

Narrative Perspective

The narrative perspective of 'The Erl-King' is strange and shifting. It begins in the third person past tense with a description of the light, making an ambiguous statement that 'perfect transparency must be impenetrable', perhaps a comment on the style of the story itself.

The second paragraph is written in the second person, present tense as 'You step between the first trees'. In the third paragraph this has changed again to the third person future tense of 'she will be'. This may even be a deliberate mirroring of perspective and paragraph number.

By the fourth paragraph, there is a first person narrator who walks through the woods which 'receded before me'. This ambiguity of narrative perspective continues throughout the story where 'she' and 'I' are sometimes used alternately.
The effect of this shifting perspective is disorienting, proving that 'it is easy to lose yourself in these woods'. Overall, this is a very ambiguous and ambitious text and the reader has to read closely to interpret it.

'The Erl-King' also makes use of a range of themes and symbols.

The Green Man

The Erl-King is synonymous with the wood. His green eyes reflect the light of the wood and these eyes 'can eat you' just as the wood 'swallows you up'. He is a being who 'came alive from the desire of the woods'. Significantly, this desire is not benign and nature in this story is harsh, like the birds that smash the shells of snails.

In many ways, the Erl-King is related to the figure of the Green Man. In folklore, the Green Man is a complex figure. He represents fertility, but can also be threatening and frightening.

Food, Eating and Being Eaten

Another theme of 'The Erl-King' is food, eating and being eaten. Many of the images and metaphors used reflect this theme. As well as the wood that 'swallows you up', the trees themselves have an 'anorexic look' and there is a lengthy description of Erl-King's cookery skills. These complex images of food and eating seem to link the theme of nature and sexuality. For example, the goblin feast has an 'appalling succulence'.

Carter is aware of Freudian psychology, in which fear of being eaten is one of the first infantile fears. Fear of being eaten is then connected to fear of sexuality. The idea of being consumed or devoured is a particular theme of this story, and of the collection as a whole.

Sexuality and the Relationships Between Men and Women

The Erl-King is possessive and jealous, another meaning of his 'green eye'. This eye operates as a 'reducing chamber' that shrinks the narrator and the other young women. The 'green eye' can therefore be seen as another embodiment of the male gaze that traps and confines women.

However, for Carter, this is no simple issue. The narrator is sexually attracted to Erl-King, although she knows 'from the first' that this powerful desire is dangerous. At times, she actually wants to become 'enormously small, so that you could swallow me'. It is because of her love for him that she almost becomes trapped. The danger of love is that it is self-annihilating.

However, the narrator realises that though she loves him, she has no desire to live in a 'very pretty' cage. This is very likely a comment on marriage, a view supported by the reference to the 'prothalamions of the larks'.

The portrayal of Erl-King himself is also very interesting in this story. Ambiguously, Erl-King is not malicious but captures the women in 'innocence'. He is far removed from the predatory patriarch of 'The Bloody Chamber' but he is no less dangerous.

The Ending of the Story

The ending of this tale is very strange. The narrator resolves to strangle the Erl-King and release the birds from their cages so that they can turn back into young women. However, the final line 'Mother, mother, you have murdered me!' seems to suggest that the narrator is the Erl-King's mother. It is unexpected and ambiguous.

Like the idea of the Green Man, this may be another reference to fertility. It may be a reminder that, for women, the fear of sex is often related to the danger of death in childbirth. It may also be a reference to another fairy tale called 'The Juniper Tree'.

You may like to think of your own interpretations for the ending of the story.

Task

Read through Christina Rossetti's poem *Goblin Market*. It is widely available online.

How does this poem influence your reading of 'The Erl-King'?

Remember that Christina Rossetti wrote this poem in 1859, before the existence of Freudian psychoanalysis. However, both writers use metaphor to illustrate the perils of sexual desire, particularly for women.

There is no commentary on this task but it is something interesting for you to think about.

Topic 36 – 'The Snow Child'

Introduction

In this topic, we will read through 'The Snow Child'. We will then consider some possible interpretations of the story.

Aims and Objectives

- To read through 'The Snow Child'
- To consider some possible interpretations of the story

Task

Read through 'The Snow Child'.

'The Snow Child'

The Snow Child' is the shortest of the stories in the collection, but in many ways it is the most shocking. It uses many of the motifs of traditional fairy stories but twists them into something much darker.

Some of the traditional elements used are the repetition of events in groups of three to form the structure of the tale and the use of vivid colour in the imagery. Indeed, many of the elements of this story feel familiar to us, such as a girl as white as snow and as red as blood. However, in most fairy stories it is a woman who wishes for a daughter with these characteristics, and many versions of Snow White begin this way.

Carter, however, twists this idea so that the girl is a male fantasy, 'the child of his desire'. It seems, therefore, to suggest the transfer of affection from an older wife to a younger mistress, as is symbolised in the transfer of the Countess's furs and boots to the snow child. Interestingly, the items themselves, boots and furs, are symbols of wealth, status and sexuality.

It might also, therefore, reflect the transitory and illusory nature of such male desire. The child appears as a fantasy and disappears after the Count has sex with her dead body, leaving only a stain on the snow. The curt description of how 'he was soon finished' is further used to mock the Count's sexual prowess and suggest his desire is shallow and fleeting.

'The Snow Child' is therefore partly about the jealousy between women. We are told that 'the Countess hated her' because she was the Count's desire. She tries in three different ways to 'be rid of her' and it is these acts to dispose of her that seem to actually cause the transfer of her own belongings to the girl.

However, Carter's attitude to this is ambiguous. Is she suggesting that competition and jealousy only hurt women? This could be indicated in the way that the rose, a traditional symbol of love, 'bites' the women who touch it. The Count, however, is unaffected.

Another Interpretation

'The Snow Child' is usually compared to the fairy tales of Snow White and Snegorotchka, a tale in which a couple make a longed-for child out of snow.[36]

Through these references, Carter may be making a further comparison between a love triangle and the triangle of mother, father and child. Many fairy tales deal with maternal jealousy, particularly of step-mothers. Freud also discussed the jealousies that exist within families in his description of the Oedipus complex.

Indeed, the girl is described as a 'child' throughout the story and the phrase 'child of his desire' could also mean a child by another mother. The Countess of 'The Snow Child' therefore represents a hostile maternal figure, typical of fairy tales. The Count's affection for her, symbolised in the rose, is therefore used by her as a weapon against the child.

This interpretation also gives a nasty, incestuous quality to the Count's act of necrophilia. It is this that makes 'The Snow Child' particularly shocking.

Answer the following questions:

1) After the snow child disappears, the Count hands the rose to his wife. How might you interpret this gesture?

---

[36] Steve Roberts, *York Notes Advanced* p.103

Commentary

1) After the snow child disappears, the Count hands the rose to his wife. How might you interpret this gesture?

The gesture is highly ambiguous. It may be that the Count wants his wife to die, as the child has.

It may, alternatively, be an attempt by the Count to obtain the forgiveness of his wife, now that his desire has been satisfied. It may be supposed, by the Count, to represent the return of his passion onto his wife, through the award of the rose that she said she wanted.

The motif of flowers as an insulting gift was also used in 'The Tiger's Bride' where the narrator comments on how flowers are thought by men to 'reconcile a woman to any humiliation'.

Topic 37 – 'The Lady of the House of Love'

Introduction

In this topic, we will read 'The Lady of the House of Love'. We will then consider the themes of fate and warfare, and we will look at the use of imagery in the story.

Aims and Objectives

- To read 'The Lady of the House of Love'
- To consider some of the themes of the story and the use of imagery within the tale

'The Lady of the House of Love'

The Lady of the House of Love is arguably the most gothic tale in *The Bloody Chamber*. In this story, Carter combines legends of vampires with the fairy tale 'Sleeping Beauty'.

Task

Read 'The Lady of the House of Love'.

Fate

The inevitability of fate and the idea of an ancestral curse is a popular theme of gothic fiction. The 'beautiful queen of the vampires' is the embodiment of this notion.

The beautiful vampire of this story is incarcerated by her own immortality. Like her caged bird, she is trapped, unable to alter her situation. She deals the cards that she knows will always be the same and she feasts on the men that she would prefer to love. Although she is a killer, she is also presented as a helpless victim, as 'the beautiful somnambulist helplessly perpetuates her ancestral crimes'.

Somewhat like the original sleeping beauty, she is caught between sleeping and waking in a state of undeath. Unlike the original sleeping beauty, however, she is eventually awakened by the handsome prince, not into life but into death. Through his innocent intervention, she finds release from her nightmarish existence.

The Gothic Tradition, The Modern World and Twentieth Century Warfare

On some levels, this story can be read as placing the gothic tradition in opposition to the modernity of the twentieth century. The 'rational' bicycle is seen as offering 'some protection against superstitious fears'. In some ways, therefore, the rational young man can be seen as defeating the monster of fantasy. This is the same theme as that of *Dracula*.

More importantly, however, the story is also situated in the context of the real horrors of industrialised warfare. The story takes place on the eve of the First World War and the young man is about to depart for the front.

There are further references to the wars and genocides of the twentieth century in the text. For example, there is a reference to 'no-man's land' where the vampire queen 'hovers...between life and death'. Carters careful choice of words also refers to the Holocaust in the phrase 'hereditary commandant of the army of shadows who camp...'. Through these references to the real horrors of war, Carter may be suggesting that gothic terrors can hold no fears in the modern world. The story ends with this idea, powerfully expressed in the simple phrase that 'Next day, his regiment embarked for France'.

Again, however, there are ambiguities here. For the young man, 'A fundamental disbelief...sustains him' and 'this lack of imagination gives his heroism to the hero'. In this, Carter may be suggesting that it is our knowledge of what can happen to us that causes us to fear and our disbelief that protects us. She then goes on to say how 'He will learn to shudder in the trenches. But this girl cannot make him shudder', further elaborating on the difference between real and imagined fears.

Carter may further be suggesting that 'her horrible reluctance for the role' mirrors the role of soldiers in wars, who are also forced to kill.

Imagery

The imagery of the story is highly gothic and is very romantically and beautifully described. The house itself is the perfect gothic setting. It is a crumbling and ruinous castle above an abandoned village in 'the land of the vampires'.

This castle is complete with winding corridors and a terrifying gallery of family portraits. The sumptuous decay of the rooms that she inhabits is beautifully described and the image of her ebony catafalque is a vivid one. Details such as the 'heavy velvet curtains', 'red figured wallpaper' and 'black satin, embroidered with tears of pearl' all work to create a lush gothic setting of darkness and decay.

The image of the vampire herself, so 'beautiful she is unnatural', sitting reading her tarot cards in an antique bridal gown is also a very gothic image, which also owes something to the character of Miss Haversham in Charles Dickens' *Great Expectations*.

Task

Is there any further significance to the idea of learning to 'shudder' in this story?

Commentary

There is a fairytale called 'The Story of the Youth Who Went Forth to Learn What Fear Was'. This story was collected by the Brothers Grimm.

In this story, a boy wants to learn how to shudder. He travels from his home and has a variety of strange and frightening experiences, but he is never afraid and does not learn how to shudder.

Eventually, he marries a king's daughter, and after an argument, she throws a bucket of freezing water over him. Shivering, he remarks that he has finally learned to shudder, but he has still not experienced fear.

This story is difficult to interpret, but seems to suggest that he lacks the imagination to fear, or that he is not aware of the possibility of supernatural threat. He is not afraid of ghosts because he does not know what they are. When he sees a ghost in the story, he is at first merely bemused, and then pushes it down the stairs.

In this fairytale, some have also read the idea of 'shuddering' as the idea of learning about sex and having sex for the first time. The story could therefore possibly relate to a fear of sexuality. This could also have significance in Carter's vampire tale, since the boy is not seduced by the beautiful vampire queen. Is Carter suggesting that innocence (of any kind) offers some protection against fear?

Topic 37 – 'The Werewolf' and 'The Company of Wolves'

Introduction

In this topic, we will read 'The Werewolf' and 'The Company of Wolves'. Both these stories are based on 'Little Red Riding Hood'.

Aims and Objectives

- To read 'The Werewolf'
- To read 'The Company of Wolves'

'The Werewolf' and 'The Company of Wolves'

In these two stories, Carter explores the fairy tale 'Little Red Riding Hood'. As in so many of her stories, she explores this fairy tale to ask questions about femininity and sexuality.

Task

Read 'The Werewolf'.

'The Werewolf'

In 'The Werewolf' a young woman goes through the forest to visit her grandmother. On the way, she encounters a dangerous wolf and cuts off its paw. When she arrives at her grandmother's house, her grandmother is sick and has had her hand cut off. The girl and the villagers conclude that she is a shape-shifting witch and stone her to death.

The Werewolf is usually interpreted by literary critics to be a story about the conflict between older and younger women. Such critics interpret the story as suggesting that young women may be forced into traditional female roles by older women, as a type of shape-shifting. The girl's defeat of her grandmother is therefore seen as the girl managing to overcome an enforced feminine role; a role she eschews through her strength and violence, severing the hand that displays her grandmother's wedding ring.

The use of 'her father's knife' is also usually taken to be a phallic symbol and her adoption of this is taken as indicative of a female use of male systems of control. The use of stoning, a method of execution used in the Bible for adulterous women, can also be considered a comment on patriarchal societies.

But consider another interpretation for this story.

In magical realist fiction, we assume that the magical events are indeed 'real'. But is there a suggestion here that they might not be? Carter opens the story by saying that people in the north have 'cold hearts', drawing attention to their hardened natures. Carter then indicates the prevalence of superstitions, arguing that they are universally believed, however unlikely they are. This is conveyed in the dismissive phrase 'anyone will tell you that'. This suggests another interpretation.

Indeed, perhaps we are not supposed to take the events of this story literally. Carter emphasises that falling snow soon obscures any tracks that 'might have been upon it'. Additionally, the wolf's paw also becomes the grandmother's hand after it is severed. In other words, there is no proof for the girl's version of events.

This could put a much darker spin on the final lines that 'she prospered'. Is there some suggestion that the girl has made up the story about her grandmother being a werewolf, knowing that it would be believed by the superstitious community, in order to obtain her house?

The title of the story also seems to add weight to this interpretation. In calling the story 'The Werewolf', Carter is questioning whether the grandmother is, in fact, a werewolf and drawing attention to the fact that there is no such thing. This interpretation also avoids having to consider a dangerous wolf as representative of a traditional female role. Indeed, if anyone is wolf-like in this story, it is the girl herself.

The story could then also be about the rivalry between women and between generations of women, but in a much more horrific way. Could Carter be suggesting that patriarchy and poverty force women to compete with each other, even using violence and deceit to do so?

An even more controversial reading is to interpret this story as a meditation on the empowering potential of violence for women.

Task

Read 'The Company of Wolves'.

'The Company of Wolves'

'The Company of Wolves' begins, like 'The Werewolf', with a discussion of superstitions, in the form of three short werewolf tales. However, here these beliefs are not discussed in the same patronising tone as in the previous story, indicating the different interpretation that we should apply to 'The Company of Wolves'. In this story, therefore, the transformation into a wolf is to be taken more seriously and aspects of the introductory tales are repeated in the main story, such as the burning of clothing to prevent transformation and the wolves surrounding a house. The descriptions of the wolves' eyes and of the ribs that 'you could count' are also repeated in the main story, providing continuity.

Carter also has some fun with the language used in this piece, such as the use of the pun the 'deer departed' near the beginning of the story. The reference to the absence of naked men in the forest before the protagonist meets the 'fully clothed one' is also humorous, as is the reference to 'His genitals, huge. Ah! huge', which echoes the use of 'What big eyes you have' in both this and in Perrault's fairy tale.

Overall, although there are also some startlingly brilliant uses of literary language and highly visual imagery used in this tale, it is also owes more to the oral tradition than many of the other tales. We get a sense of this in the first tale, where the references to 'the smell of your meat', told in the second person, include the reader directly in the tale. A less literary and more informal style is also indicated by the inclusion of spoken dialogue without speech marks.

The main narrative of 'The Company of Wolves' is a retelling of 'Little Red Riding Hood' where, although the wolf is dangerous and predatory, his threat is overcome by the protagonist's fearless resourcefulness. Like 'Wolf-Alice', it explores the idea of burgeoning sexuality through the themes of menstruation, transformation and moonlight.

The character of the main protagonist is essential to our understanding of the tale. She is a 'strong-minded child' who has been 'too much loved to ever feel scared'. This strong character is related to her loving and indulgent parents. Indeed, the generosity of her parents is shown through the plentiful contents of her basket despite the 'savage country' and this contrasts with the harsh frugality of 'The Werewolf'.

The protagonist is young, she has just begun to menstruate and her 'breasts have just begun to swell'. Her innocence is described as her protection through 'the invisible pentagram of her own virginity'. The image of the 'unbroken egg' suggests vulnerability but also strength.

When she meets with the disguised wolf she is attracted to him. Their wager for a kiss is described as 'commonplaces of a rustic seduction', but there is nothing particularly commonplace about their relationship and she is no passive victim of male desires. After the grandmother has been eaten, the protagonist, although afraid, takes control of the situation. She knows that she is 'nobody's meat' and, like the narrator of 'The Tiger's Bride', she laughs in the face of the wolf.

Indeed, there are several references to their relationship as a non-conventional 'marriage'. As she 'freely' kisses him, the wolves outside sing a wedding song called a 'prothalamion' and her act of removing lice from his hair is described as being like a 'savage marriage ceremony'. Significantly, however, in the deliberate reference to the blood on the bed sheets, the blood is not hers and this contrasts with 'The Bloody Chamber'. By burning the wolf's clothing, she transforms him permanently into a wolf and this seems to suggest that he is less dangerous to her as a wolf than as a man because 'the worst wolves are hairy on the inside'. As a wolf, she is able to tame his dangerous masculinity until as Christmas days dawns, 'all silent, all still', she can sleep safely between the paws of her 'tender wolf'.

Arguably, therefore, in 'The Company of Wolves', it is not the protagonist's innocence but her sexuality that is her strength. Through her encounter with the wolf, she grows up. She learns how to shiver.

This could even potentially be viewed as a critique of Christian morality by Carter, a committed atheist. Christian morality constrains the sexual activities of young women to marriage, and the original fairy tale is often read as a warning about the dangers of sexual relationships with strangers. Yet here it is the 'pious' old woman who is eaten by the wolf and her Bible gives her no protection from him. As in 'The Tiger's Bride', Carter may be suggesting that we can only reach (sexual and romantic) fulfilment by acknowledging our animal natures.

Task

The idea of wolves singing is an allusion to another text. From your wider reading, can you identify this text?

Commentary

The text is *Dracula*. In Chapter Two, Count Dracula refers to the howling wolves in the line:

> "Listen to them, the children of the night. What music they make!"

Topic 39 – 'Wolf-Alice'

Introduction

In this topic, we will read 'Wolf-Alice', the final story in the collection. We will then consider some of the themes of the story, including the importance of socialisation, the mirror and the male gaze.

Aims and Objectives

- To read 'Wolf-Alice'
- To consider some of the themes of the story

'Wolf-Alice'

'Wolf-Alice' is the only story in the collection that is not based on a fairy tale. Instead, it seems to be based on the documented cases of feral children raised by wolves. It also (like other stories in the collection) references the Alice novels of Lewis Carroll, most noticeably in the name of the protagonist. This story, like the other wolf stories, is also about transformation but not, as is typical of Carter, quite in the way we expect. It is the last story in *The Bloody Chamber* and one of the most interesting.

Task

Read 'Wolf-Alice'.

Nature, Socialisation and the Other

The girl in 'Wolf-Alice' is immediately defined in terms of her difference. She cannot 'speak like we do' and 'her pace is not our pace' and the use of 'we' and 'our' signifies both the narrator's complicity in the events and the reader's own place within human society. Wolf-Alice's difference to us is therefore emphasised. Indeed, we are told that 'Nothing about her is human except that she is *not* a wolf'.

However, Wolf-Alice behaves like a wolf, because she has been brought up by wolves. She sniffs the air, she does not wear clothes and she runs 'on all fours'. She lives in a world of the continuous present tense, a 'world of sensuous immediacy' that is 'without a future'. In this way, Carter is emphasising the importance of socialisation. We are who we are brought up to be.

This idea is presented as of particular importance to women, who in feminist thinking, are often constrained by the roles that patriarchal society allows them. Thus it is possibly significant that Wolf-Alice is brought up by nuns. Nuns are arguably a symbol of the idealised feminine roles of chastity and virtue.

Yet, these nuns also reject Wolf-Alice when she cannot fit into their social order. Wolf-Alice reminds us that 'human' nature is not innate. Wolf-Alice is the girl who 'showed us what we might have been'.

Maternal Nature

The relationship between nature and motherhood is also explored in this story. Maternal nature is expressed in the wolves that care for the girl and this is contrasted with her own human mother who 'bore her and left her'.

The loving kindness of the wolves is thus contrasted with unnatural mankind who shot and killed her foster mother. Wolf-Alice is also rejected by the nuns after they cannot teach her. Thus, they send her to the Duke (who is also an outsider).

The Duke

The Duke is also unnatural and non-human. We are told he came 'shrieking into the world' to 'bite his mother's nipple off and weep'. He is an eater of corpses and his 'bloody chamber' is full of the hair, clothing and finger bones of those he has eaten. He is 'the lord of cobweb castle' and is 'both less and more than a man'. He is also 'an aborted transformation' and, with his 'fictive pelt', he is neither beast nor human. Thus he is in a similar position to Wolf-Alice, although they exist in 'separate solitudes'.

Significantly, The Duke casts no reflection in a mirror. This is part of the vampire legend and often taken to signify the absence of a soul. Instead, he lives through the mirror 'as if upon the other side of things'.

The Mirror

The Mirror is an important theme of this story, as in indicated in the references to *Through The Looking Glass, and What Alice Found There*. However, as in many of the other stories, the mirror is a complex and ambiguous symbol.

Wolf-Alice gains a sense of time through understanding the relationship of her period to the full moon, but she gains a sense of self through recognising her own image. Thus the image becomes extremely important to Wolf-Alice and 'her relation with the mirror was now far more intimate since she knew she saw herself within it'. Carter is here using the mirror to show the importance of image to the concept of self.

It can therefore be suggested that the Duke has no reflection because he has no connections to others and therefore no concept of self, except as a monster or an outsider. Thus, 'nothing can hurt him since he ceased to cast an image in the mirror'. Crucially, therefore, the mirror reflects both self and society. The Duke is isolated because he sees 'nowhere in the world, a reflection of himself'. The traditional world order is therefore seen as constraining and limiting. However, it is not the only possible way to live. Indeed, the relationship between the Duke and Wolf-Alice is not reduced to standard gender roles and Carter may be suggesting that equality and happiness in human relationships can be found once we cast aside societal expectations to regain 'the Eden of our first beginnings'.

In the final image of the story, and of the collection as a whole, 'the rational glass, the master of the visible' sees her ministrations to the injured Duke. In the glass, his image appears 'brought into being by her soft, moist, gentle tongue'. This therefore symbolises a reversal of the male gaze, and a new opportunity for equality that recognises the existence of the individual.

Task

Compare and contrast the use of mirrors in the first and last stories in *The Bloody Chamber*.

Commentary

There is a certain symmetry in *The Bloody Chamber* through the repetition of the mirror motif in the first and last stories in the collection.

Again, this use of the common fairy tale motif of the mirror can be related to the concept of the male gaze. As we saw, in 'The Bloody Chamber' the narrator is confined by the idea of herself as an object of male desire. In 'Wolf-Alice' however, the protagonist gains a sense of self through the reflection that she sees. The sexuality that she discovers in the mirror is her own.

Thus, Carter may be suggesting that positive and fulfilling relationships between men and women can only be achieved once the artificial reflections of society have been cast away and replaced by women's own concept of themselves.

Topic 40 – Making Connections Between Stories

Introduction

In this topic, we will look at reading *The Bloody Chamber* as a whole and at making connections between the stories. We will also look at how to start broadening this enquiry to consider connections between *The Bloody Chamber* and *Wuthering Heights*.

Aims and Objectives

- To begin thinking about how to make connections between the stories in *The Bloody Chamber*
- To begin thinking about connecting the texts

The Collection as Whole

When considering the collection as a whole, it is important to consider Carter's use of form, as well as parallels in structure and use of language. All the stories in the collection are in the form of fairy tales. Many also draw on the forms of romance and upon the gothic tradition.

Like any collection of fairy tales, the stories are quite different and do not always hang together. 'Puss-in-Boots', for example, is a funny story while 'The Erl-King' is very mysterious and poetic. The abrupt transition between these stories is, therefore, quite jarring for the reader. Indeed, it is difficult to trace any clear pattern or arc in the arrangement of the stories. Carter may have arranged them this way to emphasise them as individual tales, to emphasise the universality of female experience, or simply to make the reader work harder at their interpretation.

Carter uses many different narrative styles, from the masculine voice of Puss to the wistful narrative of 'The Erl-King'. Indeed, most of the stories are first person narratives, each told by an individual character. Another narrative technique that Carter uses is the omniscient third person narrator. This voice often speaks to the reader directly, using the style that is typical of the fairy tale as the written form of an oral tradition.

The language therefore varies with the tone of the story. She uses either simple or complex vocabulary and sentence structures to reflect the narrative of the story. She is thus a very versatile writer who can select her style to suit the mood she wishes to create. Carter is also a highly visual writer and she uses many bright, beautiful and bloody images within these stories.

Analysing the language that Carter uses is also a very interesting way to compare the stories. Indeed, Carter frequently repeats phrases in different stories and this invites the reader to make comparisons between characters or situations. For example, the repetition of the phrase 'the lion shall lay down with the lamb' was used to compare the differences between 'The Courtship of Mr Lyon' and 'The Tiger's Bride'. The phrase 'all silent, all still' also occurs a large number of times and there are many similar repetitions. You should look out for these as you read and re-read the text.

Indeed, the constant repetitions of motif and image has lead the critic Lucy Armitt in her work 'The Fragile Frames of *The Bloody Chamber*' to write that 'one of the major problems facing the reader of these ten stories is that they seem always to be dissolving into each other'.[37]

Making Connections Between Stories

In this way, making connections across and between the stories is often very illuminating. As you read and re-read through *The Bloody Chamber*, you should look for different aspects of the stories to compare and contrast. Indeed, there are several patterns of recurring images, motifs and themes that unite the collection as a whole. One recurring image is that of the dangerous forest landscape. For example, the image of a devouring forest is used in 'The Erl-King' when the 'wood swallows you up' and in 'The Company of Wolves' when 'the forest closed upon her like a pair of jaws'. Snow is also present in many of the stories. The castle or mansion is also a recurring feature.

Motifs can also be used to compare and contrast the stories. Narrators in both 'The Bloody Chamber' and 'The Tiger's Bride' stand naked apart from their jewellery, for example. However, their situations are very different and while the Marquis's ruby choker represents a cold and impersonal male desire, the Tiger's diamond earrings are symbolic of his emotion. Therefore, jewellery can be seen as a motif which is used to compare these protagonists and their lovers.

Themes are also repeated in different stories. Transformation is a recurrent theme, for example. However, Carter's use of this theme is complex. When we consider Carter's use of the theme of transformation we have to consider whether the transformation is from a human into an animal, or the other way around. We also need to consider who it is that makes the transformation and why. Through these comparisons between different types of transformation, we can gain a deeper understanding of what Carter is really saying.

---

[37] Lucie Armitt 'The Fragile Frames of *The Bloody Chamber*' cited in Roberts *York Notes Advanced* p. 110

Paring and Comparing Stories

Some of the stories naturally fit together. For example, we have already considered 'The Courtship of Mr Lyon' and 'The Tiger's Bride' as being different re-tellings of 'Beauty and the Beast'. It is also possible to consider all three of the wolf tales together. 'The Bloody Chamber' and 'The Lady of the House of Love' make up another pairing, since they both deal with the themes of fate and both include a predator who lives in an ancient castle.

However, you should also try to consider less obvious comparisons. Both 'The Erl- King' and 'The Lady of the House of Love' include caged birds, for example. This might then link into the wider themes of entrapment and incarceration.

Remember that Carter uses these comparisons deliberately to enhance and illuminate the text. We have considered the use of jewellery and mirrors as recurrent motifs, and how these motifs draw attention to the similarities and differences between stories. You should always remember to consider why Carter uses recurrent motifs, as well as locating them.

There are too many of these comparisons to consider them all in detail here, but you should enjoy looking for these similarities in order to compare and contrast the stories.

Making Connections with Other Texts

The Bloody Chamber is dense with allusions to other texts. Carter makes repeated references to the *Alice* novels of Lewis Carroll, to other fairy tales, to Shakespeare and to works of myth and history. She also refers to many gothic texts, including *Carmilla*, *Dracula* and *The Fall of the House of Usher*.

Making Connections with *Wuthering Heights*

You should also have found many interesting connections between *The Bloody Chamber* and *Wuthering Heights*. In the exam, you will be asked to look at how both Carter and Bronte explore a particular type of encounter.

Therefore it is important to keep to thinking about the ways that similar types of encounters might be presented in both texts. Look for connections that illuminate your reading of both texts.

You might, for example, consider whether there are any encounters in The Bloody Chamber that remind you of Heathcliff's encounters with Isabella? What would this suggest about the characters, the situations, and the purposes of their respective authors?

As another example, you could explore a more abstract type of encounter. You might choose to consider violent encounters. You could then think about the ways that the different authors portray violence. How is it described? What is the author's intention and what is she trying to tell the reader? How might this connect the novels? Are both authors expressing similar ideas, or are they very different? Keep asking questions of the texts and try to get them to speak to you.

Practising thinking in this way will help you to prepare for the exam.

Task

If you have not already done so, start making a list of the types of encounters between The Bloody Chamber and Wuthering Heights.

Commentary

This is a list of some of the many types of encounters that you may have considered:

- Encounters with the other
- Encounters with animals / beasts
- Encounters with animal selves
- Encounters with the self
- Encounters with family
- Encounters between parents and children
- Encounters with society and social expectations
- Encounters between men
- Encounters between women
- Encounters between men and women
- Encounters with lovers
- Encounters with love
- Encountering sexuality
- Encountering death
- Encounters with corpses
- Gendered encounters
- Encounters with the wilderness
- Encounters with buildings

This is only a basic list for you to start from. Thinking about the connections between the texts should be a personal response that allows you to develop your own ideas.

We have now reached the end of Component 2. You are now ready to complete TMA 4.

Revision Tasks

Preparing for the Exams

In this final section, we have suggested some tips for preparing for the exams and provided some revision activities for you to complete.

Revision Methods

Finding a revision method that works well for you is an individual process and different people work in different ways.

The best revision methods are active. They involve doing something, rather than just reading passively. Note-taking, making spider diagrams, repeating and summarising information, or explaining something to a friend are all active revision methods.

Try to make your revision as exciting and creative as possible. English is a subject where original and independent thought is encouraged. Try to engage with the texts and form a personal response to them. Part of revising for an English exam is thinking about the texts and the authors and clarifying your own ideas and interpretations, so that you are ready to persuade the examiner to your view.

Familiarity with the Texts

Unlike other exams that you may have sat, English Literature is not a memory test.

Remember that you are able to take clean copies of your texts into the exam with you. The anthology text will be printed in the source booklet. Therefore, you do not need to memorise any quotations.

However, you will not have time to read through much of the text in the exam. You should make sure that you are familiar enough with the texts that you can find any material quickly.

Familiarity with the texts is key here. You should have read each of the texts at least twice. Make sure you have a good knowledge of what happens in each chapter or act of your texts. This is especially important for a longer text, such as Wuthering Heights.

Practising Past Exam Papers

The best way to prepare for the exams is to practice past exam papers. There are past papers and mark schemes on the Edexcel website.

There are many advantages to practising past papers, and you should make it an essential part of your revision. Firstly, it will make sure that you are familiar with the format of the exam and that you know what you need to do. This will help you to feel more confident.

It will also help you to practice thinking, planning and writing at speed. Answering exam questions under pressure is challenging. It is a skill that improves with practice.

A-Level exams are now quite long. Two and a half hours is a long time to concentrate (even though on the day, the time will fly by!). Make sure that you can complete the whole paper comfortably. Again, this will take practice.

It is also particularly important to also practice writing by hand, especially if you are more used to typing. You will need to make sure that you are comfortable writing for a long period of time and that your handwriting is clear and legible.

Completing past papers and then marking them for yourself using the mark scheme will also help you to learn how the examiners will approach your work and help you to evaluate your own answers. If possible, try to leave a week between answering an exam question and then marking it. After this time, you will probably have forgotten your answer and so you will be able to approach it critically. This will give you an insight into how examiners approach student work.

Checking the Exam Arrangements

Make sure that you know exactly where your exam centre is and how to get there. Check and double check the dates and times for your exams. Make your travel arrangements and aim to arrive early at your exam centre. Leave some extra time for any possible problems on the day, such as heavy traffic.

The Night Before An Exam

- Prepare your materials for the exam. Put the clean copies of your texts into your bag and make sure that you have several pens. You can store the pens in a clear pencil case or just carry them into the exam with you.
- Remember that you will need to take ID with you to your exam centre.
- Decide what clothes you are going to wear. Make sure that you have money for travel / your bus pass / etc. This will reduce stress in the morning.
- Check for any planned travel disruption, in case you have to plan a different route to your exam centre. Ensure that you know exactly where your examination centre is and how to get there. Allow plenty of time for travel on the day and aim to arrive early.
- You can spend an hour or so going over a few of your notes. You are already well-prepared. You can feel calm and confident about the exam.
- Don't stay up all night cramming.
- Don't drink energy drinks.
- Try to get to bed at your usual time. If you can't sleep, don't worry. Just close your eyes and rest. Even lying in bed this way will help you to feel more refreshed than deliberately staying awake.

In the Exam Room

Once you are in the exam room, take a deep breath and try to relax. You are well-prepared and ready. Think carefully about your answers and answer each question as fully and relevantly as you can. Engage with the material, think carefully and enjoy the challenge.

Show the examiner what you can do!

Revision Tasks

Component 1: Section A

As we saw at the end of Component 1: Section A, the best way to revise is to become very familiar with the anthology texts.

1) These are some issues to think about for each text:

- What is this text's genre and what features does this genre have? For example, think about a speech, what features might this have in common with an interview? What features does an interview share with a radio drama? What genres are most similar to blogs? What genres are most similar to podcasts? How would the text need to be altered to suit a different genre?
- Who are the audience of the piece and how can we tell? How has the author crafted the text to appeal to his audience or to different sections of his audience?
- What is the author's intention? What is he trying to tell the reader? Does his point come across effectively?
- Are there contextual factors that we need to consider? Is our reaction to the text today different to how it might have been when it was originally written.
- How does the author create a sense of voice? How do they present themselves to the reader? Do you find their personality likeable or unlikeable? Does their voice change or develop?

We suggest that you go through each text and think about the answers to these questions. Make sure that you have a good overview of all 20 texts.

2) Another good way to revise and summarise the texts is to complete the following comparison table:

	Audience	Purpose	Context	Attitudes and Values	Literary and Linguistic Features	Overall Impressions of Voice
Charlie Brooker						
Ian Birrell						
Oscar Wilde						
Maya Angelou						

Alan Bennett						
B. Neyland						
George Scott						
Past Masters						
Martin Bashir						

Jay Leno					
David Seidler					
Andrew Viner					
Chris Rainer					

Jessica Read					
Flemmich Webb					
Martin Hoyle					
JFK					
Col. Tim Collins					
D.H.Lawrence					

Paul Theroux						

This table is just a summary however. Remember that you need to take an integrated approach to each text.

Think about the connections between genres. Texts are often fitted into a genre somewhat arbitrarily. Most texts are multimodal, such as a transcript of a podcast, for instance. Try not to be too definitive. There are lots of ways that you can look at the genres and make comparisons.

The idea is to open up meanings, rather than to answer with a simplistic answer. There are no straightforward or definitive answers in English. Your role is to explore the different ways that authors create meanings. There are no strictly right or wrong answers, so long as you are making references to the text and using linguistic terminology accurately.

3) Once you are familiar with the texts, you can start practising unseen texts.

Hopefully, you have been reading a newspaper regularly, thinking about voices in everyday texts, and collecting examples of interesting articles and of other genres of writing.

You will now be able to use the texts that you have collected to practice as unseen texts. (If you have not collected any texts, then choose some now from a large Sunday newspaper.)

Muddle the texts and take one at random. Then select one of the anthology texts at random (for example, by sticking a pin in the contents page).

Practice making comparisons between these two texts. How do the authors create a sense of voice. At first, you can practice by making notes or drawing tables. Then start to practice writing full, essay-style answers.

4) You should now begin your exam practice.

Download example exam papers from the Edexcel website. Practice completing them under timed conditions. In the exam, you will have 1hr and 15mins for Section A.

Exam practice is essential. It will help you to get used to thinking, planning and writing essays in the time allowed. It is also important to get used to writing fast by hand (especially since most of us type, rather than write, most of the time.) Answering questions in the time allowed is meant to be challenging. It is a skill that improves with practice.

It is a good idea to get as much practice as possible at answering exam questions. If you run out of past papers, practice answering questions on your unseen texts (from the activity above).

Revision Tasks

Component 1: Section B

All My Sons

1) Begin your revision by re-reading All My Sons . The more times you read the text, the more you will start to notice about the play. Read over your previous notes and think about your new observations. Keep thinking about the text and developing your interpretation.

2) Think about the parallels between scenes. Read over the comparison tables that we completed during our studies. What new ideas can you add? Can you make any further comparisons?

3) Start to revise some of the themes that we have considered. These themes might include:

- Social responsibility
- Guilt and blame
- Parents and children
- Fathers and sons
- Men and masculinity (being an important man or earning money for one's family)
- Business
- Employment and social roles
- The past returning to haunt the present

Make a spider diagram for each of these themes. How is the theme presented in the play? Try to fully explore your ideas for each theme.

4) Practice your ability to compare sections of the text. Choose a theme to focus on, and then find two sections of the play that explore this theme. How is this theme treated differently in different sections? Are there parallels or are there opposite attitudes? Do the characters' attitudes change between earlier and later scenes? Think about the changing relationships between the characters and the balance of power? Do we (the audience) find out additional information that means we react differently? Identify the literary and linguistic features that support your ideas. How is Miller guiding the development of his themes?

Complete this task for as many themes as you can find. You can begin by taking notes, then move onto the next task.

5) Next, start to practise answering essay questions. Choose one of the themes that you used in the previous task and formulate an exam-style question for it. This will help you to get used to the format of the exam questions.

Plan an answer to this question. Make sure you are making comparisons between the sections and the way that Miller presents your chosen theme. How is he developing the ideas? Find literary and linguistic examples. Which contextual factors are relevant here?

6) Check back over your plan and make sure that you are making comparisons. You can write about the different sections of the play in alternate paragraphs, or you can consider one aspect of each section in the same paragraph. However, make sure that you are using comparative or connecting words such as 'similarly' or 'differently'. Don't write a separate analysis of each section. Instead, think about how Miller's presentation of the theme changes and develops.

7) Practice writing essays for each of your themes. Try to get as much practice as possible on comparing a theme across two sections of text.

In the exam, you will have 1hr and 15mins to answer Section B. Keep practising answering questions within the time allowed. This is a skill that will improve with practice.

Remember to wait a while before looking back over your answers. What would you change about them and how could you improve you response? Evaluating your own answers is a good way to practice and improve your essay technique.

8) You are now ready to begin practising past exam papers.

You are now ready to look at a whole Component 1 paper, including both Section A and Section B. Practise completing the whole paper in 2hr 30min.

Revision Tasks

Component 2: Section A

1) For this component, try to get as much practice as possible with unseen texts. Hopefully, you have been reading a newspaper regularly, and you have collected some texts that describe encounters. If not, then you should buy several newspapers or magazines now and skim them to find some texts with the theme of encounters. Remember that 'encounters' is interpreted broadly. You could consider an encounter between people, with an animal, or something more abstract, such as an encounter with the past.

2) The questions for this section take a form similar to:

> Critically evaluate how the writer conveys his experience of this encounter.

> In your answer, you must comment on linguistic and literary features and relevant contextual factors.

Practice answering this question for each of the texts that you have collected. This is the best way to prepare for the exam. Try to get as much practice with unseen texts as possible.

3) You are now ready to complete some past exam papers. Again, make sure that you can answer the question in the time allowed.

Use the mark schemes to mark your answers. How could you improve your work? Try to think about your essay writing and incorporate improvements into your next attempt.

Revision Tasks

Component 2: Section B

Wuthering Heights and *The Bloody Chamber*

1) Quickly re-read the texts of *Wuthering Heights* and *The Bloody Chamber*. Revise your notes. You will have studied our texts for Section B quite recently, so they should still be fresh in your mind.

In the exam, you will need to be able to choose appropriate encounters to write about, so you will need to be very familiar with these texts. You will need to have a good idea of the sequence of events of *Wuthering Heights*, so that you can locate an encounter quickly.

2) Start making a list of some of the types of encounters in the texts. For example, consider:

- reunions
- violent encounters
- loving encounters
- encounters between men and women
- encounters between parents (or people in parental roles) and children
- encountering a building
- encountering the environment / nature
- encountering unusual weather / storms

3) Try to find examples of each of these encounters in the texts. Look for two short examples from each text.

4) Start analysing the language that Bronte and Carter use in these extracts. How does each author describe this type of encounter? Identify some of the literary and linguistic features they use. What effect do these techniques this create? What is the author trying to convey and is their choice of method effective (successful)?

Next, start thinking about the connections between the texts. Are there similarities between the way these authors describe a particular type of encounter? If so, why might this be? Again, what effect are the authors trying to create? How is the context relevant? Are the authors trying to make a social or political point? Are they trying to draw our attention to an aspect of human nature or human relationships?

5) Start to practice writing essays, based on the encounters you have found. Use the format:

> Evaluate the effectiveness of the methods used by the writers of your two studied texts to present encounters with nature.
>
> In your response you must consider the use of literary and linguistic features, connections across texts and relevant contextual factors.

Keep practising writing these essays, and evaluating your own answers. How can they be improved?

Make sure that you can answer this question in 1hr 15mins.

6) Practise some past exam papers.

You are now ready to look at a whole Component 2 paper, including both Section A and Section B. Practise completing the whole paper in 2hr 30min.

You can use the mark schemes on the Edexcel website to mark your answers.

You have now completed your course.

We hope you have enjoyed your studies.

Good luck in your exams!

BV - #0005 - 191219 - C0 - 297/210/33 - PB - 9781326428143